CRITICAL SURVEY

OF

LONG FICTION

Detective and Mystery Novelists

Editor

Carl Rollyson

Baruch College, City University of New York

SALEM PRESS

Ipswich, Massachusetts • Hackensack, New Jersey

Cover photo:
Ray Bradbury (© Sophie Bassouls/Sygma/Corbis)

978-1-4298-3675-3

CONTENTS

CONTRIBUTORS

Patrick Adcock
Henderson State University

Anne Kelsch Breznau
Original Contributor

Susan Butterworth
Salem State College

Bill Delaney
Original Contributor

Joseph Dewey
University of Pittsburgh at Johnstown

David C. Dougherty
Original Contributor

Jack Ewing
Boise, Idaho

Kenneth Friedenreich
Original Contributor

Lucy Golsan
Stockton, California

William Hoffman
Fort Myers, Florida

Mary Anne Hutchinson
Original Contributor

Catherine Kenney
Original Contributor

Rebecca Kuzins
Pasadena, California

Michael J. Larsen
Saint Mary's University

Andrew F. Macdonald
Loyola University New Orleans

Gina Macdonald
Nicholls State University

Laurence W. Mazzeno
Alvernia College

Daniel P. Murphy
Hanover College

William Nelles
University of Massachusetts Dartmouth

Allan Nelson
Caldwell College

F. William Nelson
Original Contributor

Robert J. Paradowski
Rochester Institute of Technology

David B. Parsell
Furman University

Carl Rollyson
Baruch College, CUNY

Elizabeth D. Schafer
Loachapoka, Alabama

Thomas C. Schunk
Original Contributor

Charles L. P. Silet
Original Contributor

Roger Smith
Portland, Oregon

Gerald H. Strauss
Bloomsburg University

Dennis L. Weeks
Schenectady County Community College

Scott D. Yarbrough
Charleston Southern University

THE DETECTIVE NOVEL

The detective story is a special branch of crime fiction that focuses attention on the examination of evidence that will lead to the solution of the mystery. *The Oxford English Dictionary* records the first printed use of the noun "detective" in the year 1843. The term had become established in the language because of the formation of the first detective bureaus, the original of which was the Bow Street Runners, a group of detective-policemen organized by Henry Fielding and John Fielding in their capacities as magistrates in London. The Runners operated out of the Fielding residence on Bow Street and were the precursors of the detective branch of Scotland Yard. Some time later, early in the nineteenth century, the Sûreté Générale, the first modern police force, was formed in Paris with a detective bureau. With the establishment of such bureaus, the way was open for the detective story to be developed out of existing literary sources.

EIGHTEENTH AND NINETEENTH CENTURIES

In the eighteenth century, the chaplain of Newgate Prison in London was authorized to publish the stories of notorious criminals in *The Newgate Calendar*. From this practice sprang the often wholly fictional Newgate novels, accounts of sensational crimes. In France, François Vidocq, a criminal himself, became head of the Sûreté and later published his memoirs recounting his exploits in capturing criminals. It is also likely that some of the ambience of the early detective story was derived from the gothic novel. William Godwin's *Things as They Are: Or, The Adventures of Caleb Williams* (1794; also known as *The Adventures of Caleb Williams: Or, Things as They Are*; best known as *Caleb Williams*), for example, although not a detective novel, is a story of a crime solved in order to free an innocent man.

From these beginnings, it remained for Edgar Allan Poe to devise the detective story in its now familiar form. Poe wrote three short works that are certainly detective stories, as well as others that are sometimes included in the genre. The first of these was "The Murders in the Rue Morgue" (1841), which was followed by "The Mystery of Marie Rogêt" (1842) and "The Purloined Letter" (1845). Poe initiated the device of establishing the character of the detective and then using him for several stories. Poe's detective, M. Dupin, is a recluse, an eccentric, aristocratic young man with a keen analytical mind. He has an unnamed but admiring friend who marvels at Dupin's mental prowess and is willing to be his chronicler. Dupin examines the evidence in a given case and solves the crime after the regular police have exhausted their methods—a circumstance that was to become one of the commonplaces of detective fiction.

Apparently impressed by *Mémoires de Vidocq, chef de la police de Sûreté jusqu'en 1827* (1828-1829; *Memoirs of Vidocq, Principal Agent of the French Police Until 1827*, 1828-1829; revised as *Histoire de Vodocq, chef de la police de Sûreté: Écrite d'après lui-même*, 1829), by François Vidocq, Poe set his stories in Paris and borrowed his policemen from the Sûreté. Meanwhile, in France itself, Émile Gaboriau began to produce detective stories that also owed much to Vidocq. His detective, M. Lecoq, a representative of the official police, became the chief figure in a number of tales of detection. The detective short story was thus established and enjoyed great popularity in the century to follow.

Probably the first full-length novel of detection was *The Notting Hill Mystery* (1865), by Charles Felix, but it was quickly followed by Wilkie Collins's *The Moonstone* (1868), which critics consider to be the first important detective novel. Collins introduced Sergeant Cuff of Scotland Yard, who, with the help of amateurs, was able to solve the mystery. The first detective in English fiction, however, antedated Sergeant Cuff by fifteen years: Inspector Bucket of Charles Dickens's *Bleak House* (1852-1853, serial; 1853, book). Detective novels were published at a slow, sporadic pace until the advent of Sherlock Holmes, the most famous of all fictional detectives, in Arthur Conan Doyle's *A Study in Scarlet* (1887, serial; 1888, book).

Holmes starred in four novels and fifty-six short stories and eventually came to have a life independent of his creator, Doyle, who even killed him off in one tale only to bring him back for further adventures. A house on Baker Street in London has been identified as the place where Holmes occupied a flat and is now a tourist attraction. Clubs honor his memory with birthday parties, and a biography has been written based on incidental remarks and inferences about his "life" in the works in which he appeared. The Sherlock Holmes stories follow the pattern established by Poe's Dupin: Holmes is a bachelor given to esoteric studies, an eccentric who plays the violin and occasionally takes cocaine. A keen observer with amazing talents for analysis and deduction, an amateur boxer who performs astonishing feats of physical strength, Holmes is a virtual superman, while the commonsensical Dr. John Watson, the narrator of his exploits, provides a perfect foil.

The success of the Sherlock Holmes stories resulted in an outpouring of detective fiction; many authors adopted the basic technique of establishing the character of the detective and then recounting a series of his "cases." R. Austin Freeman introduced Dr. John Thorndyke, who based his solutions on more strictly scientific evidence rather than the deductions favored by Holmes. An American writer, Jacques Futrelle, introduced Professor S. F. X. Van Dusen, who was called "the thinking machine" and who became one of the early omniscient detectives in the tradition of Sherlock Holmes.

DETECTIVE FICTION'S GOLDEN AGE

With *Trent's Last Case* (1913, revised 1929; also as *The Woman in Black*), by E. C. Bentley, the modern era of the detective story began. Mary Roberts Rinehart modified the pattern of the detective novel by providing a female amateur as a first-person narrator who worked with the official police and who provided the key to the solution almost by accident. Another prolific writer was Carolyn Wells, who wrote seventy-four mystery novels, most of which starred Fleming Stone as the detective. She also made an important contribution to the theory of the detective story with *The Technique of the Mystery Story* (1913).

As the detective story moved closer to its "classical" stage, it became more realistic and was written with more literary skill. The detectives became less bizarre and less inclined to become involved in physical danger or in personally grappling with the criminal in the manner of the great Holmes. The adventure-mystery involving a sleuth who was proficient both physically and mentally was given over to thrillers such as the Nick Carter stories, while the strict detective tale became purely analytical. In this form, the detective story featured the detective as its chief character and the solution to an interesting mystery as its chief interest. There was generally a narrator in the Watson tradition and an absence of any love interest, and neither characterization nor the tangential demands of the plot interfered with the central business of unraveling the puzzle. With these characteristics established, the detective story moved into its golden age.

The period of 1920 to 1940 represented the golden age of the novel of detection. It included the work of Dorothy L. Sayers, Agatha Christie, Earl Derr Biggers, and S. S. Van Dine (Willard Huntington Wright). Hundreds of novels were written during this period and were enjoyed by people at all levels of literary sophistication. The expectation of the reader was that a clever detective would be faced with a puzzling crime, almost always a murder or a series of murders, that had not been committed by a professional criminal; the solution of this mystery would come about by the examination of clues presented in the novel.

Dorothy L. Sayers was perhaps the most literary writer of the practitioners of the detective novel; she attempted a combination of the detective story and the "legitimate" novel. *The Nine Tailors* (1934) is a good example of the work of her detective, Lord Peter Wimsey, and of her careful research into background material. She is considered to be one of the finest of the mystery writers of this period. Lord Peter Wimsey is a snobbish man given to airy commentary and a languid manner, but he has the analytical skills necessary to solve the mysteries.

Although she may not have had the skill in characterization or the literary quality of Sayers, Agatha Christie surpassed her rivals in the sheer ingenuity of her plots and her manipulation of the evidence that her detective, Hercule Poirot, had to evaluate. Christie used such traditional ploys as the somewhat dense associate (in this instance, Captain Hastings), the least likely person as the murderer, the unexpected turn of the plot, and an exotic manner of committing the crime. Poirot, who became the most popular fictional detective since Sherlock Holmes, appears in thirty-three of Christie's novels. Christie invented yet another fictional detective who became almost as beloved as Poirot: Miss Jane Marple is a quiet Victorian lady who figures in eleven novels and a collection of short stories. Her solutions come about from a shrewd knowledge of human behavior, keen observation, a remarkable memory, and the ability to make startling deductions from the evidence. Despite the popularity of Hercule Poirot and Miss Marple, neither stars in the book that is widely considered to be Christie's best: *Ten Little Niggers* (1939; published in the United States as *And Then There Were None*, 1940; also known as *Ten Little Indians*).

Rivaling M. Poirot and Miss Marple for the affections of detective novel fans was the Chinese Hawaiian American detective Charlie Chan, created by Earl Derr Biggers. Charlie Chan's widespread popularity was especially enhanced by the fact that his stories were turned into some forty-five motion pictures. Chan's characterization includes the frequent use of Chinese aphorisms, an extremely polite manner, and generally humane qualities. Chan is especially interesting in that come critics consider him to be the first example, in this kind of fiction, of an Asian who is a sympathetic character rather than a villain, while others consider him to be an offensive stereotype.

S. S. Van Dine is the author of twelve novels starring the detective Philo Vance, who, like Lord Peter Wimsey, is an English aristocrat, although all of his cases have an American urban setting. An extremely erudite man with a world-weary air, Vance was the best-educated and most refined detective of this era. Van Dine, under his real name of Wright, was a literary critic who made the detective story an object of research and study. The result was the publication of the "twenty rules for detective stories," only one of several efforts to define the exact characteristics of the form. Both readers and writers of this period had definite expectations and resented efforts in the field that did not follow certain specifications. The idea of fair play with the reader was essential; that is, the game must be played with all the evidence needed to solve the crime. There must be no love interest to detract from the business of solving the mystery, the detective could not be the criminal, and the solution could not come about as a result of accident or wild coincidence. During the detective novel's golden age, these rules were taken quite seriously by those who believed that a permanent form of popular fiction had been established.

While the classic detective story was being established in England and the United States, an American development turned the detective novel in a new direction. Manfred B. Lee and Frederic Dannay collaborated to create a detective who would achieve worldwide fame. Ellery Queen, ostensibly the author of the novels that describe his cases, is an amateur detective and professional writer who works with his father, Inspector Richard Queen of the New York Police Department. Inspector Queen provides the clues and investigative techniques while his son, Ellery, puts the evidence together. They are not supermen, after Sherlock Holmes, nor are they all-knowing in the manner of Philo Vance, but professionals dealing with a more realistic crime scene than that of their predecessors. Ellery Queen was thus a crossover figure leading to the police procedural story and to the kind of detective fiction that came to reflect the actual criminal class, as well as the working of the criminal justice system, in the United States.

HARD-BOILED DETECTIVE FICTION

In the 1930's, while the classic detective story was thriving, another kind of mystery story came into being—the hard-boiled detective novel. The preeminent writers of this school were Dashiell Hammett, Raymond Chandler, and—in the next generation—Ross Macdonald. Some of these writers began writing for *Black Mask*, a pulp magazine, in the

1920's. Hammett's Sam Spade, who appeared in *The Maltese Falcon* (serial 1929-1930, book 1930), is characteristic of the new detective: a private eye in a not-very-successful office who solves crimes by following people around in unsavory neighborhoods, having fights in alleys, and dealing with informers. He is cynical regarding the political dealings that go on behind the scenes and is aware of the connections between criminals and the outwardly respectable. He trusts no one, while he himself follows the dictates of a personal code. Hammett's *The Thin Man* (1934), which became the basis for a series of motion pictures, was a return to the more traditional form of detective fiction.

Another member of the hard-boiled school was Raymond Chandler, who wrote seven novels featuring his sleuth Philip Marlowe. Chandler, describing the ideal detective hero, said, "Down these mean streets a man must go who is not himself mean, who is neither tarnished nor afraid." Such a man is aware of the corruption he will find, but he is governed by a code that includes faithfulness to the client and an abhorrence of crime without an avenging or sadistic bent. Chandler specialized in complex plots, realistic settings, and snappy dialogue in novels such as *The Big Sleep* (1939), *Farewell, My Lovely* (1940), and *The Lady in the Lake* (1943). He was also a theoretician of the detective story, and his essay "The Simple Art of Murder" (1944) is an important document in the annals of crime literature.

After the introduction of the hard-boiled detective and the many stories involving the routine investigations of official law-enforcement agencies, the tradition of the superman detective declined. Fictional detectives lost their aristocratic manners and eccentricities, while the crimes being investigated gained interest not because they involved yet another bizarre or ingenious way to commit murder, but because of the influence of the psychological makeup or the social status of the criminal. The criminal was also less likely to be an amateur than a habitual malefactor. Limiting the suspects by setting the story in confined quarters—such as a country house or an ocean liner—gave way to a story that took the reader into the mean streets referred to by Chandler. These stories often involved the brutality of the police, more violence on the part of the detective, frankness in matters of sex, and the use of formerly taboo language. Mickey Spillane's Mike Hammer typified a new breed of private detectives, one who is given to acts of sadistic violence.

This often brutal social realism is also reflected in the work of Erle Stanley Gardner, best known for his creation of the lawyer-detective Perry Mason. The hero of more than eighty novels, Mason was first characterized in the hard-boiled tradition; early novels such as *The Case of the Velvet Claws* (1933) and *The Case of the Curious Bride* (1934) emphasize the fast-paced action and involuted plots that superseded the literary quality typical of Sayers's work. While retaining his early penchant for extralegal tactics, Mason gradually developed into a courtroom hero, allowing his assistant detective Paul Drake to do the research while Mason excelled in the spectacular oral combat of the cross-examination. Many of Gardner's plots were drawn from his own legal experiences as an attorney; having founded the Court of Last Resort, Gardner demonstrated a concern for the helpless. In keeping with this concern, he modified the detective genre by introducing the state as the villain and attacking the urban evils of capitalistic greed for wealth and power.

In championing the defenseless, Gardner was the voice of a modern Everyman during the decades between 1930 and 1960. Viewing themselves as vulnerable to the dictates of the state (such as the establishment of Prohibition and income tax), readers achieved vicarious satisfaction in seeing the problems of average people solved. The mass popularity of Mason's cases was the result not only of their victories over the "system" but also of the medium they employed. Gardner was, by his own admission, a "product of the paperback revolution," and he further lowered the literary standards of classical detective fiction by dictating his novels. He was also the script supervisor for the television series *Perry Mason* (starring Raymond Burr and running from 1957 to 1966), which furthered the personal appeal and accessibility of the detective. Unlike the superhuman Lord Peter Wimsey and Philo Vance, whose intellectual and aristocratic qualities are extraordinary and intimidating, Perry Mason is a successful but common professional, combining the wit of the golden-age sleuth with the cynical pertinacity of the hard-boiled detective.

POLICE PROCEDURAL NOVEL

While the hard-boiled mystery developed one element of the classic detective novel—the appeal of a recurring hero with yet another case to solve—in a strikingly new direction, the sheer fascination of deduction that characterized the golden age of the detective novel was developed in a new subgenre: the police procedural, a kind of fictional documentary often purporting to be taken from actual police files. These stories detail the routines of investigative agencies, taking the reader into forensic laboratories and describing complex chemical testing of the evidence. Hardworking police officers interview suspects, conduct stakeouts, shadow people, and investigate bank accounts. Even if there is a major figure who is in charge of the case, the investigation clearly is a matter of teamwork, with standard areas of expertise and responsibility: in short, a realistic depiction of actual police methods.

These stories date from World War II and are typified by the television series *Dragnet* and Sidney Kingsley's Broadway play *Detective Story* (1949). One of the major writers of the police procedural is Ed McBain, who wrote more than thirty novels about the "87th precinct" in a fictional urban setting that closely resembles New York City. The police procedural has proved to be a versatile form that can be used as the basis for a symbolic story with intentions far beyond that of crime solving, as in Lawrence Sanders's *The First Deadly Sin* (1973). Similarly, Tom Sharpe's *Riotous Assembly* (1971) is a police procedural set in South Africa that uses the form to ridicule apartheid, hypocrisy, and racial stereotyping.

Ostensibly, the psychological crime novels of Georges Simenon should also belong in the police procedural category; however, Inspector Jules Maigret of the Paris Police Department uses neither scientific nor rational methods to identify murderers. Similar to

Perry Mason in his bourgeois appeal (Maigret is heavyset, smokes a pipe, and is fond of domesticity) and in his delegation of research responsibilities to subordinates, Maigret solves crimes by absorbing the ambience of the place in which they were committed. By familiarizing himself with social customs, geography, and personalities, Maigret "becomes" the suspect and uses psychology and intuition to discern the criminal's identity. Patience rather than flamboyance characterizes Maigret; he relies on the hunches of his sympathetic imagination instead of on factual clues. While Maigret inhabits the sordid world of the hard-boiled detective, he sees himself as a "repairer of destinies" and acts more like a humble priest eliciting confessions than a vindictive policeman triumphing over evil.

In addition to departing from convention in Maigret's unique style of detection, Simenon also defies genre restrictions in the style of his work. *Pietr-le-Letton* (1931; *The Strange Case of Peter the Lett*, 1933; also known as *Maigret and the Enigmatic Lett*, 1963) was written in 1929, but it has little in common with the analytical works of the golden age. Accused of being too literary in his early psychological novels, Simenon probes the ambiguity of human behavior, acknowledging the capacity of people to sin while maintaining a sympathetic understanding of their actions. Readers of the Maigret novels are unable to see evil in terms of black and white, as readers of Gardner's works do, and come away with as much compassion for the murderer as for the victim. Simenon denies both the mental action of the classical period of detective fiction and the physical action of the hard-boiled period, promoting instead the action of the heart. In so doing, he demonstrates the versatility of the detective fiction genre.

New subgenres

While retaining many of its traditional core characteristics, detective fiction in the last decades of the twentieth century became increasingly varied, with many new subgenres emerging. Among the most popular and highly regarded writers that became prominent during this time were P. D. James and Dick Francis of England and Elmore Leonard of the United States. James writes in the so-called golden-age tradition of such authors as Agatha Christie and Ngaio Marsh (both of whom are still widely read). Her novels, longer and denser than most in the genre, have series detectives (Scotland Yard inspector Adam Dalgliesh and private eye Cordelia Gray) who are neither stereotypical nor two-dimensional but rather singular people whose private lives directly affect their professional activities. Dalgliesh, for example, is a poet whose wife died giving birth to their first child, a double tragedy that continues to haunt him. The cases he pursues are multifaceted; James develops complex milieus and characters, and there is always a thematic element (sometimes religious). Close to her in method is Ruth Rendell, whose Inspector Wexford novels also feature psychological probing and have equally complex puzzles but lack a thematic dimension. Both women's novels generally fall into the police procedural subgenre, as do Colin Dexter's Inspector Morse novels, which have an introspective, intellectual protagonist who is quite similar in temperament and method to Dalgliesh. Set in and around Oxford University in England, a Dexter novel usually has a religious element and a dollop of social criticism. Younger than James, Rendell, and Dexter but also a writer of procedurals is Peter Robinson, a Yorkshire native turned Canadian whose increasingly popular mysteries are set in his native northern England. His detective is the gruff but sensitive Inspector Banks (closer to Wexford than to Dalgliesh or Morse), and each novel concurrently tracks several separate crimes at once, much as Ed McBain and J. J. Marric do in their police procedurals.

The many novels of former British steeplechase jockey Dick Francis have been best sellers on both sides of the Atlantic. Each is a fast-paced thriller, but at its heart is a narrative in the golden-age manner, a standard whodunit in which the nonprofessional sleuth exposes industrial corruption, a racing scandal, or some other crime. The admirable, even exemplary, hero inevitably finds himself in an unfamiliar situation, and in a predictable Francis set piece has a life-threatening encounter with an adversary at some late point in the book. Having overcome a variety of physical, intellectual, and emotional challenges, he restores a measure of normality to the society and returns to his normal pursuits. In a departure from the norm, the hero is not an outsider dealing with a case that just came his way but rather part of a group into which criminality has intruded. Holmes, Wolfe, Archer, Maigret, and Dalgliesh may never again come into contact with the principals in their cases; Francis's detectives, however, continue to live with their erstwhile clients, seeing them regularly at the Jockey Club and other familiar spots. The novels are formulaic, but Francis has maintained a freshness over the years by eschewing the series detective, although his heroes are basically alike. Another Francis standard is the first-person narrative, through which he gains immediacy as well as increased reader empathy with the hero.

Anything but formulaic are Elmore Leonard's best sellers, which are written in the hard-boiled tradition of Chandler, Hammett, and Macdonald. Like Francis, Leonard shies away from a series detective, but he revisits characters (law enforcers and law breakers), and though his milieus range far and wide, he also returns to such places as Detroit and south Florida. While he fills his varied novels with social misfits and assorted grotesques, many of his characters are ordinary people who find themselves in extraordinary situations. Readers can also expect a spare style in the Ernest Hemingway manner, dialogue that rings true to life, and a fast-paced narrative with a chase as a central element. Leonard began his career as a writer of Westerns, and this background is evident in his plotting and style. Another hallmark is his shifting point of view. His characters, good and bad, tell their own stories; Elmore thus avoids omniscient narrators. Further, he changes the narrative point of view several times within a book, carrying the practice to an extreme in *Maximum Bob* (1991), in which part of an episode is told from an alligator's point of view. Shifts in time between the past and present are another Leonard commonplace, and this characteristic and the others may reflect his experience as a writer of screenplays. Leonard is less predictable than most of his peers, for his subjects, settings, and plots run the gamut of possibilities. *The Hot Kid* (2005), for example, is set during the Great Depression, *Pagan Babies* (2000) is set in Rwanda and Detroit, and *Get Shorty* (1990), one of several of his books that have been adapted into feature films, takes its protagonist from Miami to Las Vegas to Los Angeles. Leonard's books are full of surprising protagonists, from a midwestern couple confined in the federal witness protection program to a loan shark turned music producer to an Arizona cowboy caught up in the Spanish-American War. Before he writes, Leonard or a surrogate visits potential milieus and does on-the-spot research to ensure verisimilitude. This process, coupled with his imagination, narrative skills, and incredible ear for dialogue, has led to critical and popular acclaim for Leonard.

Another popular crime novelist who engages in extensive prewriting research is Patricia Cornwell, who, before becoming an author, worked as a police reporter and for the Richmond, Virginia, chief medical examiner as a keeper of forensic records. She also studied forensic science and rode with homicide detectives as a first responder to crime scenes. This background and the preparation she does for each project have allowed Cornwell to produce graphically realistic novels that are almost case studies in such areas as forensic anthropology (*All That Remains*, 1992) and deoxyribonucleic acid (DNA) testing (*Postmortem*, 1990). Her series detective is Kay Scarpetta, a physician who is Richmond's chief medical examiner. Talented scientist though she is, Scarpetta is a woman with a personal life that occasionally intrudes upon her professional activities. Scarpetta's niece, like Cornwell herself, is lesbian, and the novels have always treated sexual identity matter-of-factly. Despite the characters' romantic problems and their confrontations with grisly inhumanity and irrationality, Scarpetta remains a decent person who copes and ultimately triumphs, sometimes over a local, state, or federal bureaucracy, but always over criminals.

Because the boundaries separating crime writing categories are often indistinct, Cornwell sometimes is placed with the hard-boiled group of writers and at other times is placed in the police procedural genre. The police procedural flourished during the 1980's and 1990's, not only because of new Ed McBain books but also because of such varied series as Tony Hillerman's New Mexico Navajo Indian mysteries, featuring Jim Chee and Joe Leghorn; James Lee Burke's Dave Robicheaux novels set in Louisiana; Archer Mayor's Joe Gunther books, which take place primarily in Brattleboro, Vermont; Reginald Hill's Dalziel and Pascoe Yorkshire whodunits; and Stuart Kaminsky's and Martin Cruz Smith's Soviet Union books.

The traditional mystery, increasingly called the "cozy," experienced a renaissance at the end of the twentieth century. Originally pejorative, the term "cozy" refers to novels in which the setting is noncriminal and in which the detective (usually not a full-time sleuth, but rather a college professor, bookstore proprietor, or English nobleman) engages in an intellectual chess match with the reader and faces a variety of suspects. The seriousness may be tempered with some humor, and the stories shy away from graphic violence, overt sex, and crude, lowlife characters. The cozy is often associated with British writers, with whom the form originated, but Americans such as Amanda Cross, Martha Grimes, Carolyn G. Hart, and Joyce Porter are popular practitioners of the form.

The private-eye subgenre also experienced a renaissance toward the end of the century, with a major change being that the stories were set in places other than New York, San Francisco, Chicago, or Los Angeles: Cedar Rapids (Ed Gorman's Jack Dwyer), Cincinnati (Jonathan Valin's Harry Stoner), Detroit (Loren D. Estleman's Amos Walker), North Carolina (Margaret Maron's Judge Deborah Knott), and a series of national parks (Nevada Barr's Anna Pidgeon). Female private eyes, perhaps influenced by the successes of P. D. James's Cordelia Gray, also started to come to the fore. Liza Cody's London agency operative Anna Lee first appeared in *Dupe* (1980). Two years later came two important American debuts: Sue Grafton's Kinsey Milhone in *A Is for Alibi* (1982) and Sara Paretsky's V. I. Warshawski in *Indemnity Only* (1982). Noteworthy, too, is Linda Barnes's Boston private eye Carlotta Carlyle, whose first appearance in a novel is in *A Trouble of Fools* (1987). Marcia Muller's Sharon McCone is sometimes considered the first of the hard-boiled female detectives. McCone has appeared in more than twenty-five novels, including *Edwin of the Iron Shoes* (1977) and *Burn Out* (2008), and Muller was awarded the Mystery Writers of America's Grand Master award in 2005.

Several detective novel subgenres either emerged or gained in popularity during the 1980's and 1990's. Series with religious themes and clerics as detectives include William X. Kienzle's Father Robert Koesler books, Joseph Telushkin's Rabbi Daniel Winter mysteries, and Ellis Peters's medieval Brother Cadfael novels. The Amanda Cross mysteries starring Professor Kate Fansler, M. D. Lake's campus cop Peggy O'Neill novels, and Edith Skom's literature lecturer Beth Austin books are academic whodunits, mysteries set on college or university campuses. New authors began featuring African American detectives (Walter Mosely, P. J. Parrish), Native American detectives (Thomas Perry, Aimée Thurlo), and gay or lesbian detectives (Lev Raphael, Katherine V. Forrest). Historical detective fiction, in which the action is set in the past, was a rarity until the 1970's, when it became a major subgenre, as practiced not only by Ellis Peters but also by such authors as Peter Lovesey, whose Victorian mysteries feature Sergeant Cribb; Jacqueline Winspear, whose sleuth Maisie Dobbs was a nurse on the front lines in World War I; and Edward Marston (pseudonym of Keith Miles), who has authored both medieval and Elizabethan novels. Marston's eleventh century Domesday Book series is developed around the device of William the Conqueror's men traveling the countryside to review problems stemming from the ruler's census and property survey. Spurred by sibling rivalry, the desire for material gain, and the determination to purge suppressed grievances, people murder and cause havoc in a society that remains insecure two decades after the upheavals of the Norman Conquest. By the time they leave an area, the king's men have adjudicated land claims and have exorcised real and imagined evils. Another Marston series, set in England at the end of the sixteenth century, centers on a London theater group whose stage manager turns to detection when deaths occur offstage.

The several plots that Marston typically orchestrates in each of his medieval and Elizabethan mysteries exemplify such subjects as unrequited love, political and social ambition, sibling rivalry, the intrusion of the past upon the present, and questions of personal identity. They are very much like the subjects of most other detective novels, whatever their category or subgenre. In other words, however much detective fiction changes, it retains fundamentals of early and golden-age crime stories, which traditionally used murder as a dramatic means of focusing on a wide variety of human issues.

At the beginning of the twenty-first century, the publishing industry began to decline in the wake of economic downturns and the availability of online media. In 2006, retail sales of mystery fiction had accounted for about $400 million in the United States, behind only romance novels, science fiction and fantasy, and classic literary fiction. Partially in response to marketing demands, a new wave of "cozy" detective series appeared. Apparently aimed at middle-age women, these new series had hobbies and careers as their "hooks." The detectives were women (often single mothers) who solved crimes while engaged in such activities as running coffeehouses, scrapbooking, blowing glass, repairing old houses, catering, selling candies or herbs, knitting, crocheting, or working in a library. Many of these books were short and less psychologically developed than the works of authors such as P. D. James and Patricia Cornwell—meant to be consumed quickly and in quantity, like the pulp fiction of the past. With the continued publication of books by authors including Elizabeth George, Michael Connelly, Michael Chabon, and Walter Dean Myers, however, the literary detective novel continued to thrive.

F. William Nelson
Updated by Gerald H. Strauss

BIBLIOGRAPHY

Barzun, Jacques, and Wendell Hertig Taylor. *A Catalogue of Crime.* New York: Harper & Row, 1989. Highly personal compilation by two voracious readers of crime fiction contains more than five thousand brief descriptions and judgments of works in most categories of the genre as well as a variety of critical studies.

DeAndrea, William L., ed. *Encyclopedia Mysteriosa.* New York: Prentice Hall, 1994. Comprises alphabetically arranged entries about mystery authors, books, and characters as well as films and television and radio programs in the mystery genre. Includes ample cross-references and occasional longer entries (covering topics such as dime novels and the hard-boiled detective) by experts. Edited by a mystery novel writer and critic.

Frank, Lawrence. *Victorian Detective Fiction and the Nature of Evidence: The Scientific Investigations of Poe, Dickens, and Doyle.* New York: Palgrave Macmillan, 2003. Provides the framework for the development of the genre of detective fiction.

Gorman, Ed, Martin H. Greenberg, Larry Segriff, and John Breen, eds. *The Fine Art of Murder.* New York: Carroll & Graf, 1993. Collection of articles by crime fiction writers and critics is not intended as a definitive study of the genre but serves as a good introduction. Useful and entertaining, although some important writers are ignored.

Hadley, Mary. *British Women Mystery Writers: Authors of Detective Fiction with Female Sleuths.* Jefferson, N.C.: McFarland, 2002. Analyzes the works of women writers from the 1960's to the beginning of the twenty-first century, including P. D. James, Jennie Melville, Liza Cody, Val McDermid, Joan Smith, Susan Moody, Judith Cutler, and Lynda La Plante.

Kelleghan, Fiona, ed. *One Hundred Masters of Mystery and Detective Fiction.* Pasadena, Calif.: Salem Press, 2001. Collection of biographical and critical essays presents discussion of the most important figures in the genre before 1988.

Markowitz, Judith A. *The Gay Detective Novel: Lesbian and Gay Main Characters and Themes in Mystery Fiction.* Jefferson, N.C.: McFarland, 2004. Survey of series and stand-alone novels published since 1964 provides analysis of main characters, themes, and plot elements. Includes an extensive list of authors and their works.

Panek, LeRoy. *The Origins of the American Detective Story.* Jefferson, N.C.: McFarland, 2006. Covers the formative years of American detective fiction, from the late nineteenth century to the early twentieth century.

Rzepka, Charles J. *Detective Fiction.* Hoboken, N.J.: Polity Press, 2005. Presents the history of the genre from its modern beginnings in the early eighteenth century to its present state, focusing on urbanization, the rise of the professions, brain science, legal and social reform, war and economic dislocation, class-consciousness, and changing concepts of race and gender.

Symons, Julian. *Bloody Murder: From the Detective Story to the Crime Novel.* 3d rev. ed. New York: Mysterious Press, 1993. Update of a classic study by a major writer of crime novels and stories offers sound critical and historical analysis. Naturally reflects Symons's biases, but presents a balanced overview of the genre.

Thomas, Ronald R. *Detective Fiction and the Rise of Forensic Science.* New York: Cambridge University Press, 2004. Examines how the development of forensic science, from the invention of the lie detector to the uses of DNA, has influenced detective fiction in Great Britain and the United States.

PETER ABRAHAMS

Born: Brookline, Massachusetts; June 28, 1947

OTHER LITERARY FORMS

Peter Abrahams is known primarily for his novels, which have been translated into several languages, including Chinese, Dutch, Greek, Hungarian, Japanese, Polish, Russian, and Swedish, indicating the breadth of his appeal.

ACHIEVEMENTS

With the publication of his first novel, *The Fury of Rachel Monette*, Peter Abrahams was widely recognized as an important new voice in the genre of crime fiction. His subsequent novels have strengthened his hold on the imagination of critics and general readers alike. In an interview, Abrahams expressed great admiration for the works of American-Canadian crime novelist Ross Macdonald and others like him. Abrahams particularly noted that Macdonald's main character, detective Lew Archer, was developed by Macdonald to grow over the years as a human being and to become more interesting and complex. Furthermore, Archer was given a broader understanding of life and began to respond more deeply to the inevitable messiness of human experience. One recognizes the same qualities in characters created by Abrahams.

Abrahams effectively uses the conventions of the melodramatic crime thriller to create intense reader involvement. His novels also rise above others with their sophisticated rendering of flesh-and-blood individuals caught up in the dilemmas of contemporary life.

Lights Out was nominated for an Edgar Award, and *Down the Rabbit Hole* won an Agatha Award. The Edgar and Agatha awards (named for Edgar Allan Poe and Agatha Christie) are among the most prestigious awards for mystery fiction. *The Fan* was made into a 1996 feature film starring Robert De Niro and Wesley Snipes.

BIOGRAPHY

Peter Abrahams was born and reared in Massachusetts. His father was a dentist, and his mother a writer. He acquired a love of reading from his mother, from whom he also learned the basic rules of writing fiction, the most important of which is to be original. As a boy, he particularly loved adventure stories, such as Robert Louis Stevenson's *Treasure Island* (1883). Like those stories, Abrahams's works are notably effective in creating suspense.

Abrahams was graduated from Williams College in Massachusetts with a bachelor of arts degree in 1968. He then spent two years in the Bahamas, working as a spear fisherman. From there he went to Toronto, Canada, where he worked for a time in radio as a producer for the Canadian Broadcasting Corporation. His novels reflect these international experiences in a number of ways, particularly in his exploration of the United States' relationship with and impact upon other regions of the world.

In 1978, Abrahams married Diana Gray, a teacher. They had four children, two daughters and two sons. Soon after his marriage, Abrahams began to publish his critically and commercially successful fiction at the rate of one novel every other year.

The reading interests of Abrahams's children seem to have influenced him to try his hand at writing fiction for younger readers. In 2005, he published *Down the Rabbit Hole*, a mystery story with parallels to Lewis Carroll's *Alice's Adventures in Wonderland* (1865). Other mystery novels for young readers include *Behind the Curtain* and *Into the Dark*, and they, too, have enjoyed great popularity and recognition.

ANALYSIS

In his fiction, Peter Abrahams often employs variations on the double motif, that is, paired characters that suggest the duality of human beings or the self as other, such as one finds in Stevenson's *Strange Case of Dr. Jekyll and Mr. Hyde* (1886). This technique is especially useful for a writer who sees the criminal world as an inverse image of the conventional world, with disturbing correlations. In *Revolution Number Nine*, for example, a gentle, reclusive, middle-age man must confront the extremist youth he once was, after his former identity and violent past are uncovered. In *Crying Wolf*, a brilliant professor and a dim-witted thug are linked by blood and a shared conviction of their superiority to human laws and moral restraints. In *The Tutor*, a disturbed young man tries to model himself on a charismatic teacher who intends to destroy him. In *Their Wildest Dreams*, a Russian American gangster is an outsized version of the protagonist's husband in mad pursuit of the American Dream. In *The Fan*, a disturbing symbiosis develops between a professional athlete and an obsessive fan.

Where many of his American contemporaries in the crime and mystery genre have a distinct regional focus in terms of setting (Robert B. Parker's Boston, Sara Paretsky's Chicago), Abrahams is much more likely to set his stories in various locales around the United States, as well as abroad. He intends to capture as many dimensions of America as possible, with novels set in widely different states and areas of the country: New Hampshire, Vermont, Louisiana, and Arizona, among others.

A PERFECT CRIME

A Perfect Crime is a fine example of Abrahams's strengths as a novelist. Set in contemporary New England, with allusions to Nathaniel Hawthorne's *The Scarlet Letter* (1850), the story is about the adulterous affair of Francie, an art dealer, and Ned, a radio personality who dispenses advice to people with relationship problems. Francie has been married to the brilliant but brittle Roger Cullingwood for over fifteen years, but the marriage has unraveled because of his inability to father a child, his recent loss of employment, and his increasingly militant attempts to control all aspects of his domestic life, including his wife.

As with many of Abrahams's stories, *A Perfect Crime* moves back and forth between two dominant points of view, in this case from that of wife Francie, who is seeking love and fulfillment, to that of husband Roger, who moves from suspicion to blazing anger to coldly plotting "the perfect crime" when he discovers his wife's infidelity. Ned and Francie have an apparently ideal place to conduct their affair, a cottage on a small island surrounded by a lake in bucolic New Hampshire. The cottage is owned by one of Francie's wealthy clients, who is currently living in Europe. Nothing can link the cottage in any obvious way to either of the lovers. The setting, which turns from idyllic to deadly with the first snowstorm, is an effective counterpoint to the emotions generated by this affair.

Francie began her affair with Ned out of desperation, as a response to an attractive man at a time when she felt increasingly thwarted and diminished by her husband's inadequacies and abuse. She was vulnerable, Ned was sympathetic. The reader notices questionable things about Ned that Francie is inclined to overlook for some time, such as his insistence that he could never leave his wife because of its potential impact on their daughter, and his almost obsessive insistence on absolute secrecy. Nevertheless, the affair unlocks deep and powerful reserves of sexuality, creativity, and profound love in Francie, dimensions of self that she was unaware of, or despaired of being able to express. Roger, noting the changes, quickly intuits the reason, and finds a way to confirm his suspicions about his cheating wife. He immediately decides on revenge as his only possible response, assessing how to get the most satisfaction for the least amount of investment and risk.

In his portrayal of Roger, Abrahams limns the sort of character that reappears in various guises in his fiction, the calculating narcissist who thinks he is smarter than everyone else, for whom all others are chess pieces in a game to be moved about at his will. Roger is nearly as clever as he thinks he is. His plan, from which much of the story's narrative energy derives, is brilliant.

The plan is also diabolical; it brings into play a grotesque criminal who is Roger's dark double and his instrument of retribution. This criminal, an unstable mix of psychosis and sexual deviance, is on parole after long years in prison for killing a police officer's wife in the same area of the country as the hideaway cottage. It is this same police officer who has the task of piecing together the clues from a bewildering and brutal murder.

OBLIVION

In *Oblivion*, Nick Petrov is a Los Angeles private investigator specializing in missing-persons cases. In his early forties, Petrov is intelligent, imaginative, and relentless; he is also famous as the detective who solved the baffling case of a particularly gruesome serial killer named Gerald Reasoner, who preyed on young women. The case provided the basis for a television movie, and one of the interesting variations on the double motif in this novel is the counterpoint between the actual case and its widely viewed film version.

As the story opens, Liza, an attractive woman in her early thirties, hires Petrov to find her missing fifteen-year-old daughter, Amanda. Petrov is reluctant to take the case at first, because Liza's account of herself, her daughter, and the disappearance seems constructed and implausible. He is persuaded, finally, to take the case because a child is involved and the mother seems genuinely desperate. As he begins investigating, Petrov experiences a sudden, severe headache accompanied by a flood of very early childhood memories. The headaches recur periodically, and with increasing intensity.

Petrov learns that Amanda once confided to a school friend that her birth mother was murdered. This apparent bit of adolescent melodrama adds to Petrov's unease about his client's story, so he surreptitiously searches Liza's house for something that might confirm Amanda's parentage. While there, he is surprised to get a telephone call from a former professional associate, and lover, Elaine Kostelnik, whom he has not seen in years. Kostelnik, recently appointed as the first female chief of police of the Los Angeles Police Department, also played a role in solving the Reasoner case. That role propelled her professionally, owing partly to the image of her created by the film.

Petrov's sleuthing uncovers some intriguing facts. Thus, he learns that Amanda's grandfather played football in high school, coached by Kostelnik's father. Moreover, the grandfather had two daughters. Lara, the older of the two, was murdered some years earlier, reportedly the seventh and last victim of Reasoner. Liza, the younger sister, is Petrov's unreliable client. This cluster of apparent coincidences sends Petrov back to the decade-old murder case to see what connections might exist between the present and the past.

Petrov follows an acquaintance of Amanda to Reasoner's former home, where he committed the atrocities, and he discovers Amanda inside. However, instead of being grateful for a rescue, she is convinced he is there to kill her, suggesting that she has found proof that Lara was not killed by Reasoner but by others, who now want her dead as well. At this point, Petrov experiences a blinding headache; he collapses and is taken to the hospital, where he is diagnosed with a brain tumor. After days of tests, he is sent home with a grim prognosis.

One of the finest aspects of this novel, which excels in so many ways, is the portrayal of Petrov's physical deterioration and the mental and emotional adjustments he makes to what is happening to him. Also brilliant is Abrahams's innovative use of the double motif here, as he portrays Petrov in search of his own self that existed prior to his collapse.

Liza and Amanda have disappeared. So, too, has Petrov's memory of them and of much else as well. However, provocative bits and pieces of the recent case are noticeable around his home and office. Unable to resist the dictates of his nature and the habits of many years, he sets out to put those pieces together. In doing so, he discovers the shocking truth about Amanda's disappearance and Lara's murder; he also uncovers disturbing truths about himself, a self that the current Petrov is prepared to leave behind as he tries to construct a more fulfilling life in the short time he has to live.

NERVE DAMAGE

Nerve Damage is the story of Roy Valois, a Vermont artist who is working on a very large modernist steel sculpture of his late wife, Delia. Delia, it seems, had worked for the Hobbes Institute, a nongovernmental organization that addresses the needs of the developing world. She died fifteen years earlier, and according to official reports, she was killed in a helicopter accident in Central America while on a work assignment; yet she lives on in Roy's memory, imagination, and art. Early in the story, Roy learns that he has a terminal disease. The narrative is propelled by the main character's increasing sense of urgency, and is pervaded by his deepening awareness of human limitations and mortality.

While talking with his lawyer and close friend about his last will and testament, Roy begins to wonder how he will be described in his obituary. This seemingly innocuous though morbid line of thought leads to a morbid fact: Obituaries of public figures and celebrities are often prepared in advance, leaving the final details to be filled in at the appropriate time. Roy persuades a local young man to hack into the *New York Times* computer system to find the artist's draft obituary. Most of the draft is as expected, except for one detail: It reports that Delia worked for the United Nations. It is a small discrepancy, but for Roy, who idealizes his late wife, an intolerable one, and so he sets out to correct it by contacting a *New York Times* staff writer.

In very short order, the young hacker disappears, the staff writer is murdered, and ominous signs indicate that Roy himself is under surveillance, by persons unknown. Roy's sense of identity, of selfhood, is challenged by the physical threat of extinction, owing to his disease and the danger unleashed by his inquiries, but even more so by the recognition that much of his past might not be as he imagined. He sets out to find the truth about his late wife, and thus about himself and their life together.

One of the most intriguing aspects of the story is Abrahams's grimly realistic portrayal of Roy's interaction with the cancer specialist in charge of his treatment. The doctor's cool, analytical handling of Roy the patient, as he swings between hope and despair, is as chilling as the dangers Roy encounters in pursuit of the truth about Delia's real work, and the circumstances of her death. This pursuit eventually takes Roy to Washington, D.C., and to the highest offices of the U.S. government. There, he finally uncovers the secrets of his wife and her past; in doing so, he also rescues an authentic part of their shared life and love that will live on after his death.

Another important dimension of this novel is its portrait of Roy the artist. Throughout the story, Roy continues to work on Delia's sculpture, which is described in great detail as it takes shape. His quest for the facts about his wife, therefore, is partly driven by his understandable curiosity regarding the most important person in his life. It is also driven by the artist's uncompromising dedication to finding and expressing the most profound human truth through making art. In this way, and others, the novel signals Abrahams's conviction regarding the critical importance of art, its role as discovery and revelation. This conviction is amply supported by Abrahams's substantial body of work.

Michael J. Larsen

OTHER MAJOR WORKS

SHORT FICTION: *Up All Night: A Short Story Collection*, 2008 (with others).

NONFICTION: *Turning the Tide: One Man Against the Medellin Cartel*, 1991 (with Sidney D. Kirkpatrick).

YOUNG ADULT LITERATURE: *Reality Check*, 2009.

BIBLIOGRAPHY

Abrahams, Peter. http://www.peterabrahams.com. Author's Web site features biographical information, author commentary, and reviews of major works. Provides a useful introduction and overview to Abrahams's work.

Oates, Joyce Carol. "Unforgettable." Review of *Oblivion*, by Peter Abrahams. *The New Yorker*, April 4, 2005. Highly respected novelist Oates provides an overview of *Oblivion* as well as insightful commentary on Abrahams's major themes and methods.

Scaggs, John. *Crime Fiction*. New York: Routledge, 2005. Part of the New Critical Idiom series, this brief but comprehensive book surveys the field of crime fiction. An excellent general overview of the genre.

Winks, Robin, and Maureen Corrigan, eds. *Mystery and Suspense Writers: The Literature of Crime, Detection, and Espionage*. New York: Scribner & Sons, 1998. An invaluable guide to major mystery writers and genres.

PAUL AUSTER

Born: Newark, New Jersey; February 3, 1947
Also known as: Paul Benjamin Auster

PRINCIPAL LONG FICTION

City of Glass, 1985
Ghosts, 1986
The Locked Room, 1986
In the Country of Last Things, 1987
The New York Trilogy, 1987 (includes City of Glass, Ghosts, and The Locked Room)
Moon Palace, 1989
The Music of Chance, 1990
Leviathan, 1992
Mr. Vertigo, 1994
Timbuktu, 1999
The Book of Illusions, 2002
Oracle Night, 2003
The Brooklyn Follies, 2006
Travels in the Scriptorium, 2007
Man in the Dark, 2008
Invisible, 2009

OTHER LITERARY FORMS

As a young man, Paul Auster (AW-stur) distinguished himself in the literary forms of translation and poetry. His well-received translations of the works of French poets Stéphane Mallarmé, Jacques Dupin, Joseph Joubert, and André du Bouchet led to his editing a bilingual anthology titled *The Random House Book of Twentieth-Century French Poetry*, published in 1982. Beginning in 1974, his own poetry was published in reviews and by small presses. The poetry collections *Disappearances: Selected Poems* (1988) and *Ground Work: Selected Poems and Essays, 1970-1979* (1990) were published after Auster made a name for himself in fiction. His nonfiction prose collection *The Art of Hunger, and Other Essays* and his memoir *The Invention of Solitude* were originally published in 1982, and a later memoir, *Hand to Mouth: A Chronicle of Early Failure*, appeared in 1997, after Auster had published eight novels. Scriptwriting is another genre for which Auster is noted. He wrote the screenplays for the films *Smoke* (1995), *Blue in the Face* (1995), which he also codirected, as well as for *Lulu on the Bridge* (1998). *I Thought My Father Was God, and Other True Tales from NPR's National Story Project* (2001) is another edited volume for which Auster received critical notice. Auster has also been involved in musical recordings and writing song lyrics, notably for his daughter's 2005 album with the New York band One Ring Zero titled *Sophie Auster*. In 2007, Auster's film *The Inner Life of Martin Frost*, which he both wrote and directed, was released; it stars his daughter Sophie Auster as the character Anna James. He adapted his novel *In the Country of Last Things* for a 2008 feature film in English and Spanish, directed by Alejandro Chomski and filmed in Argentina.

ACHIEVEMENTS

Paul Auster's works of fiction have earned him significant recognition. *City of Glass* was nominated for an Edgar Award for best mystery novel in 1986, and *The Locked Room* was nominated for a *Boston Globe* Literary Press Award for fiction in 1990. In 1993, Auster received the Chevalier de l'Ordre des Arts et des Lettres and also won the French Prix Medicis Étranger for foreign literature, for *Leviathan*. In 2006, he was awarded the Spanish Prince of Asturias Award for Letters.

BIOGRAPHY

Paul Benjamin Auster was born in Newark, New Jersey, on February 3, 1947, and grew up in the suburbs of Newark. He benefited early from the influence of an uncle who was a skilled translator and who encouraged his nephew's developing interest in writing and literature. In the summer between high school and college, Auster traveled to Europe, returning to the United States to attend Columbia University. He supported himself during his college years with a variety of freelance jobs, including translation and interpretation. Auster graduated from Columbia in 1969 with a B.A. in English and comparative literature, and he received his M.A. in the literature of the Renaissance the following year. Auster returned to Paris in 1971 and lived in France until 1974.

Back in New York in late 1974, Auster married the writer Lydia Davis. Together they worked on translations, and Auster began to publish poetry, reviews, and essays. In 1977, their son Daniel was born. Auster was at a low point in his life at this time—his marriage was failing, and he was unhappy with his writing career and having financial difficulties. By 1979 his marriage had ended. When his father died suddenly of a heart attack and left him a small inheritance, Auster was able to write without financial worry. He continued to work on poetry and translation, but by 1980 he had begun work on *The Invention of Solitude*, which includes a tribute to his father.

In 1981, Auster met and married Siri Hustvedt. A fertile time in his writing career began, and during the 1980's he published *The Random House Book of Twentieth-Century French Poetry*, *The Art of Hunger*, and more translations. The three novels of *The New York Trilogy*, as well as *In the Country of Last Things* and *Moon Palace*, received good reviews. He worked as a teacher of creative writing at Princeton University from 1986 to 1990, and his daughter Sophie was born in 1987.

Auster's next novel, *The Music of Chance*, published in 1990, attracted the attention of the motion-picture industry, and a film version was released in 1993. At the same time, Auster's story "Auggie Wren's Christmas Story" appeared in *The New York Times*, and director Wayne Wang became interested in turning the story into a film. Auster's script became the film *Smoke*, which was followed shortly by the companion piece *Blue in the Face*. By the time the two films were released in 1995, Auster had published two more novels, *Leviathan* and *Mr. Vertigo*. In 1997, the memoir *Hand to Mouth* was released. Auster was a member of the jury for the 1997 Cannes Film Festival; in 1998, the film *Lulu on the Bridge* appeared.

Timbuktu marked Auster's return to novel writing in 1999. The novels *The Book of Illusions*, *Oracle Night*, *The Brooklyn Follies*, *Travels in the Scriptorium*, and *Man in the Dark* appeared in rapid succession through the first decade of the twenty-first century, along with volumes of his collected poetry and nonfiction, collaborations with recording and visual artists, and another film, *The Inner Life of Martin Frost*.

Auster continues to produce novels, screenplays, nonfiction, and collaborative multimedia works. He lives and works in Brooklyn, New York, a location that has influenced much of his work. At the same time, he is deeply connected to Europe, where his work is popularly and critically acclaimed.

ANALYSIS

Paul Auster is best known as a postmodernist writer. "Postmodernism" is an elusive academic term applied to unconventional fiction from the late twentieth century onward that in style and theme investigates the methods of fiction. Beneath a deceptively simple fictional form—the detective novel, science fiction, the picaresque story—lies an intellectually stimulating, thematically complex interplay between reader and author as well as between protagonist and writer. Auster's fiction is accessible on the surface level, yet the subtext is worthy of the term "experimental." The appeal of postmodern fiction is intellectual; readers are forced to think about the writer's allusions, use of unexpected devices, and breaking of the rules of conventional fiction. Auster's fiction is intelligent and puzzling, influenced by the works of Nathaniel Hawthorne, Edgar Allan Poe, Samuel Beckett, and the French Symbolists.

The three short novels collected as *The New York Trilogy* (*City of Glass*, *Ghosts*, and *The Locked Room*) constitute Auster's most often discussed work. The use of the detective-story form to introduce themes of isolation and the crisis of the individual is taken as a prime example of postmodern literature, writing that may use traditional forms in ironic or displaced ways. Characteristic of postmodernist stories, the protagonists of Auster novels do not reach solutions. Many of his heroes disappear, die mysterious deaths, or lose all of their personal possessions.

Throughout his long fiction, Auster is critically admired for his diversity of form, his intelligence, the agility of his prose, and the complexity of his structure and themes. His writing appeals to a mass audience as well as to literary scholars; his fiction has a cult following among students. He is known for the variety of genres in which he works: poetry, memoirs, essays, and screenplays.

Auster's novels are connected, in many cases by the names of characters who appear in more than one novel, but above all by their abstraction and ambiguity and by their intertwining themes: the role of chance and coincidence and the unstable nature of identity. They feature mazes of story lines and narrative twists and turns in which fiction bleeds into reality. Much of Auster's work is characterized by its examination of language. The protagonist is often a writer, sometimes Auster himself.

THE NEW YORK TRILOGY

The New York Trilogy, composed of the three short novels *City of Glass*, *Ghosts*, and *The Locked Room*, has received more attention from critics than any of Auster's subsequent work. The three novels share a common style, theme, and New York setting. Auster intentionally blurs the distinction between reality and text, placing himself as a character in the first novel. This postmodern device raises questions of identity that resonate throughout the series. Auster takes the convention of mistaken identity and develops it into a metaphor for contemporary urban life.

The first novel, *City of Glass*, opens as a standard detective novel. Quinn, a detective novelist, receives a telephone call intended for a detective named Paul Auster. Quinn decides to take on Auster's identity and accept the case. The job is to tail a madman named Stillman who has recently been released from a mental institution. Once a promising linguist, Stillman had been committed for isolating his son in a locked room for nine years to try to re-create the primitive language of Adam and Eve. Now that Stillman has been released, the son's life is in danger.

The novel subtly shifts from a standard detective story to an existential quest for identity. It moves into the realm of serious literature as it explores themes of the degeneration of language, the shifting of identity, and the struggle to remain sane in the anonymity of the metropolis. Each detail is significant. Coincidences abound, particularly coincidences involving names. Quinn the watcher becomes as seedy and degenerate as Stillman the quarry. True to its postmodern identity, and typical of Auster's work, the novel does not actually offer a resolution. Questions remain unanswered; characters simply disappear.

Ghosts, the second novel of the trilogy, explores many of the same questions of identity and blurred distinctions between watcher and prey, detective and client, but on a more abstract plane. A client named White hires a detective named Blue to follow a man named Black. The three characters merge into one as Blue passes years watching Black writing a book in a room across the street, while Blue records his observations and mails them weekly to White.

Clearly the novel is meant to be a metaphor, and after carefully paying attention to details and clues, as is necessary in a mystery story, the reader is left with the question, What does it all mean? As in the first novel, the detective hired to watch merges into the watched.

In this novel, however, neither the reader nor the protagonist knows why the detective is watching his subject.

The final volume in the trilogy, *The Locked Room*, is the richest and most accessible of the three. The narrator is summoned by the wife of his old friend Fanshawe (the name is an allusion to Hawthorne's work), who has disappeared and is presumed dead. Fanshawe, a brilliant writer, has left behind a closetful of manuscripts and instructions for his friend to have them published. The narrator moves into Fanshawe's life, marrying his wife and publishing his work. He has nearly succumbed to believing the rumors that he is actually Fanshawe, or at least the creator of the works, when he receives a communication from the real Fanshawe. The plot becomes suspenseful and dangerous as the narrator follows Fanshawe to the brink of annihilation. He so identifies with Fanshawe that he nearly joins him in his dark night of the soul. Lines between truth and fiction are dramatically blurred in a deeply satisfying conclusion to the trilogy.

IN THE COUNTRY OF LAST THINGS

For *In the Country of Last Things*, Auster also uses an established genre, this time science fiction, to achieve his postmodernist ends. This novel shares stylistic and thematic concerns with *The New York Trilogy*. The protagonist, Anna Blume, travels to a large metropolis on another continent in search of her missing brother. She discovers a city in chaos, a hellish postapocalyptic scene, a futuristic nightmare of doom. At first the reader believes this is a dystopian novel of the future in the tradition of Aldous Huxley's *Brave New World* (1932) or George Orwell's *Nineteen Eighty-Four* (1949). The reader soon realizes, however, that this world represents the ethical, spiritual, and cultural chaos of the urban jungle of the present. Auster concludes that, without art and creativity, life is bleak.

MOON PALACE

Auster's novels following *In the Country of Last Things* cannot be as easily categorized by genre. Looser in structure, *Moon Palace* is sometimes referred to as a picaresque novel, as it follows its young hero's adventures on a journey in search of his lost father. This novel employs some of the familiar motifs of the bildungsroman: the struggling orphan, the lost father, the search for self, the journey as initiation into manhood. The writer-narrator, however, seems unconcerned with creating a realistic or believable plot; in fact, he himself does not seem to believe what he has written. The writer violates realistic conventions intentionally to investigate other functions of the novel. Plot and character are secondary to structure, the relationship between reader and writer, and the act of reading.

THE MUSIC OF CHANCE

The Music of Chance is another accessible story that can be enjoyed on many levels. It opens in the manner of a road-trip novel, as protagonist Jim Nashe takes to the road in search of himself. When his money runs out, he joins a young gambler, Pozzi, in a poker game against two eccentric lottery winners. When Jim and Pozzi fall into debt, they are forced to build a stone wall for the eccentrics as payment.

Critics have faulted this novel for weakness of plot and character, yet once again these "faults" seem to be intentional. In this work, Auster takes the opportunity to explore some of his favorite themes: the roles of coincidence and random chance, the consequences of solitude, the limitations of language and free will. Character and plot are deliberately unconvincing, calling attention to the author's other literary aims. Beneath a conventional exterior, Auster's fiction is disturbing, intellectually challenging, and structurally experimental. The use of gambling as a metaphor for the role of chance in life and the allusions to Samuel Beckett's absurdist and existentialist play *Waiting for Godot* (pb. 1952) in the character names add literary depth to the novel.

LEVIATHAN

Leviathan, published in 1992, is a complex novel in the looser style Auster adopted with *Moon Palace* three years earlier. The climax of the story, the death by explosion of the New York writer Benjamin Sachs, is unveiled on the first page. Another writer, Peter Aaron, becomes obsessed with writing the story of his friend's life, not unlike the narrator's obsession with Fanshawe in *The Locked Room*. Aaron uncovers a world of secrets, multiple and exchanged identities, and previously unknown connections between characters. Readers familiar with Auster's work will recognize such elements as the references to the detective-story framework of *The New York Trilogy*, the self-referential character of the writer-narrator, shifting identities, and the importance of the written word to creating and maintaining identity.

THE BOOK OF ILLUSIONS

The Book of Illusions is a novel that is as much driven by the double themes of chance and blurred identity as any of Auster's previous books. Zimmer, a university professor who has descended into alcoholism and loneliness following the loss of his wife and sons in an accident, happens upon the films of Hector Mann, a star of silent movies who had disappeared at the height of his career some sixty years earlier. Zimmer saves his sanity by writing a book about the film star. Then a letter arrives in Zimmer's mailbox, purported to be from Hector Mann's wife, saying that Mann is alive and would like to meet him. Is this a hoax?

Critics have deemed *The Book of Illusions* Auster's richest work to date, his best book in years. Auster's trademarks—coincidence, disappearance, twists and turns of plot, a writer protagonist, characters whose lives eerily reflect one another, merging identities, random events, the thin line between sanity and madness—merge with a plot-driven, fast-moving story. Allusions to a Hawthorne plot and to a translation from the French autobiography of François-René de Chateaubriand add literary interest. There is a new maturity and tenderness in the ending as the fictional character of Zimmer, now merged with the real writer, Auster himself, reaches a reconciliation of sorts, coming to terms with the deaths of his wife and children.

ORACLE NIGHT

Oracle Night is a book within a book within a book. Its main character, Sidney Orr, is a writer with similarities to Auster, a middle-aged married man who lives in Brooklyn. After recovering from a life-threatening illness, he buys a new blue notebook and begins writing a novel, also titled *Oracle Night*. The stage is set for another novel in which fiction bleeds into reality and identities merge.

While some critics have found the plot of *Oracle Night* even more unbelievable than the plots of most of Auster's other works, others have appreciated the novel's absurdity and have praised it for its chilling ghostliness. Chance and coincidence play major roles in the novel, which has echoes of the eerie mysteries of Edgar Allan Poe. The title suggests that fiction may shape reality, yet the ambiguous ending leaves the possibility of randomness open as well.

THE BROOKLYN FOLLIES

The Brooklyn Follies is a more straightforward, down-to-earth book than Auster's previous two novels. Like *Mr. Vertigo* and *Timbuktu*, *The Brooklyn Follies* is notable for its storytelling, though chance makes an inevitable appearance. All three novels have linear plot structures, and while they are enjoyable and sold well upon publication, Auster's devoted followers have not all appreciated the author's departure in these novels from his dark existentialism.

The protagonist of *The Brooklyn Follies* is Nathan Glass, a survivor of lung cancer who has come to Brooklyn to die, seeking only solitude and anonymity. He unexpectedly connects with an estranged nephew working in the bookstore of a former forger. In one of Auster's familiar references to Nathaniel Hawthorne, one of the plot twists involves a forgery of the first page of *The Scarlet Letter* (1850). Glass begins work on his own book, which he calls *The Book of Human Folly*, but his own despair is superseded by unexpected connections with other people. A collection of vignettes of typical Brooklyn characters is one of the pleasures of the book. In a novel that is warmer and more cheerful than most of Auster's work, Nathan finds redemption, but the ending darkens as a happy Nathan steps out into the bright sunshine of the morning of September 11, 2001.

TRAVELS IN THE SCRIPTORIUM

Travels in the Scriptorium, a spare, fable-like novella, is pure distilled Auster, reminiscent of *Ghosts* in its abstractness. Mr. Blank has lost all memory of his identity. He finds himself in a locked room, with a few labeled objects—DESK, CHAIR, LAMP—the labels of which mysteriously change places. Language itself is not to be trusted. Blank appears to be undergoing some kind of treatment; he feels a vague sense of guilt. In the room is a manuscript, the story within the story, and Blank begins to read. The narrative seems to be a report, but his doctor tells him it is fiction and suggests that he create an ending to the story as an exercise in "imaginative reasoning." As characters enter the room, Blank writes down their names so that he can remember them. The names he lists have appeared in previous Auster novels. The locked room appears to be Auster's own.

Stories with changing endings, objects with changing labels, characters that move from book to book, fact that is indistinguishable from fiction, loss of identity, a violent and chaotic dystopian society—reading Auster is like wandering in a maze or working a puzzle for which there is no solution. The more Auster one has read, the more intricate the layers become, but the message seems to recede further into abstraction. The elements of the novel are familiar, but the whole is outside conventional meaning.

Susan Butterworth

OTHER MAJOR WORKS

POETRY: *Disappearances: Selected Poems*, 1988; *Ground Work: Selected Poems and Essays, 1970-1979*, 1990; *Collected Poems*, 2004.

SCREENPLAYS: *"Smoke" and "Blue in the Face": Two Screenplays*, 1995; *Lulu on the Bridge*, 1998; *The Inner Life of Martin Frost*, 2007.

NONFICTION: *The Art of Hunger, and Other Essays*, 1982 (also known as *The Art of Hunger: Essays, Prefaces, Interviews*, 1991); *The Invention of Solitude*, 1982, 1988; *Hand to Mouth: A Chronicle of Early Failure*, 1997; *The Red Notebook: True Stories*, 2002; *The Story of My Typewriter*, 2002.

TRANSLATIONS: *A Tomb for Anatole*, 1983 (of Stéphane Mallarmé's poetry); *The Notebooks of Joseph Joubert: A Selection*, 1983.

EDITED TEXTS: *The Random House Book of Twentieth-Century French Poetry*, 1982; *I Thought My Father Was God, and Other True Tales from NPR's National Story Project*, 2001.

MISCELLANEOUS: *Collected Prose: Autobiographical Writings, True Stories, Critical Essays, Prefaces, and Collaborations with Artists*, 2003.

BIBLIOGRAPHY

Auster, Paul. "Interview, 1989-90." Interview by Larry McCaffery and Sinda Gregory. In *The Art of Hunger, and Other Essays*. Berkeley, Calif.: SBD, 1982. Long interview is a rich resource for readers interested in Auster's approach to writing.

Barone, Dennis, ed. *Beyond the Red Notebook: Essays on Paul Auster*. Philadelphia: University of Pennsylvania Press, 1995. Collection of critical essays on Auster's poetry and prose, some previously published in periodicals, addresses many different aspects of his work. Includes a detailed bibliography of works by and about Paul Auster.

_____. "Paul Auster/Danilo Kis Issue." *Review of Contemporary Fiction* 14, no. 1 (Spring, 1994): 7-96. Special issue devoted to the works of these two authors includes essays by scholars such as Charles Baxter, Sven Birkerts, Paul Bray, Mary Ann Caws, Robert Creeley, Alan Gurganus, Mark Irwin, Mark Osteen, Mark Rudman, Katherine Washburn, and Curtis White.

Bloom, Harold, ed. *Paul Auster.* Philadelphia: Chelsea House, 2004. Collection of sixteen critical essays includes discussion of *The New York Trilogy* and the themes of fear of identity loss, chance, and confinement in Auster's novels. Literary critic Bloom provides an informative introduction.

Brown, Mark. *Paul Auster.* New York: Palgrave, 2007. Offers extended analysis of Auster's essays, poetry, fiction, films, and collaborative projects. Traces how Auster's representations of New York and city life have matured from a position of urban nihilism to qualified optimism.

Donovan, Christopher. *Postmodern Counternarratives: Irony and Audience in the Novels of Paul Auster, Don DeLillo, Charles Johnson, and Tim O'Brien.* New York: Routledge, 2005. Explores the role of Auster and three other major contemporary ironic novelists amid questions of social realism and morality in the twenty-first century.

Martin, Brendan. *Paul Auster's Postmodernity.* New York: Routledge, 2008. Theorizes that in creating fictional protagonists who appear to be versions of himself, Auster constructs postmodern autobiography.

Shiloh, Ilana. *Paul Auster and Postmodern Quest: On the Road to Nowhere.* New York: Peter Lang, 2002. Discusses Auster's work from the perspective of the narrative of the quest, focusing on eight novels written between 1982 and 1992.

Springer, Carsten. *A Paul Auster Sourcebook.* New York: Peter Lang, 2001. Outlines many of the real-life sources for Auster's fictions. Also contains an extensive bibliography of his writings and further secondary sources in print, including an extensive list of interviews, newspaper articles, and Web sites.

ROBERTO BOLAÑO

Born: Santiago, Chile; April 28, 1953
Died: Barcelona, Spain; July 15, 2003
Also known as: Roberto Bolaño Ávalos

PRINCIPAL LONG FICTION

Consejos de un discípulo de Morrison a un fanático de Joyce, 1984 (with
    Antoni García Porta)
La pista de hielo, 1993
La senda de los elefantes, 1993 (also known as *Monsieur Pain*, 1999)
Estrella distante, 1996 (*Distant Star*, 2004)
La literatura Nazi en América, 1996 (*Nazi Literature in the Americas*, 2008)
Los detectives salvajes, 1998 (*The Savage Detectives*, 2007)
Amuleto, 1999 (*Amulet*, 2006)
Nocturno de Chile, 2000 (*By Night in Chile*, 2003)
Una novelita lumpen, 2002
2666, 2004 (English translation, 2008)

OTHER LITERARY FORMS

Roberto Bolaño (boh-LAWN-yoh) was primarily a poet. He published his first chapbook, *Reinventar al amor* (reinventing love), in 1976. In 1979, he edited a collection of poetry, *Muchachos desnudos bajo el arcoiris de fuego* (naked guys under a rainbow of fire), which reflects the work of an aesthetic movement he cofounded. He continued writing and publishing poetry until his death. Bolaño also wrote reviews, journalistic columns, critical articles, commentaries on literature and society, and autobiographical essays. Some of these are collected in the volume *Entre paréntesis: Ensayos, artículos, y discursos, 1998-2003* (2004; in parentheses: essays, articles, and speeches).

ACHIEVEMENTS

The publication of *Los detectives salvajes* in 1998 made Roberto Bolaño a sensation among readers of the Spanish language, as did the novel's 2007 translation, *The Savage Detectives*, for English readers. In 1999, the novel earned him the prestigious Rómulo Gallegos Prize, the Spanish equivalent of the Pulitzer Prize, as well as the Herralde Prize the same year. Among his other awards is the Municipal Prize of Santiago for the short-story collection *Llamadas telefónicas* (1997; phone calls). Many critics consider him the greatest Latin American fiction writer of the second half of the twentieth century, particularly because he departed from the tradition of Magical Realism of writers such as Gabriel García Márquez.

BIOGRAPHY

Roberto Bolaño was born Roberto Bolaño Ávalos on April 28, 1953, in Santiago, Chile. His father was a truck driver and amateur boxer, and his mother was a mathematics teacher. The family lived in a series of small cities in south-central Chile before moving to Mexico City, Mexico, in 1968.

Bolaño thrived in the Mexican capital, reading voraciously and eclectically, and he dropped out of school to immerse himself in political and literary culture. He was especially devoted to poetry. Very much in the spirit of the hippie era, he joined a Mexican communist group and traveled to El Salvador to take part in the leftist ferment there. In 1973, he returned to Chile to support the Socialist government of President Salvador Allende. Not long afterward, General Augusto Pinochet Ugarte staged a coup. Bolaño was briefly placed under arrest.

In 1974, Bolaño was again in Mexico City, where he cofounded the reactionary literary movement infrarealism, which was influenced by Dadaism and the French Surrealist poet André Breton. Intent upon disrupting the staid establishment poetry of the era, Bolaño and his friends soon became notorious for disrupting poetry readings by shouting out their own poetry from the audience.

Infrarealism, however, proved short-lived. The movement's brief life, and a failed romance, led Bolaño to leave Mexico in 1977. After a year traveling through France, Spain, and North Africa, he settled for a while in Barcelona. He worked as an itinerant laborer in a variety of jobs—including salesman, night watchman, dock worker, and grape picker—and continued to write poetry.

In 1982, Bolaño married Carolina Lopez, a Catalonian, and settled in the resort town of Blanes on the Catalonian coast. In 1984, he published his first novel, *Consejos de un discípulo de Morrison a un fanático de Joyce* (advice of a disciple of Morrison to a Joyce fanatic). He and his wife had a son, Lautaro, in 1991 and later a daughter, Alexandra. To earn a living for his family, which he called his "only motherland," Bolaño concentrated on writing fiction. He became a prolific writer, able to devote himself to the craft for long periods of time. By 1996, he was publishing at least one novel every year, as well as poems, essays, and newspaper columns.

Widely considered a major new writer, Bolaño remained a maverick, outspoken and often caustic. Nevertheless, his reputation steadily grew. At the same time, his health declined. Aware that he was dying, he rushed to complete his last novel to ensure financial security for his family. He passed away on July 15, 2003, in Barcelona. His novel *2666* was edited by his literary executor, Ignacio Echevarría, and published in 2004. In its original edition, the novel is more than eleven hundred pages long, and it became an immediate success. It was hailed by some critics as one of the most significant fictional works in a generation of Latin Americans.

ANALYSIS

Roberto Bolaño was a writer's writer. Literature was his subject matter. The fictions that people make out of their own lives constitute his primary theme, and the dangers of those fictions, especially as manifest in obsession, ambition, and self-deception, provide the narrative suspense of his plots. Moreover, he readily displays his debt to his favorite authors: Nicanor Parra of Chile, Jorge Luis Borges, Julio Cortázar of Argentina, Thomas Pynchon of the United States, and James Joyce of Ireland. Scores more are mentioned in his works, and he includes in his fiction discussion of topics such as aesthetics and literary movements, their contests, prizes, and films. Each novel opens a panorama on modern literature.

Bolaño himself frequently appears as a character in his fiction under his own name, as "B," or as his alter ego, Arturo Belano. He draws much of his material from his own experience and that of people he knew. *The Savage Detectives*, for instance, borrows from his times with friends in Mexico City, so much so that its second section is practically a roman à clef. This foundation in actual history helps give his fiction its exuberant immediacy and restlessness. Nearly all of his characters live a wandering existence, and the hint is that those who settle down lose the vitality that sets them apart, for better or worse. Many fictional characters also appear in more than one novel, and passages in some novels give rise to later novels, as is the case with *Distant Star*, which expands on the ending of *Nazi Literature in the Americas*.

Bolaño makes use of several genres, mixing them so that his narratives emerge from literary conventions but are not bound by them. The pursuit of a mystery is central to his plots, through detectives such as Romero in *Nazi Literature in the Americas*, amateur detectives such as Belano and Ulises Lima, or scholars such as those in the first section of *2666*. There are also scenes appropriate to satire, crime thrillers, romantic comedy, and the coming-of-age novel. Many stories are told by first-person narrators, a technique that intensifies the immediacy of the narratives. Other times, however, Bolaño creates a prismatic effect: Such novels as *The Savage Detectives* use dozens of narrators, so that a story is not so much told as pieced together from every available viewpoint.

Bolaño undermines conventions and foils the expectations of genre. His protagonists end up antiheroes, usually near death or left in fear and doubt at a novel's end. The effect is to remove literature from its usual status as an artifact, an entertainment created by satisfying typical plot and character patterns, and to impel readers to see the characters as not simply literary creations but also possible lives. Accordingly, Bolaño's fiction expresses human relationships and thereby reflects society—politics in particular. Having himself lived through political turmoil, he is able to investigate the mechanics of moral failure and competition for power under the guise of ideology. Above all, Bolaño possesses a superior ability among modern writers to involve readers in the chancy, vital world of his tales.

THE SAVAGE DETECTIVES

The Savage Detectives recounts the history of avant-garde poets from 1975 in Mexico City until 1996 in Africa. Their literary movement, visceral realism, begins with a mischievous revolutionary fervor but spins apart through jealousy, murder, exile, despair, insanity, and, in a very few cases, self-discovery. Although the underlying plot line is straightforward, the narrative structure and multiple points of view belong uniquely to this novel. The book is divided into three sections that present the story out of temporal order.

The section "Mexicans Lost in Mexico" concerns the last two months of 1975 and takes place wholly in Mexico City. It is told through the diary entries of Juan García Madero, a seventeen year old whose ambition is to study literature and become a poet. He encounters two older poets, Belano and Lima. They are the leaders of the visceral realism movement, which is defined mostly by its vigorous opposition to mainstream Mexican literature. By chance the pair discovers that another poet, Cesárea Tinajero, also had used the term "visceral realism" to describe a literary movement. Tinajero was a shadowy figure from the 1920's, known for a single published poem. Belano and Lima decide to track her down, along with García Madero and Lupe, a prostitute on the run from her pimp.

The novel's long middle section, "The Savage Detectives," leaps forward in time, after Belano and Lima have fled to Europe in 1976. It comprises a series of testimonies about Lima and Belano by former visceral realists and some older literati, whom the pair interviewed about Tinajero. The reader learns that Lima and Belano live like lost souls, bouncing from one place to another in Nicaragua, France, Spain, Austria, and Israel. Lima eventually turns up again in Mexico City, years later and a broken man. Belano, although continuing to write, develops a mortal illness and goes to Africa as a correspondent, hoping to be killed in action. He is last seen near Monrovia, Liberia, in 1996, trying to evade a rebel army.

The final section, "The Sonora Desert," reverts to García Madero's diary, which records the events of the first six weeks of 1976. Belano, Lima, Lupe, and García Madero speed north in a borrowed car, pursued by Lupe's pimp and his henchman. The four find Tinajero in a border town of down-and-out killers. Her life having turned into a long decline into poverty, she is killed by Lupe's pursuers before Belano and Lima can interview her about visceral realism. The four fugitives then split up. García Madero finds and reads Tinajero's secret notebooks. Expecting access to the thoughts of a brilliant literary rebel, the notebooks disappoint him, and he is forced to see beyond his own ambition to become a poet. An earlier character's observation about his own literary experience applies to García Madero as well: "It gave us a glimpse of ourselves in our common humanity. It wasn't proof of our idle guilt but a sign of our miraculous and pointless innocence." These words define the true savagery of *The Savage Detectives*.

BY NIGHT IN CHILE

By Night in Chile opens with Father Sebastián Urrutia Lacroix on his deathbed confessing to the reader that although once at peace with himself, he is no longer. He is tormented by accusations from a mysterious "wizened youth" and struggles to justify his life. What follows, printed in a single paragraph, is a turbulent montage of images, anecdotes, stories, allegories, laments, and delusions.

After seminary, Urrutia allies himself to Chile's preeminent critic, an old-fashioned example of the Western literati: effete, independently wealthy, and sterile. Through him, young Urrutia socializes with the cultural elite (meeting such luminaries as Pablo Neruda), eventually becoming a prominent critic and university professor himself. However, he is suborned by politics and sent on a seriocomic mission to save the Catholic Church by agents of Opus Dei and a second mission to educate the generals of the ruling military junta about communism.

Urrutia comes to recognize that his appreciation of Chile's underlying culture, like that of many of his literary compatriots, is selective, often precious, and self-deceiving. He asks piteously, "Is it *always* possible for a man to know what is good and what is bad?" He understands at last that the answer is no and that he, like other intellectuals, has let himself be used, out of vanity, by those in power for the maintenance of power. He recognizes, further, that the wizened youth tormenting him is in reality the withered remnant of his own conscience.

NAZI LITERATURE IN THE AMERICAS

Nazi Literature in the Americas has the appearance of a biographical encyclopedia. The entries, varying in length from half a page to nearly thirty pages, discuss writers from throughout the two continents and from early in the twentieth century to as late as 2029. They are writers of nearly all genres. Through most of the book the tone is detached, judicious, and scholarly. Gradually, however, as Bolaño discusses thirty-one authors with fascist sensibilities under thirteen headings, it becomes clear to the reader that he is far from detached and that his purpose is ridicule. Moreover, he becomes involved in their world despite himself.

All these writers yearn for an autocracy that is based, variously, on race, creed, ideology, or class. While espousing family values and other standards of conduct, few of the writers practice what they preach. Herein lies the book's mordant humor. The writers are violent (soccer thugs, mercenaries, torturers, and murderers), sexually promiscuous and deviant, sometimes ignorant, and treacherous. The last of them is a figure of horror.

Chilean Carlos Ramírez Hoffman is a military pilot who creates poetic skywriting over Santiago. He is also a member of a death squad; he murders several people and tortures others, then he disappears. At this point Bolaño enters the novel as a character. Abel Romero, a private investigator on the trail of Ramírez Hoffman, asks for Bolaño's help. Together they track him down, but Bolaño begs Romero not to kill Ramírez Hoffman: "'He can't hurt anyone now,' I said. But I didn't really believe it. 'Of course he could. We all could. I'll be right back,' said Romero." The ending insists that literature, even that by the lunatic fringe, has a way of turning personal.

Roger Smith

OTHER MAJOR WORKS

SHORT FICTION: *Llamadas telefónicas*, 1997; *Putas asesinas*, 2001; *El gaucho insufrible*, 2003 (includes short stories and essays); *Last Evenings on Earth*, 2006; *El secreto del mal*, 2007.

POETRY: *Reinventar al amor*, 1976; *Fragmentos de la universidad desconocida*, 1993; *Los perros románticos: Poemas, 1980-1998*, 2000 (*The Romantic Dogs, 1980-1998*, 2008); *Tres*, 2000.

NONFICTION: *Entre paréntesis: Ensayos, artículos, y discursos, 1998-2003*, 2004.

EDITED TEXT: *Muchachos desnudos bajo el arcoiris de fuego*, 1979.

BIBLIOGRAPHY

Andrews, Chris. "Varieties of Evil." *Meanjin* 66 (September, 2007): 200-206. Andrews discusses Bolaño's portrayal of state-sponsored crime in Latin America in his works of fiction.

Corral, Will H. "Portrait of the Writer as a Noble Savage." *World Literature Today* 80 (November/December, 2006): 4-8. A concise but comprehensive literary biography of Bolaño that discusses the influences on his choice of subjects and styles for his works of fiction.

Deb, Siddhartha. "The Wandering Years: Roberto Bolaño's Nomadic Fiction." *Harper's*, April, 2007. In this magazine article, Deb analyzes the types of protagonist included in Bolaño's novels *Distant Star* and *By Night in Chile*.

Ocasio, Rafael. *Literature of Latin America*. Westport, Conn.: Greenwood Press, 2004. A good, updated survey of modern Latin American poetry and fiction.

Zalewski, Daniel. "Vagabonds: Roberto Bolaño and His Fractured Masterpiece." *The New Yorker*, March 26, 2007. Zalewski provides much biographical information on Bolaño in this magazine article to aid readers in an examination of the novel *The Savage Detectives*.

RAY BRADBURY

Born: Waukegan, Illinois; August 22, 1920
Also known as: Ray Douglas Bradbury

OTHER LITERARY FORMS

Ray Bradbury's principal literary form has been the short story, and he has published several important collections, including *Dark Carnival* (1947), *The Illustrated Man* (1951), *The Golden Apples of the Sun* (1953), and *I Sing the Body Electric!* (1969). Two important extensive collections of his short stories are *The Stories of Ray Bradbury* (1980) and *Bradbury Stories: One Hundred of His Most Celebrated Tales* (2003). In addition to his short stories and novels, he has published in a wide variety of literary forms, from light verse and poetry to plays for radio, television, films, and the stage. One of his notable screenplays, which he wrote in collaboration with the director John Huston, is *Moby Dick* (1956). His poetry has been collected in such volumes as *The Complete Poems of Ray Bradbury* (1982) and *I Live by the Invisible: New and Selected Poems* (2002). A representative example of his nonfiction is the widely and well-reviewed *Zen in the Art of Writing: Essays on Creativity* (1989).

ACHIEVEMENTS

Although Ray Bradbury became arguably the best-known science-fiction writer in the United States, the majority of his work, which ranges from gothic horror to social criticism, centers on humanistic themes. Aficionados of the genre have criticized his science-fiction stories for their scientific and technological inaccuracies, a criticism he shrugs off, stating that his dominating concerns are social, cultural, and intellectual issues, not scientific verisimilitude. His stories, which often explore the dehumanizing pressures of technocracies and the mesmerizing power of the imagination, are widely anthologized and translated into many foreign languages. His ascent from pulp magazines to literary respectability has been intermittently recognized with several awards, including appearances in Martha Foley's annual best American short-story collections, two O. Henry Prizes, the Benjamin Franklin Magazine Award, the National Institute of Arts and Letters Award, an Academy Award nomination, an Emmy Award for his television adaptation of his 1972 children's book *The Halloween Tree*, and a Golden Eagle Award for his 1961 screenplay *Icarus Montgolfier Wright*.

In 2000 the National Book Foundation honored Bradbury with a medal for Distinguished Contribution to American Letters, and in 2004 President George W. Bush presented him with the National Medal of Arts. In 2007 he received a special citation from the Pulitzer Board for his outstanding work in science fiction and fantasy, and the French paid tribute to him with the medal of Commandeur, Ordre des Arts et des Lettres. Bradbury has been honored with a star on the Hollywood Walk of Fame, and his hometown of Waukegan, Illinois, has named a park for him. Astronomers have named an asteroid in his honor, and a crater on the Moon is named for his novel *Dandelion Wine*. His best novels are cautionary tales of the dangers of unrestricted scientific and technological progress, and his work has a strong moral core, encouraging the hope that humanity will deal creatively and ethically with the new worlds it seems driven to construct.

BIOGRAPHY

Ray Douglas Bradbury was born on August 22, 1920, in Waukegan, Illinois. His father, Leonard Spaulding Bradbury, whose distant ancestor Mary Bradbury was among those tried for witchcraft in Salem, Massachusetts, in the seventeenth century, was a lineman with the Waukegan Bureau of Power and Light; his mother, Esther Marie (née Moberg) Bradbury, emigrated to the United States from Sweden when she was a child. When he was three years old, his mother took him to his first film, *The Hunchback of Notre Dame* (1923), and he was frightened and entranced by Lon Chaney's performance in this film and, later, in *The Phantom of the Opera* (1925). As a child, Bradbury passed through a series of enthusiasms, from monsters to circuses to dinosaurs and eventually to the planet Mars. His development through childhood was aided by an older brother and by an aunt, Neva Bradbury, a costume designer, who introduced him to the theater and to the stories of Edgar Allan Poe.

In 1932, Bradbury's family moved to Arizona, where they had previously spent some time in the mid-1920's, largely because of his father's need to find work. In 1934 the family left behind both Arizona and Waukegan, settling in Los Angeles, which became Bradbury's permanent home. He attended Los Angeles High School and joined the Science Fiction Society (he had earlier begun reading Hugo Gernsback's magazine *Amazing Stories*, which, he said, made him fall in love with the future). After graduation, Bradbury worked for several months in a theater group sponsored by the actor Laraine Day, and for several years he was a newsboy in downtown Los Angeles. He took these jobs to support his writing, an avocation that he hoped would soon become a vocation.

His poor eyesight prevented him from serving in the military during World War II, which left him free to launch his writing career. During the early 1940's he began to publish his stories in such pulp magazines as *Weird Tales* and *Amazing Stories*, but by the late 1940's his work was appearing in such mass-market magazines as *Collier's*, the *Saturday Evening Post*, *The New Yorker*, *Harper's Magazine*, and *Mademoiselle*. Because these magazines paid well, he was able, on September 27, 1947, to marry Marguerite Susan McClure, a former English teacher at the University of California in Los Angeles. He continued, during the 1950's, to write for the pulp and mass-market magazines, and he routinely collected his stories for publication in books. In the mid-1950's he traveled to Ireland in connection with a screenplay of *Moby Dick* that he wrote with John Huston. Upon his return to the United States, Bradbury composed a large number of television scripts for such shows as *Alfred Hitchcock Presents*, *Suspense*, and *The Twilight Zone*. During the late 1950's and early 1960's, Bradbury's stories and novels focused mostly on his midwestern childhood—for example, *Dandelion Wine* and *Something Wicked This Way Comes*, the latter his favorite book.

During the 1960's and 1970's, Bradbury's output of fiction decreased, and his ideas found outlets in such forms as plays, poems, and essays. He also became involved in a number of projects such as "A Journey Through United States History," the exhibit that occupied the upper floor of the United States Pavilion for the New York World's Fair in the mid-1960's. Because of this display's success, the Walt Disney organization hired him to help develop the themes for Spaceship Earth, an important part of Epcot Center at Disney World in Florida. Bradbury also helped design a twenty-first century city near Tokyo. In the 1980's he continued to diversify his activities by collaborating in projects to turn his novel *Fahrenheit 451* into an opera and his novel *Dandelion Wine* into a musical, and he developed a series, *Ray Bradbury Theater*, that ran on cable television from 1986 to 1992 and has continued its influence on DVD.

In 1990 Bradbury published *A Graveyard for Lunatics* with the publishing house Alfred A. Knopf, but after 1992 Avon became his publisher because Bradbury was unhappy that Knopf had allowed several of his books to go out of print and had been dilatory in publishing his new works. Avon has kept his backlist in print and has brought out such short-story collections as *Quicker than the Eye* (1996) and *Driving Blind* (1997).

In 1999 a stroke temporarily interfered with Bradbury's writing, and as he regained his ability to walk with a four-pronged cane, he also returned to creating stories, now aided by one of his daughters, who transcribed his telephone-dictated works. His poststroke novels include *From the Dust Returned* and *Farewell Summer*. As his health improved, he traveled to various ceremonies honoring him not just for his contributions to science fiction and fantasy but also to American literature. In 2004 he made news with his impassioned objection to the misuse of the title of his novel *Fahrenheit 451* for the title of Michael Moore's documentary film *Fahrenheit 9/11*. Deaths of family members and friends along with his own health problems have heightened Bradbury's awareness of his own race with death, a theme that is prominent in his twenty-first century short stories and novels.

ANALYSIS

Paradoxically, Ray Bradbury's stories look both backward and forward. For him, each story is a way of discovering a self, and the self found in one story is different from the self found in another. Bradbury, like all human beings, is made of time, and human beings, like rivers, flow and change. Adapting the ancient Greek philosopher Heraclitus's famous statement that one cannot step into the same river twice, one could say that no person ever steps twice into the same self. Sometimes Bradbury discovers a self in the past, and sometimes, particularly in his science fiction, he discovers a self in the future. Several critics have pictured him as a frontiersman, ambivalently astride two worlds, who has alternately been attracted to an idealized past, timeless and nostalgic, and to a graphic future, chameleonic and threatening. This creative tension is present both in his own life and in the generation of Americans he likes to depict. It is also intimately connected with the genre—science fiction—with which he became so closely identified.

Bradbury has been called a romantic, and his romanticism often surfaces in the themes he investigates: the conflict between human vitality and spiritless mechanism, between the creative individual and the conforming group, between imagination and reason, between intuition and logic, between the innocence of childhood and the corruptions of adulthood, and between the shadow and the light in every human soul. His stories make clear that, in all these conflicts, human beings, not machines, are at the center of his vision. An ambivalence about technology characterizes his life and work. For example, he never learned to drive, even while spending most of his life in Los Angeles, a city that has made the automobile not only an apparent necessity but also an object of worship. He also refused to use a computer, and he successfully avoided flying in an airplane for the first six decades of his life. Each of these attitudes is rooted in some profoundly emotional experience; for example, he never learned to drive because, as a youth, he witnessed the horrible deaths of five people in an automobile accident. Because of his emphasis on basic human values against an uncritical embracing of technical progress, because of his affirmation of the human spirit against modern materialism, and because of his trust in the basic goodness of small-town life against the debilitating indifference of the cities, several critics have accused him of sentimentality and naïveté. Bradbury has responded by saying that critics write from the head, whereas he writes from the heart.

The poetic style that he developed is admirably suited to the heartfelt themes that he explores in a cornucopia of highly imaginative stories. He cultivated this style through eclectic imitation and dogged determination. As an adolescent, he vowed to write several hundred words every day, for he believed that quantity would eventually lead to quality. Experience and the example of other writers would teach him what to leave out. According to Bradbury, his style was influenced by such writers as Charles Dickens, Mark Twain, Thomas Wolfe, and Ernest Hemingway. On another occasion, however, he stated that his style came as much from silent-film actor Charles Chaplin as from Aldous Huxley, as much from Tom Swift as from George Orwell, as much from cowboy actor Tom Mix as from Bertrand Russell, and as much from Edgar Rice Burroughs as from C. S. Lewis.

Bradbury was also influenced by such poets as Alexander Pope, Gerard Manley Hopkins, and Dylan Thomas, and such dramatists as William Shakespeare and George Bernard Shaw. Furthermore, and surprisingly, such painters as El Greco and Tintoretto and such composers as Wolfgang Amadeus Mozart and Joseph Haydn showed him how to add color and rhythm to his writing. According to him, all these influences—writers, poets, painters, and musicians—gloried in the joy of creating, and their works overflow with animal vigor and intellectual vitality. Their ardor and delight are contagious, and their honest response to the materials at hand calls forth a similar response in their readers, viewers, and listeners. This enchanting of the audience, similar to casting a magic spell, is what Bradbury attempts to do with his kaleidoscopic style: to transform colorful pieces of reality into a glittering picture that will emotionally intensify the lives of his readers.

Bradbury's writing is profoundly autobiographical, and childhood, adolescent, and adult experiences generated many of his stories. Graham Greene once said that there is always one moment in childhood when the door opens and lets the future in. Actually, for Bradbury, there were many such moments. He once said that everything he had ever done—all his activities, loves, and fears—were created by the primitive experiences of monsters and angels he had when he was five years old. He also said, however, that the most important event in his childhood occurred when he was twelve years old, at a carnival, when the performance of a magician, Mr. Electrico, so energized his imagination that he began to write stories to communicate his fervid visions to others.

Several critics have detected a decline in the quality of Bradbury's later work, but the standard he set in the 1950's was very high. Because he has worked in so many different literary forms, and because, within each of these forms, his treatment of a potpourri of subjects has been equally variegated, it is difficult to make neat generalizations about this author's oeuvre. The public has recognized Bradbury as the world's premier science-fiction writer, but only a third of his work has been in the genre. Certainly, his science-fiction stories have revealed that cultivated and craftsmanlike writing is possible in what was seen, before he began to publish, as a vulgar genre. Within the science-fiction community, however, sharp differences of opinion exist about Bradbury's contributions. A sizable segment sees his work as reactionary, antitechnological, and anti-utopian. As one of these critics has put it, Bradbury is a science-fiction writer for people who do not really like science fiction. On the other hand, a large group, which includes a significant segment of the literary community (viewing him as one of their own), sees him as a humanist and a regional writer. This group draws some good arguments from Bradbury's stories: For example, even when he writes about Mars, the planet symbolizes for him the geography—emotional and intellectual—of the American Midwest. In this sense, his regionalism is one of the mind and heart.

Actually, both sides of this debate can find evidence for their views in Bradbury's motley work. He can be both enthusiastic about a future transformed by technology and critical of the dangers posed by technocracies. Ultimately, for Bradbury, technology is a human creation, and it is therefore subject to the labyrinthine goods and evils of the human heart. Although his best work is deeply humanistic and includes a strong critique of unrestrained technology, he is no Luddite. It is true that the technological society has produced many problems—pollution, for example—but human beings love to solve problems; it is a defining characteristic of the species.

Those who see only Bradbury's critique of technology view him as a pessimistic writer. In the proper light, however, his work is really profoundly optimistic. His fiction may rest upon the gloomy foundation of the Fall, but, in traditional theology, the counterpart of the Fall is Redemption, and Bradbury believes that human beings will renew themselves, particularly in space, which he sees as modern humankind's religious quest. Space, then, is Bradbury's new wilderness, with an infinity of new challenges. In that inexhaustible wilderness, human beings will find themselves and be saved.

DARK CARNIVAL

Numerous Bradbury stories, including several in his first collection, *Dark Carnival*, have as their provenance specific childhood events. For example, "The Small Assassin," which metamorphoses some of his childhood experiences and fears, tells of a newborn infant, terrified at finding himself thrust into a hostile world, taking revenge on his parents by first terrorizing, then murdering them. This story also reveals that Bradbury's view of childhood innocence is more complex than many critics realize, for, in Bradbury's view, beneath the facade of innocence lies a cauldron of sin—a dark vision of the human condition that some critics have called Calvinistic. Another tale, "The Lake," is based on Bradbury's experience as a seven-year-old, when his cousin nearly drowned in Lake Michigan. These and other early stories, which he first published in such pulp magazines as *Weird Tales*, *Amazing Stories*, and *Astounding Science Fiction*, served as his apprenticeship, an opportunity to perfect his style, deepen his vision, and develop the themes on which he would play variations in his later, more accomplished short stories, novels, poems, and dramas.

One of these early themes that also haunted his later fiction is alienation. Bradbury himself experienced cultural alienation when he traveled to Mexico in 1945. Americans were then mostly Protestant, individualistic, and preoccupied with getting ahead. Mexicans, on the other hand, were mostly Catholic, communalistic, and preoccupied with death. On his trip to Guanajuato, northwest of Mexico City, Bradbury was both horrified and fascinated by the catacombs, with their rows of propped-up mummified bodies. A story collected in *Dark Carnival*, "The Next in Line," grew out of this experience. In this story, a young American wife finds herself, after her traumatic ordeal in the Guanajuato crypts, alienated both from the strange Mexican society and from her own body, which she obsessively realizes is a potential mummy. Bradbury uses the metaphor of death to help the reader comprehend one reality, life, in terms of another, death. Metaphor thus becomes a medicine, a way of healing ourselves by envisioning ourselves into new modes of experiencing, learning, and surviving.

THE MARTIAN CHRONICLES

Although, at first glance, many of Bradbury's early stories seem notable for their great variety, he did deal, especially in his stories about Mars, with a set of conflicts that had a common theme, and so, when an editor suggested in 1949 that he compose a continuous narrative, he took advantage of the opportunity, since several of his stories about the colonization of Mars by Earthlings lent themselves to just such a treatment. Using the chronological frame of 1999 to 2026, Bradbury stitched these stories together with bridge passages that gave the book a semblance of unity. (It also presented categorizers of his works with a problem: Some have listed the book as a novel, others as a short-story collection.) Many critics have called *The Martian Chronicles* (1950) Bradbury's masterpiece, a magical and insightful account of the exploitation of a new frontier, Mars, by Earthlings whose personalities appear to have been nurtured in small midwestern American towns. By placing these normal human beings in an extraordinary setting, Bradbury was able to use the strange light of an alien world to illuminate the dark regions of human nature.

The apparatus of conventional science fiction makes an appearance, including monsters and supermachines, but Bradbury's basic intent is to explore the conflicts troubling postwar America: imperialism, alienation, pollution, racism, and nuclear war. He therefore depicts not a comforting human progress but a disquieting cycle of rises and falls. He also sees the Martian environment, itself transformed by human ingenuity, transforming the settlers. Thus his ultimate view seems optimistic: Humanity will, through creative adaptation, not only survive but also thrive. In *The Martian Chronicles* Earthlings metamorphose into Martians, an action that serves as a Bradburian metaphor for the human condition, which is to be always in the process of becoming something else.

Even though scientists criticized *The Martian Chronicles* for its portrayal of Mars as a planet with a breathable atmosphere, water, and canals (known by astronomers in 1950 to be untrue), and even though science-fiction devotees found Bradbury's portrayal of Martian colonies implausible, the book was a triumphant success, largely, some have suggested, because of these "weaknesses." Bradbury's Mars mirrored the present and served as the stage on which his eccentric characters—the misfits, opportunists, and romantics—could remake Mars in their own images (only to find themselves remade by Mars in the process). *The Martian Chronicles* has proved to be enduringly popular. It has passed through several editions, sold millions of copies, and been translated into more than thirty foreign languages.

THE ILLUSTRATED MAN

Another book of interlinked stories, *The Illustrated Man*, followed soon after the publication of *The Martian Chronicles*. In *The Illustrated Man* the device linking the stories together is the tattoo art on the skin of one of the characters. Bradbury sets some of his stories on Mars, and a few bear some relation to the cycle of stories in *The Martian Chronicles*. By the early 1950's, Bradbury was a well-established writer, able to place his stories in both pulp and popular magazines and able to profit again when his collections of these stories were published as books. His fourth collection, *The Golden Apples of the Sun*, abandoned the frame narrative that he had been using and instead simply juxtaposed stories from a wide variety of genres—science fiction, fantasy, crime, and comedy.

John Huston, the film director, was impressed by a dinosaur story that Bradbury had written and asked him to come to Ireland to develop a screenplay for Huston's film about another great beast, *Moby Dick*. Bradbury's experiences in Ireland in 1953 not only led to an excellent screenplay but also gave him material for several stories and plays about the Irish. Furthermore, the trip gave him the chance to meet the English philosopher Bertrand Russell and art historian Bernard Berenson, two of his heroes. Berenson had written a fan letter to Bradbury in which he praised the American's attitude toward writing as a "fascinating adventure."

FAHRENHEIT 451

During this most prolific period in Bradbury's literary life, he also published the book that would generate, along with *The Martian Chronicles*, his greatest success and influence. The story that came to be called *Fahrenheit 451* went through several transformations. In 1947 he had written a short story, "Bright Phoenix," in which the residents of a small town counter government book-burning edicts by memorizing the banned books. In 1951 he expanded this idea into a long story, "The Fireman," which appeared in *Galaxy Science Fiction*. A fire chief informed him that book paper first bursts into flame at 451 degrees Fahrenheit, which gave him the title for his novel-length story set in a future totalitarian state. Some critics interpreted this dystopian novel as an attack against McCarthyism, then at the height of its power, but the book also attacks the tyrannical domination of mass culture, especially in this culture's tendency to eschew complexity of thought and to embrace the simple sentiments of pressure groups. The central irony of the novel concerns firefighters whose job is to set fires (burn books) rather than to extinguish them.

Bradbury, a lifelong book lover, used *Fahrenheit 451* to show how important books are to freedom, morality, and the search for truth. The novel concludes with Montag, a fireman who has rejected his role as book burner, joining a community that strives to preserve books by memorizing them. Some critics have pointed out that this new society, where individuals abandon their identities to "become" the books they have memorized, inculcates a mass behavior as conformist as the one from which they and Montag have escaped, but Bradbury would respond that this new culture allows for a multiplicity of ideas and attitudes and thus provides the opportunity for human creativity to shape a hopeful legacy for the next generation.

DANDELION WINE

From the mid-1950's to the mid-1960's, Bradbury's writings tended to center on his midwestern childhood, without being camouflaged by science-fiction or fantasy settings. His novel *Dandelion Wine* is a nostalgic account of a small Illinois town in the summer of 1928. Again, as was the case with so much of his earlier work, this novel was composed of previously published stories, and the superficial unity that Bradbury imposed on the material was not sufficiently coherent to satisfy some critics. Another similarity to his previous work was his theme of the twin attractions of the past and the future. The twelve-year-old hero finds himself between the secure, uncomplicated world of childhood and the frightening, complex world of adulthood. Despite the loneliness, disease, and death that seem to plague adults, the young man, like the colonists in *The Martian Chronicles*, must transform his past to create his future. Critics accused Bradbury of sentimentality in *Dandelion Wine*, pointing out how depressed and ugly Waukegan, Illinois—the model for Green Town—was at this time. Bradbury answered that he was telling his story from the viewpoint of the child, and factories, trains, pollution, and poverty are not ugly to children. Adults teach children what is ugly, and their judgments about ugliness are not always sound. For a child, as for Bradbury, Green Town was like William Butler Yeats's Byzantium, a vision of creativity and a dream for action.

SOMETHING WICKED THIS WAY COMES

Bradbury returned to some of these themes in another novel, *Something Wicked This Way Comes*, in which a father tries to save his son and his son's friend from the evil embodied in a mysterious traveling carnival. The friend, Jim Nightshade (a name indicative of the symbolic burden the characters in this novel must bear), is particularly susceptible to the carnival's temptations, since his shadow side is so powerful. The father ultimately achieves victory by using the power of laughter as his weapon; however, the father also points out that human victories are never final and that each individual must constantly struggle never to permit the good that is in him or her to become a passive rather than an activating force. The potential for evil exists in every human being (a Christian idea, original sin, that surfaces in many of Bradbury's stories), and unless humans keep their goodness fit through creativity, evil will take over. For Bradbury, love is the best humanizing force that human beings possess.

Something Wicked This Way Comes marked a turning point in Bradbury's career. After this work failed to enhance his status as a significant American novelist, he turned increasingly to plays, poems, and essays. His turn to drama was essentially a return, since he had acted, as a boy, on the stage and on radio, and since he had written several plays when he was young (they were so bad that he vowed never to write plays again until he learned to write competently in other forms). Many of his plays are adaptations of his stories, and most of them have been staged in California, though a few have had productions Off-Broadway in New York. The majority of his plays have been published. His first collection, *The Anthem Sprinters and Other Antics*, appeared in 1963 (the "anthem sprinters" are Irishmen who flee from motion-picture theaters before the national anthem is played). Although his short-story writing diminished during the 1960's, it did not vanish, and in 1969 he published another collection, *I Sing the Body Electric!*, which was a miscellany of science-fiction and fantasy stories.

Throughout his life, Bradbury has also been an avid reader of poetry. He has often made use of poetic diction in his stories, but, as in the case of his playwriting, he refrained from publishing his poetry until late in his career, because he wanted it to be accomplished and stylistically refined. Heavily indebted to Gerard Manley Hopkins, Dylan Thomas, Walt Whitman, and others, his poetry has not had the success of his stories. Much of the poetry, whimsical in tone, can be categorized as light verse.

THE TOYNBEE CONVECTOR

In 1988 Bradbury published his first new collection of short stories in eighteen years, *The Toynbee Convector* (a retrospective of one hundred stories, *The Stories of Ray Bradbury*, was published in 1980). As in some of his other collections, the stories of *The Toynbee Convector* contain a number of genres, subjects, and themes. The title story centers on a returned time traveler (the convector is his time machine, named for the historian Arnold Toynbee). He enthralls people with his message that, in the future world he visited, most of Earth's problems have been solved: The planet's waters have been cleansed, the dolphins and whales have been preserved, and the Moon and Mars have been colonized. In the story's concluding twist, however, it turns out that the time traveler had faked his trip to provide twentieth century humans with hope. Again, the reader encounters one of Bradbury's favorite themes: A lie can create a reality. In this story, a lie was needed to shake the world from its despair. For Bradbury, then, lies are like dreams, in that they are truths waiting to be born.

GREEN SHADOWS, WHITE WHALE

During the last decade of the twentieth and the first decade of the twenty-first century, Bradbury published four novels and three novellas as well as a graphic novel. Like his previous writings, these stories are rooted in his childhood experiences, or in his relationships with other writers, both living and dead, or in films. For example, in *Green Shadows, White Whale*, he fictionalizes his mid-1950's experiences in Ireland while working with John Huston on the screenplay for *Moby Dick*. Unlike the motion picture, this memoir, which interweaves facts and fabrications, is lighthearted, emphasizing the tall tales of the eccentrics in Heeber Finn's pub rather than the quest for a perfect script. Some critics have described this novel as the "most entertaining" of Bradbury's career and his vignettes of the Irish as perceptively humorous, but others have found it disappointing, complaining that the Irish characters, situations, and stories are stereotypical and that the "Irish green" disproportionately overshadows the "white whale."

AHMED AND THE OBLIVION MACHINES

Many of Bradbury's creative efforts throughout his life have appealed to adolescents as well as adults, and in *Ahmed and the Oblivion Machines* (1998) he wrote "a fable for adults and children alike" (the "oblivion machines" are unsuccessful aircraft of the past). This novella's central character is a twelve-year-old Arab boy whose fall from a camel accidentally separates him from his father's caravan. Before finding his way back to his father, Ahmed experiences several adventures that help him to understand who he truly is and what humankind should be. His guide in his desert wanderings is a god, whose statue Ahmed's tears vivify. This god not only teaches Ahmed to fly but also teaches him to interpret history correctly. Because this is a fable, this knowledge will enable Ahmed to create a world better than his father's. Critics have tended to compare this novella unfavorably with Bradbury's earlier fables, finding the story line weak and the symbolism either arcane or overelaborate.

FROM THE DUST RETURNED

Published on Halloween, 2001, *From the Dust Returned* provides another example of how Bradbury often constructs his novels from previous short stories. For more than fifty years he had made the Elliots, a family of supernatural eccentrics, central characters in a series of stories. Using the device of a family gathering at a vacated midwestern mansion, eerily depicted on the dust jacket by a Charles Addams painting, Bradbury stitches old and new stories together through an investigation of the family's history, meaning, and destiny. Unlike many of his other horror tales, this story's tone is blithesome, and the Thousand Times Great Grandmother, the green-winged uncle, the sleeping and dream-traveling daughter, and assorted other extramundane relatives, along with an adopted earthly son, are all meant to inspire affection rather than fear. Some commentators have situated this novel among Bradbury's "most enduring masterworks," and others have asserted that some of the individual stories rank with his best. On the other hand, some critics have detected in this novel a deterioration of the once-lauded Bradburian style, citing numerous solecisms, absurd images, and overwritten passages.

CRUMLEY MYSTERIES

During the decade 1980-1990, Bradbury returned to the literary forms that had made him famous. He published a novel, *Death Is a Lonely Business*, his first in twenty-three years, in 1985. This novel and *A Graveyard for Lunatics*, published in 1990, make use of some of the same characters, and both are detective stories with a strong dose of fantasy. In 2003 he completed what had become a trilogy with *Let's All Kill Constance*, which he began in a hospital while recuperating from a stroke. All three novels have a common setting (Southern California) and such recurring characters as the nameless writer-narrator and his detective friend Elmo Crumley.

The story of the final novel, with its tongue-in-cheek tone, begins on a stormy night in

Venice, California, in 1960, when a Hollywood has-been frantically knocks on the writer's door. The once-glamorous, now lusterless Constance Rattigan believes her life is in danger, because she has received a 1900 Los Angeles telephone directory with red markings indicating not only already dead Hollywood stars but also those who are about to die, including Constance. After leaving the directory and her address book with the writer, she disappears. With the help of Crumley, the narrator travels around Los Angeles, warning and interviewing other possible victims. In the course of these peregrinations the narrator paints a squalid picture of the ruthless, greedy, and heartless Hollywood scene.

Several reviewers found the clash of genres in the first two novels—detective and fantasy—too disorienting to make the stories effective, but others found Bradbury's re-creation of a bygone era in Southern California history appealing. Critical response to the last novel of the trilogy was largely favorable, although some have called it the weakest member of the trilogy, while others have noted numerous flaws in Bradbury's writing, which the charitable have attributed to his ill health.

FAREWELL SUMMER

Among the novels of Bradbury's late period, *Farewell Summer* was the most eagerly anticipated, as it is the sequel to the much-loved *Dandelion Wine*, published nearly fifty years before. Following this gestation, which has been called one of the longest in literary history, the sequel, though it makes use of material removed from the original manuscript of *Dandelion Wine*, profits from the life experiences that Bradbury had in the interim. *Farewell Summer* was written by a man approaching death who has existential knowledge that life, in the end, takes away youth, love, friends, and happiness, leaving nothing but darkness. However, in telling this story he hopes that his spirit will in some way live on.

The story takes place in Green Town, Illinois, during an Indian summer in October, 1929, and it centers on a conflict between a thirteen-year-old boy, Douglas Spaulding, and an elderly "school board despot," Calvin C. Quartermain. The conflict begins when the sound of Doug's cap-pistol accidentally precipitates the death of an old man, and Quartermain is determined to discover the "killer" among the group of "rebellious rapscallions." Making use of American Civil War imagery and an elegiac tone, Bradbury describes intergenerational battles that occur in relation to the courthouse clock and a haunted house on the edge of a ravine. Both the clock and the house are part of the "immense frightening machinery of the Enemy" because of their connections to death. In the story's resolution the boys repair the clock that they had stopped, and Quartermain has a birthday party for a girl who gives Doug his first kiss. In the final part of the novel, titled "Appomattox," Quartermain and Doug meet to share the lessons that this "civil war" has taught them. Many readers and critics have described *Farewell Summer* as moving, unforgettable, and wise, though some have asserted that it lacks the enchantment of *Dandelion Wine*.

NOW AND FOREVER

In 2007 Bradbury published two novellas under the cover title *Now and Forever*. Like several of his books of the new century, this one also includes discussions of the provenance of each story. The first novella, *Somewhere a Band Is Playing*, owes its origin to Bradbury's time in Tucson, Arizona, as a child and his encounters with actor Katharine Hepburn in his life and in her 1955 film *Summertime*. In 1956, when he started writing the story, he intended it as a starring vehicle for the actor, but by the time he completed it, Hepburn, one of the novella's dedicatees, was gone. Nefertiti, the most intriguing resident of the unmapped Summerton, Arizona, would have been the Hepburn role, and her relationship with the visiting journalist, James Cardiff, is, along with the town itself, the focus of the story. Cardiff discovers that the town has no children, doctors, or dead bodies in the cemetery. He falls in love with the ageless "Nef" and is confronted with the agonizing choice between remaining in Summerton forever or returning to the joys and sufferings of his conventional mortal life. Although this novella was conceived by a young writer, it was finished by an old man attempting to age gracefully.

Time and death are also themes in the second novella in *Now and Forever*, *Leviathan '99*. This story derives from Bradbury's experiences while he was writing the screenplay for *Moby Dick*. He here transforms Herman Melville's story into a science-fiction adventure. The spaceship *Cetus* replaces the *Pequod*, and a planet-destroying comet stands in for the great white whale. Melville's narrator, Ishmael, becomes the astronaut Ishmael Hunnicut Jones, the South Pacific island native Queequeg becomes the alien Quell, and Ahab becomes a monomaniacal, blind starship captain. Before its incarnation as this novella, *Leviathan '99* had been a radio drama starring Christopher Lee as the captain. In another version it had been a poorly received play, and Bradbury hoped that this new telling would be successful. On the whole, these novellas have met with favorable critical response, with some reviewers praising their imaginative visions that have assumed an honored place in the ever-growing Bradburian canon.

Robert J. Paradowski

OTHER MAJOR WORKS

SHORT FICTION: *Dark Carnival*, 1947; *The Martian Chronicles*, 1950 (revised 1997); *The Illustrated Man*, 1951; *The Golden Apples of the Sun*, 1953; *The October Country*, 1955; *A Medicine for Melancholy*, 1959; *Twice Twenty-Two*, 1959; *The Machineries of Joy*, 1964; *Autumn People*, 1965; *Vintage Bradbury*, 1965; *Tomorrow Midnight*, 1966; *I Sing the Body Electric!*, 1969; *Long After Midnight*, 1976; *"The Last Circus," and "The Electrocution,"* 1980; *The Stories of Ray Bradbury*, 1980; *Dinosaur Tales*, 1983; *A Memory of Murder*, 1984; *The Toynbee Convector*, 1988; *Quicker than the Eye*, 1996; *Driving Blind*, 1997; *One More for the Road: A New Short Story Collection*, 2002; *The Best of Ray Bradbury: The Graphic Novel*, 2003; *Bradbury Stories: One Hundred of His Most Celebrated Tales*, 2003; *The Cat's Pajamas*, 2004; *Summer Morning, Summer Night*, 2008.

PLAYS: *The Anthem Sprinters and Other Antics*, pb. 1963; *The World of Ray Bradbury: Three Fables of the Future*, pr. 1964; *The Day It Rained Forever*, pb. 1966; *The Pedestrian*, pb. 1966; *Dandelion Wine*, pr. 1967 (adaptation of his novel); *Madrigals for the Space Age*, pb. 1972; *The Wonderful Ice Cream Suit, and Other Plays*, pb. 1972; *Pillar of Fire, and Other Plays for Today, Tomorrow, and Beyond Tomorrow*, pb. 1975; *That Ghost, That Bride of Time: Excerpts from a Play-in-Progress*, pb. 1976; *The Martian Chronicles*, pr. 1977 (adaptation of his story collection); *Fahrenheit 451*, pr. 1979 (musical; adaptation of his novel); *A Device Out of Time*, pb. 1986; *On Stage: A Chrestomathy of His Plays*, 1991.

POETRY: *Old Ahab's Friend, and Friend to Noah, Speaks His Piece: A Celebration*, 1971; *When Elephants Last in the Dooryard Bloomed: Celebrations for Almost Any Day in the Year*, 1973; *Where Robot Mice and Robot Men Run Round in Robot Towns: New Poems, Both Light and Dark*, 1977; *The Bike Repairman*, 1978; *Twin Hieroglyphs That Swim the River Dust*, 1978; *The Aqueduct*, 1979; *The Haunted Computer and the Android Pope*, 1981; *The Complete Poems of Ray Bradbury*, 1982; *Forever and the Earth*, 1984; *Death Has Lost Its Charm for Me*, 1987; *Dogs Think That Every Day Is Christmas*, 1997 (illustrated by Louise Reinoehl Max); *With Cat for Comforter*, 1997 (illustrated by Louise Reinoehl Max); *I Live by the Invisible: New and Selected Poems*, 2002.

SCREENPLAYS: *It Came from Outer Space*, 1952 (with David Schwartz); *Moby Dick*, 1956 (with John Huston); *Icarus Montgolfier Wright*, 1961 (with George C. Johnson); *The Picasso Summer*, 1969 (with Ed Weinberger).

NONFICTION: *Teacher's Guide to Science Fiction*, 1968 (with Lewy Olfson); *"Zen and the Art of Writing" and "The Joy of Writing": Two Essays*, 1973; *Mars and the Mind of Man*, 1973; *The Mummies of Guanajuato*, 1978; *The Art of the Playboy*, 1985; *Zen in the Art of Writing: Essays on Creativity*, 1989; *Yestermorrow: Obvious Answers to Impossible Futures*, 1991; *Bradbury Speaks: Too Soon from the Cave, Too Far from the Stars*, 2005.

CHILDREN'S/YOUNG ADULT LITERATURE: *Switch on the Night*, 1955; *R Is for Rocket*, 1962; *S Is for Space*, 1966; *The Halloween Tree*, 1972; *Fever Dream*, 1987; *Ahmed and the Oblivion Machines: A Fable*, 1998.

EDITED TEXTS: *Timeless Stories for Today and Tomorrow*, 1952; *The Circus of Dr. Lao, and Other Improbable Stories*, 1956.

BIBLIOGRAPHY

Bloom, Harold, ed. *Ray Bradbury*. New York: Chelsea House, 2001. Critical essays cover the major themes in Bradbury's works, looking at, among other topics, his Martian stories, his participation in the gothic tradition, the role of children in his work, and his use of myth.

_____. *Ray Bradbury's "Fahrenheit 451."* New York: Chelsea House, 2001. Eight essays address various aspects of one of Bradbury's most important novels. Includes an informative editor's introduction, a chronology, and a bibliography.

Eller, Jonathan R., and William F. Touponce. *Ray Bradbury: The Life of Fiction*. Kent, Ohio: Kent State University Press, 2004. Described as "the first comprehensive textual, bibliographical, and cultural study of sixty years of Bradbury's fiction," this book makes use of manuscripts, correspondence, charts, and graphs to bring out the interconnections among the many versions that led to Bradbury's published works and the events in his life. Includes index.

Greenberg, Martin Henry, and Joseph D. Olander, eds. *Ray Bradbury*. New York: Taplinger, 1980. Anthology of Bradbury criticism includes essays that defend Bradbury against the charge that he is not really a science-fiction writer but an opponent of science and technology; others defend him against the charge that his work is mawkish. Includes extensive bibliography and index.

Mogen, David. *Ray Bradbury*. Boston: Twayne, 1986. Provides a brief introduction to Bradbury's career, focusing on analyses of the literary influences that shaped the development of his style and the themes that shaped his reputation. Includes detailed notes, bibliography, and index.

Reid, Robin Ann. *Ray Bradbury: A Critical Companion*. Westport, Conn.: Greenwood Press, 2000. Offers biographical information as well as critical discussion of Bradbury's major works and their critical reception. Includes bibliography and index.

Touponce, William F. *Naming the Unnameable: Ray Bradbury and the Fantastic After Freud*. Mercer Island, Wash.: Starmont House, 1997. Argues that the psychoanalytic ideas of Sigmund Freud and Carl Jung are helpful in plumbing the effectiveness of much of Bradbury's work (though in a letter to the author, Bradbury himself denies any direct influence, saying he has "read little Freud or Jung"). Asserts that Bradbury has produced stories of a modern consciousness that often forgets its debt to the unconscious.

Weist, Jerry. *Bradbury: An Illustrated Life—A Journey to Far Metaphor*. New York: William Morrow, 2002. Celebratory book, with an introduction by Bradbury, has, as its principal attraction, its numerous illustrations, carefully chosen and presented by an auction-house expert in science-fiction and fantasy collectibles. Includes index.

Weller, Sam. *The Bradbury Chronicles: The Life of Ray Bradbury*. New York: William Morrow, 2005. Authorized biography, based on extensive research in Bradbury's personal archives and on many interviews, presents an inspirational account of the highly imaginative writer. Includes detailed bibliographic notes, selected bibliography, and index.

RITA MAE BROWN

Born: Hanover, Pennsylvania; November 28, 1944

PRINCIPAL LONG FICTION

Rubyfruit Jungle, 1973
In Her Day, 1976
Six of One, 1978
Southern Discomfort, 1982
Sudden Death, 1983
High Hearts, 1986
Bingo, 1988
Wish You Were Here, 1990 (with Sneaky Pie Brown)
Rest in Pieces, 1992 (with Sneaky Pie Brown)
Venus Envy, 1993
Dolley: A Novel of Dolley Madison in Love and War, 1994
Murder at Monticello: Or, Old Sins, 1994 (with Sneaky Pie Brown)
Pay Dirt: Or, Adventures at Ash Lawn, 1995 (with Sneaky Pie Brown)
Murder, She Meowed: Or, Death at Montpelier, 1996 (with Sneaky Pie Brown)
Riding Shotgun, 1996
Murder on the Prowl, 1998 (with Sneaky Pie Brown)
Cat on the Scent, 1999 (with Sneaky Pie Brown)
Loose Lips, 1999
Outfoxed, 2000
Pawing Through the Past, 2000 (with Sneaky Pie Brown)
Alma Mater, 2001
Claws and Effect, 2001 (with Sneaky Pie Brown)
Catch as Cat Can, 2002 (with Sneaky Pie Brown)
Hotspur, 2002
Full Cry, 2003
The Tail of the Tip-Off, 2003 (with Sneaky Pie Brown)
Whisker of Evil, 2004
Cat's Eyewitness, 2005 (with Sneaky Pie Brown)
The Hunt Ball, 2005
The Hounds and the Fury, 2006
Sour Puss, 2006
Puss 'n Cahoots, 2007 (with Sneaky Pie Brown)
The Tell-Tale Horse, 2007
Hounded to Death, 2008
The Purrfect Murder, 2008 (with Sneaky Pie Brown)
The Sand Castle, 2008

OTHER LITERARY FORMS

Rita Mae Brown is a versatile and prolific writer. In addition to her novels, many of which she says she wrote with her cat, Sneaky Pie Brown, she has published an autobiography, *Rita Will: Memoir of a Literary Rabble-Rouser* (1997); a collection of political articles, *A Plain Brown Rapper* (1976); and two books of poetry, *The Hand That Cradles the Rock* (1971) and *Songs to a Handsome Woman* (1973). In 1982, she produced a screenplay, *The Slumber Party Massacre*, and a teleplay, *I Love Liberty*, followed by the creation of other film and television scripts. She has published articles, book reviews, and short stories in periodicals including *Horse Country*, *Sports Illustrated*, the *Los Angeles Times*, *Ms.* magazine, and *Vogue*. Brown has also written introductions for reprinted editions of her novels and for several other authors' books, including *The Troll Garden* (1905) by Willa Cather.

ACHIEVEMENTS

The Massachusetts Council on Arts and Humanities presented Rita Mae Brown with a grant in 1974. That year she was also given a National Endowment for the Arts Creative Writing Fellowship. Brown was a member of the Literature Panel for the National Endowment for the Arts from 1978 to 1982, and she received the National Endowment for the Arts fiction grant in 1978. In 1982, her teleplay *I Love Liberty* was nominated for an Emmy Award for Best Variety Show, and it received the Writers Guild of America Award for Best Variety Show on Television. She received another Emmy nomination for *The Long Hot Summer* in 1985. Brown was named a Literary Lion by the New York Public Library in 1987. She is a member of the International Academy of Poets and the International Association of Poets, Playwrights, Editors, Essayists, and Novelists (PEN). Wilson College awarded Brown an honorary doctorate in humanities in 1992.

Several of Brown's mysteries have been Library of Virginia Literary Awards nominees. Many of her books have been *New York Times* best sellers and commercial book club selections, and many have been translated into numerous languages, including German, French, Spanish, Italian, Dutch, Swedish, Danish, and Hebrew. Her landmark 1973 novel *Rubyfruit Jungle* has retained literary interest and has remained in print into the twenty-first century.

BIOGRAPHY

Rita Mae Brown was born in Hanover, Pennsylvania, on November 28, 1944, to Juliann Young, a single mother, and weightlifter James Gordon Venable. Within two weeks, Young gave Rita Mae up for adoption to Ralph and Julia Ellen Buckingham Brown, Young's half cousin. Brown began school in Pennsylvania, where she dealt with ostracism due to her illegitimate birth and her family's lower socioeconomic status, then, in 1955, moved with her family to Fort Lauderdale, Florida, where she thrived because people did not discriminate against her. She began writing stories as a child. A voracious reader, Brown frequented area libraries. Her Latin classes at school enhanced her reading and writing abilities. As a teenager, she was a gifted tennis player.

After graduating from Fort Lauderdale High School in 1962, Brown enrolled with a scholarship at the University of Florida in Gainesville. In 1964, she was dismissed from that university for civil rights activism and for being a lesbian. She returned to Fort Lauderdale and attended the Junior College of Broward County, where she earned an A.A. in 1965. Following her graduation, Brown relocated; she earned a B.A. in English and classics from New York University in 1968 and a certificate in cinematography from Manhattan's School of Visual Arts that same year. While she lived in New York, Brown worked for several publishers and composed articles that were published in underground newspapers. She also became active in publicly addressing feminist, lesbian, and anti-Vietnam War issues.

In 1971, Brown went to Washington, D.C., as a fellow at the Institute for Policy Studies while she attended graduate courses. She published two poetry collections in the early 1970's and began her professional career as a novelist with the publication of *Rubyfruit Jungle* in 1973. Brown completed a Ph.D. in English and political science at the Institute for Policy Studies in 1976. During the next four years, she became a writing instructor at Goddard College in Vermont as well as at the Cazenovia, New York, Women Writers Center and continued to write in a variety of genres, including nonfiction and screenplays.

Brown then settled in Charlottesville, Virginia, her biological father's hometown, and also bought a farm at Afton in Nelson County, Virginia, near Crozet, the setting of her feline mystery series. Brown identifies Afton, where she raises horses and foxhounds on her farm, as her primary residence. Devoted to equine sports, Brown organized the Blue Ridge Polo Club and the Piedmont Women's Polo Club. She reestablished the Oak Ridge Foxhunt Club in 1993, serving as its master of foxhounds. She also is a Virginia Hunt Week director. An animal advocate, she supports humane shelters and rescues abandoned and mistreated animals. In 2005, Brown accepted a two-year visiting faculty position at the University of Nebraska at Lincoln, where she taught writing.

ANALYSIS

Critics of Rita Mae Brown often assert that she is too radical and too argumentative in her works. Others point out that she is dealing with a problem of acceptance that has been the plight of many minor writers. Brown is no more "defensive" about her sexuality than are many other lesbian or gay writers, such as Allen Ginsberg in his poetic statement *Howl* (1956).

What sets Brown's work apart is that she does not disguise her prolesbian stance and does not become an apologist, as did some writers before her. Brown's work is feminist and thus has put off some conservative readers. She began writing in the early 1970's and was influenced by the National Organization for Women (NOW, an organization that asked her to leave because of her political views), the women's movement, and the movement against the Vietnam War. Most important, Brown reacted to her own sense of freedom, discovered upon her relocation to New York City, where she could be open as a lesbian.

Structure is the basic element Brown considers when writing fiction, carefully planning the framework of each story and how characters, plot, and other literary elements will be placed. Brown's relatives inspired her to write the Hunsenmeir novels, *Six of One*, *Bingo*, and *Loose Lips*, featuring the complexities of several generations of an extended southern family at different times in the twentieth century. Brown appropriated autobiographical elements for those books, in which character Nickel Smith, depicted at various ages, shares many of Brown's own characteristics. Interested in ancient literature, Brown acknowledges being inspired by the intricate Greek plays of Aristophanes and other early dramatists. She frequently incorporates tall tales, lies, legends, and historical and literary references in her novels to develop characterizations and settings. Humor and absurdity often lighten the intense tone of Brown's fiction, helping to expose facts and enabling broader awareness of nuances and secrets that would otherwise remain obscured.

During the late 1980's, Brown deviated from her previous literary endeavors by beginning to publish mysteries. She published her eighth novel, *Wish You Were Here*, in 1990; it features a Virginia sleuth and her pets, including a cat named Mrs. Murphy. The Mrs. Murphy mysteries, which reviewers have described as cozies, have attracted readers who might have been unfamiliar with Brown's previous works. Brown continued to produce both literary novels and Mrs. Murphy mysteries during the remainder of the 1990's before developing a foxhunting mystery series. By the early twenty-first century, Brown was concentrating mostly on writing her two mystery series, both of which feature heterosexual female protagonists, weaving her social and political commentary more subtly into plots than she had done in her 1970's novels.

Brown's agrarian interests shape her mystery fiction, which emphasizes protecting natural resources and educating people to respect the environment. Sensory details, such as noting weather conditions and seasonal changes, enhance the landscape descriptions. Brown has noted that each mystery she writes occurs in a particular season, and she cycles consecutively through the seasons of the year in four novels. Emphasizing pastoral aspects of her settings, Brown devotes passages to the praise of nature and animals, inserting Bible verses occasionally. Her portrayals of settings as sanctuaries from modern stresses often convey a spiritual tone.

Brown's affinity for animals has resulted in her giving some animal characters, both domestic and wild, names, and she has attributed some of her writing to their insights, including anthropomorphic dialogue and scenes from animals' points of view; this has caused many literary critics to dismiss certain of her works. The resilience of people and of creatures remains an enduring theme in Brown's fiction, in which characters become empowered by their experiences and interactions.

RUBYFRUIT JUNGLE

Brown's novels draw on her own life; most of her work is clearly autobiographical. In her autobiography, Rita Will, Brown writes that when *Rubyfruit Jungle* was released, she received hate mail and threats on her life. The book is radical, and many readers found it upsetting.

Rubyfruit Jungle is a coming-of-age novel for protagonist Molly Bolt; it is also a direct statement of Brown's own coming-of-age. It describes the early life of Bolt, an adopted daughter of a poor family living in Coffee Hollow, Pennsylvania. Brown traces Molly's life from Coffee Hollow to Florida to New York City and takes Molly from a naïve young girl of seven to a mature, worldly-wise woman in her mid-twenties. Molly Bolt's life story is exactly that of Rita Mae Brown. In most cases, Brown presents all of the characters as merely renamed family members and friends from her childhood through her time in New York. During the course of the novel, the reader sees Molly defy local authority figures of every kind: parents, educators, family members, employers, and lovers. Molly has been described by at least one critic as similar to Huckleberry Finn in his rebellion against authority. Like that of Mark Twain, Brown's style employs folk humor and observations about the world. Unlike Twain, however, Brown does not rely on dialect or local color, though Brown's style is in the vein of other southern American writers, such as Flannery O'Connor, Eudora Welty, and Alice Walker, who have a sharp eye for idiosyncratic behavior.

Molly moves to Florida, as did Brown. While there, she becomes aware of her feelings for other women, falls in love with her college roommate at the University of Florida, and is expelled for this love, just as Brown was expelled from the university for being a lesbian. Molly leaves Florida and arrives in New York City, where she establishes herself in the gay community of Greenwich Village. There she finds a menial job, puts herself through school, and meets a beautiful woman who becomes her lover. From this point on, the novel concentrates on Molly's life as a lesbian.

When Molly left for New York, she was estranged from her mother. Only when she returns to Florida to film her mother as a final project for her degree does Molly really understand that the choices she has made have helped her to develop as an individual who can face the reality of her world. Breaking away from the homogeneity of family, friends, and society has been a difficult ordeal for Molly; however, it is something she had to do in order to grow. Brown explores a similar situation in her 2001 novel *Alma Mater*, in which female college students also make sexual and romantic decisions that counter their friends' and families' social expectations.

IN HER DAY

In Her Day, which treats the difficulties and divisions within the women's movement of the 1970's, was Brown's second novel. The focus is on Carole, an art historian at New York University (NYU). Other characters include LaVerne and Adele, women in their forties who are friends of Carole; Bon and Creampuff, a couple who are friends of the first three women; and a young woman named Ilse, a waitress in a feminist café where all the women dine one night. Ilse is attracted to Carole, and the two begin a relationship. The novel details the age conflict between Carole and Ilse and the even greater conflicting political views of the two women. Eventually, a radical newspaper exposes Carole as a lesbian to her misogynist chairman at NYU, and, when she suffers at his hands, she realizes that perhaps she is too conservative. In the meantime, Ilse's moderate views are influenced by Carole, and she begins to become more conservative. Although the women are unable to reach a common ground that will support their unstable relationship, the novel does illustrate a sense of compromise, which is clearly a nod from Brown to the feminist movement that disowned her when she was young and living in New York.

This novel is weaker than *Rubyfruit Jungle*. Brown tries too hard to be humorous, and her humor is too dark and crude for the novel. Also, *In Her Day* is somewhat harsh and off-putting, with its political diatribes.

VENUS ENVY

Venus Envy, another autobiographical novel, revolves around Mary Frazier Armstrong, owner of a successful art gallery in Charlottesville, Virginia. The heroine, known as Frazier to her family and friends, is hospitalized with what is thought to be terminal cancer. In a drug-induced state, Frazier writes letters to all the people who are important to her, including her mother, father, alcoholic brother, business partner, and two gay male friends. In these letters, Frazier sums up her relationship with each recipient and then informs each one that she is a lesbian. The next time the doctor visits the hospitalized Frazier, he tells her he has made a mistake, and she will not die. The rest of the novel portrays Frazier dealing with the consequences of her letters.

With *Venus Envy*, Brown reclaims her stature as a writer who is able to use humor, in this case derived from the plot, to make her point that people should be accepted as they are and should be allowed to lead their own lives. The novel redeems Brown as a radical of the 1960's and 1970's. While *Rubyfruit Jungle* is clearly her best work, *Venus Envy* shows that by eliminating the harsh tone of *In Her Day*, Brown could recapture her unique style and voice.

THE TELL-TALE HORSE

In *The Tell-Tale Horse*, the sixth volume in her foxhunting mystery series, Brown depicts the complex social dynamics and rivalries of a central Virginia foxhunting community. The novel's protagonist, seventy-three-year-old Jane Arnold, first introduced in the novel *Outfoxed*, serves as the Jefferson Hunt Club's master of foxhounds. The widowed Arnold, who is known as Sister, has the freedom and financial resources to pursue her interests on her farm, where she maintains well-bred foxhounds and horses. Foxhunting introduces a diverse cast of characters into Sister's world, ranging from her lover, Gray

Lorillard, to employees, friends, and enemies. Conflicts between characters often escalate into crimes, including embezzlement, fraud, and murder.

In *The Tell-Tale Horse*, Sister and her friend Marion Maggiolo find a nude woman's corpse perched atop a large horse figure promoting Marion's store, Horse Country; the dead woman has been shot through the heart. It is discovered that the victim, Aashi Mehra, was the mistress of billionaire telecommunications entrepreneur Lakshmi Vajay, who foxhunts with Sister. Brown's adept characterization provides insights, as reasons for characters' antagonism and disdain for specific individuals are revealed. Sister ponders whether Lakshmi's wife, Madhur, murdered Aashi for vengeance or perhaps a wireless service competitor killed Aashi to protect technological secrets. As subplots consume Sister's attention, two additional murders occur. She maintains contact with Sheriff Ben Sidell, whose investigative skills she trusts. Although she fears being the next victim, especially after finding bloodied white roses in her stable, Sister often displays more interest in foxhunting than in sleuthing; through this device, Brown provides some relief from suspense and tension.

Nature is a prevailing theme in the novel, with digressions taking such form as Sister's discussion of how to tend foxes; she stresses that she wants to protect, not kill, wildlife and to promote responsible land conservation. Brown juxtaposes an emphasis on rural endeavors by locals to improve natural landscapes with the encroachment of urban outsiders who have acquired fortunes from telecommunications technology using cellular towers erected on nearby mountains. In this series of novels, Brown addresses various social issues in addition to ecological concerns, including racism, drug abuse, and teenage pregnancy. Her knowledge of both southern American culture and the culture of foxhunting enthusiasts provides authenticity, although at times her digressions related to these cultures seem excessive and disrupt the narrative flow.

THE PURRFECT MURDER

Greed provokes chaos in *The Purrfect Murder*, one of Brown's Mrs. Murphy mysteries. During the autumn after her fortieth birthday, Mary Minor Haristeen, known as Harry, focuses on managing her Crozet, Virginia, farm and her remarriage to equine veterinarian Pharamond (Fair) Haristeen. As in this series' previous fifteen novels, crime upsets Harry's rural community, which is populated by diverse personalities, including characters with deep roots in Crozet and newcomers who have substantial wealth to build elaborate homes there. Past and present relationships fuel emotions of jealousy and revenge, triggering confrontations as characters seek to acquire the things they desire, such as money and power.

Harry contemplates who murdered Dr. Will Wylde, a local gynecologist who performed abortions. Harry's recurring friends from prior books, including Cynthia Cooper, a local deputy, consider possible culprits; suspects include pro-life activists and Dr. Harvey Tillach, whose wife Wylde had seduced. Harry—along with Tee Tucker, a corgi, and cats Mrs. Murphy and Pewter—visits area residents, Wylde's widow, Benita, and his office staff. She discusses the murder while planning an elaborate fund-raiser with her closest friend, Susan Tucker. The omniscient narrative shifts, observing various characters' activities, such as smug building inspector Mike McElvoy visiting construction sites and arguing with owners, including arrogant Carla Paulson.

Tension escalates when an attacker kills Paulson at the fund-raiser, and police arrest Harry's friend Tazio Chappers, an architect, who is found holding a knife near the corpse. Determined to exonerate Tazio, Harry, often oblivious to her own vulnerabilities, intensifies her investigation into both Wylde's and Paulson's deaths. Brown gives voice to her animal characters, which communicate with each other and try to alert Harry to notice subtle details that may offer clues to the crimes. (She uses the stylistic technique of italicized dialogue to indicate her animal characters' communication with each other.) She often uses comic scenes with animal characters to counter the serious tone of passages describing crimes or villains. By including in her narrative the discussion of such topics as building codes and abortion, Brown suggests the disruption that urban concerns pose to rural tranquillity at the same time she increases her ability to hide clues for Harry and her pets to comprehend.

THE SAND CASTLE

Family conflicts reveal people's capacity for forgiveness and tolerance in *The Sand Castle*. As an adult, Nickel Smith recalls an August, 1952, trip with her mother, aunt, and cousin, characters Brown featured in three prior Hunsenmeir novels. In this story, Nickel, the narrator, is seven years old and her cousin, Leroy, is eight. Leroy's grandmother, Louise, whom Nickel calls Wheezie, and her sister Juts, who is Nickel's mother, drive the children to a Maryland beach in an attempt to comfort Leroy, who is mourning his mother's death from cancer six months prior. Wheezie, also bereft after losing her daughter, quarrels with Juts regarding their contrasting religious beliefs. Enjoying the bickering between her mother and aunt, Nickel teases Leroy, who is emotionally paralyzed. His passivity contrasts with Nickel's outspokenness.

The sisters reminisce about beach trips during their youth, telling the children about a prank they played that embarrassed their aunt and sharing details of their family's history. At the beach, Wheezie and Juts start building a sand castle, assigning the children the task of toting buckets of water and sand. The sisters continue to spar verbally, each criticizing the other's choices regarding marriage and lifestyle. Juts views the sand castle as her opportunity to construct something grander in design than the home she desires but cannot afford. Nickel digs a moat to protect the castle, but Juts realizes the sea will eventually wash it away, making a biblical reference that offends Wheezie. Fighting between the sisters escalates, and Wheezie abandons Juts and Nickel at the beach. Eventually she returns, however, and they eat soft-shell crabs at a local restaurant. Leroy, horrified by Nickel's tale of crabs eating flesh, rejects that delicacy.

The group returns to the beach, where the castle still stands but is occupied by a crab; the crab crawls into Leroy's swimming trunks and pinches his genitalia. Soon the beachgoers unite in an effort to resolve Leroy's predicament and avert castration. On the drive home, their attempts to comfort Leroy in his physical pain also contribute to healing their emotional distress, reinforcing their love and acceptance of one another despite their differences. Brown's use of humor to depict this day provides a realistic glimpse of the family dynamics that often surround grieving. By telling this story, adult Nickel keeps her promise, made in *Loose Lips*, that the Hunsenmeir sisters will remain alive in her memories.

Dennis L. Weeks
Updated by Elizabeth D. Schafer

OTHER MAJOR WORKS

POETRY: *The Hand That Cradles the Rock*, 1971; *Songs to a Handsome Woman*, 1973.

SCREENPLAY: *The Slumber Party Massacre*, 1982; *Mary Pickford: A Life on Film*, 1997.

TELEPLAYS: *I Love Liberty*, 1982; *The Long Hot Summer*, 1985; *My Two Loves*, 1986 (with Reginald Rose); *Rich Men, Single Women*, 1989; *The Woman Who Loved Elvis*, 1993.

NONFICTION: *A Plain Brown Rapper*, 1976; *Starting from Scratch: A Different Kind of Writer's Manual*, 1988; *Rita Will: Memoir of a Literary Rabble-Rouser*, 1997; *Sneaky Pie's Cookbook for Mystery Lovers*, 1999.

TRANSLATION: *Hrotsvitha: Six Medieval Latin Plays*, 1971.

BIBLIOGRAPHY

Boyle, Sharon D. "Rita Mae Brown." In *Contemporary Lesbian Writers of the United States: A Bio-bibliographical Critical Sourcebook*, edited by Sandra Pollack and Denise D. Knight. Westport, Conn.: Greenwood Press, 1993. Profiles Brown's life and work. Includes an extended discussion of *Rubyfruit Jungle* and a useful bibliography.

Davies, Julia A. "Rita Mae Brown (1944-   )." In *Significant Contemporary American Feminists: A Biographical Sourcebook*, edited by Jennifer Scanlon. Westport, Conn.: Greenwood Press, 1999. Analyzes how Brown's political activities influenced her literary endeavors, particularly her novels featuring unconventional female protagonists and characters who challenge traditional gender roles.

Day, Frances Ann. "Molly Bolts and Lifelines: Rita Mae Brown's *Rubyfruit Jungle* (1973)." In *Women in Literature: Reading Through the Lens of Gender*, edited by Jerilyn Fisher and Ellen S. Silber. Westport, Conn.: Greenwood Press, 2003. Addresses the classroom study of Brown's *Rubyfruit Jungle* as it relates to the censorship of literature in schools. Identifies attributes of the novel's protagonist, such as individualism, that are universal to most students.

Greenya, John. "Virginia Foxhunting, Murder." *The Washington Times*, March 25, 2007. Reviews Brown's *The Hounds and the Fury*, expressing criticism that the abundance of foxhunting details overwhelm the novel's plot development. Also comments on the strengths and weaknesses of Brown's approach to writing mysteries.

Perry, Carolyn, and Mary Louise Weaks, eds. *The History of Southern Women's Literature*. Baton Rouge: Louisiana State University Press, 2002. Collection of essays includes discussion of themes in Brown's literature within the context of the work of contemporary southern female authors. A biographical sketch of Brown by Harold Woodell discusses her works through her early mysteries.

Van Dover, J. K., and John F. Jebb. *Isn't Justice Always Unfair? The Detective in Southern Literature*. Bowling Green, Ohio: Bowling Green State University Popular Press, 1996. Devotes a chapter to the examination of how rural settings, including those in Brown's mysteries, are depicted and influence literary techniques to create characters, crimes, and plots in the mystery genre. Also addresses Brown's portrayal of animals as sleuths.

Ward, Carol Marie. *Rita Mae Brown*. New York: Twayne, 1993. Provides a comprehensive introductory overview of Brown's life, writings, and philosophy and presents critical analysis of her works. Includes a chronology and an annotated bibliography.

Zimmerman, Bonnie. *The Safe Sea of Women: Lesbian Fiction, 1969-1989*. Boston: Beacon Press, 1990. Insightful study of contemporary lesbian prose that explores the interaction between fiction and community, specifically how lesbian novels and short stories have both reflected and shaped the lesbian community. Zimmerman describes *Rubyfruit Jungle* as the quintessential coming-out novel.

JAMES M. CAIN

Born: Annapolis, Maryland; July 1, 1892
Died: University Park, Maryland; October 27, 1977
Also known as: James Mallahan Cain

OTHER LITERARY FORMS

James M. Cain began his career as a novelist relatively late in life. Cain first wrote professionally as a journalist. Long after he had become famous for his fiction, he would describe himself in *Who's Who in America* as a "newspaperman." Cain used his newspaper work as a springboard to a broader literary career in the 1920's. As a member of the editorial staff of the *New York World* he commented acerbically on contemporary American culture. Cain also authored a number of short stories that never appeared in hardcover during his lifetime. Following Cain's death, Roy Hoopes edited three collections of his journalistic writing and short fiction, *The Baby in the Icebox, and Other Short Fiction* (1981), *Sixty Years of Journalism* (1986), and *Career in C Major, and Other Fiction* (1986). Cain long dreamed of becoming a playwright, but success eluded him. An early effort, *Crashing the Gates* (pr. 1926), failed before reaching Broadway. A dramatization of *The Postman Always Rings Twice* (pr. 1936) ran for seventy-two performances in New York. Cain spent many years in Hollywood as a screenwriter but received screen credit for only three films, *Algiers* (1938), *Stand Up and Fight* (1939), and *Gypsy Wildcat* (1944).

ACHIEVEMENTS

James M. Cain's standing as a novelist has long been the subject of critical controversy. His first novel, *The Postman Always Rings Twice*, became a sensational best seller, but the work's lurid mix of sex and violence inevitably led to doubts about Cain's literary seriousness. In the years that followed, Cain never strayed from his twin themes of crime and sexual obsession. Critical opinion was divided among those who appreciated Cain as a poet of tabloid murder, such as writer Edmund Wilson, and those who believed that Cain exploited rather than explored the material of his books, such as the novelist James T. Farrell. After his period of greatest notoriety during the Depression and the World War II years, Cain's work was largely ignored by critics and scholars. He never received a literary prize for his novels, though late in life he received a lifetime achievement award from the Mystery Writers of America. Cain himself tended to dismiss critical commentary on his artistry, preferring instead to quote his sales figures. Novels such as *The Postman Always Rings Twice*, *Double Indemnity*, and *Mildred Pierce* endure as classic examples of the "hard-boiled" or "tough guy" school of writing that flourished in the 1930's and 1940's, and inspired American film noir. Along with such contemporaries as Dashiell Hammett and Raymond Chandler, James M. Cain will be remembered as a writer who illuminated an existential terror lying just beneath the often-glittering surface of American life.

BIOGRAPHY

James Mallahan Cain was the eldest of two sons and three daughters born to James William Cain and Rose Mallahan Cain. His father was a professor of English and a college administrator who became the president of Washington College. His mother was a trained opera coloratura who gave up her professional ambitions to raise a family. Later in life Cain repeatedly expressed a sense of resentment and rivalry regarding his handsome and accomplished father. He revered his mother and imbibed from her an abiding love of the opera. After graduating from Washington College in 1910, Cain attempted to realize his dreams of a career in the opera by studying to be a singer. Unfortunately his voice could not match his aspiration, and he quit after a year of frustration. Between 1910 and 1914, Cain worked at a succession of jobs as he searched for a direction in life. He decided to become a writer, though he always regarded writing as a second choice because of his failure to express himself in music. He moved home and began writing short stories and sketches, none of which he could sell. Cain supported himself by teaching mathematics and English at Washington College and earned a master's degree in drama.

Restless, Cain moved to Baltimore in 1917 and found work as a newspaper reporter. He volunteered for service in World War I and edited the Seventy-ninth Division newspaper. Upon demobilization, Cain returned to Baltimore and journalism. He embarked on a course that made him a successful man of letters in the 1920's. He began publishing essays and stories in journals such as *The Atlantic Monthly*, *The Nation*, and the *Saturday Evening Post*. He became friends with editor H. L. Mencken and contributed a series of satiric dialogues to Mencken's *The American Mercury*, published in *Our Government* in 1930. After a brief stint teaching at St. John's College in Annapolis, Cain moved to New York City in 1924. He joined the editorial staff of the *New York World*. There he wrote witty commentaries on life during the Jazz Age. When the *World* failed in 1931, Cain moved to *The New Yorker* as managing editor. He stayed at *The New Yorker* only nine months. Like many other writers, Cain traveled to Hollywood, taking advantage of a lucrative offer to write screenplays.

Cain never became a great success at screenwriting, and by 1933 he was out of a job. Financially pressed, he wrote his first novel that spring and summer. *The Postman Always Rings Twice* appeared in 1934 and was a literary sensation and popular triumph. The success of the novel revived Cain's Hollywood career, and he made California the setting of his most powerful works. During the 1930's, Cain produced a string of rough-edged novels that evoked some of the darkest shadows of life in Depression-era America. With the 1940's, however, Cain's inspiration seemed to fade, though he published for another thirty years. In 1946-1947, he attempted to establish an organization called the American Authors' Authority, which would have protected the economic rights of writers, but the effort failed. Cain proved a poor husband to three wives, but in 1947 he married for the fourth time, successfully, to Florence Macbeth, an opera singer like his mother. In 1948, Cain returned home to Maryland, moving to Hyattsville. He lived there quietly, continuing to write until his death in 1977.

ANALYSIS

James M. Cain's strengths as a novelist are inextricably bound to his weaknesses. He has often been praised for the economy of his style and the speed with which he moves his narrative. Readers experience a delicious sense of surrender to the headlong impetus of his storytelling, yet motion in Cain's work often masks wayward prose and manipulative plotting. Critics have remarked on the cinematic quality of his writing. His protagonists live in his pages with the vibrant immediacy of Hollywood icons on the big screen. Cain's actors flirt with caricature; his characterizations are often so primitive and mechanical that they are ludicrous in retrospect.

Cain explores elemental passions in his novels. Sex, jealousy, and greed drive his characters as they thrust themselves into webs of crime and deceit. The intensity of Cain's evocation of this raw emotionalism imbues certain of his most notorious scenes with a surreal naturalism. Frank and Cora's frenzied lovemaking next to the body of the man they have killed in *The Postman Always Rings Twice* and Sharp's rape of Juana in a church in *Serenade* transcend and transfigure the more mundane trappings of Cain's stories. Moments like these also open Cain to the charge that he is trafficking in sensationalism, reveling in the sordid for its own sake. There is a voyeuristic quality to Cain's writing. He exposes his readers to the scabrous underside of the American Dream. Although he occasionally referred to his novels as morality tales, Cain rarely provides any moral alternative to the obsessive dreams of his characters, other than the faceless brutality of authority.

In Cain's universe the only law is chance. His protagonists enjoy no dignity with their various ends. Unlike the heroes of classical tragedy, their destinies do not illuminate the contours of a higher moral order. They are simply victims of an impersonal and blindly malevolent fate. This nihilism gives Cain's writings much of their enduring power. He captured the desperation of people leading blighted lives in a world wracked by the Great Depression. As long as men and women continue to sense their own powerlessness in a modern, mass-produced society, Cain's fables of reckless desire will resonate with readers.

THE POSTMAN ALWAYS RINGS TWICE

Cain's first novel is generally considered his greatest. It adumbrates themes and techniques that characterize his fiction. *The Postman Always Rings Twice* is cast in the form of a confession written by Frank Chambers on the eve of his execution. Frank, like many of Cain's protagonists, is doomed by his relationship with a woman. A homeless drifter, Frank wanders into a roadside "bar-b-que" and meets Cora, the frustrated wife of the Greek owner. Immediately drawn together by an overwhelming sexual chemistry, Frank and Cora kill the Greek in a fake auto accident. The murder drives the lovers apart, however, as their passion is clouded by suspicion and fear. Ironically, Cora dies in a real car crash, and Frank is then condemned for a murder he did not commit.

Cain's grim tale proved very influential. French writer Albert Camus acknowledged *The Postman Always Rings Twice* as an inspiration for *L'Étranger* (1942; *The Stranger,* 1946), his own existential meditation on crime and punishment.

DOUBLE INDEMNITY

Double Indemnity first appeared as a magazine serial. Cain wrote it for money, and he did not regard it very highly. Over time, the novel has come to be regarded as one of Cain's greatest achievements. Like *The Postman Always Rings Twice*, it is written in confessional form and tells a story of the fatal consequences of the wrong man meeting the wrong woman. Walter Huff, an insurance salesman, encounters Phyliss Nirdlinger, a beautiful, unhappily married woman. Desire and villainy blossom together as Huff sees an opportunity to win the woman he loves while at the same time beating the system he has long served. Huff and Phyliss kill Mr. Nirdlinger, making it look like an unusual accident, worth a double indemnity on his life insurance. As always in Cain, however, success in crime brings only anxiety and distrust. The lovers' mutual doubts and jealousy culminate in a deadly meeting on a cruise ship.

SERENADE

Serenade provided sensational reading in the 1930's. It is Cain's psychologically outlandish commentary on sex and artistry. The protagonist and narrator, John Sharp, is an opera singer who has retreated to Mexico because of the failure of his voice. Cain's premise is that Sharp cannot sing because of his receptiveness to the sexual advances of conductor Stephen Hawes. Sharp falls under the spell of Juana, an uneducated earth mother, whose embraces restore his sexual and vocal potency. Sharp returns to California and stardom. His success is challenged when Hawes appears. Juana kills Hawes, almost ritually, during a mock bullfight. Sharp insists on fleeing with Juana and inadvertently causes her death.

MILDRED PIERCE

Mildred Pierce marked a departure for Cain: The book contains no murders; it is told in the third person; its protagonist is a woman. The novel remains true, however, to Cain's dark vision of human relationships. Mildred Pierce is a middle-class housewife who rejects her philandering husband. Forced to support herself, she begins as a waitress and becomes the owner of a chain of restaurants. Mildred's undoing is her extravagant, almost incestuous, love for her daughter Veda, an aspiring opera singer. Mildred mortgages her restaurants to finance Veda's career. Veda responds by leaving, taking with her Mildred's second husband. Mildred lives on, ruined and alone, her career a perverse distortion of America's Horatio Alger myth.

THE BUTTERFLY

Cain's originality and intensity seemed to dissipate with the end of the Depression and the advent of World War II. Some critics think highly of *The Butterfly*, a tale of incest and murder set in the mountains of eastern Kentucky. In this novel Cain ambitiously attempts to delineate the psychology of a delusional and obsessive personality as he traces the agonies of a self-righteous mountaineer sexually drawn to a young woman he believes to be his daughter. Cain's lofty intentions never attain fruition, however, because he allows his mountaineer and supporting characters to dissolve into vulgar and simplistic stereotypes. Flawed as it is, *The Butterfly* is the best of Cain's later writing, which separates into unrealized historical romances and diffident echoes of his earlier work. Cain's reputation as a novelist will always rest on the bitter existential melodramas he produced in the 1930's.

Daniel P. Murphy

OTHER MAJOR WORKS

SHORT FICTION: "Pastorale," 1928; "The Taking of Monfaucon," 1929; "Come-Back," 1934; "The Birthday Party," 1936; "Brush Fire," 1936; "Dead Man," 1936; "Hip, Hip, the Hippo," 1936; "Coal Black," 1937; "Everything but the Truth," 1937; "The Girl in the Storm," 1940; *Career in C Major, and Other Stories*, 1943; "Payoff Girl," 1952; "Cigarette Girl," 1953; "Two O'Clock Blonde," 1953; "The Visitor," 1961; *The Baby in the Icebox, and Other Short Fiction*, 1981 (Roy Hoopes, editor); *Career in C Major, and Other Fiction*, 1986 (Hoopes, editor).

PLAYS: *Crashing the Gates*, pr. 1926; *Theological Interlude*, pb. 1928 (dialogue); *Trial by Jury*, pb. 1928 (dialogue); *Citizenship*, pb. 1929 (dialogue); *Will of the People*, pb. 1929 (dialogue); *The Governor*, pb. 1930; *Don't Monkey with Uncle Sam*, pb. 1933 (dialogue); *The Postman Always Rings Twice*, pr. 1936 (adaptation of his novel); *7-11*, pr. 1938.

SCREENPLAYS: *Algiers*, 1938; *Stand Up and Fight*, 1938; *Gypsy Wildcat*, 1944.

NONFICTION: *Our Government*, 1930; *Sixty Years of Journalism*, 1986 (Roy Hoopes, editor).

MISCELLANEOUS: *The James M. Cain Cookbook: Guide to Home Singing, Physical Fitness, and Animals (Especially Cats)*, 1988 (essays and stories; Roy Hoopes and Lynne Barrett, editors).

BIBLIOGRAPHY

Cain, James M. "An Interview with James M. Cain." Interview by John Carr. *Armchair Detective* 16, no. 1 (1973): 4-21. Cain reveals interesting highlights of his career as a reporter and explains the influence of Vincent Sergeant Lawrence, a journalist and screenwriter, on his work. Cain's comments on his three major novels are particularly informative. Includes an annotated list of people important in Cain's life and a bibliography of Cain's writings.

Hoopes, Roy. *Cain*. New York: Holt, Rinehart and Winston, 1982. Comprehensive biography is divided into four chronological parts, covering his years in Maryland and France, New York, Hollywood, and Hyattsville. Includes an afterword on Cain as newspaperman. Supplemented by extensive source notes, a list of Cain's publications, a filmography, and an index.

Madden, David. *Cain's Craft*. Metuchen, N.J.: Scarecrow Press, 1985. One of Cain's earliest academic champions explores the author's literary techniques. Compares some of Cain's works to novels by other writers and addresses the ways in which Cain's books have been adapted to the screen.

_____. *James M. Cain*. New York: Twayne, 1970. Well-written introductory volume takes note of Cain's varied reputation as an excellent, trashy, important, and always popular writer. Approaches every major aspect of his work on several levels, including his life in relation to his writing, analysis of his characters, and his technical expertise. Complemented by notes, a bibliography of primary and secondary sources, and an index.

Marling, William. *The American Roman Noir: Hammett, Cain, and Chandler*. Athens: University of Georgia Press, 1995. Intriguing exercise in literary criticism links the hard-boiled writings of Cain, Dashiell Hammett, and Raymond Chandler to contemporary economic and technological changes. Marling sees these writers as pioneers of an aesthetic for the postindustrial age.

Nyman, Jopi. *Hard-Boiled Fiction and Dark Romanticism.* New York: Peter Lang, 1998. Examines the fiction of Cain, Dashiell Hammett, Ernest Hemingway, and Horace Mc- Coy and asserts that the romanticism and pathos in these works reflects the authors' nostalgia for a lost world of individualism and true manhood.

Oates, Joyce Carol. "Man Under Sentence of Death: The Novels of James M. Cain." In *Tough Guy Writers of the Thirties*, edited by David Madden. Carbondale: Southern Il- linois University Press, 1968. Brief but wide-ranging essay approaches Cain's novels as significant for the light they throw on his relationship with the American audience of the 1930's and 1940's.

Shaw, Patrick W. *The Modern American Novel of Violence.* Troy, N.Y.: Whitson, 2000. Analysis of violence in American novels includes an examination of *The Postman Al- ways Rings Twice.* Concludes that in writing this "sadistic" novel, Cain created a "sar- donic, unencumbered narrative style that proved more influential than the story it conveyed."

Skenazy, Paul. *James M. Cain.* New York: Continuum, 1989. Comprehensive study of Cain's work. Skenazy is more critical of the author's writing than are some other com- mentators (including Madden, cited above) but acknowledges Cain's importance and his continuing capacity to attract readers.

Wilson, Edmund. "The Boys in the Back Room." In *Classics and Commercials.* New York: Farrar, Straus and Giroux, 1950. Personal essay by an astute social and cultural commentator groups Cain with John Steinbeck, John O'Hara, William Saroyan, and others in the 1930's and 1940's who were influenced by Ernest Hemingway. Wilson considers Cain to be the best of these writers.

MICHAEL CHABON

Born: Washington, D.C.; May 24, 1963
Also known as: Leon Chaim Bach; Malachi B. Cohen; August Van Zorn

<small>PRINCIPAL LONG FICTION</small>
The Mysteries of Pittsburgh, 1988
Wonder Boys, 1995
The Amazing Adventures of Kavalier and Clay, 2000
The Final Solution: A Story of Detection, 2004
Gentlemen of the Road, 2007
The Yiddish Policemen's Union, 2007

OTHER LITERARY FORMS

Although known primarily as a novelist, Michael Chabon (SHAY-bahn) has also distinguished himself as a writer of short fiction, publishing the collections *A Model World, and Other Stories* (1991) and *Werewolves in Their Youth* (1999). His second book, *A Model World*, helped cement Chabon's emerging reputation as a writer of emotional depth and lyrical intensity. His novel *The Amazing Adventures of Kavalier and Clay* inspired a comic-book series, published by Dark Horse Comics, based on the novel's comic-book superhero character the Escapist; Chabon has contributed but is not a primary writer for the series. He has published articles and essays in a variety of magazines such as *Esquire*, *The New Yorker*, and *The Paris Review*. He served as the editor for the anthology *McSweeney's Mammoth Treasury of Thrilling Tales* (2003) and *McSweeney's Enchanted Chamber of Astonishing Stories* (2004). He has worked on screenplays for a number of films, most notably *Spider-Man 2* (2004). A collection of Chabon's essays (largely made up of his magazine publications) titled *Maps and Legends: Essays on Reading and Writing Along the Borderlands* was published in 2008.

ACHIEVEMENTS

After having initially made a splash as a novelist, Michael Chabon was also lauded for his collections of short fiction; the story "Son of the Wolfman" won an O. Henry Award in 1999. Chabon's star climbed higher with the 2000 film adaptation of *Wonder Boys* and reached even greater heights when *The Amazing Adventures of Kavalier and Clay* won the Pulitzer Prize in 2000 and was nominated for the National Book Critics Circle Award as well as short-listed for the PEN/Faulkner Award. Chabon's subsequent foray into adolescent fantasy, *Summerland*, won the Mythopoeic Fantasy Award for Children's Literature in 2003. His further work in genre fiction has been rewarded as well; a brief version of his novel *The Final Solution* won the 2003 Aga Khan Prize for fiction for best work published in *The Paris Review* that year. Furthermore, *The Yiddish Policemen's Union* won the Edgar

Award for best mystery novel, the Nebula Award for best science-fiction novel, and the Locus Award for best science-fiction novel and was nominated for a Hugo Award for best science-fiction novel as well as the Sidewise Award for Alternate History. His historical swashbuckling novel *Gentlemen of the Road* was first serialized in *The New York Times Magazine.*

BIOGRAPHY

Michael Chabon was born on May 24, 1963, in Washington, D.C., and raised partly in Columbia, Maryland, and partly in Pittsburgh, Pennsylvania. His parents divorced when Chabon was an adolescent. During this time the young Chabon turned to comic books and works of genre fiction (such as Arthur Conan Doyle's Sherlock Holmes stories) to escape the domestic strife in his life. He attended the University of Pittsburgh, earning a B.A. in English in 1984; from there he attended the master of fine arts program at the University of California at Irvine, where he would earn his degree in 1987. More important, one of his advisers at Irvine, novelist Donald Heiney, was so impressed with Chabon's thesis that he sent the manuscript to his own agent; the novel was purchased for $155,000 (almost an unheard-of sum for a first literary novel in 1987) and was published to great advance praise. That same year, Chabon married poet Lollie Groth, a union that would end with their divorce in 1991.

For the next several years, Chabon worked on a novel that he planned to title "Fountain City," about environmental activism and a baseball park in Florida, among other things; the novel became longer and longer, until Chabon realized that it was not succeeding and put it aside to begin work on a novel about a man unable to finish a sprawling novel, *Wonder Boys.* Chabon married attorney Ayelet Waldman in 1993, with whom he would eventually have three children (Sophie, Ezekiel, and Ida-Rose). The successful adaptation of *Wonder Boys* into a film (directed by Curtis Hanson) released in 2000 combined with the author's thriving sales to make him financially independent and able to focus on his work. Chabon's second wife, Waldman has published a number of mystery novels in a series known as the Mommy-Track Mysteries; her successful work in genre fiction parallels Chabon's own interest in the field. Since his work on *Spider-Man 2* (directed by Sam Raimi), Chabon has balanced his busy life writing fiction with work on screenplays.

ANALYSIS

As might be expected of a novelist who first gained acclaim at the age of twenty-five and who has not escaped the limelight since, Michael Chabon has produced work that displays significant evolution over the succeeding two decades. While all his novels have shown Chabon's gift for fluid, lyrical prose, the tones of the works have stretched from wistful (*The Mysteries of Pittsburgh*) to wryly comic (*Wonder Boys*) to cynical and laconic (*The Yiddish Policemen's Union*). Structurally, Chabon's methods have also changed. Where his first two novels are tightly focused first-person narratives about small numbers of people over a brief time, *The Amazing Adventures of Kavalier and Clay* takes place over several years and includes an expansive cast; *The Yiddish Policemen's Union* evokes an alternative version of the world in which Sitka, Alaska, has been the Jewish homeland since World War II; and *Gentleman of the Road* is a short, quickly paced novel of historical adventure.

As Chabon's plots and style have evolved, so too have his interests and subject matter. *The Mysteries of Pittsburgh* is a book by a young man, not too long out of college, about a young man just out of college. The distance between the writer and the creation is greater in *Wonder Boys*, but at some level Grady Tripp's struggle to complete a new novel is surely based on Chabon's similar experience. With *The Amazing Adventures of Kavalier and Clay*, however, Chabon broke into new territory: The novel is set in the years before and after World War II and deals with such broad themes as art, creativity, Jewish identity, romantic happiness, and the closeted lives of gays at a time when such lives were subject to scrutiny and persecution.

Chabon's novels have often portrayed gay characters and aspects of gay lifestyle. After the success of *The Mysteries of Pittsburgh*, which is partly about a bisexual man making a choice between a relationship with a man and a relationship with a woman, Chabon became identified as an author who writes about and is sympathetic to gay characters. Similarly, although Chabon's Jewish heritage seems to have had relatively little influence on his first two novels, Jewish culture and identity are primary issues in *The Amazing Adventures of Kavalier and Clay*, *The Yiddish Policemen's Union*, and *Gentlemen of the Road*.

Chabon has also become increasingly interested in fiction genres such as detective, horror, and science fiction. In addition to editing genre collections for McSweeney's and writing a new "final chapter" to the life of Sherlock Holmes, Chabon has incorporated both science fiction and the detective story in the long consideration of Jewish identity and Zionism that is *The Yiddish Policemen's Union*. Similarly, although ostensibly a historical adventure novel, *Gentlemen of the Road* is in many ways patterned on the fantasy works of such writers as Fritz Leiber and Michael Moorcock; the primary characters are again Jewish, and the setting is an ancient Turkish city-state of Jews.

THE MYSTERIES OF PITTSBURGH

The Mysteries of Pittsburgh is primarily a coming-of-age novel. Art Bechstein is poised on the precipice of several new worlds: He is not only trying to unravel his future as a new college graduate but also coming to terms with his own troubling (to him, at first) bisexuality as well as the realization that his father is a shadowy underworld figure. Even as Art is seduced by both Arthur Lecomte and Phlox Lombardi, he is pulled between their world and his own. Both names are symbolic in their way; Arthur has more or less the same name as Art, and at some level he represents an outward manifestation of Art's previously unacknowledged bisexuality. A phlox is a kind of flower, and in truth Art's world is in flower, blooming and changing; at the same time, phlox serves as a homonym for "flux," a perfect description of Art's emotional state.

Arthur and Phlox introduce Art to Cleveland, a charming and literate aspiring young criminal who wishes to use Art to gain an introduction to Art's father. As Phlox and Arthur represent different aspects of Art's life, Cleveland represents the allure of rebellion and the thrill of unplanned and unchecked danger. By the end of the novel, the triangle of friendships that has stretched Art in different directions has fallen apart under tragedy, and Art must make his own way into adulthood.

WONDER BOYS

Wonder Boys was published seven years after *The Mysteries of Pittsburgh*. The novel tells of a middle-aged creative-writing professor, Grady Tripp, who learns that his third wife, Emily, is leaving him even as he finds out that his mistress, college chancellor Sara Gaskell (and wife to the English Department's chair, Walter), is pregnant with Grady's child. Grady has been drinking too much and smoking too much marijuana, typing away all the while at his sprawling novel *Wonder Boys*, which is seven years overdue and at this point more than two thousand pages long. The events of the novel take place over the weekend of the small fictional Pennsylvania college's WordFest literary festival. Grady's editor, Terry Crabtree, is in town to attend the festival and to inquire about Grady's novel, which Grady has implied—untruthfully—is nearing completion.

Wonder Boys is, in some ways, nominally autobiographical; like Tripp, Chabon worked on an abortive second novel ("Fountain City") for several years, watching it grow to more than fifteen hundred pages before realizing that he had to abandon it. In most ways, however, Grady Tripp is a character in his own right, and throughout the novel his name proves apt as he trips repeatedly over his own feet literally and figuratively. Even as he tries to navigate between Emily's leaving and Sara's announcement, he must also try to guide his naïve, gay, and vulnerable young wunderkind student James Leer around the pitfalls represented by Grady's lecherous gay friend Terry and James's own budding talent and vulnerabilities.

The novel becomes a kind of picaresque series of adventures, with Grady stumbling from misadventure to misadventure, accompanied by James, who stitches together lies about his background. Interposed throughout the narrative are Grady's memories of cult horror writer Albert Vetch, who died forgotten and alone. Grady eventually realizes that, unless he wants to mimic Vetch's life, he too must put away childish things and fully embrace maturity.

THE AMAZING ADVENTURES OF KAVALIER AND CLAY

The Amazing Adventures of Kavalier and Clay in many ways demonstrates Chabon's coming-of-age. Early in the novel, eighteen-year-old Jewish art student and part-time escape artist Joseph Kavalier is smuggled out of Prague; the year is 1939. Sent to the United States, he meets his distant cousin Sammy Klayman (also known as Sammy Clay). Before long, Sammy has introduced Joe to the budding medium of comic books, and together they invent their own character, the Escapist. The allure of the Escapist in their lives is obvious: Millions of European Jews are being persecuted and are unable to escape the horror of the Holocaust; conversely, the Escapist is able to escape from any trap and turn the tables on his enemies. In addition, even as Sammy fears a second kind of persecution—as a closeted young gay man—the Escapist is empowered and fearless.

As the novel progresses, Joe confronts both his fear of persecution and his fear of intimacy when he joins the war effort and is sent on a mission to Antarctica; similarly, Sammy (although involved in a marriage of convenience with Joe's lover Rosa, who becomes pregnant with Joe's child just before he leaves for the war) takes more and more chances as he seeks to live a fully integrated life. Joe, too, eventually realizes that he needs family when he rejoins Sammy, Rosa, and his son, Tommy.

THE FINAL SOLUTION *and* GENTLEMEN OF THE ROAD

Both the young adult novel *Summerland* and *The Final Solution* indicate the different directions that Chabon's interests took in the years following *The Amazing Adventures of Kavalier and Clay*. *Summerland* is a fantasy novel (similar in style to J. K. Rowling's Harry Potter series) about a boy named Ethan Feld who hates baseball, which his father makes him play. Along with his friend, Native American pitcher Jennifer Rideout, Ethan is recruited to lead a team of misfit players (from a variety of dimensions) in a series of baseball games to save the world from destruction by the mysterious Coyote, a godlike avatar of chaos. *The Final Solution* returns to where Chabon's interest in genre fiction began—Sherlock Holmes. Set in 1944 during World War II, the eighty-nine-year-old character is never named but is clearly Holmes (or based completely on Holmes). The title refers both to Adolf Hitler's plan to exterminate the Jews of Europe and to "The Final Problem" (1893), the story wherein Holmes author Arthur Conan Doyle temporarily killed off his detective hero. Like *The Amazing Adventures of Kavalier and Clay* and *The Yiddish Policemen's Union*, *The Final Solution* deals with issues of Jewish identity; the aged Holmes's last case involves a young Jewish refugee from Germany. Although Holmes can find answers to the more overt problems in the case, others are insoluble.

Like *The Final Solution*, *Gentlemen of the Road* is a short novel; it was originally serialized in *The New York Times Magazine*. Set in the tenth century C.E., this swashbuckling adventure novel follows two mercenaries, an African Jew named Amram and a long-haired Jewish Frank named Zelikman, as they work to bring the rightful heir of the Jewish Khazars back to the throne.

THE YIDDISH POLICEMEN'S UNION

The Yiddish Policemen's Union represents a culmination of Chabon's interests in Jewish identity and in genre fiction. The novel posits an alternate history: The creation of Israel in 1948 fails, and instead a temporary homeland for Jews is created in Sitka, Alaska. The novel is set at the end of the sixty-year period following establishment of that homeland, soon before the Alaskan region is to revert to American control. The language in *The Yiddish Policemen's Union* is more tightly controlled and terse than in most of Chabon's work, in keeping with its crime-novel milieu. The protagonist is a down-on-his-luck homicide detective named Meyer Landsman, who, true to his genre, drinks too much and has recently seen his marriage fall apart.

Teamed with partner and cousin Berko Shemets (half Jewish and half Tlingit native), Landsman sets out to uncover the murder of a mysterious man who has died in Landsman's own apartment building. Like his hard-boiled predecessors Philip Marlowe (the detective creation of Raymond Chandler, 1888-1959) and Sam Spade (created by Dashiell Hammett, 1894-1961), Landsman solves his crimes more through persistence and toughness than through brilliant insights; the more the various communities of Sitka try to warn him away, the deeper he digs. Chabon uses the detective-novel framework of *The Yiddish Policemen's Union* to investigate questions of Jewish American culture, Zionism, and Anti-Semitism.

Scott D. Yarbrough

OTHER MAJOR WORKS

SHORT FICTION: *A Model World, and Other Stories*, 1991; *Werewolves in Their Youth: Stories*, 1999.

NONFICTION: *Maps and Legends: Essays on Reading and Writing Along the Borderlands*, 2008.

YOUNG ADULT LITERATURE: *Summerland*, 2002.

EDITED TEXTS: *McSweeney's Mammoth Treasury of Thrilling Tales*, 2003; *McSweeney's Enchanted Chamber of Astonishing Stories*, 2004.

MISCELLANEOUS: *Michael Chabon Presents: The Amazing Adventures of the Escapist*, 2004 (2 volumes).

BIBLIOGRAPHY

Binelli, Mark. "The Amazing Story of the Comic Book Nerd Who Won the Pulitzer Prize for Fiction." *Rolling Stone*, September 27, 2001. Provides an overview of Chabon's life and career as well as brief discussion of each of his novels.

Cahill, Bryon. "Michael Chabon: A Writer with Many Faces." *Writing!* 27, no. 6 (April/ May, 2005): 16-20. Presents a detailed examination of Chabon's developing interests and the inspirations behind many of his works.

Chabon, Michael. "On *The Mysteries of Pittsburgh*." *The New York Review of Books*, June 9, 2005. Brief history by the author explains the genesis of his first novel and some of the less overt autobiographical elements in the work.

_____. "Secret Skin: Superheroes, Escapism, Realism." *The New Yorker*, March 10, 2008. Examines the comic-book and superhero genres, with emphasis on the costumes as well as on the ways in which the comic-book medium differs from traditional prose fiction. Discusses the superhero motif in *The Amazing Adventures of Kavalier and Clay.*

Fowler, Douglas. "The Short Fiction of Michael Chabon: Nostalgia in the Very Young." *Studies in Short Fiction* 32, no. 1 (Winter, 1995): 75-82. Offers analysis of Chabon's *The Mysteries of Pittsburgh* and various of his short stories, with comparisons drawn to F. Scott Fitzgerald's *The Great Gatsby* (1925).

Munson, Sam. "Slices of Life." *Commentary* 115, no. 6 (June, 2003): 67-71. Focuses on Chabon's editing of the McSweeney's anthologies as well as on the development of his interests in genre fiction.

Perle, Liz. "Alternate Reality: Author Profile of Michael Chabon." *Publishers Weekly,* September 24, 2007. Discusses Chabon's creativity and interest in genre categories, as demonstrated by his novel *Gentlemen of the Road.*

RAYMOND CHANDLER

Born: Chicago, Illinois; July 23, 1888
Died: La Jolla, California; March 26, 1959
Also known as: Raymond Thornton Chandler

PRINCIPAL LONG FICTION

The Big Sleep, 1939
Farewell, My Lovely, 1940
The High Window, 1942
The Lady in the Lake, 1943
The Little Sister, 1949
The Long Goodbye, 1953
Playback, 1958
The Raymond Chandler Omnibus: Four Famous Classics, 1967
The Second Chandler Omnibus, 1973
Poodle Springs, 1989 (incomplete manuscript finished by Robert B. Parker)
Later Novels and Other Writings, 1995

OTHER LITERARY FORMS

Raymond Chandler began his literary career with a false start in England in his early twenties, publishing an assortment of journalistic sketches, essays, poems, and a single story; most of these pieces are collected in *Chandler Before Marlowe: Raymond Chandler's Early Prose and Poetry* (1973), edited by Matthew J. Bruccoli. His real career as a writer was launched more than twenty years later, when he began publishing short stories in crime magazines. Chandler published twenty-three stories during his lifetime, most of which appeared in pulp magazines such as *Black Mask* and *Dime Detective Magazine*. Although the stories rarely approach the literary merit of his novels, they are representative of a popular type of American writing. They also show a versatility within the mystery formula that Chandler would later develop in his novels.

Chandler forbade the reissue during his lifetime of eight of his stories, but three of these were published, apparently without the author's consent. Chandler insisted that these stories be withheld because of a curious professional scruple. The materials had been incorporated in subsequent novels—in Chandler's word, "cannibalized"—and he felt that their republication would be unfair to readers of the novels. Some of the best of Chandler's stories are in this group and have, since his death, been published in the collection *Killer in the Rain* (1964).

Like William Faulkner and F. Scott Fitzgerald, Chandler was invited to Hollywood to write film scripts. He collaborated on several important screenplays and, with Billy Wilder, was nominated for an Academy Award for the 1944 screen adaptation of James

Raymond Chandler
(Library of Congress)

M. Cain's novel *Double Indemnity* (1936). His original screenplay *The Blue Dahlia* also received an Oscar nomination, despite the fact that Chandler remained dissatisfied with that 1946 film. In 1948 he wrote, under contract with Universal Pictures, an original screenplay, *Playback*, that was not filmed; Chandler rewrote this work, with new characters, as a novel during his final years.

ACHIEVEMENTS

More than any of his contemporaries, Raymond Chandler attempted to use the devices of mystery fiction for serious literary purposes. The peculiarly American school of detective fiction came of age during the years of the Great Depression in the 1930's. The most influential outlet for this fiction was *Black Mask*, a pulp magazine founded by H. L. Mencken and George Jean Nathan and later edited by Captain Joseph T. Shaw. The American detective character that had its origins in *Black Mask* and similar pulp magazines is often called the "hard-boiled detective"—this character differs sharply from that of the traditional British sleuth. Chandler's heroes are not charming eccentrics in the tradition of

Dorothy L. Sayers's Lord Peter Wimsey, nor are they masters of unbelievable powers of deduction, such as Arthur Conan Doyle's Sherlock Holmes. When Chandler's Philip Marlowe tells his client (in *The Big Sleep*) that he is not Holmes or Philo Vance and humorously introduces himself as Philo Vance in *The Lady in the Lake*, Chandler is calling attention to the distance he intends to create between his character and the traditional heroes of detective literature. The American detective of fiction as created by Chandler, Dashiell Hammett, and a host of lesser contemporaries is a loner, a man of ordinary intellect but of unusual perseverance and willingness to confront whatever adversary he encounters, whether that adversary be the criminal or the legal establishment. Kenneth Millar, who under the pen name Ross Macdonald would become the most worthy of Chandler's successors, said that from the *Black Mask* revolution came "a new kind of detective hero, the classless, restless men of American democracy, who spoke the language of the street."

Chandler found the formulaic plots of traditional detective fiction limiting and confining. He was less interested in challenging the deductive skills of the reader than in examining the milieu and sociocultural effects of criminal behavior. Chandler once told his publisher that he disliked those popular mystery titles that emphasized sheer deduction because such titles "put too much emphasis on the mystery itself, and I have not the ingenuity to devise the sort of intricate and recondite puzzles the purest aficionados go for." His mention of a lack of ingenuity is characteristic of the diffidence with which Chandler sometimes spoke of his own work; what is certain, both from his letters and from his 1944 essay "The Simple Art of Murder," is that such plots did not interest Chandler.

Although he should be credited, along with Hammett and other *Black Mask* writers, with the development of a peculiarly American form of detective fiction, Chandler himself always consciously sought to transcend the limitations of the genre. He regarded himself as a serious novelist who wrote detective fiction. His intent was to study the modern landscape of evil, and his work bears striking affinities with T. S. Eliot's *The Waste Land* (1922) and with Ernest Hemingway's novels. His evocation of a world dominated by malicious, sadistic, self-centered, ruthless, and psychopathic types led W. H. Auden, in his 1948 essay "The Guilty Vicarage: Notes on the Detective Story, by an Addict," to conclude that Chandler's interest was not in detective fiction at all, but in "serious studies of a criminal milieu, the Great Wrong Place"; Auden argues that Chandler's "powerful but extremely depressing books should be read and judged, not as escape literature, but as works of art."

Auden states, admirably, only half the case. Chandler's books should be judged as works of art, but not merely as studies of the world of crime or of the world gone bad. In his novels there is a constant quest, a search for heroic possibility in the ruined moral landscape of modern California. Chandler's fiction continually considers whether authentic heroism is possible in the modern world, and Marlowe's attempt to take heroic action places him at odds with the world he inhabits. By the time he was ready to write *The Long*

Goodbye, Chandler had indeed transformed the detective story: In that book the elements of detection and mystery are clearly subordinate to psychological and cultural realism.

The achievement of Chandler thus discloses a paradox. Although he was instrumental in the discovery of an American style for detective fiction and has been widely and rightly respected for that accomplishment, his real achievement was to merge detective fiction with serious literature.

BIOGRAPHY

Although his early ambition was to be a writer, Raymond Thornton Chandler did not begin the literary career that would win him fame until he was forty-five years old. This is only one of several incongruities in the life of one of America's original literary talents.

Chandler was born in Chicago, in 1888, the only child of a railroad employee and an Irishwoman. The marriage was marred by his father's alcoholism and ended in divorce when the boy was seven. Chandler and his mother moved to London and became dependent on his maternal uncle, a successful solicitor. Chandler went to Dulwich College, where he received the solid classical education characteristic of English public schools. He was at the head of his class in most of his subjects. After his graduation from Dulwich, Chandler claimed dual citizenship so that he could take the English civil service examinations, but he was unable to adapt to the bureaucratic environment and resigned his civil service appointment. He supported himself briefly by writing for magazines and newspapers and by publishing some undistinguished poems and a single story. He left England for the United States in 1912.

Chandler made his way to Southern California, where he began a relationship that was to dominate his literary life. Chandler despised the superficiality and pretentiousness of the California culture as well as its lack of tradition or continuity, but he intuited that this would be the culture of the future. One aim of his writing would be to record and comment on that culture. His immediate concern upon arriving was to find work, and he was involved in a variety of minor jobs until he completed a three-year bookkeeping course in six weeks. Thereafter, he was involved in various business enterprises until 1917, when he joined the Canadian army. He saw action in France during World War I; Chandler was the sole survivor of a raid on his outfit and was decorated for valor. When he returned to California, he briefly tried banking and eventually established himself as an extremely successful executive of the Dabney Oil Syndicate. He became vice president of the concern and was at one time director of eight subsidiary firms and president of three.

Shortly after he joined the Dabney firm, Chandler married Cissy Pascal, who filed for divorce in order to marry him. An accomplished pianist and a beauty, she was also eighteen years older than Chandler, a fact she deliberately concealed from him: He was thirty-five; she was fifty-three. Their marriage was a lasting but troubled one.

Perhaps discoveries about his marriage, as well as problems and pressures in his business, led to the first appearance of what became Chandler's lifelong struggle with alcoholism. In fact, several of Chandler's early stories, such as "Pearls Are a Nuisance," feature a hero who must contend with a drinking problem. In 1932, Dabney fired Chandler because of chronically poor job performance traced directly to excessive drinking.

Chandler took the shock of his firing as an indication that he had to take control of his life, and he turned again to the literary aspirations of his youth. Chandler was then reading and being influenced by Hemingway rather than by Henry James, whom he had read avidly in England, and he soon found the outlet his creative talent needed in the emerging American detective story. His first story appeared in *Black Mask* in 1933; he would be a successful novelist within the decade.

Fame and success came to Chandler in the 1940's. His sales were solid, studios sought the film rights to his novels, his books were being translated into several languages, and he was lured to Hollywood to write screenplays. There he enjoyed material success and stimulating camaraderie with other writers. Soon the pressures of studio deadlines, artistic compromise, and the pretentiousness around him—much of the satire of *The Little Sister* is directed at the phoniness of Hollywood—combined with personal ill health sent Chandler back to the bottle. His career in Hollywood ended in frustration, petty squabbles, and bitterness.

With material success and public acclaim, Chandler spent the final decade of his life alternating between despair and the hope for new beginnings. Always a lonely man, he became depressive after his wife died in 1954. He attempted suicide, but after his recovery divided his time between life in London and La Jolla, California, between bouts with the bottle and the admiration of an appreciative public. He fell in love with his agent, Helga Greene, but the two were unable to marry. Chandler's death in 1959 ended the career of a shy, quiet man who was quite unlike his fictional hero Marlowe except for the essential loneliness and decency Chandler could not avoid projecting onto his most important creation.

ANALYSIS

Many people who have never read a single word of Raymond Chandler's recognize the name of his fictional hero Philip Marlowe. This recognition results in part from the wide exposure and frequent dilution Chandler's works have received in media other than print. Several of his novels have been adapted to film repeatedly; *Farewell, My Lovely* and *The Big Sleep*, in particular, have been made into motion pictures numerous times—both most recently in the 1970's. Marlowe has been interpreted on film by such diverse actors as Humphrey Bogart, Dick Powell, Robert Montgomery, George Montgomery, Robert Mitchum, James Garner, and Elliot Gould. Both radio and television series have been based somewhat loosely on Chandler's character.

This recognition amounts to more than exposure in multiple media; it is an indication of the legendary or even mythic proportions of Chandler's creation. Marlowe has become a central figure in the myth of the detective; the only comparable characters would be Arthur Conan Doyle's Sherlock Holmes and Agatha Christie's Hercule Poirot, even though they are quite different from Marlowe. Dashiell Hammett's Sam Spade, although well known, is developed in only one book and lacks the psychological depth of Marlowe. Marlowe has taken his place among characters of American myth, with Natty Bumppo, Captain Ahab, Huckleberry Finn, and Thomas Sutpen. There is something uniquely American about the self-reliance of this character, something that goes beyond Chandler's brilliant descriptions of the burned-out landscape of modern California.

Marlowe is in fact Chandler's great achievement, but that accomplishment in itself imposed a limitation of a sort. Because Marlowe had the dual role of central character and observer in all seven of Chandler's novels, the author was not consistently pressed to explore other characters except as they interacted with his hero. In his final novel, *Playback*, Chandler leads Marlowe through an ill-conceived plot at the expense of two neglected characters who had shown real literary promise. In this final project, the author had fallen victim to the temptation to rely on his primary character, and Marlowe's character suffers as a result.

Nevertheless, Marlowe remains an impressive artistic creation because of his remarkable combination of the detective with more traditional American heroic types, a combination Chandler discusses in his famous essay "The Simple Art of Murder." In this essay, Chandler attempts to define his intentions as a writer of detective fiction; the work has since become one of the classic texts concerning the scope and intention of mystery writing. Although a major point of "The Simple Art of Murder" is Chandler's rejection of the stylized mystery and his often-quoted tribute to Hammett—his claim that Hammett took murder "out of the Venetian vase and dropped it in the alley"—the essay makes its most important point in an argument for detective fiction as a heroic form in which modern readers can still believe. Claiming that all art must contain the quality of redemption, Chandler insists, perhaps too stridently, that the detective is "the hero; he is everything." In the character of Marlowe, Chandler tests the possibility of heroism in the modern cultural and spiritual wasteland of Southern California, to see whether traditional heroic values can survive the test of a realistic portrait of modern society.

In precisely this way, Chandler had to face a limitation that did not affect his American predecessors: the disappearance of the frontier. American heroes acted out the myth of Emersonian self-reliance against the background of a vast, unspoiled frontier. In the twentieth century, William Faulkner, attempting to study the ambivalent role of the hero, moved his fiery character Thomas Sutpen to the frontier in *Absalom, Absalom!* (1936). Most American novelists in the twentieth century despaired of the possibility of reviving the heroic tradition and concentrated instead on victims, common people, and even criminals.

Ernest Hemingway stood alone among the serious novelists looking for an affirmation by means of the code hero, and Chandler's intellectual debt to Hemingway is profound. He acknowledged that debt in two ways. In "The Simple Art of Murder," he points out that what is excellent in Hammett's (and by inference his own) work is implicit in Hemingway's fiction. In a more celebrated reference, a policeman in *Farewell, My Lovely* is called Hemingway by Marlowe. When Galbraith, the officer, asks who this Hemingway is, Marlowe explains, "A guy that keeps saying the same thing over and over until you begin to believe it must be good." This is of course a joke about the terse Hemingway style, and the character whom Marlowe calls Hemingway is indeed terse. The jest is not, however, a slap at Hemingway. Galbraith is one of the few men with integrity whom Marlowe encounters in *Farewell, My Lovely.* He is a policeman who wants to be honest but who has to work in a corrupt system. By contrast, in the story from which this portion of *Farewell, My Lovely* was "cannibalized," "The Man Who Liked Dogs," Galbraith was as corrupt as any of the criminals Carmady (the detective) encountered. He was merely a sadistic cop who participated in cover-ups and even murder. The verbal association of this character with Hemingway corresponds nicely with Chandler's changing the personality of the officer so that he would represent the quality Chandler most admired in Hemingway's heroes, resignation to defeat while maintaining some measure of integrity.

The world Marlowe inhabits is, like that of Hemingway's characters, not conducive to heroism. Chandler coined a memorable phrase, "the mean streets," to describe the environment in which his hero would have to function. Marlowe was created to indicate that it is possible to maintain integrity in these surroundings, even if one cannot be uninfluenced by them. As Chandler put it, "down these mean streets a man must go who is not himself mean, who is neither tarnished nor afraid." Chandler emphasized that Marlowe is part of that environment—by necessity—but is not contaminated by it—by choice. He is not without fear. Marlowe often expresses the fear of a normal man in a dangerous situation, and in this way he differs from the heroes of the tough-guy school and from those of Chandler's apprentice stories. Like Hemingway's heroes, he must learn to control and to disguise his fear. Most important, he is not intimidated by his environment. As Chandler puts it in his essay, the detective "must be, to use a rather weathered phrase, a man of honor."

Although commonly used, the phrase "the mean streets" is somewhat misleading. Chandler's target is not merely, or even primarily, the cruelty and brutality of life at the bottom of the social and economic ladder. For him, the mean streets extend into the posh apartments and mansions of Hollywood and suburban Los Angeles, and he is more interested in exploring cruelty and viciousness among the very rich than among the people of the streets. Each of the novels treats the theme of the quest for and ownership of money and power as the source of evil; Chandler constantly emphasizes Marlowe's relative poverty as a symbol of his incorruptibility. *The High Window,* for example, is more a study in the corrupting influence of wealth than in the process of detection. Marlowe is shocked to discover that his client Mrs. Murdock not only murdered her husband to collect his life insurance but also systematically conditioned her timid and neurotic secretary to believe that she was the murderess, dependent on Mrs. Murdock for forgiveness as well as for protection from the law. This instance is typical of Chandler's novels. The mean streets originate in the drawing rooms of those who may profit by exploiting others.

Marlowe's code of behavior differs from those of other fictional detectives, though his descendants, particularly Ross Macdonald's Lew Archer and Robert B. Parker's Spenser, resemble Chandler's hero. Marlowe is not, in the final analysis, a tough guy. He is a compassionate man who, as he half-ironically tells a policeman in *The Long Goodbye*, hears "voices crying in the night" and goes to "see what's the matter." Marlowe is instinctively the champion of the victims of the rich and powerful; in *The High Window* he insists that the secretary, Merle Davis, be set free of the psychological exploitation by the Murdock family and be allowed to return to her home in Kansas. To those who aspire to wealth and power, Marlowe is not so kind. In *The Little Sister*, he knowingly allows the amoral, ruthless murderess Dolores Gonzales to be killed by her husband.

This instinctive compassion for the weak accounts for much of Marlowe's fundamental decency, but it often gets him into trouble, for he is human enough to be occasionally deceived by appearances. The apparently innocent client in *The Little Sister*, Orfamay Quest from Kansas, deceives Marlowe with her piety and sincerity, and he is eventually depressed to learn that his compassion for her is wasted, that despite her apparent innocence she is compulsively materialistic and is willing to exploit even her brother's murder if she can profit by his scheme to blackmail a gangster.

Marlowe's compassion is what makes him interesting as a character, but it is also what makes him vulnerable in the mean streets. His defense against that vulnerability is to play the role of the tough guy. His wisecracks, which have since become obligatory in stories about private detectives, are nothing more than a shield. Chandler says in "The Simple Art of Murder" that the detective is a proud man who will take "no man's insolence without a due and dispassionate revenge." The mean streets have taught Marlowe that corrupt politicians, tired policemen, ambitious actresses, rich people, and street toughs will insult and abuse him readily; his defense is the wisecrack. It is the attempt of an honorable man to stand up to a world that has gone sour.

THE BIG SLEEP

The Big Sleep, Chandler's first full-length novel, makes explicit use of the associations with myth that had been implicit in the stories he had published over six years. It was in this book that the author settled on the name Marlowe for his detective, after he had experimented with such names as Carmady and Dalmas. In his first detective story, "Blackmailers Don't Shoot," he had called the detective Mallory, an obvious allusion to the chronicler of the Arthurian legends, Sir Thomas Malory. The association with the quest romance is worked out in several important ways in *The Big Sleep*. When the detective first arrives at the home of his client, he notices a stained-glass panel "showing a knight in dark armor rescuing a lady" and concludes that, "if I lived in the house, I would sooner or later have to climb up and help him." Much later, upon returning to the house, the detective notes that the knight "wasn't getting anywhere" with the task of rescuing the lady.

These two references remind the reader of a heroic tradition into which Marlowe, a citizen of the twentieth century, is trying to fit his own experiences. Malory's knights lived in an age of faith, and the quest for the Holy Grail was a duty imposed by that faith as well as a test of the worthiness of the knight himself. Marlowe's adventures entangle him with a pornographer who is murdered, a small-time blackmailer whose effort to cut himself into the action leads to his death, a trigger-happy homosexual, a powerful criminal the law cannot touch, a district attorney eager to avoid scandal that might touch a wealthy family, and a psychopathic murderess. The environment is impossible to reconcile with the values suggested by the knight in the panel. At midpoint in the novel, Marlowe has a chess problem laid out (his playing chess against the problems defined in classical matches gives him an intellectual depth uncharacteristic of the tough-guy detective), and, trying to move a knight effectively on the board, he concludes that "knights had no meaning in this game. It wasn't a game for knights."

The implication of this set of images is that Marlowe aspires to the role of the traditional knight, but that such an aspiration is doomed to failure in the mean streets. His aspiration to the role of the knight is a hopeless attempt to restore order to the modern wasteland. At the same time, it is proof of his integrity that he tries to maintain that role in the face of certain and predictable frustration. In a subsequent novel, *The High Window*, a minor character invents a phrase that eloquently describes Marlowe's association with the romance tradition; he calls the detective a "shop-soiled Galahad," a reminder both of the knight who, in the romance, could not be corrupted, and of the pressures that wear down the modern hero.

Another important reference to the romance tradition in *The Big Sleep* is the client himself. General Sternwood is a dying man; he has to meet Marlowe in a greenhouse because the general needs the artificial warmth. He is lame, impotent, and distressed at the moral decay of his daughters. Chandler implicitly associates this character with the Fisher King of the archetypal romance, and *The Big Sleep* takes on revealing connections with T. S. Eliot's *The Waste Land*, another modern version of this quest. Like Eliot's poem, Chandler's version of the quest is a record of failure. Marlowe's success in the work of detection points paradoxically to the failure of his quest. He is able to complete, even to go beyond, his assignment. His instinctive sympathy for the helpless general leads him to try to find out what happened to the general's son-in-law, Rusty Regan, whose charm and vigor had restored some vitality to the old man, much as the traditional knight might restore the Fisher King. Marlowe discovers that Regan has been murdered, hence, there is no hope that the general might be restored. He can only prepare to join Regan in "the big sleep."

"It was not a game for knights." This knight is able to sort through the many mysteries of *The Big Sleep*, to discover the killers of the various victims. He outsmarts a professional killer in a shoot-out and feels that in doing so he achieves some revenge for Harry Jones, a tough little victim whom Marlowe had respected. His actions do not, however, restore order to his surroundings. He is unable to reach, through law or intimidation, Eddie Mars, the operator of a gambling casino and several protection rackets, a parasite of society. His discovery that Regan was murdered leads him to the conclusion that all he can do is try to protect the general from "the nastiness," the inescapable and brutal facts of life. Even his discovery that Regan's killer was the general's daughter, Carmen, does not resolve anything: She is a psychopath, and her actions are gratuitous, not subject to reform. All Marlowe can do, ironically, is the same thing Eddie Mars and Regan's widow, Vivian, tried to do—protect the general from knowing that his own daughter was responsible for the death of the one person who brought happiness to his life. Marlowe's method differs from that of Mars. Rather than cover up the fact, he uses the leverage of his knowledge of the cover-up to force Vivian Regan, Carmen's sister as well as Rusty's widow, to have Carmen committed to a mental hospital. He makes this deal only after Vivian has tried to buy his silence.

What makes *The Big Sleep* such a rich novel, in addition to its mythic associations, is the question of what keeps Marlowe going. He knows that justice is not possible in a world controlled by Eddie Mars, and he learns that his efforts lead only to compound frustrations and personal danger. He continues to work, against the warnings of the criminal element, the official police, and the family of his client. Both Vivian and Carmen offer sexual bribes if Marlowe will get off the case. He is so personally affected by "the nastiness" around him that he has a nightmare after having encountered the perverse scene in which the pornographer Geiger was killed—a dream in which Marlowe implicates himself as an ineffective pornographer. He dreams about a "man in a bloody Chinese coat" (Geiger) who was chasing "a naked girl with long jade earrings" (Carmen) "while I ran after them and tried to take a photograph with an empty camera." This exposure to the corruption around him makes Marlowe doubt, in his nightmare, even his own ability to resist corruption.

He is able to continue in the face of these pressures because, like Joseph Conrad's Marlow in *Heart of Darkness* (1902), he believes in something greater than his personal interests. His idealism is of course shattered by the corruption around him, but like Conrad's character or Hemingway's heroes, he believes in a code: loyalty to his client. In the absence of a belief in an absolute good, Marlowe guides his behavior by weighing his options in the context of the principle of loyalty to the client. When the police and the district attorney threaten him, he explains that all he has to sell is "what little guts and intelligence the Lord gave me and a willingness to get pushed around in order to protect a client." He refuses an invitation to have sex with each of the attractive Sternwood daughters because of this principle. He tells Carmen, "It's a question of professional pride" after he has told Vivian that as a man he is tempted but as a detective, "I work at it, lady. I don't play at it." Many bribes, monetary and sexual, are offered Marlowe in *The Big Sleep*. Even more threats, from criminals, police, and his client's family, are hurled at him. What gives him his sense of purpose in a world that seems to resonate to no moral standard is one self-imposed principle. This is the main theme of Chandler's fiction: If standards of behavior do not exist outside the individual, as they were believed to in the age of chivalry, then one must create them, however imperfect they may be, for oneself.

By the end of the 1940's, Chandler was well established as a master of detective fiction, but he was becoming increasingly impatient with the limitations of the form. Classically educated and somewhat aristocratic in his personal tastes, he found the conventions of the hard-boiled genre increasingly confining. He was not willing to dispose of Marlowe, however, partly because the detective had brought his creator success. More important, as biographer Frank MacShane has pointed out, Chandler's real interest was the variety of the life and the essential formlessness of Los Angeles, so his detective's ability to cut across class lines, to meet with criminals, police, the seedier citizens as well as the wealthy, gave the author a chance to explore in fiction the life of the entire community, much as two of his favorite novelists, Charles Dickens and Honoré de Balzac, had done for the cities in which they had lived.

Chandler had already pushed the mystery novel somewhat beyond its inherent limits, but he remained unsatisfied with what must be regarded as an impressive achievement. He had altered the formula to apply the quest myth in *The Big Sleep*; to study phony psychics and corrupt police in *Farewell, My Lovely*; to examine psychological and legal exploitation by the very wealthy in *The High Window*; to work with the devices of disguise and the anxieties of those who merely aspire to wealth and power in *The Lady in the Lake*; and to satirize the pretentiousness of Hollywood as well as to comment on the corrosive influence of materialism in *The Little Sister.*

THE LONG GOODBYE

The Long Goodbye abandons so many of the conventions of the detective formula that it simply uses what is left of the formula as a skeleton around which to build serious psychological and cultural themes. The actual detective work Marlowe is hired to perform is merely to search for the novelist Roger Wade, who has disappeared on a drunken spree, and eventually Marlowe discovers that the search itself was unnecessary. Wade's wife knew where Roger was but hired Marlowe to get him involved in Roger's life, so that he might possibly be persuaded to take a job as Wade's bodyguard. The search for Wade allows for some discussion of physicians who dispense drugs freely to the wealthy, but it depends more on persistent following of leads than on brilliant deduction. The real detective work in which he engages is entirely independent, work from which he is discouraged by the police, a gangster named Menendez, a wealthy businessman, and the Wades. It is a work of sentiment, not professionalism, and the book discloses that this task is worth neither the effort nor integrity that Marlowe puts into it.

The Long Goodbye is finally a study in personal loyalties. The sustaining ethic of the earlier novels, loyalty to a client, does not really apply in this book, for most of the time Marlowe has no client or refuses to take up the assignments offered him. He is no longer satisfied with his work as a detective, and one of the book's best chapters details the monotony and triviality of a day in the life of a private investigator. His own ambivalence about his role is summed up after a series of absurd requests for his services: "What makes a man stay with it nobody knows. You don't get rich, and you don't often have much fun. Sometimes you get beaten up or shot at or tossed in the jailhouse." Each of these unpleasant things happens to Marlowe. He stays in business, but he has ceased to understand why.

At the heart of the book is Marlowe's relationship with Terry Lennox, who drifts into Marlowe's personal life. Lennox, a man with a mysterious past but at present married for the second time to the nymphomaniac daughter of a tycoon, impresses Marlowe with a jaded version of the Hemingway code. Lennox knows he is little more than a gigolo, but he has accepted himself with a kind of refined drunkenness. He and Marlowe become friends, but after his wife is brutally murdered, Lennox asks Marlowe to help him escape to Mexico. Marlowe, who agrees out of friendship rather than loyalty to Lennox as a client, is thus legally implicated as a possible accessory after the fact.

His action brings him into inevitable conflict with the police, and he is roughly treated by a detective and his precinct captain. Marlowe's being at odds with the official police is far from a new occurrence in Chandler's work. His fiction always contains an innate distrust of the legal establishment, from the exposé of police corruption in *Farewell, My Lovely* through the abuse of police power by one of the killers in *The Lady in the Lake*. A lawyer in *The Long Goodbye* tells Marlowe, "The law isn't justice, it's a very imperfect mechanism. If you press exactly the right buttons and are also lucky, justice may show up in the answer." This distrust of the mechanism of law usually led Chandler to condemn separate kinds of justice for the wealthy and the powerless. Marlowe's reaction to his disillusionment includes verbal and physical conflict with the police as well as the routine concealment of evidence that might implicate a client.

What differentiates this conflict from previous ones in Chandler's work is that Marlowe is not really protecting the interests of a client. He acts out of a personal loyalty, based partly on his belief that Lennox could not have committed the sadistic murder of which he is accused. He keeps his silence during a week in jail, during which he is pressed to give evidence that would implicate both himself and Lennox.

Lennox's confession and suicide render Marlowe's actions futile. The arrival of a letter and a large sum of money rekindles a sentimental interest in the Lennox matter, and as it becomes clear that some connection exists between Lennox and the Wades, who have tried to hire him to help Roger stay sober long enough to finish his book, Marlowe continues to fit together evidence that points to Lennox's innocence. Proving Lennox innocent is another source of disillusionment: Marlowe learns that both the confession and the suicide were faked. In their final interview, Marlowe tells Lennox, "You had standards and you lived by them, but they were personal. They had no relation to any kind of ethics or scruples." Marlowe has himself come close to this moral relativism in his uncritical loyalty to Lennox, and has perhaps seen in his friend an example of the vague standard of ethical conduct to which such moral relativism can lead. The difference between Lennox and Marlowe is that the detective still recognizes the importance of having a code. He tells

Lennox, "You're a moral defeatist." His work on behalf of Lennox has been a disappointment of the highest order, for he has seen the paralysis of will toward which the cynicism both men share leads. By returning Lennox's money, Marlowe implies that Lennox was not worth the risk and labor of proving his innocence.

The Long Goodbye is populated by "moral defeatists." Another character, Roger Wade, has given up on himself as a man and as a writer. Chandler creates in this character a representation of the writer who knowingly compromises his artistic talent for personal gain. Knowing that he is "a literary prostitute," Wade is driven to alcoholic sprees and personal despair. When he seeks Marlowe's sympathy for his predicament, Marlowe reminds him of Gustave Flaubert, an example of the genuine artist who was willing to sacrifice success for his art.

Marlowe's association with Wade develops the central theme of *The Long Goodbye*: personal responsibility. Wade's publisher and his wife want Marlowe to protect Wade from his depressive and suicidal tendencies. Realizing that Wade is trying to escape something inside himself, Marlowe knows that only Wade can stop his rush toward self-destruction. He refuses to take the lucrative job as Wade's bodyguard because he realizes he cannot prevent the author from being self-destructive. In fact, Marlowe is in the Wade house the day Roger Wade apparently commits suicide. Although he does try to remove Wade's gun from its customary desk drawer, he makes no effort to stop Wade from drinking. He knows that restraining Wade, whether by physical force or coercion, would be an artificial substitute for a real solution. If Wade's self-loathing makes him suicidal, Marlowe recognizes that nothing he can do will prevent the self-destructive act from taking place.

The theme of personal responsibility is even more directly apparent in Marlowe's relation with Eileen Wade. Initially, she impresses him as an ideal beauty, and the erotic implications of their relationship are always near the surface. In a scene after he has put the drunken Roger to bed, the detective comes close to his first sexual consummation in the novels. In this episode, it becomes clear that Eileen is mentally disturbed, and Marlowe's subsequent investigation reveals that she was once married to Lennox, who served in the war under another name. Her attempt to seduce Marlowe is in fact a clumsy attempt to establish a relationship with the Terry Lennox she knew before his cynicism turned to moral defeatism. From these premises, Marlowe deduces that Eileen murdered both Sylvia Lennox and Roger, who had been having an affair with Sylvia, a perverse revenge for her being twice defeated by a woman whose vulgarity she despised.

Marlowe has sufficient evidence to prove Lennox's innocence and to show that Wade's death was not suicide, but he does not go to the police. He confronts Eileen with the evidence and gives her time to commit suicide. He refers to himself as a "one-man death watch" and takes no action to prevent the self-destruction of this woman to whom he is so powerfully attracted. When he has to explain his conduct to the one policeman he trusts, Bernie Ohls, he says, "I wanted her to take a long look at herself. What she did about it was her business." This is a ruthless dismissal of a disturbed, though homicidal, person. What Chandler intends to emphasize is the idea that all humans must ultimately take full responsibility for their actions.

Even Marlowe's relationship with Bernie Ohls deteriorates. Ohls, the only policeman Marlowe likes or trusts, consents to leak a document so that Marlowe will use it unwittingly to flush out the racketeer Menendez, knowing that Marlowe will be abused psychologically and physically in the process. The ruse works, and Ohls ruthlessly sends Menendez off to possible execution by his fellow criminals. In the image used by another character, Marlowe has been the goat tied out by the police to catch the tiger Menendez. Marlowe understands why the police have used him this way, but the novel ends with a new note of mistrust between Marlowe and Ohls. Yet another human relationship has failed.

In *The Long Goodbye*, the business of detection is subordinate to the themes of personal responsibility, betrayal, and the mutability of all human relationships. The book is a powerful indictment of the shallowness of public values in midcentury America, and the emphasis is on characterization, theme, and atmosphere rather than on the matters typical of the mystery novel. It represents a remarkable transition from the detective novel to the realm of serious fiction, a transition that has subsequently been imitated but not equaled.

David C. Dougherty

OTHER MAJOR WORKS

SHORT FICTION: *Five Murderers*, 1944; *Five Sinister Characters*, 1945; *Finger Man, and Other Stories*, 1946; *Red Wind*, 1946; *Spanish Blood*, 1946; *The Simple Art of Murder*, 1950; *Trouble Is My Business*, 1950; *Pick-up on Noon Street*, 1952; *Smart-Aleck Kill*, 1953; *Pearls Are a Nuisance*, 1958; *Killer in the Rain*, 1964 (Philip Durham, editor); *The Smell of Fear*, 1965; *The Midnight Raymond Chandler*, 1971; *The Best of Raymond Chandler*, 1977; *Stories and Early Novels*, 1995; *Collected Stories*, 2002.

SCREENPLAYS: *And Now Tomorrow*, 1944 (with Frank Partos); *Double Indemnity*, 1944 (with Billy Wilder); *The Unseen*, 1945 (with Hager Wilde); *The Blue Dahlia*, 1946; *Strangers on a Train*, 1951 (with Czenzi Ormonde).

NONFICTION: *Raymond Chandler Speaking*, 1962 (Dorothy Gardiner and Katherine Sorely Walker, editors); *Chandler Before Marlowe: Raymond Chandler's Early Prose and Poetry*, 1973 (Bruccoli, editor); *The Notebooks of Raymond Chandler and English Summer*, 1976 (Frank MacShane, editor); *Raymond Chandler and James M. Fox: Letters*, 1978; *Selected Letters of Raymond Chandler*, 1981 (Frank MacShane, editor); *The Raymond Chandler Papers: Selected Letters and Non-fiction, 1909-1959*, 2000 (Tom Hiney and Frank MacShane, editors); *Philip Marlowe's Guide to Life: A Compendium of Quotations*, 2005 (Martin Asher, editor).

BIBLIOGRAPHY

Bruccoli, Matthew J., and Richard Layman, eds. *Hardboiled Mystery Writers: Raymond Chandler, Dashiell Hammett, Ross Macdonald.* New York: Carroll & Graf, 2002. Compilation presents interviews, articles, letters, and previously published studies about the three writers. Lavishly illustrated with personal photographs, reproductions of manuscript pages, print advertisements, film promotional materials, dust jackets, and paperback covers.

Chandler, Raymond. *Raymond Chandler Speaking.* Edited by Dorothy Gardiner and Katherine Walker. 1962. Reprint. Berkeley: University of California Press, 1997. Chandler discusses a wide range of subjects, including his life, the mystery novel in general, his mystery novels in particular, the craft of writing, his character Philip Marlowe, and cats. Includes a chronology.

Freeman, Judith. *The Long Embrace: Raymond Chandler and the Woman He Loved.* New York: Pantheon Books, 2007. Interesting work illuminates Chandler's personality and psyche. Freeman believed that Chandler's life was a greater mystery than his novels, so she traveled to the almost two dozen Southern California houses and apartments where he and his wife lived and uncovered information about Chandler's wife, Cissy, who played a crucial role in his understanding of women and of himself.

Hiney, Tom. *Raymond Chandler: A Biography.* New York: Atlantic Monthly Press, 1997. Brief biography discusses Chandler's education in England, his relationship to Los Angeles, and the plots and characters of his most important detective novels and stories.

Jameson, F. R. "On Raymond Chandler." In *The Poetics of Murder: Detective Fiction and Literary Theory,* edited by Glenn W. Most and William W. Stowe. San Diego, Calif.: Harcourt Brace Jovanovich, 1983. Critical essay starts with the observation that Chandler's English upbringing in essence gave him an outsider's view of American life and language. Presents an informative discussion of the portrait of American society that emerges from Chandler's works.

Lehman, David. "Hammett and Chandler." In *The Perfect Murder: A Study in Detection.* New York: Free Press, 1989. Describes Chandler as one of the authors who brought out the parable at the heart of mystery fiction. Part of a comprehensive study of detective fiction that is valuable both for its breadth and for its unusual appendixes, one a list of further reading and the other an annotated list of the critic's favorite mysteries.

MacShane, Frank. *The Life of Raymond Chandler.* New York: E. P. Dutton, 1976. Standard biography draws on Chandler's interviews and correspondence with colleagues and lovers to describe the author's life and to provide insights into his novels.

Marling, William H. *The American Roman Noir: Hammett, Cain, and Chandler.* Athens: University of Georgia Press, 1995. Interprets the works of the three writers of hardboiled detective fiction within the context of American social and cultural history of the 1920's and 1930's. Includes three chapters about Chandler: one a biography and the other two analyses of *The Big Sleep* and *Farewell, My Lovely.*

Phillips, Gene D. *Creatures of Darkness: Raymond Chandler, Detective Fiction, and Film Noir.* Lexington: University Press of Kentucky, 2000. Focuses largely on Chandler's Hollywood output but also presents some discussion of his novels.

Van Dover, J. K., ed. *The Critical Response to Raymond Chandler.* Westport, Conn.: Greenwood Press, 1995. Collection of essays includes discussions of Chandler's Los Angeles, *The Big Sleep* (both the novel and the film), *Farewell, My Lovely,* and the function of simile in Chandler's novels. Includes bibliographical references and index.

Widdicombe, Toby. *A Reader's Guide to Raymond Chandler.* Westport, Conn.: Greenwood Press, 2001. Features entries, arranged alphabetically, on Chandler's works, characters, places, allusions, and major topics. Appendixes contain information on Chandler's screenwriting, other writers' adaptations of Chandler, and the portrayal of the character of Philip Marlowe in film, radio, and television.

G. K. CHESTERTON

Born: London, England; May 29, 1874
Died: Beaconsfield, Buckinghamshire, England; June 14, 1936
Also known as: Gilbert Keith Chesterton

<small>PRINCIPAL LONG FICTION</small>

The Napoleon of Notting Hill, 1904
The Man Who Was Thursday: A Nightmare, 1908
The Ball and the Cross, 1909
The Innocence of Father Brown, 1911
Manalive, 1912
The Flying Inn, 1914
The Wisdom of Father Brown, 1914
The Incredulity of Father Brown, 1926
The Return of Don Quixote, 1926
The Secret of Father Brown, 1927
The Floating Admiral, 1931 (with others)
The Scandal of Father Brown, 1935
Basil Howe: A Story of Young Love, 2001 (wr. 1894)

<small>OTHER LITERARY FORMS</small>

G. K. Chesterton was a prolific writer, and in addition to novels he produced works in numerous other genres. Throughout his life he wrote poetry; his first two published books were poetical works. He also produced short fiction, especially detective stories. In addition, he wrote plays, but he was not always comfortable in the medium of drama, as he was at heart an essayist. He published a large number of nonfiction works in such areas as autobiography, biography, essays, history, and literary criticism.

<small>ACHIEVEMENTS</small>

Among the primary achievements of G. K. Chesterton's long writing career are the wide range of subjects he wrote about, the large number of genres he employed, and the sheer volume of publications he produced. Chesterton was primarily a journalist and essayist who wrote articles, book reviews, and essays for newspapers and periodicals. In addition to these pieces, however, he also wrote poetry, biographies, plays, history, and literary criticism as well as novels and short stories.

In his approach to fiction Chesterton rejected the "modern realistic short story" and the realistic novel. Instead, in the first instance, he turned to the detective short story and wrote extensively on its legitimacy as a literary art form. Chesterton himself helped to develop the definition of the detective story; he contended that it was the sole popular literary struc-

G. K. Chesterton
(Library of Congress)

ture expressing "some sense of the poetry of modern life," and he helped to popularize detective fiction with his fifty-one Father Brown stories and short novels.

As a novelist, Chesterton argued that "sensational novels are the most moral part of modern fiction." He liked tales about death, secret groups, theft, adventure, and fantasy. There was no genre in his day that embraced his ideas, and so he crafted his own literary structure, the "fantastic novel." In his novels Chesterton stressed such themes and issues as family, science versus religion, moral and political integrity, and local patriotism versus empire building. He also introduced such subthemes as the common man, nature, and womanhood. Above all, Chesterton's novels illustrate his "love of ideas."

BIOGRAPHY

Gilbert Keith Chesterton was born in London on May 29, 1874, to a middle-class family. His father, Edward, was an estate agent who liked literature and art, and his mother, Marie, was the daughter of a Wesleyan lay preacher. Both parents were Unitarians, but they baptized their son in the Anglican Church. Chesterton attended the Colet Court preparatory school and then, in 1887, went to St. Paul's School. His academic record was not good, but he finally began to demonstrate literary capability as a member of the Junior Debating Club, which he and some of his fellow students established during the summer of 1890. Two years later he won the Milton Prize for his poem "St. Francis Xavier."

From 1892 to 1895, Chesterton attended the Slade School to study art and took some courses in French, English, and Latin at University College, London. He did not do well, however, except in his English courses, and he left the Slade School in 1895 without taking a degree. For the next six years he worked in publishing houses, reading authors' manuscripts, and at night he did his own writing. In 1900 his first two books appeared, *Greybeards at Play: Literature and Art for Old Gentlemen—Rhymes and Sketches* and *The Wild Knight, and Other Poems*, both works of poetry. The next year he began to submit articles regularly to the *Speaker* and the *Daily News* and thus started a career as a journalist that was to last until his death. He became known for his opposition to the Boer War and his support of small nations.

In 1901 Chesterton married Frances Blogg after a courtship of five years. The couple lived first in London, and then in 1909 they moved to Beaconsfield, forty miles outside London. They had no offspring, but they enjoyed the company of the children of their friends, relatives, and neighbors.

In 1904 Chesterton's first novel, *The Napoleon of Notting Hill*, was published, and by 1914 he had written five more novels and numerous other works, including biographies (*Robert Browning*, 1903; *Charles Dickens: A Critical Study*, 1906), as well as *Heretics* (1905), which criticized what he saw as the mistakes of some contemporary writers, *Orthodoxy* (1908), a defense and support of Christianity, and a study of his friend and disputant, *George Bernard Shaw* (1909). In 1911 the first of his volumes of detective stories appeared, featuring a Catholic priest, Father Brown, as the sleuth.

Chesterton wrote his best work prior to 1914; in November of that year he became gravely ill with a form of dropsy, and it was not until June of the following year that he recovered. During the years after World War I, he traveled, visiting Palestine, the United States, Poland, and Italy. In 1922 he became a Roman Catholic, a faith that had attracted him for some time, as is reflected in his writing. The most notable nonfiction works of his later years are *The Everlasting Man* (1925) and another biography, *St. Thomas Aquinas* (1933). Chesterton's health declined during the first half of 1936, and on June 14 he died in Beaconsfield.

ANALYSIS

Between 1904 and 1927, G. K. Chesterton wrote six full-length novels, not including the long Father Brown mysteries. All of them stressed the sensational, and they illustrated life as a fight and a battle. Chesterton thought that literature should portray life as perilous rather than as something listless. Tales of death, robbery, and secret groups interested him, and he did not think that what he called the "tea table twaddle" type of novels approached the status of significant art. The sensational story "was the moral part of fiction."

Fantasy was an important part of Chesterton's novels, and the methodology used in his long fiction emphasized adventure, suspense, fantasy, characterization, satire, narrative technique, and humor. He needed a medium to employ these techniques, so he produced the "fantastic novel." Fanstasy also involves ideas, and in all Chesterton's novels ideas are a central, indispensable feature.

Chesterton's novels served as vehicles for the dissemination of whatever his political and social ideas were at the time, and to this extent they were propagandistic. His critics have had difficulty in deciding the merits of his various writings in terms of separating propaganda from literary art. Often Chesterton used allegory as a device for conveying his controversial ideas. Critic Ian Boyd has called Chesterton's works of long fiction "political fables, parables, and allegories or more simply and conveniently . . . novels."

In Chesterton's novels, the state of bachelorhood predominates; this situation is appropriate, since this status is a fundamental element of adventure. Moreover, women rarely appear in any significant roles in his long fiction. There is no female character in his first novel, *The Napoleon of Notting Hill*, and the woman in *The Man Who Was Thursday* is a passing character. In *The Ball and the Cross* and *The Flying Inn*, women are minor figures, but they do play significant roles in *Manalive* and *The Return of Don Quixote*, works that are more involved with the family and society.

The weakest of Chesterton's nondetective novels are perhaps *Manalive*, published in 1912, and *The Return of Don Quixote*, which appeared in 1927. In *The Return of Don Quixote*, Chesterton concludes that the only good future for England involves "a remarriage" of the country with the Catholic Church, as was the case in the Middle Ages. The first three of Chesterton's novels, published from 1904 to 1909, are widely considered his best.

THE NAPOLEON OF NOTTING HILL

The Napoleon of Notting Hill is Chesterton's first novel. The first two chapters are distinct from the main plot, the first being an essay on prophecy showing the author working in a genre that was always congenial to him. The next chapter concerns a luncheon discussion among three government clerks and the former president of Nicaragua, Juan del Fuego. The content of their talk brings out one of the main themes of the novel, "the sanctity of small nations," a concept dear to Chesterton that stemmed from his opposition to the Boer War.

The subsequent death of del Fuego eliminates him from the work, but one of the three clerks, Auberon Quin, a zany individual and joker, is subsequently selected king in the futuristic utopian England of 1984, where a mild political despotism exists. The monarch is chosen by lot. Once crowned as king, Quin reorganizes the sections of London into separate municipalities and thus re-creates the smallness of medieval cities, complete with costumes and heraldry. Quin then encounters Adam Wayne, first as a youth and then as the serious-minded provost of Notting Hill, one of the municipalities; Wayne has embraced the king's "Charter of Cities" wholeheartedly.

Wayne, however, much to the dismay of the provosts of other London municipalities, refuses to give up a street in his domain, Pump Street, which contains several shops, so that a thoroughfare connecting three boroughs can be built. The result is a war, which Wayne wins by encouraging the patriotism of Pump Street residents and by following excellent strategy, despite being outnumbered by the opposing forces. Quin with his "Charter of Cities" and Wayne in his defense of Notting Hill both illustrate Chesterton's small-nation theme. The concluding chapters of the novel concern London twenty years later, when the powerful and dominant Notting Hill has become corrupt; the corruption causes a revolt of subject municipalities. Wayne fights in the second war but realizes that there is no longer a noble cause involved. Conflict in the novel lies in the confrontation between Wayne and Quin, the fanatic and the joker. Wayne's opponents had accused him of being mad, but Quin asserts that the only sane individuals are himself and Wayne. The last chapter is a discussion between the two men, now dead and in the afterlife, in which Wayne argues that in order to be complete both men needed each other, because the joker was without seriousness and the fanatic lacked laughter.

THE MAN WHO WAS THURSDAY

Chesterton's second novel, *The Man Who Was Thursday*, has been described by some critics as his best. Ronald Knox called it "an extraordinary book written as if the publisher had commissioned him to write something rather like the *Pilgrim's Progress* in the style of the *Pickwick Papers*." Chesterton himself called it a protest against the pessimism of the 1880's, and this protest gives rise to one of two allegories in the novel, a personal one. The other is a public or political allegory concerning an individual's clash with a world conspiracy that does not really exist. The story concerns a young poet, Gabriel Syme, who, wishing to fight a gigantic conspiracy supposedly being plotted by anarchists, joins the police and becomes a member of an undercover squad of detectives.

As a result of a bit of trickery and luck, he becomes a member of the top anarchist council, called the Council of Seven Days because each member has the name of a day of the week. Syme's name is Thursday. The council's leader, named Sunday, is an ambiguous figure. While working to stop a bombing planned for Paris, Thursday discovers that, except for Sunday, all his fellow council members are undercover police detectives. Each had been interviewed by a figure whom nobody saw in a dark room at Scotland Yard. By the conclusion of the novel, it is revealed that Sunday is both the head of the detectives and the leader of the anarchists. Some critics have seemed to think that Chesterton is condoning evil in the novel, but he himself asserted that he is questioning in the novel whether everything is evil and whether one can find good in the pessimism of the age.

THE BALL AND THE CROSS

A review published a year after the publication of *The Ball and the Cross* stated that the novel is about two individuals dueling over "the most vital problem in the world, the truth of Christianity." This work definitely deals with religion and the nature of good and evil, subjects either ignored or addressed ambiguously in Chesterton's first two novels. The book opens with Professor Lucifer depositing a captured Bulgarian monk, Michael, from a flying machine atop the cross and ball of St. Paul's Cathedral in London.

The plot continues with a confrontation between a Catholic highland Scot, Evan McIan, and another Scot, John Turnbull, an atheist and publisher of works on atheism. The two fight a duel over what McIan perceives as an insult to the Virgin Mary. The duelists are constantly interrupted, however; they go through a series of adventures and ultimately become friends. The book ends with the two men in an insane asylum, which is set on fire by a satanic figure. The inmates are led out by a monk, Michael, who had been a prisoner there. Ultimately Turnbull becomes a Christian. The novel contains much symbolism and many allegories. The ball on St. Paul's dome, for example, is the rational and independent world, while the cross represents religion. Martin Gardner views the work as reflecting the clash between St. Augustine's City of God, which in Chesterton's view is the Catholic Church, and the City of Man, which is dominated by Satan. The novel also attacks modern science and accuses modern culture of being "lukewarm."

Allan Nelson

OTHER MAJOR WORKS

SHORT FICTION: *The Tremendous Adventures of Major Brown*, 1903; *The Club of Queer Trades*, 1905; *The Perishing of the Pendragons*, 1914; *The Man Who Knew Too Much, and Other Stories*, 1922; *Tales of the Long Bow*, 1925; *Stories*, 1928; *The Sword of Wood*, 1928; *The Moderate Murder and the Honest Quack*, 1929; *The Poet and the Lunatics: Episodes in the Life of Gabriel Gale*, 1929; *The Ecstatic Thief*, 1930; *Four Faultless Felons*, 1930; *The Paradoxes of Mr. Pond*, 1936; *The Vampire of the Village*, 1947.

PLAYS: *Magic: A Fantastic Comedy*, pr. 1913; *The Judgment of Dr. Johnson*, pb. 1927; *The Surprise*, pb. 1953.

POETRY: *Greybeards at Play: Literature and Art for Old Gentlemen—Rhymes and Sketches*, 1900; *The Wild Knight, and Other Poems*, 1900 (revised 1914); *The Ballad of the White Horse*, 1911; *A Poem*, 1915; *Poems*, 1915; *Wine, Water, and Song*, 1915; *Old King Cole*, 1920; *The Ballad of St. Barbara, and Other Verses*, 1922; *Poems*, 1925; *The Queen of Seven Swords*, 1926; *Gloria in Profundis*, 1927; *Ubi Ecclesia*, 1929; *The Grave of Arthur*, 1930.

NONFICTION: *The Defendant*, 1901; *Robert Louis Stevenson*, 1902 (with W. Robertson Nicoll); *Thomas Carlyle*, 1902; *Twelve Types*, 1902 (revised as *Varied Types*; 1903; also known as *Simplicity and Tolstoy*); *Charles Dickens*, 1903 (with F. G. Kitton); *Leo Tolstoy*, 1903 (with G. H. Perris and Edward Garnett); *Robert Browning*, 1903; *Tennyson*, 1903 (with Richard Garnett); *Thackeray*, 1903 (with Lewis Melville); *G. F. Watts*, 1904; *Heretics*, 1905; *Charles Dickens: A Critical Study*, 1906; *All Things Considered*, 1908; *Orthodoxy*, 1908; *George Bernard Shaw*, 1909 (revised 1935); *Tremendous Trifles*, 1909; *Alarms and*

Discursions, 1910; *The Ultimate Lie*, 1910; *What's Wrong with the World*, 1910; *William Blake*, 1910; *Appreciations and Criticisms of the Works of Charles Dickens*, 1911; *A Defence of Nonsense, and Other Essays*, 1911; *The Future of Religion: Mr. G. K. Chesterton's Reply to Mr. Bernard Shaw*, 1911; *The Conversion of an Anarchist*, 1912; *A Miscellany of Men*, 1912; *Thoughts from Chesterton*, 1913; *The Victorian Age in Literature*, 1913; *The Barbarism of Berlin*, 1914; *London*, 1914 (with Alvin Langdon Coburn); *Prussian Versus Belgian Culture*, 1914; *The Crimes of England*, 1915; *Letters to an Old Garibaldian*, 1915; *The So-Called Belgian Bargain*, 1915; *Divorce Versus Democracy*, 1916; *A Shilling for My Thoughts*, 1916; *Temperance and the Great Alliance*, 1916; *Lord Kitchener*, 1917; *A Short History of England*, 1917; *Utopia of Usurers, and Other Essays*, 1917; *How to Help Annexation*, 1918; *Charles Dickens Fifty Years After*, 1920; *Irish Impressions*, 1920; *The New Jerusalem*, 1920; *The Superstition of Divorce*, 1920; *The Uses of Diversity*, 1920; *Eugenics and Other Evils*, 1922; *What I Saw in America*, 1922; *Fancies Versus Fads*, 1923; *St. Francis of Assisi*, 1923; *The End of the Roman Road: A Pageant of Wayfarers*, 1924; *The Superstitions of the Sceptic*, 1924; *The Everlasting Man*, 1925; *William Cobbett*, 1925; *The Catholic Church and Conversion*, 1926; *A Gleaming Cohort, Being from the Words of G. K. Chesterton*, 1926; *The Outline of Sanity*, 1926; *Culture and the Coming Peril*, 1927; *Robert Louis Stevenson*, 1927; *Social Reform Versus Birth Control*, 1927; *Do We Agree? A Debate*, 1928 (with George Bernard Shaw); *Generally Speaking*, 1928 (essays); *G. K. C. as M. C., Being a Collection of Thirty-seven Introductions*, 1929; *The Thing*, 1929; *At the Sign of the World's End*, 1930; *Come to Think of It*, 1930; *The Resurrection of Rome*, 1930; *The Turkey and the Turk*, 1930; *All Is Grist*, 1931; *Is There a Return to Religion?*, 1931 (with E. Haldeman-Julius); *Chaucer*, 1932; *Christendom in Dublin*, 1932; *Sidelights on New London and Newer York, and Other Essays*, 1932; *All I Survey*, 1933; *G. K. Chesterton*, 1933 (also known as *Running After One's Hat, and Other Whimsies*); *St. Thomas Aquinas*, 1933; *Avowals and Denials*, 1934; *Explaining the English*, 1935; *The Well and the Shallows*, 1935; *As I Was Saying*, 1936; *Autobiography*, 1936; *The Man Who Was Chesterton*, 1937; *The End of the Armistice*, 1940; *The Common Man*, 1950; *The Glass Walking-Stick, and Other Essays from the "Illustrated London News," 1905-1936*, 1955; *Lunacy and Letters*, 1958; *Where All Roads Lead*, 1961; *The Man Who Was Orthodox: A Selection from the Uncollected Writings of G. K. Chesterton*, 1963; *The Spice of Life, and Other Essays*, 1964; *Chesterton on Shakespeare*, 1971.

EDITED TEXTS: *Thackeray*, 1909; *Samuel Johnson*, 1911 (with Alice Meynell); *Essays by Divers Hands*, 1926.

MISCELLANEOUS: *Stories, Essays, and Poems*, 1935; *The Coloured Lands*, 1938; *The Collected Works of G. K. Chesterton*, 1986-1999 (35 volumes).

BIBLIOGRAPHY

Ahlquist, Dale. *G. K. Chesterton: The Apostle of Common Sense*. San Francisco, Calif.: Ignatius Press, 2003. Provides an introductory overview of Chesterton's life and work designed for general readers, with analyses of some of Chesterton's novels, including books in the Father Brown series. Designed to complement a television series of the same title created by Ahlquist, president of the American Chesterton Society.

Bloom, Harold, ed. *G. K. Chesterton.* New York: Chelsea House, 2006. Collection of essays analyzes various aspects of Chesterton's work, including the author's view of the grotesque and "terror and play" in his imagination. Editor's introduction provides an overview to Chesterton's life and work.

Boyd, Ian. *The Novels of G. K. Chesterton: A Study in Art and Propaganda.* New York: Barnes & Noble Books, 1975. Good study examines Chesterton's major novels as well as his collections of short stories. Discusses the novels chronologically, with a chapter each about novels in his early years, pre-World War I, postwar, and later years.

Clipper, Lawrence J. *G. K. Chesterton.* New York: Twayne, 1974. Useful introduction to the works of Chesterton does a fine job of describing the recurring themes in his fictional and nonfictional writings. Includes informative analysis also of Chesterton's poetry and literary criticism. Contains an excellent annotated bibliography.

Coates, John D. *G. K. Chesterton as Controversialist, Essayist, Novelist, and Critic.* Lewiston, N.Y.: Edwin Mellen Press, 2002. Refutes Chesterton's reputation as a minor writer, maintaining that his detective novels remain important and relevant works. Places Chesterton's fiction within the context of modernism and the Edwardian novel of ideas.

Conlon, D. J., ed. *Chesterton: A Half Century of Views.* New York: Oxford University Press, 1987. Contains numerous short essays on Chesterton published during the first fifty years after his death. The wide diversity of positive critical reactions shows that not only his popular fiction but also his writings on literature and religion continue to fascinate readers.

Hollis, Christopher. *The Mind of Chesterton.* Coral Gables, Fla.: University of Miami Press, 1970. Especially thoughtful study explores above all Chesterton's evolution as a writer before his conversion to Catholicism in 1922. Final chapter, titled "Chesterton and His Survival," explains why Chesterton's work continues to fascinate readers who do not share his religious beliefs.

Lauer, Quentin. *G. K. Chesterton: Philosopher Without Portfolio.* New York: Fordham University Press, 1988. Thought-provoking study addresses Chesterton's philosophical reflections on the uses and limitations of reason, Christian humanism, religious tolerance, and moral values.

Pearce, Joseph. *Wisdom and Innocence: A Life of G. K. Chesterton.* San Francisco, Calif.: Ignatius Press, 1996. Scholarly, well-written biography examines Chesterton's life and provides interesting analysis of many quotations from his works.

Ward, Maisie. *Gilbert Keith Chesterton.* New York: Sheed & Ward, 1943. Well-researched biography remains the essential resource concerning Chesterton. Ward had full access to Chesterton's manuscripts and spoke with many people who had known him personally. Reveals much about his evolution as a writer and the importance of friendship in his life.

Wills, Garry. *Chesterton.* New York: Doubleday, 2001. Biography is an updated edition of Wills's *Chesterton, Man and Mask* (1961), with a new introduction. Wills is a Catholic intellectual and best-selling author who has written several books about religion in the United States.

AGATHA CHRISTIE

Born: Torquay, Devon, England; September 15, 1890
Died: Wallingford, Oxfordshire, England; January 12, 1976
Also known as: Agatha Mary Clarissa Miller; Mary Westmacott; Agatha Mary
  Clarissa Mallowan

PRINCIPAL LONG FICTION

The Mysterious Affair at Styles: A Detective Story, 1920
The Secret Adversary, 1922
The Murder on the Links, 1923
The Man in the Brown Suit, 1924
The Secret of Chimneys, 1925
The Murder of Roger Ackroyd, 1926
The Big Four, 1927
The Mystery of the Blue Train, 1928
The Seven Dials Mystery, 1929
Giants' Bread, 1930 (as Mary Westmacott)
The Murder at the Vicarage, 1930
The Floating Admiral, 1931 (with others)
The Sittaford Mystery, 1931 (also known as *The Murder at Hazelmoor*)
Peril at End House, 1932
Lord Edgware Dies, 1933 (also known as *Thirteen at Dinner*)
Murder in Three Acts, 1934
Murder on the Orient Express, 1934 (also known as *Murder on the Calais
  Coach*)
Unfinished Portrait, 1934 (as Westmacott)
Why Didn't They Ask Evans?, 1934 (also known as *Boomerang Clue*, 1935)
Death in the Clouds, 1935 (also known as *Death in the Air*)
The A. B. C. Murders: A New Poirot Mystery, 1936
Cards on the Table, 1936
Murder in Mesopotamia, 1936
Death on the Nile, 1937
Dumb Witness, 1937 (also known as *Poirot Loses a Client*)
Appointment with Death: A Poirot Mystery, 1938
Hercule Poirot's Christmas, 1939 (also known as *Murder for Christmas: A
  Poirot Story*)
Murder Is Easy, 1939 (also known as *Easy to Kill*)
Ten Little Niggers, 1939 (also known as *And Then There Were None*, 1940)
One, Two, Buckle My Shoe, 1940 (also known as *The Patriotic Murders*, 1941)

Sad Cypress, 1940

Evil Under the Sun, 1941

N or M? The New Mystery, 1941

The Body in the Library, 1942

Five Little Pigs, 1942 (also known as *Murder in Retrospect*)

The Moving Finger, 1942

Poirot on Holiday, 1943

Absent in the Spring, 1944 (as Westmacott)

Death Comes in the End, 1944

Towards Zero, 1944

Sparkling Cyanide, 1945 (also known as *Remembered Death*)

The Hollow: A Hercule Poirot Mystery, 1946

Poirot Knows the Murderer, 1946

Poirot Lends a Hand, 1946

Murder Medley, 1948

The Rose and the Yew Tree, 1948 (as Westmacott)

Taken at the Flood, 1948 (also known as *There Is a Tide . . .*)

Crooked House, 1949

A Murder Is Announced, 1950

Blood Will Tell, 1951

They Came to Baghdad, 1951

A Daughter's a Daughter, 1952 (as Westmacott)

Mrs. McGinty's Dead, 1952

They Do It with Mirrors, 1952 (also known as *Murder with Mirrors*)

After the Funeral, 1953 (also known as *Funerals Are Fatal*)

A Pocket Full of Rye, 1953

Destination Unknown, 1954 (also known as *So Many Steps to Death*, 1955)

Hickory, Dickory, Dock, 1955 (also known as *Hickory, Dickory, Death*)

The Burden, 1956 (as Westmacott)

Dead Man's Folly, 1956

4:50 from Paddington, 1957 (also known as *What Mrs. McGillicuddy Saw!*)

Ordeal by Innocence, 1958

Cat Among the Pigeons, 1959

The Pale Horse, 1961

The Mirror Crack'd from Side to Side, 1962 (also known as *The Mirror Crack'd*, 1963)

The Clocks, 1963

A Caribbean Mystery, 1964

At Bertram's Hotel, 1965

Third Girl, 1966

Endless Night, 1967
By the Pricking of My Thumbs, 1968
Hallowe'en Party, 1969
Passenger to Frankfurt, 1970
Nemesis, 1971
Elephants Can Remember, 1972
Postern of Fate, 1973
Curtain: Hercule Poirot's Last Case, 1975
Sleeping Murder, 1976

OTHER LITERARY FORMS

Agatha Christie published approximately thirty collections of short stories, fifteen plays, a nonfiction book (*Come Tell Me How You Live*, 1946), and many omnibus editions of her novels. Under the pen name Mary Westmacott, Christie published six romance novels. At least ten of her detective works have been made into motion pictures, and *An Autobiography* (1977) was published because, as Christie told *Publishers Weekly* in 1966, "If anybody writes about my life in the future, I'd rather they got the facts right." Sources disagree on the total number of Christie's publications because of the unusual quantity of titles, the reissue of so many novels under different titles, and especially the tendency to publish the same book under differing titles in England and the United States.

ACHIEVEMENTS

Among her many achievements, Agatha Christie bears one unusual distinction: She is the only writer whose main character's death precipitated a front-page obituary in *The New York Times*. Christie was a fellow of the Royal Society of Literature; received the New York Drama Critics' Circle Award for Best Foreign Play of the year in 1955 for *Witness for the Prosecution* (which was first produced in 1953); was knighted Dame Commander, Order of the British Empire, in 1971; received the Film Daily Poll Ten Best Pictures Award in 1958 (for the film adaptation of *Witness for the Prosecution*, directed by Billy Wilder); and was made a doctor of literature at the University of Exeter.

BIOGRAPHY

Agatha Mary Clarissa Miller was born in Torquay, England, on September 15, 1890; the impact of this location on her was enormous. Near the end of her autobiography, Christie indicates that all other memories and homes pale beside Ashfield, her parents' home in Torquay: "And there you are again—remembering. 'I remember, I remember, the house where I was born. . . .' I go back to that always in my mind. Ashfield." The roots of Christie's self-contained, quiet sense of place are found in her accounts of life at Ashfield. Her love of peace, routine, and order was born in her mother's well-ordered household, a household cared for by servants whose nature seemed never to change, and sparked by the

Agatha Christie
(Library of Congress)

sudden whims of an energetic and dramatic mother. Christie's father was Fred Miller, an American, many years older than her English mother, Clara. They were distant cousins and had an exceptionally harmonious marriage because, according to Christie, her father was an exceptionally agreeable man. Nigel Dennis, writing for *Life* magazine in May, 1956, noted that Christie is at her best in "orderly, settled surroundings" in which she can suddenly introduce disruption and ultimately violence. Her autobiographical accounts of days upon days of peace and routine followed by sudden impulsive adventures initiated by her mother support the idea that, as she says, all comes back to Ashfield, including her mystery stories at their best.

In writing her autobiography, Christie left a detailed and insightful commentary on her works. To one familiar with her autobiography, the details of her life can be found in the incidents and plots of her novels. Frequently, she barely disguises them. She writes, for example, of a recurring childhood dream about "the Gunman," whose outstanding characteristics were his frightening eyes appearing suddenly and staring at her from absolutely any person around her, including her beloved mother. This dream forms almost the entire basis for the plot of *Unfinished Portrait*, a romance novel Christie wrote under the pen name Mary Westmacott. That dream may have been the source of her willingness to allow absolutely any character the role of murderer. No one, including her great Hercule Poirot, is exempt from suddenly becoming the Gunman.

Christie was educated at home chiefly by her parents and her nurse. She taught herself to read before she was five and from then on was allowed to read any available book at Ashfield. Her father taught her arithmetic, for which she had a propensity and which she enjoyed. She hated spelling, on the other hand, because she read by word sight and not by the sound of letters. She learned history from historical novels and a book of history that her mother expected her to study in preparation for a weekly quiz.

She also had tutors. A stay in France at about age seven and an ensuing return with a Frenchwoman as her companion resulted in her speaking and reading French easily. She had piano and voice tutors and attended a weekly dancing class. As she grew older, she attended the theater weekly, and, in her teens, she was sent to a boarding school in France.

She was always allowed to use her imagination freely. Her sensible and beloved nurse went along with her early construction of plots and tales enlisting the nurse as well as dolls and animals to be the characters. She carried on a constant dialogue with these characters as she went through her days. The absence of playmates and the storytelling done within the family also contributed to the development of her imagination. Her mother invented ongoing bedtime tales of a dramatic and mysterious nature. Her elder sister, Madge, liked to write, and she repeatedly told Agatha one particular story: the "Elder Sister" tale. Like the Gunman, the Elder Sister became a frequent personage in Christie's later novels. As a child, Agatha would ask her sister, feeling a mixture of terror and delight, when the elder sister was coming; Madge would indicate that it would be soon. Then a few days later, there would be a knock on Agatha's door and her sister would enter and begin talking in an eerie voice as if she were an elder, disturbed sister who was normally locked up somewhere but at large for the day. The pattern seems similar to that of the Gunman: the familiar figure who is suddenly dangerous. One of Christie's book in particular, *Elephants Can Remember*, concerns a crazy identical twin sister who escapes from a mental institution, kills her twin, and takes her place in marriage to a man they had both known and loved as young girls.

In addition to her sister, Agatha had an elder brother, Monty, whom she adored. He allowed her to join him frequently in his escapades and was generally agreeable but, like her father, did not amount to much otherwise and was managed and even supported by his sisters later in his life. "Auntie Grannie" was another strong figure in Agatha's early life. She was the aunt who had reared Clara Miller and was also Fred's stepmother, hence her title. Many critics see in her the basis for the character of Miss Marple.

The picture of Christie that emerges is one of a woman coming from an intensely female-dominated household where men were agreeable and delightful but not very effective. Female servants and family members provided Agatha with her rigorous, stable values and independent behavior. She grew up expecting little of men except affection and loyalty; in return, she expected to be sensible and self-supporting when possible. Another possible explanation for Christie's self-sufficiency is the emotional support that these surrounding females provided for her. Even after her mother's death in the late 1920's, Christie always sought the companionship of loyal female servants and secretaries who, in the British Victorian fashion, then became invaluable to her in her work and personal life. Especially in her marriage to Archibald Christie, she relied on her female relatives and servants to encourage, assist, and even love her. The Miss Marples of her world, the Constance Sheppards (*The Murder of Roger Ackroyd*), and the servants were her life's bedrock.

In 1914, Agatha Miller married Colonel Archibald Christie in a hasty wartime ceremony. They had one daughter, Rosamund, whom Agatha adored but considered an "efficient" child. She characterized Rosamund in her Mary Westmacott novel *A Daughter's a Daughter.*

Agatha started writing on a dare from her sister but only began writing novels seriously when her husband was away in World War I and she was employed as a chemist's (pharmacist's) assistant in a dispensary. Finding herself with extra time, she wrote *The Mysterious Affair at Styles.* Since she was familiar with both poisons and death because of her hospital and dispensary work, she was able to distinguish herself by the accuracy of her descriptions. Several other books followed that were increasingly successful, until *The Murder of Roger Ackroyd* became a best seller in 1926.

The death of her mother and a divorce from Archie Christie took place about the same time Agatha Christie was beginning to experience success. These events sent her into a tailspin that ended in her famous eleven-day disappearance. She reappeared at a health spa unharmed but, to her embarrassment, the object of a great deal of attention; in addition, the public was outraged at the large expense of the search that had been mounted for the author.

In 1930, Christie married Sir Max Mallowan, an archaeologist, perhaps a more "agreeable" man than Archie Christie. Certainly her domestic life after the marriage was peaceful; in addition, she was able to travel with Mallowan to his archaeological dig sites in the Middle East. This gave her new settings and material for her books and enabled her to indulge in one of her greatest pleasures: travel.

In 1930, *The Murder at the Vicarage* was published; it introduced Christie's own favorite sleuth, Miss Jane Marple, village spinster and observer of the village scene. By this time, Christie was an established author, and in the 1940's her books began to be made into plays and motion pictures. In 1952, *The Mousetrap* was launched in a London theater and eventually became one of the longest-running plays in that city's history. The film version of *Witness for the Prosecution* received awards and acclaim in the late 1950's. *Murder in the Calais Coach* became *Murder on the Orient Express*, a popular American film directed by Sidney Lumet and released in 1974.

Producing approximately one book per year, Christie has been likened to an assembly line, but, as her autobiography indicates, each book was a little puzzle for her own "grey cells," the conceiving of which gave her great enjoyment and the writing of which took about six to twelve weeks and was often tedious. In 1971, she was made Dame Agatha Christie by Queen Elizabeth II and had what she considered one of her most thrilling experiences, tea with the queen. In 1975, she allowed the book *Curtain: Hercule Poirot's Last Case* to be published and the death of her chief sleuth, Hercule Poirot, to occur. This was of sufficient interest to warrant a front-page obituary in *The New York Times*.

By the time of Christie's own death in 1976, history writer Ellsworth Grant wrote that Christie's writings had "reached a wider audience than those of any author who ever lived." More than 400 million copies of her novels and short stories had been sold, and her works had been translated into 103 languages.

ANALYSIS

Agatha Christie's trademarks in detective fiction brought to maturity the classical tradition of the genre, which was in its adolescence when she began to write. The tradition had some stable characteristics, but she added many more and perfected existing ones. The classical detective hero, for example, from Edgar Allan Poe on, according to Ellsworth Grant, is of "superior intellect," is "fiercely independent," and has "amusing idiosyncrasies." Christie's Hercule Poirot was crafted by these ground rules and reflects them in *The Mysterious Affair at Styles* but quickly begins to deplore this Sherlock Holmes type of detecting. Poirot would rather think from his armchair than rush about, magnifying glass in hand, searching for clues. He may, by his words, satirize classical detection, but he is also satirizing himself, as Christie well knew.

Christie's own contributions to the genre can be classified mainly as the following: a peaceful, usually upper-class setting into which violence intrudes; satire of her own heroes, craft, and genre; a grand finale in which all characters involved gather for the dramatic revelation of truth; the careful access to all clues; increased emphasis on the "who" and the "why," with less interest in the "how"; heavy use of dialogue and lightning-quick description, which create a fast-paced, easy read; a consistent moral framework for the action; and the willingness to allow absolutely any character to be guilty, a precedent-setting break with tradition. Her weakness, critics claim, is in her barely two-dimensional characters, who lack psychological depth.

Christie created, as Grant puts it, a great many interesting "caricatures of people we have met." Grant excuses her on the grounds that allowing every character to be a possible suspect limits the degree to which each can be psychologically explored. One might also attribute her caricatures to her great admiration for Charles Dickens, who also indulged in caricatures, especially with his minor characters. Christie herself gave a simple explanation. She judged it best not to write about people she actually knew, preferring to observe strangers in railroad stations and restaurants, perhaps catching fragments of their conversations. From these glimpses, she would make up characters and plots. Character fascinated her endlessly, but, like Miss Marple, she believed the depths of human iniquity were in everyone, and it was only in the outward manifestation that people became evil or good. "I could've done it," a juvenile character cries in *Evil Under the Sun*. "Ah, but you didn't and between those two things there is a world of difference," Poirot replies.

DEATH COMES IN THE END

In spite of Christie's simplistic judgment of human character, she manages, on occasion (especially in her novels of the 1940's and later), to make accurate and discerning forays into the thought processes of some characters. In *Death Comes in the End*, considerable time is spent on Renisenb's internal musings. Caught in the illiterate role that her time (Egypt, 2000 B.C.E.) and sex status decree for her, Renisenb struggles to achieve language so she can articulate her anxieties about evil and good. Her male friend, Hori, speaks at great length of the way that evil affects people. "People create a false door—to deceive," he says, but "when reality comes and touches them with the feather of truth—their truth self reasserts itself." When Norfret, a beautiful concubine, enters a closed, self-contained household and threatens its stability, all the characters begin to behave differently. The murderer is discovered precisely because he is the only person who does *not* behave differently on the outside. Any innocent person would act guilty because the presence of evil touches self-doubts and faults; therefore, the one who acts against this Christie truth and remains normal in the face of murder must, in fact, be guilty.

THE MYSTERIOUS AFFAIR AT STYLES

Although *The Mysterious Affair at Styles* is marred by overwriting and explanations that Christie sheds in later books, it shows signs of those qualities that would make her great. The village of Styles St. Mary is quiet, and Styles House is a typical country manor. The book is written in the first person by Hastings, who comes to visit his old friend John Cavendish and finds him dealing with a difficult family situation. Cavendish's mother has married a man who everyone agrees is a fortune hunter. Shortly afterward, she dies of poison in full view of several family members, calling her husband's name. Hastings runs into Hercule Poirot at the post office; an old acquaintance temporarily residing at Styles, Poirot is a former police inspector from Belgium. Christie's idea in this first novel seems to be that Hastings will play Watson to Poirot's Holmes, although she quickly tires of this arrangement and in a later book ships Hastings off to Argentina.

Every obvious clue points to the husband as the murderer. Indeed, he is the murderer and has made arrangements with an accomplice so that he will be brought to a speedy trial. At the trial, it would then be revealed that the husband had an absolute alibi for the time when the poison must have been administered; hence, he and his accomplice try to encourage everyone to think him guilty. Poirot delays the trial and figures out that the real poison was in the woman's own medicine, which contained a substance that would become fatal only if released from other elements. It then would settle to the bottom of the bottle, and the last dose would be lethal. Bromide is an ingredient that separates the elements. Bromide was added at the murderer's leisure, and he had only to wait until the day when his wife would take the last dose, making sure that both he and his accomplice are seen by many people far distant from the household at the time she is declared to have been poisoned. The plot is brilliant, and Christie received congratulations from a chemists' association for her correct use of the poisons in the book.

THE MURDER OF ROGER ACKROYD

By the time she published *The Murder of Roger Ackroyd*, her sixth book, Christie had hit her stride. Although Poirot's explanations are still somewhat lengthy, the book is considered one of her best. It is chiefly noted for the precedent it set in detective fiction. The first-person narrator, Dr. Sheppard, turns out to be the murderer. The skill with which this is concealed and revealed is perhaps Christie at her most subtle. The reader is made to like Dr. Sheppard, to feel he or she is being taken into his confidence as he attempts to write the history of Roger Ackroyd's murder as it unwinds. Poirot cultivates Dr. Sheppard's acquaintanceship, and the reader believes, because the information comes from Dr. Sheppard, that Poirot trusts him. In the end, Dr. Sheppard is guilty. Christie allows herself to gloat at her own fiendish cleverness through the very words that Sheppard uses to gloat over his crime when he refers back to a part of his narrative (the story itself is supposedly being written to help Poirot solve the crime) where a discerning reader or sleuth ought to have found him out.

THE BODY IN THE LIBRARY

The Body in the Library, executed with Christie's usual skill, is distinctive for two elements: the extended discussions of Miss Marple's sleuthing style and the humorous dialogue surrounding the discovery of the body of an unknown young woman in the library of a good family. Grant says of Jane Marple that she insists, as she knits, that human nature never changes. O. L. Bailey expands on this in an article that appeared in *Saturday Review* in 1973: "Victorian to the core," he writes, "she loves to gossip, and her piercing blue eyes twinkle as she solves the most heinous crimes by analogy to life in her archetypal English village of St. Mary Mead."

Marple, as well as the other characters, comments on her methods. Marple feels her success is in her skeptical nature, calling her mind "a sink." She goes on to explain that "the truth is . . . that most people . . . are far too trusting for this wicked world." Another character, Sir Henry, describes her as "an old lady with a sweet, placid, spinsterish face and a mind that has plumbed the depths of human iniquity and taken it as all in the day's work."

Through a delightfully comic conversation between Mr. and Mrs. Bantry, the possibility of a dead body in the library is introduced, and, once it is discovered, the story continues in standard sleuth style; the opening dialogue, however, is almost too funny for the subject matter. Ralph Tyler, in an article published in *Saturday Review* in 1975, calls this mixture of evil and the ordinary a distancing of death "by bringing it about in an upper-middle-class milieu of consummate orderliness." In that milieu, the Bantrys' dialogue is not too funny; it is quite believable, especially since Mr. and Mrs. Bantry do not yet know the body is downstairs.

THE SECRET ADVERSARY

Perhaps real Christie aficionados can be identified by their reactions to Tommy and Tuppence Beresford of *The Secret Adversary*, an engaging pair of sleuths who take up adventuring because they cannot find work in postwar England. Critics for the most part dismiss or ignore the pair, but Christie fans often express a secret fondness for the two. In Tommy and Tuppence, readers find heroes close to home. The two blunder about and solve mysteries by luck as much as by anything else. Readers can easily identify with these two and even feel a bit protective of them.

Tommy and Tuppence develop a romance as they establish an "adventurers for hire" agency and wait for clients. Adventure begins innocently when Tommy tells Tuppence he has overheard someone talking about a woman named Jane Finn and comments disgustedly, "Did you ever hear such a name?" Later they discover that the name is a password into an international spy ring.

The use of luck and coincidence in the story is made much of by Christie herself. Christie seems to tire of the frequent convenient circumstances and lets Tommy and Tuppence's romance and "high adventure" lead the novel's progress. When Tommy asks Mr. Carter, the British spy expert, for some tips, Carter replies, "I think not. My experts, working in stereotyped ways, have failed. You will bring imagination and an open mind to the task." Mr. Carter also admits that he is superstitious and that he believes in luck "and all that sort of thing." In this novel, readers are presented with a clever story, the resolution of which relies on elements quite different from deductive reasoning or intuition. It relies on those qualities that the young seem to exude and attract: audacity and luck.

N OR M? THE NEW MYSTERY

In *N or M? The New Mystery*, Tommy and Tuppence (now married and some twenty years older) are again unemployed. Their two children are both serving their country in World War II. The parents are bemoaning their fate when a messenger from their old friend Mr. Carter starts them on a spy adventure at the seacoast hotel of Sans Souci. They arrive with the assumed names Mr. Meadowes and Mrs. Blenkensop. Mrs. Blenkensop, they agree, will pursue Mr. Meadowes and every now and then corner him so they can exchange information. The dialogue is amusing and there is a good deal of suspense, but too many characters and a thin plot keep this from being one of Christie's best.

At times, it seems that Christie withholds clues; the fact that all evidence is presented to the reader is the supreme test of good detective fiction. Mrs. Sprot, adopted mother of Betty, coolly shoots Betty's real mother in the head while the woman is holding Betty over the edge of a cliff. The reader cannot be expected to know that the woman on the cliff is Betty's real mother, nor can the reader be expected to decipher Tuppence's mutterings about the story of Solomon. In the story of Solomon, two women claim the same baby, and Solomon decrees that the woman who is willing to give up her child rather than have it split in half is the real mother. Since both women in this scene *appear* willing to jeopardize the baby's life, the reader is likely, justifiably, to form some wrong conclusions. This seems less fair than Christie usually is in delivering her clues.

SLEEPING MURDER

In her last novel, *Sleeping Murder*, written several years before its 1976 publication date, Christie achieves more depth in her portrayal of characters than before: Gwenda, her dead stepmother, Dr. Kennedy, and some of the minor characters such as Mr. Erskine are excellent examples. The motivation in the book is, at least, psychological, as opposed to murder for money or personal gain, which are the usual motives in Christie's novels. In comparison with others of Christie's works, this novel seems, in short, to display much more probing into the origins and motivations of her characters' actions.

Sleeping Murder ends with the romantic young couple and the wise old Miss Marple conversing on the front porch of a hotel in, of all places, Torquay, Christie's beloved birthplace. Christie had come full circle, celebrating her romantic and impulsive youth and her pleasant old age in one final reunion at home in Torquay, England.

Anne Kelsch Breznau

OTHER MAJOR WORKS

SHORT FICTION: *Poirot Investigates*, 1924; *Partners in Crime*, 1929; *The Mysterious Mr. Quin*, 1930; *The Thirteen Problems*, 1932 (also known as *The Tuesday Club Murders*, 1933); *The Hound of Death, and Other Stories*, 1933; *The Listerdale Mystery, and Other Stories*, 1934; *Parker Pyne Investigates*, 1934 (also known as *Mr. Parker Pyne, Detective*); *Murder in the Mews, and Other Stories*, 1937 (also known as *Dead Man's Mirror, and Other Stories*); *The Regatta Mystery, and Other Stories*, 1939; *The Mystery of the Baghdad Chest*, 1943; *The Labours of Hercules: Short Stories*, 1947 (also known as *Labors of Hercules: New Adventures in Crime by Hercule Poirot*); *The Witness for the Prosecution, and Other Stories*, 1948; *The Mousetrap, and Other Stories*, 1949 (also known as *Three Blind Mice, and Other Stories*); *The Under Dog, and Other Stories*, 1951; *The Adventures of the Christmas Pudding, and Selection of Entrées*, 1960; *Double Sin, and Other Stories*, 1961; *Star over Bethlehem, and Other Stories*, 1965 (as A. C. Mallowan); *Thirteen Clues for Miss Marple: A Collection of Mystery Stories*, 1965; *The Golden Ball, and Other Stories*, 1971; *Hercule Poirot's Early Cases*, 1974; *Miss Marple's Final Cases*, 1979; *The Harlequin Tea Set, and Other Stories*, 1997.

PLAYS: *Black Coffee*, pr. 1930; *Ten Little Niggers*, pr. 1943 (also known as *Ten Little Indians*, pr. 1944); *Appointment with Death*, pr., pb. 1945; *Murder on the Nile*, pr., pb. 1946; *The Hollow*, pr. 1951; *The Mousetrap*, pr. 1952; *Witness for the Prosecution*, pr. 1953; *Spider's Web*, pr. 1954; *Towards Zero*, pr. 1956 (with Gerald Verner); *The Unexpected Guest*, pr., pb. 1958; *Verdict*, pr., pb. 1958; *Go Back for Murder*, pr., pb. 1960; *Afternoon at the Seaside*, pr. 1962; *The Patient*, pr. 1962; *The Rats*, pr. 1962; *Fiddlers Three*, pr. 1971; *Akhnaton*, pb. 1973 (also known as *Akhnaton and Nefertiti*).

POETRY: *The Road of Dreams*, 1925; *Poems*, 1973.

NONFICTION: *Come Tell Me How You Live*, 1946; *An Autobiography*, 1977.

CHILDREN'S LITERATURE: *Thirteen for Luck: A Selection of Mystery Stories for Young Readers*, 1961; *Surprize! Surprize! A Collection of Mystery Stories with Unexpected Endings*, 1965.

BIBLIOGRAPHY

Bunson, Matthew. *The Complete Christie: An Agatha Christie Encyclopedia.* New York: Pocket Books, 2001. Comprehensive reference volume contains alphabetical entries on all characters in Christie's works, cross-referenced to the works in which they appear; plot synopses; listings of all film, television, and radio adaptations of Christie's works and of documentaries about Christie; a biography; and a bibliography.

Christie, Agatha. *An Autobiography.* New York: Dodd, Mead, 1977. Although published the year after her death, this book, which was written over a fifteen-year period, concludes in 1965, when the author was seventy-five years old. Although she does not explain her mysterious disappearance in the 1920's, probably because of her desire for privacy, she provides interesting details about happier events and invaluable commentary on the creation of her works.

Gill, Gillian. *Agatha Christie: The Woman and Her Mysteries.* New York: Free Press, 1990. Short and highly readable biography is definitely of the popular, rather than critical, variety, employing as chapter titles seven different names used at one time or another by the mystery writer (including the assumed name she used during her infamous disappearance in 1926). Still, Gill goes out of her way to emphasize Christie's dedication to her art and the discipline of her life.

Irons, Glenwood, and Joan Warthling Roberts. "From Spinster to Hipster: The 'Suitability' of Miss Marple and Anna Lee." In *Feminism in Women's Detective Fiction*, edited by Glenwood Irons. Toronto, Ont.: University of Toronto Press, 1995. Discusses Christie's creation of Miss Marple as the archetypal British sinister detective figure in stories and novels. Analyzes Marple's basic methodology in *The Tuesday Club Murders*.

Makinen, Merja. *Agatha Christie: Investigating Femininity.* New York: Palgrave Macmillan, 2006. Sets out to disprove what many critics have asserted: that Agatha Christie created her female characters to be weak and inferior to their male counterparts.

Emphasizes the ways in which the female characters play vital roles outside the domestic sphere and therefore challenge traditional notions of femininity.

Osborne, Charles. *The Life and Crimes of Agatha Christie: A Biographical Companion to the Works of Agatha Christie*. New York: St. Martin's Press, 2001. Presents a chronological listing of Christie's works accompanied by biographical notes that place the writings within the context of the events of the author's life. Includes bibliographical references and index.

Paul, Robert S. *Whatever Happened to Sherlock Holmes? Detective Fiction, Popular Theology, and Society*. Carbondale: Southern Illinois University Press, 1991. A study of detective fiction based on the general premise that detective stories mirror the morals and theological assumptions of their time. The chapter on Agatha Christie explores how her stories reflect what happens in a society when compassion is lacking.

Shaw, Marion, and Sabine Vanacker. *Reflecting on Miss Marple*. New York: Routledge, 1991. Presents a brief chronology of Christie's life and then devotes four chapters to one of her most memorable detectives, making a case for viewing Miss Marple as a feminist heroine. Reviews the history of women writers and the golden age of detective fiction as well as the social context of Christie's Miss Marple books. Asserts that the spinster Miss Marple is able to solve her cases by exploiting prejudices against unmarried older women.

Thompson, Laura. *Agatha Christie: An English Mystery*. London: Headline Review, 2007. Comprehensive biography, written with the cooperation of Christie's family and with full access to the author's unpublished letters and notebooks. Includes information about Christie's eleven-day disappearance in 1926 and about the novels she wrote under the pseudonym Mary Westmacott.

Wagoner, Mary S. *Agatha Christie*. Boston: Twayne, 1986. Scholarly but readable study of Christie and her writings. A brief biography of Christie in the first chapter is followed by analytical chapters focusing on the different genres of her works, such as short stories. Contains a good bibliography, an index, and a chronological table of Christie's life.

York, R. A. *Agatha Christie: Power and Illusion*. New York: Palgrave Macmillan, 2007. Reevaluates Christie's novels, which traditionally have been described as "cozy" mysteries. Asserts that although these works may appear to depict a stable world of political conservatism, conventional sex and class roles, and clear moral choices, this world is not as safe as it appears to be. Notes how Christie's mysteries also depict war, social mobility, ambiguous morality, violence, and, of course, murder.

WILKIE COLLINS

Born: London, England; January 8, 1824
Died: London, England; September 23, 1889
Also known as: William Collins

PRINCIPAL LONG FICTION

Antonina: Or, The Fall of Rome, 1850
Basil: A Story of Modern Life, 1852
Hide and Seek, 1854
The Dead Secret, 1857
The Woman in White, 1860
No Name, 1862
Armadale, 1866
The Moonstone, 1868
Man and Wife, 1870
Poor Miss Finch: A Novel, 1872
The New Magdalen, 1873
The Law and the Lady, 1875
The Two Destinies: A Romance, 1876
My Lady's Money, 1878
The Fallen Leaves, 1879
The Haunted Hotel: A Mystery of Modern Venice, 1879
A Rogue's Life, 1879
Jezebel's Daughter, 1880
The Black Robe, 1881
Heart and Science, 1883
I Say No, 1884
The Evil Genius: A Dramatic Story, 1886
The Guilty River, 1886
The Legacy of Cain, 1889
Blind Love, 1890 (completed by Walter Besant)

OTHER LITERARY FORMS

In addition to his novels, Wilkie Collins produced a biography of his father in 1848 as well as travel books, essays and reviews, and a number of short stories. He also wrote and adapted plays, often in collaboration with Charles Dickens.

ACHIEVEMENTS

Wilkie Collins's reputation more than a century after his death rests almost entirely on two works: *The Woman in White*, first published serially in *All the Year Round* from November 26, 1859, to August 25, 1860; and *The Moonstone*, published in 1868. Mystery author Dorothy L. Sayers called the latter work "probably the finest detective story ever written." No chronicler of crime and detective fiction can fail to include Collins's important contributions to the genre; simply for the ingenuity of his plots, Collins earned the admiration of T. S. Eliot. *The Woman in White* and *The Moonstone* have also been adapted numerous times for the stage, film, radio, and television. For an author so conscientious and industrious, however—Collins averaged one "big" novel every two years in his maturity—to be known as the author of two books would hardly be satisfactory. The relative obscurity into which most of Collins's work has fallen cannot be attributed completely to the shadow cast by his friend and sometime collaborator Charles Dickens, to his physical infirmities and his addiction to laudanum, or to the social vision that led him to write a succession of thesis novels. Indeed, the greatest mystery Collins left behind concerns the course of his literary career and subsequent reputation.

BIOGRAPHY

A pencil drawing of the author titled "Wilkie Collins by his father William Collins, R. A." survives; it shows a pretty, if serious, round face. The features beneath the end of the boy's nose are shaded, giving particular prominence to the upper face and forehead. The viewer is at once drawn to the boy's eyes; they are large, probing, mysterious—hardly the eyes of a child. Perhaps the artist-father sought to impart to his elder son some of his own austere, pious nature. William Collins (1788-1847), whose life began on the verge of one great European revolution and ended on the verge of another, was no revolutionary himself, nor was he the bohemian others of his calling imagined themselves. Instead, he was a strict Sabbatarian, an individual who overcame by talent and perseverance the disadvantages of poverty. The novelist's paternal grandfather was an art dealer, a restorer, and a storyteller who lovingly trained and cajoled his son in painting and drawing. William Collins did not begin to taste success until several years after the death of his father in 1812, but gradually commissions and patrons did come, including Sir Robert Peel. Befriended by noted artists such as Sir David Wilkie and Washington Allston, William Collins was at last elected to the Royal Academy in 1820. Two years later, he married Harriet Geddes. The names of both of their sons, born in 1824 and 1828, respectively, honored fellow artists: William Wilkie Collins and Charles Allston Collins.

Little is known of Wilkie Collins's early years, save that they appear to have been relatively tranquil. By 1833, Collins was already enrolled at Maida Hill Academy. In 1836, William Collins elected to take his family to Italy, where they remained until the late summer of 1838. The return to London required taking new lodgings at Regent's Park, and the fourteen-year-old Wilkie Collins was sent to boarding school at Highbury. By the close of 1840, he was presumably finished with school. His father's health began to fail, and the senior Collins made known his wish that Wilkie take holy orders, though the son apparently had no such inclination. The choice became university or commerce. Wilkie Collins chose business, and he became an apprentice to the tea merchants Antrobus and Company in 1841. He performed well there and was able to take a leave in order to accompany his father to Scotland the following summer. While still an apprentice, Collins began to write occasional pieces, and in August, 1843, the *Illuminated Magazine* published his first signed story, "The Last Stage Coachman." A novel about Polynesia was also written but discarded. In 1844, Collins traveled to Paris with his friend Charles Ward, and he made a second visit in 1845. While William Collins's health began to deteriorate more rapidly, his son was released from his apprenticeship and decided on the study of law. In February, 1847, William Collins died.

Wilkie Collins emulated his father's self-discipline, industry, and especially his love of art and beauty, yet if one judges by the series of self-serving religious zealots who populate Collins's fiction, one must assume that, while he respected his father's artistic sensibilities, he did not admire his pious ardor. Instead, Wilkie Collins seems in most things to have taken the example of his mother, a woman of loving good nature and humor with whom both he and his brother Charles remained close until her death. Nevertheless, William Collins near the end of his life had asked Wilkie to write his biography, providing the opportunity for the young man's first published book, *Memoirs of the Life of William Collins, R. A.*, published in 1848 in two volumes. While the narrator tends toward self-effacement and burdens his readers with minute detail, the work is nevertheless a formidable accomplishment. His research in preparing the book led Collins into correspondence with the American writer Richard Henry Dana, Jr., and with a circle of established and rising artists, including E. M. Ward (brother of his friend Charles), Augustus Egg, John Everett Millais, Holman Hunt, and the Rossettis. At this time, Collins completed his historical novel *Antonina*, which is filled with gothic violence and adventure, a work that attracted the serious attention of John Ruskin. It was published in 1850, the same year that saw the production of Collins's first publicly staged dramatic work, *A Court Duel*, which he had adapted from the French. With the success of his play and the surprisingly positive reception of *Antonina*, Collins began to enjoy a rising reputation.

In January, 1851, Richard Bentley published Collins's account of a Cornwall hiking trip taken during the summer of 1850 as *Rambles Beyond Railways*. Two months later, Egg introduced the twenty-seven-year-old Collins to Dickens, and the initial contact resulted in Collins's taking part in Dickens's theatrical *Not So Bad as We Seem: Or, Many Sides to a Character* (pb. 1851), written by Edward Bulwer-Lytton. Until Dickens's death in 1870, he and Collins remained staunch friends, though there is some indication that there was friction between the two authors following Collins's success with *The Moonstone* and Dickens's supposed attempt to outdo his junior with his novel *The Mystery of Edwin Drood* (1870), which remained unfinished at Dickens's death.

In 1852, after having tried to sell the version of a story that would become "Mad Monkton" to Dickens, Collins published the story "A Terribly Strange Bed" (anthologized often since) in *Household Words*, a magazine edited by Dickens from 1850 to 1859.

The following years saw considerable collaboration between the two authors, not the least of which were Collins's stories for the Christmas annuals such as *Mr. Wray's Cash-Box: Or, The Mask and the Mystery* (1852), the collaboration *The Seven Poor Travellers* (1854), *The Wreck of the Golden Mary* (1856), a work often attributed to Dickens until the late twentieth century, the novel *The Dead Secret*, and numerous other stories and articles. In 1853, Collins, Dickens, and Egg traveled together in Italy and Switzerland. Four years later, Dickens produced Collins's play *The Frozen Deep*, later noting that the self-sacrifice of the central character, Richard Wardour (played by Dickens), provided the germ for *A Tale of Two Cities* (1859). Although never published as a play, *The Frozen Deep* was published in 1866 as part of a collection of short stories.

The impact each had on the writing of the other has long been a topic of controversy and speculation for critics and biographers; generally unchallenged is the influence of Collins's meticulous plotting on the work of his senior. In turn, Dickens often corrected and refined by suggestion Collins's fiction, although he never agreed with Collins's practice of including prefaces that upbraided critics and the public alike. When Collins published *Basil* (having included for Bentley's publication in book form the first of those vexing prefaces), he forwarded the volume to Dickens. After a two-week silence, there came a thoughtful, admiring reply: "I have made Basil's acquaintance," wrote Dickens at the end of 1852, "with great gratification, and entertain high respect for him. I hope that I shall become intimate with many worthy descendants of his, who are yet in the limbo of creatures waiting to be born." Collins did not disappoint Dickens on that count over their years of friendship and collaboration; indeed, they became "family" when Charles Allston Collins married Dickens's daughter Kate.

Household Words faded in 1859 along with Dickens's association with the publishers Bradbury and Evans. Dickens's new periodical, *All the Year Round* (1859-1870), began auspiciously with the publication of *A Tale of Two Cities*. After the run of that novel, he needed something to keep public interest in the new magazine from abating, and Collins provided it with *The Woman in White*. This work's monumental success put Collins into that rarest literary circle: that of well-to-do authors. Its success also coincided with important personal events in Collins's life.

Collins had lived the life of a bachelor, residing with his brother and mother at least into his early thirties. Their house was often open to guests. On one such evening, the author and his brother escorted home the artist John Everett Millais through then-rural North London. Suddenly, a woman appeared to them in the moonlight, attired in flowing robes, all in white. Though distraught, she regained her composure and vanished as quickly as she had appeared. The author was most astounded and insisted he would discover the identity of the lovely creature. J. G. Millais, the painter's son, who later narrated this anecdote in a life of his father, did not reveal the lady's ultimate identity, saying, "Her subsequent history, interesting as it is, is not for these pages." The woman was Caroline Elizabeth Graves, born 1834, mother of a little girl, Harriet. Her husband, G. R. Graves, may or may not have been dead. Of him, only his name is known. Clearly, however, the liaison between Caroline Graves and Wilkie Collins was fully under way when he began to write *The Woman in White.*

From at least 1859, the couple lived together in a secret relationship known only to their closest friends, until the autumn of 1868, when for obscure reasons Caroline married the son of a distiller, John C. Clow. Collins, not one to waste time, started a new liaison with Martha Rudd. This union produced three children: Marian (1869), Harriet Constance (1871), and William Charles (1874). The children took the surname Dawson, but Collins freely admitted his paternity. By this time, too, Caroline and her daughter returned, and Harriet Graves for a time served as her mother's lover's amanuensis; Collins adopted her as his daughter. A lover of hearty food, fine champagne, and good cigars, Collins appears to have lived in private a life that would have shocked many of his readers. Still, Collins treated his "morganatic family" quite well: He provided handsomely for his natural and adopted children and for their mothers. When she died in 1895 at age sixty-one, Caroline Elizabeth Graves was interred beside the author of *The Woman in White.*

As Collins's private life began taking on its unconventional proportions in the 1860's, his public career grew more distinguished. His output for *All the Year Round* in shorter forms declined; he simply did not need the money. In March, 1861, his novel *No Name*, a didactic work about inheritance, began its run in the magazine; it was published in volume form in December, 1862. A year later, Collins resigned his editorial assignment for Dickens's periodical and also published, with Sampson Low, Son, and Company, *My Miscellanies*, bringing together, in two volumes, work that had first appeared in the two Dickens periodicals. After about seven years of almost obsessive productivity, Collins relented, but only for a time; he began his novel *Armadale* in the spring of 1864, for serial publication in the *Cornhill Magazine* in Britain and *Harper's Monthly* in the United States. This exploration of inherited and personal guilt remains one of Collins's most adept and popular novels; it is also his longest. He wrote a dramatic version of the novel in 1866, but the play was not produced until it appeared in 1876 as *Miss Gwilt.*

In 1867, Collins and Dickens began their last collaboration, the play *No Thoroughfare* (pr., pb. 1867), an adventure set in the Alps and perhaps not unaffected by the two men's shared Swiss journey many years before. By this time, too, Collins began to suffer tremendously from the good living he had long enjoyed—gout of the areas around the eyes caused him excruciating pain, requiring the application of bandages for weeks at a time. To allay the ache, Collins developed a habit for laudanum, that tincture of opium that fills the darker recesses of middle-Victorian culture. It was in this period of alternating pain and bliss that Collins penned *The Moonstone*, for *All the Year Round*, beginning in January, 1868. The novel was an uncontestable triumph; Collins himself thought it wonderfully wrought.

The Moonstone had hardly begun its run, however, when Collins's mother died, and later that same year, Caroline married Clow. When the novel was finished, Collins again turned to the stage, writing *Black and White* with his friend Charles Fechter, an actor; the play successfully opened in March, 1869. At the end of the year, the serialization of *Man and Wife* began in *Harper's Weekly* and in January, 1870, in *Cassell's Magazine*. Posterity has judged *Man and Wife* more harshly than did its first readers. It was a different kind of novel from *The Moonstone*: It attacked society's growing obsession with athleticism and castigated marital laws that Collins believed to be cruel, unfair, and unrealistic. According to Collins's modern biographer Kenneth Robinson, *Man and Wife* was the turning point in Collins's career, the start of the "downhill" phase of the writer's life. The novel sold well after its serialization; Collins also wrote a four-act dramatic version that was not produced on the stage until 1873.

At the same time, Collins adapted *No Name* for the theater and, in 1871, *The Woman in White*. The stage version of *The Woman in White* opened at the Olympic Theatre in October and ran for five months before going on tour. The same year saw the beginning of a new novel in serial form, *Poor Miss Finch*, about a blind woman who falls in love with an epileptic whose cure turns him blue. When she is temporarily cured of her affliction, she finds herself in a dilemma about her blue lover, whose healthy twin also desires her love. A year later, the indefatigable Collins published *The New Magdalen* in a magazine called *Temple Bar*; the novel's heroine, a virtuous prostitute, outraged contemporary critics, but the work's dramatization in 1873 was greeted with enthusiasm.

As his work increasingly turned to exposing social hypocrisies, Collins sought, as a writer of established repute, to regulate the body of his published work. Since *Basil*, wholesale piracy of his writings had angered him and hurt his finances. By the early 1870's, he had reached agreements with the German publisher Tauchnitz and with Harper & Brothers in the United States, and, by 1875, with Chatto & Windus in Britain. Chatto & Windus not only bought all extant copyrights to Collins's work but also became his publisher for the rest of his life. This arrangement was finalized in the year after Collins, like his friend Dickens before him, had undertaken a reading tour of the United States and Canada.

The years 1875 and 1876 saw the publication of two popular but lesser novels, *The Law and the Lady* and *The Two Destinies*. The next year was marked, however, by the successful dramatization of *The Moonstone* and the beginning of Collins's friendship with Charles Reade. In 1879, Collins wrote *The Haunted Hotel* for the *Belgravia Magazine*, a ghost story fresh in invention that extends one's notions about the genre. Meanwhile, however, Collins's health became less certain and his laudanum doses became more frequent and increasingly potent. The decade took away many close friends, beginning with Dickens and, later, his brother Charles, then Augustus Egg.

In the last decade of his life, Collins became more reclusive, although not much less productive. He adapted his 1858 play *The Red Vial* into the novel *Jezebel's Daughter*. He also began, for serialization in the *Canadian Monthly*, the novel *The Black Robe*, the central figure of which is a priest plotting to encumber the wealth of a large estate. This work has been regarded as the most successful of his longer, late novels. It was followed by a more controversial novel, *Heart and Science*, a polemic against vivisection that appeared in 1883. The same year saw Collins's last theatrical work, *Rank and Riches*, an unqualified disaster that brought the leading lady to tears before the first-act curtain and that led her leading man, G. W. Anson, to berate the audience. Collins thereafter gave up writing for the stage, save a one-performance version of *The Evil Genius* in 1885; the work was quickly recast as a novel that proved his single most lucrative publication.

Although 1884 saw the passing of Reade, his closest friend of the time, Collins continued to write steadily. *The Guilty River* made its appearance in the *Arrowsmith Christmas Annual* for 1886; in 1887, Chatto & Windus published *Little Novels*, collecting earlier stories. Two works also appeared that ended the battle Collins had long waged with critics. A young man, Harry Quilter, published an encomiastic article for the *Contemporary Review*, "A Living Story-Teller." Collins himself wrote "How I Write My Books" for the newspaper *The Globe*, an account of his work on *The Woman in White*. As his health at last began to fail precipitously in 1888, Collins completed his final serial novel, *The Legacy of Cain*. It appeared in three volumes the following year, at a time when he was finishing the writing of *Blind Love* for the *Illustrated London News*. On the evening of June 30, 1889, Collins suffered a stroke. He requested that Walter Besant, then traveling in the north, return and complete the tale.

Collins had long before befriended Dickens's physician and neighbor, Frank Beard, who did what little could be done to comfort Collins in his final days. Just past midmorning on September 23, 1889, Wilkie Collins died, Beard at his bedside. Four days following his death, Collins was buried at Kensal Green; his procession was headed by Caroline Graves, Harriet Graves, and his surviving literary, theatrical, and household friends. Despite infirmities, Collins had lived a life long and full, remaining productive, industrious, and successful throughout his career.

ANALYSIS

At its best, Wilkie Collins's fiction is characterized by a transparent style that occasionally pleases and surprises the reader with an apt turn of word or phrase, by a genius for intricate plots, by a talent for characterization that in at least one instance must earn the epithet "Miltonic," and by an eye for detail that seems to make the story worth telling. These are the talents of an individual who learned early to look at things like a painter, to see the meaning, the emotion behind the gesture or pose—a habit of observation that constituted William Collins's finest bequest to his elder son.

NARRATIVE STYLE AND PLOTTING

The transparency of Collins's style rests on his adherence to the conventions of the popular fiction of his day. More so than contemporaries, he talks to readers, cajoles them, often protesting that the author will recede into the shadows in order that readers may judge the action for themselves. The "games"—as one critic has observed—that Collins plays with readers revolve about his mazelike plots, his "ingenuous" interruptions of the narrative, and his iterative language, symbolic names, and metaphors. Thus, at the beginning of "Mrs. Zant and the Ghost," published in *Little Novels*, the narrator begins by insisting that this tale of "supernatural influence" occurs in the daylight hours, adding, "The writer declines to follow modern examples by thrusting himself and his opinions on the public view. He returns to the shadow from which he has emerged, and leaves the opposing forces of incredulity and belief to fight the old battle over again, on the old ground." The apt word is "shadow," for certainly, this story depicts a shadow world. At its close, when the preternatural events have occurred, the reader is left to assume a happy resolution between the near victim Mrs. Zant and her earthly rescuer, Mr. Rayburn, through the mood of the man's daughter:

> Arrived at the end of the journey, Lucy held fast by Mrs. Zant's hand. Tears were rising in the child's eyes. "Are we to bid her good-bye?" she said sadly to her father.
>
> He seemed to be unwilling to trust himself to speak; he only said, "My dear, ask her yourself."
>
> But the result justified him. Lucy was happy again.

Here, Collins's narrator has receded like Mrs. Zant's supernatural protector, leaving the reader to hope and to expect that Mrs. Zant can again find love in this world.

This kind of exchange—direct and inferred—between author and reader can go in other directions. For example, when, near the middle of *The Woman in White*, one realizes that Count Fosco has read—as it were—over one's shoulder the diary of Miss Halcolmbe, the author surely intends that one should feel violated while at the same time forced into collusion with the already attractive, formidable villain.

Because Collins's style as narrator is so frequently self-effacing, it sustains the ingenuity of his plots. These are surely most elaborate in *The Woman in White* and *The Moonstone*. In both cases, Collins elects to have one figure, party to the main actions, assemble the materials of different narratives into cohesive form. It is a method far less tedious than that of epistolary novels and provides for both mystery and suspense. Although not the ostensible theme in either work, matters of self-identity and control over one's behavior operate in the contest between virtue and vice, good and evil. Thus, Laura Fairlie's identity is obliterated in an attempt to wrest from her her large fortune; thus, Franklin Blake, heavily drugged, unconsciously removes a gem that makes him the center of elaborate investigation. In each novel, the discovery of the actual circumstances restores identity to the character. The capacity to plot allows Collins to surprise his readers profoundly: In *The Woman in White*, one is astounded to be confronted by Laura Fairlie standing in the churchyard, above her own grave. In *The Moonstone*, one is baffled when the detective, Sergeant Cuff, provides a plausible solution to the theft of the diamond that turns out to be completely incorrect.

Collins's novels of the 1860's find the author having firmly established his transparent detachment from the subjects at hand, in turn giving full scope to his meticulous sense of plot. *No Name* and *Armadale* are no less complex in their respective actions than their more widely read counterparts. It is interesting to note, however, that all of these novels explore matters of identity and motive for action; they attest to Collins's ability to relate popular tales that encompass more serious issues.

CHARACTERIZATION

Because he had a painter's eye for detail, Collins was a master of characterization, even when it appears that a character is flat. Consider, for example, this passage from "Miss Dulane and My Lord," published in *Little Novels*:

> Mrs. Newsham, tall and elegant, painted and dyed, acted on the opposite principle in dressing, which confesses nothing. On exhibition before the world, this lady's disguise asserted she had reached her thirtieth year on her last birthday. Her husband was discreetly silent, and Father Time was discreetly silent; they both knew that her last birthday had happened thirty years since.

Here an incidental figure in a minor tale remains fixed, the picture of one comically out of synchronization with her own manner; before she has uttered a syllable, one dislikes her. Consider, on the other hand, the initial appearance of a woman one will grow to like and admire, Marian Halcolmbe, as she makes her way to meet Walter Hartright in *The Woman in White*:

> She turned towards me immediately. The easy elegance of every movement of her limbs and body as soon as she began to advance from the far end of the room, set me in a flutter of expectation to see her face clearly. She left the window—and I said to myself, The lady is dark. She moved forward a few steps—and I said to myself, The lady is young. She approached nearer—and I said to myself (with a sense of surprise which words fail me to express), The lady is ugly!

This passage reveals not only Collins's superb sense of pace, his ability to set a trap of astonished laughter, but also some of Hartright's incorrect assumptions about the position he has taken at Limmeridge House; for example, that the two young women he will instruct are pampered, spoiled, and not worth his serious consideration. Preeminently, it shows the grace of Marian Halcombe, a grace that overcomes her lack of physical beauty in conventional senses and points to her indefatigable intelligence and loyalty, so crucial to future events in the novel. Marian is, too, a foil for her half sister, Laura Fairlie, the victim of the main crimes in the book. While one might easily dismiss Laura Fairlie with her name—she is fair and petite and very vulnerable—she also displays a quiet resilience and determination in the face of overwhelming adversaries.

The most memorable of Collins's characters is Count Fosco in the same novel, whose name immediately suggests a bludgeon. Collins gives the job of describing Fosco to Marian Halcombe: "He looks like a man who could tame anything." In his characterization of Fosco, Collins spawned an entire race of fat villains and, occasionally, fat detectives, such as Nero Wolfe and Gideon Fell. One is not surprised that Sydney Greenstreet played both Fosco and his descendant, Caspar Gutman, in the 1948 film version of *The Woman in White* and the 1941 film version of Dashiell Hammett's *The Maltese Falcon* (1930). In one of his best speeches, Fosco reveals the nature of his hubris, his evil genius:

> Crimes cause their own detection, do they? . . . there are foolish criminals who are discovered, and wise criminals who escape. The hiding of a crime, or the detection of a crime, what is it? A trial of skill between the police on one side, and the individual on the other. When the criminal is a brutal, ignorant fool, the police in nine cases out of ten win. When the criminal is a resolute, educated, highly-intelligent man, the police in nine cases out of ten lose.

In pitting decent people against others who manipulate the law and social conventions to impose their wills, Collins frequently creates characters more interesting for their deficiencies than for their virtues. His novels pit, sensationally at times, the unsuspecting, the infirm, or the unprepossessing against darker figures who are usually operating under the scope of social acceptance. Beneath the veneer of his fiction, one finds in Collins a continuing struggle to legitimate the illegitimate, to neutralize hypocrisy, and to subvert the public certainties of his era.

Kenneth Friedenreich

OTHER MAJOR WORKS

SHORT FICTION: *Mr. Wray's Cash-Box: Or, The Mask and the Mystery*, 1852; *The Seven Poor Travellers*, 1854; *After Dark*, 1856; *The Wreck of the Golden Mary*, 1856; *The Lazy Tour of Two Idle Apprentices*, 1857 (with Charles Dickens); *The Queen of Hearts*, 1859; *The Frozen Deep*, 1866; *Miss or Mrs.?, and Other Stories*, 1873; *The Frozen Deep, and Other Stories*, 1874; *Alicia Warlock: A Mystery, and Other Stories*, 1875; *The Guilty River*, 1886; *Little Novels*, 1887; *The Yellow Tiger, and Other Tales*, 1924.

PLAYS: *The Lighthouse*, pr. 1855; *The Red Vial*, pr. 1858; *No Thoroughfare*, pr., pb. 1867 (with Charles Dickens); *The Woman in White*, pr., pb. 1871 (adaptation of his novel); *Man and Wife*, pr. 1873 (adaptation of his novel); *The New Magdalen*, pr., pb. 1873 (adaptation of his novel); *The Moonstone*, pr., pb. 1877 (adaptation of his novel).

NONFICTION: *Memoirs of the Life of William Collins, R. A.*, 1848 (2 volumes); *Rambles Beyond Railways*, 1851; *The Letters of Wilkie Collins*, 1999 (William Baker and William M. Clarke, editors); *The Public Face of Wilkie Collins: The Collected Letters*, 2005 (4 volumes; William Baker, editor).

MISCELLANEOUS: *My Miscellanies*, 1863; *The Works of Wilkie Collins*, 1900, 1970 (30 volumes).

BIBLIOGRAPHY

Bachman, Maria K., and Don Richard Cox, eds. *Reality's Dark Light: The Sensational Wilkie Collins.* Knoxville: University of Tennessee Press, 2003. Collection of fourteen essays analyzes Collins's novels, focusing on the themes and techniques that he introduced to the genre. Includes analysis of *The Moonstone* and *The Woman in White* as well as some of his lesser-known novels.

Gasson, Andrew. *Wilkie Collins: An Illustrated Guide.* New York: Oxford University Press, 1998. Well-illustrated volume provides an alphabetical guide to the characters, titles, and terms in Collins's works. Also includes a chronology, the Collins family tree, maps, and a bibliography.

Nayder, Lillian. *Wilkie Collins.* New York: Twayne, 1997. Good introductory study of the author features analysis of his novels and other works, placing them within the context of the political and cultural issues of Collins's time.

O'Neill, Philip. *Wilkie Collins: Women, Property, and Propriety.* New York: Macmillan, 1988. Seeks to move the discussion of Collins away from popularist categories by using modern feminist criticism deconstructively to open up a more considered version of his thematic material. Contains a full bibliography.

Peters, Catherine. *The King of Inventors: A Life of Wilkie Collins.* Princeton, N.J.: Princeton University Press, 1991. Comprehensive biography draws on a newly discovered autobiography by Collins's mother and on thousands of Collins's unpublished letters. Supplemented by detailed notes and bibliography.

Pykett, Lyn. *Wilkie Collins.* New York: Oxford University Press, 2005. Traces the various debates that have arisen since 1980, when literary critics began seriously reevaluating Collins's work. The essays focus on Collins's preoccupation with the themes of social and psychological identity, class, gender, and power.

_____, ed. *Wilkie Collins.* New York: St. Martin's Press, 1998. Provides an excellent introduction to Collins for the beginning student. In addition to essays that discuss Collins's place within Victorian detective fiction and the "sensation novel," some essays analyze his individual works, including *The Woman in White.* Includes bibliographical references and an index.

Taylor, Jenny Bourne, ed. *The Cambridge Companion to Wilkie Collins.* New York: Cambridge University Press, 2006. All aspects of Collins's writing are discussed in this collection of thirteen essays. His common themes of sexuality, marriage, and religion are examined, as well as his experiences with publishing companies and the process of adapting his works for film. Includes a thorough bibliography and index.

Thoms, Peter. *The Windings of the Labyrinth: Quest and Structure in the Major Novels of Wilkie Collins.* Athens: Ohio University Press, 1992. Focuses on seven major novels, analyzing the theme of the quest in *Basil, Hide and Seek, The Dead Secret, The Woman in White, No Name, Armadale,* and *The Moonstone.*

ARTHUR CONAN DOYLE

Born: Edinburgh, Scotland; May 22, 1859
Died: Crowborough, East Sussex, England; July 7, 1930
Also known as: Arthur Ignatius Conan Doyle

PRINCIPAL LONG FICTION

A Study in Scarlet, 1887 (serial), 1888 (book)
The Mystery of Cloomber, 1888
Micah Clarke, 1889
The Firm of Girdlestone, 1889
The Sign of Four, 1890 (also known as *The Sign of the Four*)
Beyond the City, 1891
The Doings of Raffles Haw, 1891
The White Company, 1891
The Great Shadow, 1892
The Refugees, 1893
The Parasite, 1894
The Stark Munro Letters, 1895
The Surgeon of Gaster Fell, 1895
Rodney Stone, 1896
The Tragedy of the Koroska, 1897 (also known as *A Desert Drama*)
Uncle Bernac, 1897
A Duet, with an Occasional Chorus, 1899 (revised 1910)
The Hound of the Baskervilles, 1901-1902 (serial), 1902 (book)
Sir Nigel, 1905-1906 (serial), 1906 (book)
The Lost World, 1912
The Poison Belt, 1913
The Valley of Fear, 1914-1915 (serial), 1915 (book)
The Land of Mist, 1926

OTHER LITERARY FORMS

In his lifetime, Arthur Conan Doyle (doyuhl) was far better known for his short stories than for his novels. Until he became interested in science fiction (a medium he found better suited to shorter fiction) after 1900, Doyle concentrated his creative energies on his novels, those works by which he felt posterity would judge him, and took a purely monetary interest in the short-story format. Ironically, contemporary readers and critics continue to value the Sherlock Holmes short stories and largely ignore Doyle's historical novels.

One of the most prolific in an era of prolific authors, Doyle also dabbled in the theater. The most commercially successful of his dramas was the stage version of *Sherlock*

Arthur Conan Doyle
(Library of Congress)

Holmes, first produced in 1899, starring William Gillette. Doyle frequently financed his own plays, such as the violent and realistic *The Fires of Fate* (pr. 1909, from his novel *The Tragedy of the Koroska*), a dramatization of a river-pirate raid on a party of English tourists in Egypt, an adventure based—like so many of Doyle's works—on his own experiences.

Doyle's nonfiction was largely polemical. He chronicled and defended the course of the British involvement in the Boer War in his *The Great Boer War*, published in 1900, and *The War in South Africa: Its Cause and Conduct* (1902). His efforts at defending government policy, as well as his own medical service during the war, were largely responsible for his knighthood. Doyle also wrote extensively about other causes: the reform of the divorce laws, the denial of the vote for women, the abolition of ostrich-feather hats. He reserved his greatest energy, however, for his popularizing and propagandizing of spiritualism, a doctrine with which he had toyed from his youth and to which he became devoted after the death of his eldest son in World War I. Indeed, the last fifteen years of his life were spent in furthering the spiritualist cause through writings and lectures.

Achievements

"Come, Watson. The game's afoot." Few words by any author evoke a clearer picture in the public's mind. Individuals who have never read a Sherlock Holmes story can immediately conjure up a vision of two distinctive figures leaving the fog-shrouded entrance to 221-B Baker Street: Sherlock Holmes, tall and skeletal, pale from his sedentary existence and haggard from his addiction to cocaine, wearing his famous deerstalker cap; Dr. Watson, short and stolid, though limping from an old bullet wound, one hand nervously hovering over the pocket that holds his trusted revolver. Indeed, few, if any, imaginary addresses have received the bulk of mail that continues to be sent to Holmes's Baker Street apartment; few fictional characters have been the subject of even a single "biography," let alone the great number of books that purport to document the life of Sherlock Holmes; and certainly few authors have cursed the success of one of their creations as much as Arthur Conan Doyle did that of Sherlock Holmes.

When the struggling young Portsmouth physician first wrote down the name of "Sherringford Hope," soon changed to "Sherlock Holmes" in honor of the American writer Oliver Wendell Holmes, he did not dream of fame or literary immortality but merely of some means of augmenting his income, for he had a wife as well as a younger brother and an impoverished mother to support. In fact, as soon as *A Study in Scarlet* had been sent off to a prospective publisher in early 1887, Doyle was hard at work on *Micah Clarke*, the novel he felt would represent "a door . . . opened for me into the Temple of the Muses." Two years later, Doyle wrote the second Holmes novel, *The Sign of Four*, as a *jeu d'esprit* after a convivial dinner with Oscar Wilde, an unlikely admirer of *Micah Clarke*, and James Stoddart, the editor of *Lippincott's Monthly Magazine*, who challenged both Doyle and Wilde to supply him with suitable mystery manuscripts. Doyle's real interest at the time was in the completion of his "masterpiece," the historical novel *The White Company*, and its acceptance for serialization in the *Cornhill Magazine* beginning in January, 1891, seemed to him a far better harbinger of literary fame.

The unexpected success of Sherlock Holmes stories as they appeared in *The Strand Magazine* in the early 1890's quickly established Doyle's reputation as, in the opinion of Greenough Smith, literary editor of the magazine, the greatest short-story writer since Edgar Allan Poe, but Doyle continued to churn out a seemingly endless series of historical and semiautobiographical novels, most of which are read today only by scholars. The commercial success of these novels (*The Firm of Girdlestone, Beyond the City, The Great Shadow, The Refugees, The Parasite, The Stark Munro Letters, Rodney Stone, Uncle Bernac*, and *Sir Nigel*, among others), his numerous collections of short stories, his occasional ventures into drama, and his essays and pamphlets on social and political issues (such as reform of the divorce laws and the conduct of the Boer War) all depended in large part on Doyle's popularity as the creator of Sherlock Holmes. Throughout his life, however, he never saw the stories and novels featuring Holmes and Watson as much more than potboilers. Even the famous "resurrection" of Holmes in 1903 was an attempt to capitalize financially on the success of the London opening of the play *Sherlock Holmes*, starring William Gillette. Doyle saw his real life's work, up until he became a propagandist for spiritualism at the end of his life, as writing fiction that would amuse and distract "the sick and the dull and the weary" through the evocation of the heroic past.

BIOGRAPHY

The idealization of the past served other purposes for Arthur Ignatius Conan Doyle, who had been born into genteel poverty in Edinburgh on May 22, 1859, and named for King Arthur: It gave him a model to live by and to instill in his sons, and it diverted him from the disappointments of life that frequently threatened to overwhelm him. From his earliest childhood, his mother, Mary Doyle, the daughter of the keeper of a lodging house who believed herself a descendant of the Plantagenets, indoctrinated her eldest son in tales of his aristocratic ancestry and the virtues of medieval chivalry. Doyle's father, Charles, although employed throughout his son's childhood as a municipal architect in Edinburgh, was the youngest son of a highly gifted and artistic family. Charles Doyle's father, John Doyle, was the talented caricaturist "H. B."; his maternal uncle Michael Edward Conan was an artist as well as the art and drama critic and Paris correspondent for *Art Journal*; his brother Richard was a graphic artist for *Punch* and later an illustrator for John Ruskin, Charles Dickens, and William Makepeace Thackeray; another brother, Henry, was a painter before becoming director of the National Gallery of Ireland; a third brother, James, was a famous mid-Victorian portrait painter. Charles Doyle himself, who had suffered since early childhood from epilepsy and emotional disturbances, supplemented his salary with sketches of famous criminal trials and illustrations of fairy tales and historical romances. By the time his older son reached adulthood, Charles Doyle had descended through alcoholism into incurable insanity, retreating from a world he found uncongenial to his artistic temperament.

Mary Doyle necessarily became the central figure in her children's lives and continued to be so after they grew up. When Doyle first considered killing off Sherlock Holmes in November, 1891, his mother convinced him not to do so, thus reprieving the famous detective for a year. She also supplied her son with ideas for the Holmes stories. Throughout his childhood, Doyle's mother managed the practical necessities of life for an improvident husband and eight children on £180 per year and also instilled a vision of the ideal gentleman in her eldest son. In contrast to his father's instability and impracticality, Doyle grew into the epitome of the Victorian male: respectable, decent, cautious, thrifty, stolid. Only his writing—with its predilection for the codes of chivalry and honor and its preoccupation with a romantic past and his later obsession with spiritualism—betrayed the influences of Doyle's belief in his descent from kings and his father's retreat into a world of fantasy.

Doyle's family was Catholic, and he was educated first at a Catholic preparatory school and then at Stonyhurst, the foremost Jesuit educational institution in England. He hated both, finding Stonyhurst rigid, backward, superstitious, narrow, and, above all, dull. Unpopular with the masters because of his frequent protests against physical punishment, Doyle survived his school days because of his ability at games, his preeminence among his schoolmates, and his aptitude at diverting himself through reading and writing about a more glorious and exciting past. In his five years at Stonyhurst he had no formal holidays, but he managed one visit to his uncle Richard Doyle in London, where the highlight of his stay was a visit to the Chamber of Horrors at Mme Tussaud's on Baker Street. During this period, he began to read the short stories of Poe, which later influenced him through their fascination with the macabre as well as through the characterization of Poe's intellectual detective, C. Auguste Dupin, who was one of the models for Sherlock Holmes. When Doyle entered Stonyhurst, the Jesuits had offered free tuition if he would train for the priesthood; fortunately, his mother refused the offer for him in spite of the advantages such an arrangement would have held. Ironically, the reactionary atmosphere at Stonyhurst contributed to Doyle's loss of faith, a faith he would not regain until his adoption of spiritualism forty years later.

Leaving school, Doyle found himself with three choices: the priesthood, law, or medicine. His loss of faith ruled out the first alternative and his lack of influential connections the second, so he entered Edinburgh University to study medicine in 1877. Although he was once again not a particularly brilliant student, he was deeply influenced by two of his professors, Dr. Joseph Bell, who became a prototype for Sherlock Holmes, and Dr. Andrew Maclagan, an instructor of forensic medicine, who served as a model for Professor Challenger in Doyle's later science-fiction novels. The School of Medicine at Edinburgh formed both the setting and the subject of his early and happily forgotten novel *The Firm of Girdlestone*.

Doyle's university days were punctuated with two spells as a ship's surgeon. The first voyage was aboard the *Hope*, an Arctic fishing boat. The seven-month trip was one of the highlights of Doyle's life. Seemingly indifferent to the bloody spectacle of the slaughter of whales and seals, he remembered only the sense of adventure and camaraderie among the crew. After graduation, he took a similar job aboard the passenger ship *Mayumba* on a voyage to the Gold Coast. This trip was in stark contrast to the first. Passengers and crew were struck down with tropical fevers that the young doctor was unable to treat. This experience so depressed Doyle that he gave up his plans for a career as a ship's surgeon and took up a position as an assistant to a doctor who turned out to be incompetent. When Mary Doyle objected to this association, her son left his employer and went to Portsmouth, where he opened his first practice.

Since the first years of his practice were not prosperous, Doyle returned to writing to occupy his time and to supplement his earnings. He also began to toy with an interest in the supernatural that is reflected in his later fiction and in his obsession with spiritualism. He attended his first séance in 1879 and worked on a number of bizarre stories. His poverty was such (he earned only about fifty pounds a year from his writing, and not much more from his practice) that his nine-year-old brother Innes, who was living with him at the time, had to usher patients into his surgery. His mother sent sheets and other household necessities from Edinburgh.

One of Doyle's greatest strokes of good fortune was the death of a patient. When a young boy collapsed of meningitis, then an incurable illness, outside his office, Doyle took the patient in and nursed him until his death. The boy's mother was so grateful for the doctor's solicitude, if not his medical skill, that she introduced Doyle to her daughter, Louise Hawkins, known as Touie. The young couple were married on August 6, 1885, and Touie Doyle became the perfect Victorian wife. Not only was she gentle, undemanding, and industrious but she also possessed a small yearly income that nicely supplemented her husband's earnings. The Doyles eventually had two children, Mary Louise and Alleyne Kingsley, before Touie developed consumption, the disease that doomed her to an early death and Doyle to years of celibacy.

Doyle's *Beyond the City* and *A Duet, with an Occasional Chorus* chronicle their married life. *Beyond the City* is set in Upper Norwood, the London suburb to which they moved in 1891, and details the days of their early married life: quiet afternoons spent bicycling together, equally quiet evenings with Touie sewing and her husband reading or writing. *A Duet*, written after Touie's fatal illness had been diagnosed, is silly and sentimental but ends with the deaths of the main characters in a train crash. Although Doyle remained devoted to assuring his wife's happiness until her death in 1906, he had fallen in love again in the mid-1890's. How much the fictionalized death of Touie in *A Duet* may have represented wish fulfillment remains conjecture.

The 1890's were years of contradiction for Doyle. His rise to literary prominence was paralleled by great personal distress. Although he had enjoyed moderate success as an author beginning with the publication of *A Study in Scarlet* in 1887, he still doubted that he could support his family by his pen. Early in 1891, he and Touie went to Austria, where he attempted to study ophthalmology; unsuccessful in this, he returned to England and moved his wife and daughter to London, where he set up a practice that drew even fewer patients than the one in Portsmouth. He had arrived back in England at a fortuitous moment for his career as a writer, however, as *The Strand Magazine* had decided to bolster its circulation by abandoning the traditional serial novel for a series of short stories featuring a continuing character. Hearing of this, Doyle decided to revive his Sherlock Holmes character. In less than two weeks, he wrote two more Holmes stories, "A Scandal in Bohemia" and "The Red-Headed League," which were immediately accepted by Greenough Smith, literary editor of *The Strand Magazine*. The two stories, which were published with illustrations by Sidney Paget, were instant and enormous successes. Doyle found himself an overnight celebrity.

This, however, was not the type of literary fame for which Doyle had hoped. Although he continued to turn out Holmes stories for *The Strand Magazine*, he worked more diligently on two new novels, *The Refugees*, another historical tale, and *Beyond the City*. By

November, 1891, just five months after Holmes first appeared in *The Strand*, his creator had decided to end the detective's life. Only the influence of Mary Doyle and the temptation of the one thousand pounds the magazine was offering for a new series to run throughout 1892 made Doyle reconsider.

The second Holmes series confirmed Smith's opinion that Doyle was among the masters of the short-story form. Doyle himself found the format tedious; he always thought up the solution to the mystery first and then concocted the story in such a fashion as to obscure the true outcome from the reader as long as possible. His real affinity was for the historical novel, which he felt comfortable in writing and which he felt represented the true and highest purposes of art. In 1892, *The Great Shadow*, another example of his fondness for this genre, was published. It was extremely popular only because its author was the creator of Sherlock Holmes.

The continued ill health of Doyle's wife (her tuberculosis was finally diagnosed in 1893) required frequent journeys to the Continent. Churning out a story a month to meet his commitment to *The Strand Magazine*, concerned about Touie's health, constantly on the move, unhappy with the format in which he was forced to write, Doyle became more and more dissatisfied with his literary detective. If he did not exactly grow to hate Sherlock Holmes, he found the process of inventing new adventures for him more and more distasteful. He informed the magazine that Holmes's final case, recorded in "The Final Problem," would appear in their December, 1893, issue. No entreaties or offers of higher payments would change his mind. After the account of Holmes's death was published, more than twenty thousand subscribers to *The Strand* canceled their subscriptions.

With Sherlock Holmes seemingly permanently out of his life, Doyle devoted himself to a renewed interest in the psychic research of his youth and to public affairs. Since his wife's illness precluded sexual intercourse, Doyle's writings of this period reverted to his earlier preoccupation with a connection between sex and death. Doyle's 1894 novel *The Parasite* deals with the relationship between Professor Gilroy, a Holmesian figure who has retreated to the world of the intellect, and Helen Penclosa, a beautiful clairvoyant. At first a skeptic, Gilroy becomes increasingly obsessed with the beautiful young woman until, unable to withstand the passion that has made him lock himself in his own room, he rushes to her flat and makes love to her. Overcome immediately by guilt, he flees from her room, only to discover later that she has mesmerized him and forced him to rob a bank. As his obsession grows, Gilroy is dismissed from his post at the university and becomes increasingly erratic in his behavior. The more unstable Gilroy becomes, the weaker Penclosa grows, her power obviously transferring itself into his mind. In a moment of madness, Gilroy attempts to murder his fiancé, then decides to free himself by killing Penclosa. When he arrives at her flat, he finds her already dead and himself returned to sanity.

The public Doyle, however, continued to be the respectable man of affairs. Another historical novel, *Rodney Stone*, the story of a Regency dandy who becomes a "man" in the end, appeared in 1896. *Round the Red Lamp: Being Fact and Fancies of Medical Life*, a collection of ghost stories Doyle wrote for his children, was published in 1894. He continued his travels in search of renewed health for Touie, journeying back and forth to Switzerland and spending the winter of 1896-1897 in Egypt.

In private, Doyle was increasingly troubled by the complications of his love for Jean Leckie, to whom he was originally attracted because of her descent from the Scottish hero Rob Roy. Although he confessed his love for Jean to his mother and other family members, he resisted all their advice that he divorce Touie. Vowing never to consummate his relationship with Jean until Touie's death, he instructed his family never even to hint of the affair to his wife. His "code of honor" as a gentleman mandated that he cherish and protect Touie at the cost of his own happiness. Jean, with whom he had never quarreled, agreed. They continued to see each other, but Touie was kept ignorant of her husband's love for another woman. Doyle and Jean even waited the requisite year of mourning after Touie's death before they were finally married in 1907.

Although he had returned to an English setting for *Rodney Stone*, Doyle was fascinated by the events of the French Revolution and the Napoleonic Wars. In 1896 and 1897, after a spell in Egypt as a war correspondent during the Sudanese War, he published *The Exploits of Brigadier Gerard*, the first of a series of stories about the picaresque hero to appear in novel form. He also wrote *Uncle Bernac*, another Napoleonic novel, and *The Tragedy of the Koroska*, a melodrama about his adventures with paddleboat bandits in Egypt.

In the late 1890's and the first years of the new century, Doyle increasingly turned to the horror story. One particular story, "Playing with Fire," published in 1900, combined his interest in psychic phenomena with his love for animals and suggested that animals, too, survive the grave. "The King of Foxes" (1903) dealt with Jean Leckie's favorite sport, foxhunting, in a bizarre and macabre form. Also in this period, to make money and to forestall another dramatist from seizing on the idea, Doyle adapted the character of Sherlock Holmes for the American stage, emphasizing that the play that would make actor William Gillette famous was not a new adventure but related events that had occurred before Holmes's "death."

The outbreak of the Boer War in October, 1899, gave Doyle the outlet he needed for his interest in public affairs. He first attempted to enlist in the army and then accepted the position of senior surgeon with John Longman's private field hospital. He saw his service at Bloemfontein in 1900 as that of a medieval knight seeking to help those less fortunate than he. His heroic efforts with inadequate equipment, his propaganda pamphlet *The War in South Africa: Its Cause and Conduct*, and later his history of the war, *The Great Boer War*, combined to win him knighthood in 1902.

While in South Africa, Doyle had read of the story of the Cabell family, which was haunted by a ghostly hound. He saw in this the germ of a new Holmes novel, and *The Hound of the Baskervilles* was duly published in 1901-1902. He was still not committed to bringing Holmes back to life and insisted once again that *The Hound of the Baskervilles* was an earlier adventure only now coming to light. Although he continued to write horror stories, he was unable to resist the financial lure of more Holmes tales, and, consequently, in October, 1903, the first adventure of the "resurrected" Sherlock Holmes appeared.

During the last two decades of Doyle's life, his fame and finances were assured by the popularity of Sherlock Holmes. His private life, after his marriage to Jean Leckie and the birth of their three children, was that of an Edwardian paterfamilias. With the exception of *Sir Nigel*, he finally abandoned the historical novel in favor of science fiction. Politically reactionary, Doyle nevertheless was respected for his warnings about the outbreak of World War I. His greatest preoccupation, however, was with the cause of spiritualism; his final "conversion" to absolute belief in the phenomenon that had fascinated him for years resulted from the deaths of his brother Innes and eldest son Kingsley during World War I. To the end of his life, he was convinced that he was in frequent touch with the spirits of his loved ones and thus devoted all the proceeds from his novels and lectures to the "cause."

In the early 1920's, he once again announced Holmes's departure, this time to honorable retirement as a beekeeper on the Sussex Downs. Doyle brought him back only once, in a 1924 story written expressly for Queen Mary's Dolls' House, an elaborate dollhouse created for Queen Mary in the 1920's. His literary reputation suffered because of his involvement in spiritualism, and his excellent science-fiction novels, many of which rival those of Jules Verne, were ridiculed by the critics more for their author's peculiarities than for their own lack of merit. Doyle died on July 7, 1930; his wife Jean claimed to receive a spirit message from him less than twenty-four hours later. His epitaph, however, looked back to earlier decades, to the little boy named after King Arthur who had resolved to live his life according to knightly ideals: "STEEL TRUE/BLADE STRAIGHT."

ANALYSIS

Arthur Conan Doyle's epitaph can also serve as an introduction to the themes of his novels, both those that feature actual medieval settings and those that center on Sherlock Holmes. Doyle's central character is always the knight on a quest, living and battling according to chivalric ideals. Micah Clarke, Alleyne Edricson, and Sir Nigel Loring all engage in real battles; Sherlock Holmes combats villains on behalf of distressed young women and naïve and frightened young men; Professor Challenger takes on the unknown—a prehistoric world, the realm of the spirit, the threatened extinction of life on Earth.

MICAH CLARKE

Doyle's first historical novel, *Micah Clarke*, is set in seventeenth century England against the background of Monmouth's Rebellion. As he always did in his historical fiction, in which he intended to portray the actual conditions of life at the time the novels were set, he paid meticulous attention to actual detail. In the Sherlock Holmes stories, Doyle seems not to have cared whether Dr. Watson's old war wound was in his shoulder or his knee, whether the good doctor's Christian name was John or James, whether there were one or two Mrs. Watsons, but his period novels show none of this casualness. For *Micah Clarke*, the author had carefully explored the area around Portsmouth, where most of the action takes place. He also did careful research into the dress, customs, and speech of the era. Indeed, it was its "mode of speech" that caused both Blackwoods and Bentley, Ltd. to reject the novel; this same period diction makes the novel extremely slow going for the modern reader.

Like most of Doyle's characters, those in *Micah Clarke* are modeled on real individuals. Micah Clarke, the gallant young man fighting zealously for a lost cause, is largely based on young Doyle himself, protesting hopelessly at Stonyhurst against outmoded courses of study, unfair punishments, and censorship of his letters home. Ruth Timewell, the cloyingly sweet young heroine, depicts the quiet, meek Touie Doyle, who at the time the novel was written represented her husband's ideal of womanhood. In spite of the critical acclaim *Micah Clarke* received when it was originally published, few people would consider it the stirring tale of adventure that its author did, although parts of it, especially the description of the climactic Battle of Sedgmoor and the portrait of the evil Judge Jeffreys, retain some interest for the modern reader.

THE WHITE COMPANY

The White Company, Doyle's second venture into the historical genre, and its companion piece, *Sir Nigel*, have worn slightly better. Like its predecessor, *The White Company* is distinguished by its scrupulous re-creation of the entire spectrum of life in fourteenth century England. Once again, Doyle's preoccupation with noble causes is reflected in the interests of his characters, members of a small but dedicated mercenary company who set off for the Continent to fight for England during the Hundred Years' War.

The hero of *The White Company*, after whom Doyle later named his eldest son, is Alleyne Edricson, a landless young squire who leaves the monastery where he has been reared with his two companions, the lapsed monk Hortle John and the former serf Samkin Aylward, to join the White Company under the command of Sir Nigel Loring. Alleyne, his friends, his leader, and later his prince represent a microcosm of English society in the Middle Ages, depicting an idealized vision of the English character and contrasting with that of the country's main enemies: the French, the Spanish, and the Germans. Departing from his usual historical accuracy, Doyle presents the Germans as the worst foes of the English, reflecting his own late Victorian perspective. Alleyne and his friend are mercenaries who live by their wits, but their fighting, looting, and pillaging are always conducted according to the rules of the chivalric game. At the end of the novel, Alleyne wins his knighthood, his inheritance, and his lady fair in the person of Sir Nigel's daughter Maude. The virtues Sir Nigel embodies and Alleyne learns are those that Doyle taught his own sons: sympathetic treatment of social inferiors, courtesy and respect for women, and honesty in financial dealings.

The novel is particularly interesting for its two main themes: the rise of the English middle class and of English patriotism. *The White Company* depicts a world where individuals are judged not by their birth but by their accomplishments, in much the same manner as Doyle rose from poverty to affluence through his own efforts. The book, however, also reflects its author's belief that the English character was the best in the world; Doyle clearly insists that the language, history, customs, and beliefs of England are far superior to those of any other nation.

SHERLOCK HOLMES NOVELS

At first glance, the four Sherlock Holmes novels (*A Study in Scarlet, The Sign of Four, The Hound of the Baskervilles*, and *The Valley of Fear*) might seem to have little in common with Doyle's historical fiction. A closer look, however, shows that whatever the surface differences, the author's underlying concerns and prejudices are the same. Indeed, Sherlock Holmes can be seen as a knight-errant who ventures forth from Baker Street on a series of quests. In the earlier novels and stories, he battles dragons of crime on behalf of individuals. Mary Morstan in *The Sign of Four* is the epitome of a damsel in distress. In Holmes's later adventures, both the suppliants and the dragons are different. There is an increasing tendency for those seeking Holmes's assistance to be representatives of the government itself or, as in "The Illustrious Client," a person no less exalted than King Edward VII himself, and for the villains to be international criminals or even foreign governments.

Holmes's relationship with Dr. Watson reflects that of a knight and his squire. The detective and his intellect operate according to the rules of detection that Holmes himself establishes at the beginning of *The Sign of Four*, rules analogous to the chivalric code, and squire Watson accompanies Holmes as much to learn how to conduct himself according to these rules as to assist in the solution of the crime. Dull, plodding, faithful Watson may never win his spurs, but at least he wins the hand of Mary Morstan.

The Holmes novels also exhibit Doyle's characteristic xenophobia. With the possible exception of Moriarty, who, after all, is an international rather than an English criminal, the villains with whom Holmes contends frequently are foreigners, or else the crimes he investigates have their origins in foreign or distant events. *A Study in Scarlet* is a story of the revenge exacted for a crime committed in the mountains of Utah twenty years earlier. The novel's "victims" are in fact villains who have mistreated an old man and a young girl, those most deserving of protection, and so deserve their own deaths, while its "villain" is a just avenger who is saved from the gallows by a "higher judge" and dies with a smile on his face as if looking back on a deed well done. The crime in *The Sign of Four* similarly has its origins years before in India, and its victims also turn out to have brought their doom on themselves. Rodger Baskerville, the father of Stapleton the naturalist, who perpetrated the hoax in *The Hound of the Baskervilles*, had fled to South America before his son was born. As in the fictional press report at the end of *A Study in Scarlet*, Doyle appears eager to distance the true Englishman from responsibility for crime.

THE LOST WORLD

Although Doyle himself favored his historical fiction while the public preferred the Sherlock Holmes adventures, the author's finest works have largely been ignored. *The Lost World, The Poison Belt*, and *The Land of Mist* are novels that belong to a series of science-fiction works featuring the eccentric Professor George Edward Challenger. By the time *The Lost World* was published in 1912, Doyle was already becoming a figure of fun among the intelligentsia because of his ardent defense of psychic phenomena and his reactionary political views. The critics' disdain for this series unfortunately affected its popularity, and in subsequent years scholars and others have had a consequent tendency to overlook them as examples of Doyle's literary skill at its finest.

The Lost World resulted from Doyle's interest in prehistoric footprints near his home in the New Forest. After he made casts of the prints, he consulted with zoologist Edwin Ray Lankester and came away with the idea for the novel. *The Lost World* is narrated by Edward Dunn Malone, a journalist who comes to act as a Watson-like chronicler of the exploits of Professor Challenger, an eccentric scientist with a great physical resemblance to Arthur Conan Doyle. After knocking Malone down the stairs at their first meeting, Challenger recruits him for a proposed expedition to South America in search of a prehistoric monster believed to exist on a plateau in the Amazon River basin.

Doyle's penchant for realistic description deserts him in *The Lost World*. His details are fifty years out of date; he instead presents a fantastically imaginative vision of the unexplored jungle wilderness. The beauty of the jungle vanishes as the explorers reach the historic plateau. With almost surrealistic horror, Doyle depicts the filthy, fetid nesting ground of the pterodactyls and the dank and dirty caves of the ape-men who inhabit the plateau. A marvelous comic ending has Challenger revealing the results of the expedition to a skeptical London audience of pedants by releasing a captured pterodactyl over their heads.

The characterization in *The Lost World* is among Doyle's finest achievements. The members of the expedition are well balanced: the eccentric and pugnacious Challenger, the naïve and incredulous Malone, the cynical and touchy Summerlee, and the great white hunter Lord John Roxton. The one woman in the novel, Malone's fiancé, Gladys, bears no resemblance to the Ruth Timewells and Lady Maudes of Doyle's earlier work. She is spunky and independent, refusing to marry Malone until he has done something worth admiring, and in his absence marrying someone else because she decides money is a more practical basis for marriage than fame.

LATER WORKS

The series retains its high quality in *The Poison Belt*, but the subsequent related works are less consequential. In *The Land of Mist*, Challenger becomes a spiritualist convert when the spirits of two men whom he believes he has killed return to tell him of his innocence. "When the World Screamed," one of the stories in *The Maracot Deep, and Other Stories* (1929), reverts to the morbid sexuality of *The Parasite*. When Challenger attempts to drill a hole to the center of the earth, the world turns out to be a living female organism. When Challenger's shaft penetrates the cortex of her brain, she screams, setting off earthquakes and tidal waves.

Few of Doyle's writings from the last decade of his life are read by other than specialists, dealing as they do with the propagation of spiritualism. The canon of his fiction can thus be said to have ended with science-fiction novels. These novels too all deal with Doyle's characteristic themes and concerns. Challenger and Maracot uncover hidden truths about the nature of the past, the present, the future, and life after death much in the same way Sherlock Holmes discovered the truth about human nature in the course of his investigation of crime. The historical fiction had sought to explore the truth about a specialized human nature, that of the archetypal Englishman, in the same manner. Even the obsession with spiritualism that cost him his credibility among intellectual circles was but another example of Doyle's lifelong search for the truth about human existence.

In whatever guise he portrayed that search, Doyle never deviated from the devotion to the ideals that were instilled in him in childhood and that are recorded on his gravestone. Similarly, all his literary protagonists embody these same ideals: a devotion to truth and a belief in the rightness of their cause. Few other authors have managed to create such a coherent body of work as did Arthur Conan Doyle, and fewer have matched the content of their work so closely to the conduct of their lives.

Mary Anne Hutchinson

OTHER MAJOR WORKS

SHORT FICTION: *Mysteries and Adventures*, 1889 (also known as *The Gully of Bluemansdyke, and Other Stories*); *The Captain of Polestar, and Other Tales*, 1890; *The Adventures of Sherlock Holmes*, 1892; *My Friend the Murderer, and Other Mysteries and Adventures*, 1893; *The Great Keinplatz Experiment, and Other Stories*, 1894; *The Memoirs of Sherlock Holmes*, 1894; *Round the Red Lamp: Being Fact and Fancies of Medical Life*, 1894; *The Exploits of Brigadier Gerard*, 1896; *The Man from Archangel, and Other Stories*, 1898; *The Green Flag, and Other Stories of War and Sport*, 1900; *The Adventures of Gerard*, 1903; *The Return of Sherlock Holmes*, 1905; *Round the Fire Stories*, 1908; *The Last Galley: Impressions and Tales*, 1911; *One Crowded Hour*, 1911; *His Last Bow*, 1917; *Danger!, and Other Stories*, 1918; *Tales of Terror and Mystery*, 1922 (also known as *The Black Doctor, and Other Tales of Terror and Mystery*); *Tales of the Ring and Camp*, 1922 (also known as *The Croxley Master, and Other Tales of the Ring and Camp*); *Tales of Twilight and the Unseen*, 1922 (also known as *The Great Keinplatz Experiment, and Other Tales of Twilight and the Unseen*); *Three of Them*, 1923; *Last of the Legions, and Other Tales of Long Ago*, 1925; *The Dealings of Captain Sharkey, and Other Tales of Pirates*, 1925; *The Case-Book of Sherlock Holmes*, 1927; *The Maracot Deep, and Other Stories*, 1929; *The Final Adventures of Sherlock Holmes*, 1981 (revised and expanded 2001); *Uncollected Stories: The Unknown Conan Doyle*, 1982.

PLAYS: *Foreign Policy*, pr. 1893; *Jane Annie: Or, The Good Conduct Prize*, pr., pb. 1893 (with J. M. Barrie); *Waterloo*, pr. 1894 (also known as *A Story of Waterloo*); *Halves*, pr. 1899; *Sherlock Holmes*, pr. 1899 (with William Gillette); *A Duet*, pb. 1903; *Brigadier Gerard*, pr. 1906; *The Fires of Fate*, pr. 1909; *The House of Temperley*, pr. 1909; *The Pot of Caviare*, pr. 1910; *The Speckled Band*, pr. 1910; *The Crown Diamond*, pr. 1921; *Exile: A Drama of Christmas Eve*, pb. 1925; *It's Time Something Happened*, pb. 1925.

POETRY: *Songs of Action*, 1898; *Songs of the Road*, 1911; *The Guards Came Through, and Other Poems*, 1919; *The Poems: Collected Edition*, 1922.

NONFICTION: *The Great Boer War*, 1900; *The War in South Africa: Its Cause and Conduct*, 1902; *The Case of Mr. George Edalji*, 1907; *Through the Magic Door*, 1907; *The Crime of the Congo*, 1909; *The Case of Oscar Slater*, 1912; *Great Britain and the Next War*, 1914; *In Quest of Truth, Being a Correspondence Between Sir Arthur Conan Doyle and Captain H. Stansbury*, 1914; *To Arms!*, 1914; *The German War: Some Sidelights and Reflections*, 1915; *Western Wanderings*, 1915; *The Origin and Outbreak of the War*, 1916; *A Petition to the Prime Minister on Behalf of Roger Casement*, 1916(?); *A Visit to Three Fronts*, 1916; *The British Campaign in France and Flanders*, 1916-1919 (6 volumes); *The New Revelation*, 1918; *The Vital Message*, 1919; *A Debate on Spiritualism*, 1920 (with Joseph McCabe); *Our Reply to the Cleric*, 1920; *Spiritualism and Rationalism*, 1920; *The Evidence for Fairies*, 1921; *Fairies Photographed*, 1921; *The Wanderings of a Spiritualist*, 1921; *The Case for Spirit Photography*, 1922 (with others); *The Coming of the Fairies*, 1922; *Our American Adventure*, 1923; *Memories and Adventures*, 1924; *Our Second American Adventure*, 1924; *The Early Christian Church and Modern Spiritualism*, 1925; *Psychic Experiences*, 1925; *The History of Spiritualism*, 1926 (2 volumes); *Pheneas Speaks: Direct Spirit Communications*, 1927; *What Does Spiritualism Actually Teach and Stand For?*, 1928; *A Word of Warning*, 1928; *An Open Letter to Those of My Generation*, 1929; *Our African Winter*, 1929; *The Roman Catholic Church: A Rejoinder*, 1929; *The Edge of the Unknown*, 1930; *Arthur Conan Doyle on Sherlock Holmes*, 1981; *Essays on Photography*, 1982; *Letters to the Press*, 1984; *Arthur Conan Doyle: A Life in Letters*, 2007 (Jon Lellenberg, Daniel Stashower, and Charles Foley, editors).

TRANSLATION: *The Mystery of Joan of Arc*, 1924 (of Léon Denis's biography).

EDITED TEXTS: *Dreamland and Ghostland*, 1886; *D. D. Home: His Life and Mission*, 1921 (by Mrs. Douglas Home); *The Spiritualist's Reader*, 1924.

MISCELLANEOUS: *The Sir Arthur Conan Doyle Reader*, 2002.

BIBLIOGRAPHY

Barsham, Diana. *Arthur Conan Doyle and the Meaning of Masculinity*. Burlington, Vt.: Ashgate, 2000. Examines Doyle's depiction of masculinity, delving into all of his works, including his war correspondence and travel writings. Demonstrates how Doyle sought to alter the idea of manliness at a time of shifting gender identity.

Booth, Martin. *The Doctor, the Detective, and Arthur Conan Doyle: A Biography of Ar-

thur Conan Doyle. London: Hodder & Stoughton, 1997. Well-written, astute biography provides details about the full range of Doyle's activities and writings. Demonstrates how Doyle's accomplishments extended far beyond his creation of Sherlock Holmes.

Carr, John Dickson. *The Life of Sir Arthur Conan Doyle.* London: John Murray, 1949. One of the first biographies of Doyle not written by a relative, this straightforward account gives a good overview of Doyle's life. Quotes copiously from Doyle's letters, but offers little discussion of the stories. Includes a list of sources and an index.

Edwards, Owen Dudley. *The Quest for Sherlock Holmes: A Biographical Study of Arthur Conan Doyle.* New York: Barnes & Noble Books, 1983. Concentrates on the first twenty-three years of Doyle's life. Explains how various aspects of Doyle's early life influenced his writing, such as his love of history and Celtic lore, the impoverished and Catholic Edinburgh of his youth, and his alcoholic father.

Jaffee, Jacqueline A. *Arthur Conan Doyle.* Boston: Twayne, 1987. Solid study combines biography and a critical discussion of Doyle's novels and stories. Supplemented by an index, a bibliography of Doyle's work, and an annotated bibliography.

Jann, Rosemary. *The Adventures of Sherlock Holmes: Detecting Social Order.* New York: Twayne, 1995. Slim volume is divided into two parts, the first of which places the great detective in a literary and historical context, followed by Jann's own reading of Arthur Conan Doyle's Sherlockian approach to detective fiction. Includes a brief chronology of Doyle's life and work as well as a selected bibliography.

Lycett, Andrew. *The Man Who Created Sherlock Holmes: The Life and Times of Sir Arthur Conan Doyle.* New York: Free Press, 2007. Comprehensive and detailed biography is based in part on materials in Doyle's personal archive that were not available to researchers until 1997. Describes the events of the author's life and the variety of his writings, explaining how the author who created one of the world's most rational detectives was a believer in spiritualism and the supernatural.

Orel, Harold, ed. *Critical Essays on Sir Arthur Conan Doyle.* New York: G. K. Hall, 1992. Collection of essays presents both evaluations by Doyle's contemporaries and later scholarship, some of it commissioned specifically for inclusion in this volume. Divides the discussion into three sections: "Sherlock Holmes," "Other Writings," and "Spiritualism." Orel opens the collection with a lengthy and comprehensive essay, which is followed by essays by such literary lights as Dorothy L. Sayers, George Bernard Shaw, Max Beerbohm, and Heywood Broun.

Simmons, Diane. *The Narcissism of Empire: Loss, Rage, and Revenge in Thomas De Quincey, Robert Louis Stevenson, Arthur Conan Doyle, Rudyard Kipling, and Isak Dinesen.* Brighton, England: Sussex Academic Press, 2007. Analyzes the works of five authors who helped popularize the goals of imperialism, arguing that they all bore scars of traumatic childhoods and sought to bolster their fragile egos through dreams of imperial domination.

Stashower, Daniel. *Teller of Tales: The Life of Arthur Conan Doyle.* New York: Henry Holt, 1999. Excellent, thorough biography focuses less on the Holmes novels than have other biographers and more on Doyle's historical novels, personal crusades, and spiritualism. This work received the 1999 Edgar Award for Best Biographical Work.

JOHN GREGORY DUNNE

Born: Hartford, Connecticut; May 25, 1932
Died: New York, New York; December 30, 2003

OTHER LITERARY FORMS

In addition to his novels, John Gregory Dunne produced a distinguished body of nonfiction, including a memoir, *Harp* (1989), and other personal and autobiographical essays. One of his primary subjects was Hollywood, the focus of both *The Studio* (1969) and *Monster: Living off the Big Screen* (1997). His first book, *Delano: The Story of the California Grape Strike* (1967, revised 1971), reflects his early career in journalism. He combined his talents as autobiographer and reporter in *Vegas: A Memoir of a Dark Season* (1974), which recounts a time of crisis in his marriage and in his writing career, set in the milieu of a stunning cast of characters who thrive in the mecca of legal gambling. Dunne's travel writing is featured in *Crooning* (1990), a collection of essays that also contains a number of his reflections on Hollywood, the American West, and politics. *Quintana and Friends* (1978), another collection of essays, is autobiographical (Quintana is the name of his adopted daughter) and focuses on his personal account of moving from his roots in the eastern United States to a career as a Hollywood screenwriter. Uniting much of Dunne's fiction and nonfiction are his concerns with his Irish background and sensibility as well as the world of urban crime and scandal and the role of institutions such as the family, the Roman Catholic Church, politics, and the entertainment industry. *Regards: The Selected Nonfiction of John Gregory Dunne* (2006) includes several essays published in the last fifteen years of his life and previously uncollected in book form, as well as his 1996 *Paris Review* interview.

ACHIEVEMENTS

John Gregory Dunne's fiction falls within the tradition of the crime novel as developed by Dashiell Hammett and Raymond Chandler. Like Hammett's, Dunne's novels feature a gritty realism, although his detectives tend to be less hard-boiled and romanticized than those of his predecessors. Dunne shares much of Chandler's fascination with Los Angeles. In other words, Dunne's obsession with crime and detection reveals a profound concern with the corruption of urban society. Also like Hammett and Chandler, Dunne is an elegant stylist. Although his sense of plot construction is not as acute as that of the greatest detective novelists, his probing of characters and milieu is reminiscent of writers such as F. Scott Fitzgerald and Nathanael West. Like Fitzgerald and West, Dunne sets some of his fiction in Hollywood, where Americans seem particularly free to invent themselves.

Dunne's fiction recalls Fitzgerald's *The Last Tycoon* (1941) and *The Great Gatsby* (1925), for it takes up the theme of the easterner who moves West to find his fortune and a new identity. Dunne, however, adds a keen concern with ethnicity and religion that earlier crime and mystery writers confront only fleetingly and with embarrassing stereotypes. Dunne's Irish men and women, for example, are not only sophisticated and working class, white and blue collar, powerful politicians and churchmen, but also immigrants and criminals. Dunne's unique contribution to the crime novel was to give it a sociological context and a depth of background without sacrificing the drama and intense curiosity about events and people that are requisite in mystery fiction. Dunne's final novel, published in 2004 shortly after his death, exploits his deft understanding of politics and the legal system and shows no diminution of his narrative powers or of his ability to create memorable characters.

BIOGRAPHY

John Gregory Dunne, born on May 25, 1932, in Hartford, Connecticut, was the fifth of six children born to Richard Edward and Dorothy Burns Dunne. In many ways, Dunne's family enjoyed the typical immigrant success story. His maternal grandfather arrived in the United States from Ireland shortly after the American Civil War, an uneducated boy who could not read. He became a grocer and then a banker in Frog Hollow, Hartford's Irish ghetto. Dunne grew up with stories about his Irish ancestors' assimilation in America and with a sense of being a "harp," a derogatory term for the Irish, who were considered inferior by the city's Anglo-Saxon establishment.

An indifferent student, Dunne nevertheless managed to complete four years at Princeton University and earn an undergraduate degree. Not knowing what to do after graduation, he enlisted in the U.S. Army, a decision he credits in *Harp*, his autobiography, with helping to ground him with a sense not only of society's complexity but also of its very rich resources in humanity. Had he remained in the elitist milieu of Princeton, Dunne suggests, his career as a writer would have been seriously limited, if not entirely vitiated, by the lack of worldly experience he deemed necessary for a writer.

Dunne's development as a novelist proceeded slowly. He began writing short pieces for newspapers before landing a job on the staff of *Time* magazine. There he labored for six years in New York City, meeting writer Joan Didion, whom he married on January 30, 1964. Although she was already an accomplished journalist and novelist, Didion found herself undergoing a creative crisis, and the couple decided to move to California, where Didion had grown up and where Dunne hoped to find the material to begin writing both fiction and nonfiction. Husband and wife also began collaborating on screenplays as a way of supporting themselves while they worked on longer fiction and nonfiction projects. After two decades of residence in California, Dunne and Didion moved back to New York City, continuing to collaborate on screenplays as well as working separately on their fiction and nonfiction. Dunne continued to write essays for *The New York Review of Books*. He suffered from a heart condition that worsened during the last decade of his life, and he died of a heart attack at his Manhattan home on December 30, 2003.

ANALYSIS

All of John Gregory Dunne's novels are about power and personal integrity. The power is exercised by Roman Catholic prelates, the police, criminals, studio bosses and producers, quasi-legitimate businessmen, and politicians. The person of integrity is often the estranged member of a family, such as Jack Broderick in *The Red White and Blue* and *Playland* or Tom Spellacy in Dunne's brilliant debut novel, *True Confessions*. The head of the family—Jack's father, Hugh Broderick, or Tom Spellacy's brother, Des (Desmond), for example—stands for the patriarchal and corrupt aspects of society. Tom Spellacy may have spurned his brother Des's ambitious careerism in the Church, but he has also been a bagman for a local crime king. Jack Broderick has not followed his father into the world of high-stakes politics and business, yet he writes screenplays for craven Hollywood producers. In other words, even Dunne's moral characters are compromised. They come by their moral code precisely because they are flawed figures. Dunne's early exposure to Roman Catholicism is most telling in his awareness of how virtue and vice coincide.

TRUE CONFESSIONS

True Confessions begins and ends in the 1970's, when Tom Spellacy has retired from the police department and his brother Des, an ambitious Catholic clergyman, is spending the last of his thirty years of exile in a small, neglected parish. Somehow Tom's actions have led to his brother's downfall, and the heart of the novel, "Then" (set in the 1940's), tells the story that leads to "Now," the first and last chapters.

The first "Now" section centers on Des's call to his brother Tom. Why, Tom wonders, has Des summoned him to his parish in the desert? The brothers have been intensely preoccupied with each other and yet estranged. Although one has chosen a career in the police department and the other the Church, they are both worldly men. Tom cannot seem to live down his corrupt period on the vice squad, when he was "on the take," a bagman for Jack Amsterdam, a supposedly legitimate contractor and a pillar of the Church, but in fact a thug with numerous illicit enterprises. Amsterdam is the link between the careers of the two brothers, since Des has relied on Amsterdam to construct many of his parish's impressive church buildings, even though Des knows that Amsterdam has padded his payroll and physically intimidated other contractors so that they have not put in bids for the construction projects. Des has also functioned as a kind of enforcer for Cardinal Danaher, who is trying to centralize power by depriving parish priests of their autonomy.

When the two brothers meet in the opening section of the novel, Des tells Tom that he is dying. It is this announcement that precipitates the action of the novel, as Tom remembers the events that have led to his brother's dramatic announcement.

"Then" begins as a traditional murder mystery. A woman is found with her body hacked in two. There is no blood, which suggests the body has been moved from another location. The cut is clean, indicating that a very sharp instrument was used.

Tom Spellacy is goaded into action by his boss, Fred Fuqua, who is yearning to become chief of police. Fuqua is a systems man. He claims to be able to find patterns in crime, though he has little sense of street life or of how crimes are committed. What also goads Tom, however, is his intuition that larger forces—namely, Jack Amsterdam—are somehow connected to the mutilated body. Tom's search for the murderer and his gunning for Amsterdam also set in motion the forces that expose Des's complicity in evil and lead to his banishment from the center of power.

DUTCH SHEA, JR.

Dutch Shea, Jr. is one of Dunne's darkest novels. It includes an epigraph by the poet Gerard Manley Hopkins, "I awake and feel the fell of dark, not day." Its second epigraph provides a hint of understanding, if not redemption: "for we possess nothing certainly except the past"—a line from novelist Evelyn Waugh. Significantly, both Hopkins and Waugh were Catholics who found in their religion a way of analyzing and coping with the world's corruption and blindness. This novel of occluded vision is reminiscent of Saint Paul's admonition that "we see as through a glass darkly."

Dutch Shea's father was sent to prison for embezzlement, and attorney Dutch is well on the way to committing a similar crime, having held back money owed to one of his clients, now in a nursing home. Dutch's demons also drive him, however, to defend criminal suspects that other attorneys spurn. His wife has left him, and he is carrying on a covert relationship with a female judge. He mourns his adopted daughter, who was blown up in an Irish Republican Army (IRA) bombing in London, but he has also seduced his surrogate father's Irish immigrant servant. He suspects that his surrogate father was somehow involved in the crime that put his father in prison, and much of the novel deals with Dutch's conflicted feelings: He is at once burning to know exactly how and why his father turned to crime and terribly afraid of knowing the worst. What Dutch never sees, however, is that the story he is investigating—his attempt to find the Irish immigrant girl he seduced—will lead him to a confrontation not only with the mystery of why his father sinned and committed suicide in prison but also with his own failings as husband and lover.

Like *True Confessions*, *Dutch Shea, Jr.* thrives on lively dialogue and shrewd character assessments. It lacks the drive of Dunne's first novel, however, perhaps because it does not have a tightly constructed plot and its themes seem not only derivative of *True Confessions* but also devoid of fresh treatment.

THE RED WHITE AND BLUE

Whereas *True Confessions* centers on Los Angeles and is tightly woven around the tensions between Tom and Des, and *Dutch Shea, Jr.* explores the career of a disaffected and down-and-out lawyer trying to regain a coherent life for himself and a tolerable vision of the world, *The Red White and Blue* functions on a broader canvas, as an ambitious novel that represents Dunne's bid to encompass the epic sweep of contemporary American history. The Broderick family of the novel vaguely resembles the Kennedy family of American politics. Again there is a struggle between two brothers, Bro (another ambitious churchman) and Jack (the less determined screenwriter). Both brothers, however, disappoint their father, Hugh, a kind of Joseph Kennedy figure, the confidant of presidents and other power brokers, an amoral man who finds Bro's talents wasted on the Church and Jack's lack of drive pathetic and almost beneath his notice.

As the novel's narrator, Jack resembles Tom Spellacy, for, as is true of Tom, it is Jack's nearness to power coupled with his distaste for it that makes him both keen observer and critic. Each of the male Brodericks focuses, in turn, on Leah Kaye, a radical attorney whose moral and political principles are opposed to the Brodericks'. Leah becomes sexually involved with all three of the Broderick men, and her personal and political entanglements are further examples of the difficulty of separating the worlds of virtue and vice in Dunne's fiction.

Like *Dutch Shea, Jr.*, *The Red White and Blue* seems a falling off from *True Confessions*. All three novels are immensely polished performances, yet only the first seems original in its intensity and language, while the second seems repetitive and the third too diffuse. The machinations of the Brodericks are less intricate and tawdry than those of their real-life models, the Kennedys.

PLAYLAND

Dunne's fourth novel represents a recovery of the author's full novelistic powers. It not only has the intensity of *True Confessions* but also manages to incorporate the broader canvas that seems too thin in *The Red White and Blue*. Jack Broderick is the narrator, and Dunne puts his own experience as a Hollywood screenwriter into full play, as Jack sets off on a quest to find the reclusive Blue Tyler, a child star of the 1930's rumored to be living in a trailer park in Hamtramck, Michigan.

As Jack is researching Tyler's life and interviewing her, he is negotiating with Hollywood producer Marty Magnin to turn the project into a film. Bits of screenplay are interwoven throughout the narrative, as Broderick writes and rewrites Tyler's life, realizing that he is often speculating, turning guesses into narrative even as he tries to resist the Hollywood touches on which his producer insists.

Playland's gangster character, Jacob King, is reminiscent of Fitzgerald's Jay Gatsby, and Jack's quest to understand the King-Tyler love affair by interviewing various witnesses also calls to mind the 1941 film *Citizen Kane*. The humor, sex, and violence are as crude as in the cheapest crime novels, but Jack's desire to get the story right, even as he realizes there cannot be a single authentic version, elevates *Playland* to the ranks of the most distinguished works about Hollywood, including Fitzgerald's *The Last Tycoon* and Norman Mailer's play *The Deer Park* (pb. 1967). *Playland* also includes stunning settings in Las Vegas and Detroit, giving the novel the all-encompassing geographic and historical reach that Dunne had been working toward since the brilliant success of *True Confessions*.

NOTHING LOST

Dunne's last novel is set in the small town of Regent, South Midland—apparently a fictional version of South Dakota. At any rate, this heartland setting is the locus for a brutal murder: A well-liked African American man is bludgeoned to death and then stripped of his flesh. Although this would seem an obvious case of a racially motivated crime, in fact the story of Edgar Parlance's gruesome death is far more elusive and ambiguous than either the court system or the press can fathom. The novel's narrator, Max Cline, a prosecutor turned defense attorney, gradually pieces together part of what happened to Parlance, assembling testimony from a cast of characters with varying degrees of reliability. In the end, vital aspects of the Parlance case remain unresolved in favor of a nuanced and sharply observant portrayal of a people and a place reminiscent of William Faulkner's best work, such as *Absalom, Absalom!* (1936), or of the greatest nonfiction as exemplified in Rebecca West's classic essay "Mr. Setty and Mr. Hume" in *A Train of Powder* (1955).

Cline is a superb choice for a narrator because he has worked for the establishment and yet is an outsider. Jewish and gay, he had only a short-lived career in the attorney general's office, and his switch to defense work makes him a pariah among law-enforcement types and in his community, since he is regarded as protecting the very kinds of criminals he used to incarcerate. Cline sports his outsider credentials wryly, so that while he may irritate the establishment, nothing in his behavior actually can be charged with causing offense. He thus insinuates himself into the action, so to speak, avoiding confrontations but picking up bits of evidence overlooked by the police. In the Parlance case, he has a cocounsel, Teresa Kean, whose own story and affair with J. J. McClure, the prosecutor and ostensibly her adversary, complicates Cline's work but also leads him closer to the reality of what happened to Parlance.

Cline works with the sensibility of a novelist. Indeed, it has been noted that Cline's voice resembles the one Dunne employed in his nonfiction. Perhaps because Cline has been the object of hate and ridicule, he is slow to sit in judgment of McClure's and Kean's unethical behavior and Kean's efforts to hide her affair from Cline. Kean, like Duane Lajoie, the man she is defending, is the product of a fraught background and of forces she ultimately finds it impossible to control.

Not much more can be said of the plot of *Nothing Lost* without giving away the secrets Cline so assiduously explores. Suffice it to say that a number of critics have asserted that *Nothing Lost* is Dunne's finest novel. It has been compared to the best work of John D.

MacDonald and John O'Hara because of Dunne's sure handling of both the novel's mystery elements and its social observations.

Carl Rollyson

OTHER MAJOR WORKS

SCREENPLAYS: *The Panic in Needle Park*, 1971 (with Joan Didion); *Play It as It Lays*, 1972 (with Didion); *A Star Is Born*, 1976 (with Didion); *True Confessions*, 1981 (with Didion); *The War*, 1994 (with Didion); *Up Close and Personal*, 1996 (with Didion).

TELEPLAYS: *Hills Like White Elephants*, 1990; *L.A. Is It*, 1991.

NONFICTION: *Delano: The Story of the California Grape Strike*, 1967 (revised 1971); *The Studio*, 1969; *Vegas: A Memoir of a Dark Season*, 1974; *Quintana and Friends*, 1978; *Harp*, 1989; *Crooning: A Collection*, 1990; *Monster: Living off the Big Screen*, 1997; *Regards: The Selected Nonfiction of John Gregory Dunne*, 2006.

BIBLIOGRAPHY

Dunne, John Gregory. *Harp*. New York: Simon & Schuster, 1989. Dunne's memoir is one of the best sources available for both biographical information on the author and insight into the sources and themes of his fiction.

Edwards, Thomas R. "The Awful Truth." *The New York Review of Books*, June 24, 2004. Long, thoughtful review of *Nothing Lost* takes into account the entire trajectory of Dunne's career. Provides especially perceptive discussion of the connections between Dunne's fiction and his nonfiction.

Fanning, Charles. *The Irish Voice in America: 250 Years of Irish-American Fiction*. 2d ed. Lexington: University Press of Kentucky, 2000. Comprehensive scholarly work includes discussion of Dunne as an Irish American writer.

Keane, James. T. "Savagery in South Midland." *America*, February 21, 2005. Review of *Nothing Lost* commends Dunne for creating a notable cast of characters and for his satiric portrayal of the American media as well as of the conniving practices of both local, state, and national politicians.

Thomson, David. "*Playland*." *The New Republic*, August 22, 1994. Highly critical review of the novel includes an astute assessment of Dunne's style and his handling of Hollywood themes.

Winchell, Mark Roydon. *Joan Didion*. Rev. ed. Boston: Twayne, 1989. Includes brief discussion of Dunne's work and the Dunne-Didion marriage. Chapter 1 provides a good overview of Dunne's and Didion's reactions to the American East and West Coasts in their writing.

_____. *John Gregory Dunne*. Boise, Idaho: Boise State University Press, 1986. Brief work provides a solid introduction to Dunne's biography and to the backgrounds of his fiction. Discusses only the first two novels and Dunne's early nonfiction. Includes a useful bibliography.

KEN FOLLETT

Born: Cardiff, Wales; June 5, 1949
Also known as: Symon Myles; Zachary Stone; Bernard L. Ross; Martin Martinsen

PRINCIPAL LONG FICTION

The Big Black, 1974 (as Symon Myles)
The Big Needle, 1974 (as Myles; also known as *The Big Apple*, 1975)
The Big Hit, 1975 (as Myles)
The Shakeout, 1975
Amok: King of Legend, 1976 (as Bernard L. Ross)
The Bear Raid, 1976
The Modigliani Scandal, 1976 (as Zachary Stone)
Paper Money, 1977 (as Stone)
Capricorn One, 1978 (as Ross)
The Eye of the Needle, 1978 (also known as *Storm Island*)
Triple, 1979
The Key to Rebecca, 1980
The Man from St. Petersburg, 1982
Lie Down with Lions, 1985
The Pillars of the Earth, 1989
Night over Water, 1991
A Dangerous Fortune, 1993
Pillars of the Almighty, 1994
A Place Called Freedom, 1995
The Third Twin, 1996
The Hammer of Eden, 1998
Code to Zero, 2000
Jackdaws, 2001
Hornet Flight, 2002
Whiteout, 2004
World Without End, 2007

OTHER LITERARY FORMS

In addition to his many novels, Ken Follett (FAHL-iht) has written nonfiction, including *On Wings of Eagles* (1983), about American businessman Ross Perot's 1979 rescue of two corporate executives imprisoned in Tehran, Iran; screenplays such as *Fringe Banking* (1978) and *A Football Star* (1979); and children's stories such as *The Secret of Kellerman's Studio* (1976) and *The Power Twins and the Worm Puzzle: A Science Fantasy for Young People* (1976).

ACHIEVEMENTS

Among the youngest millionaire authors, Ken Follett has created best sellers characterized by clear-cut prose with multiple subplots and characters. Set amid chaotic sociopolitical milieus, these works suggest the conflicts of an age or of a historical period through the plight of individuals, and depend on ordinary women rising to life's challenges with strength, fortitude, and vision. Follett was not yet thirty years old when he wrote his novel *The Eye of the Needle*, an international success that sold more than ten million copies, was translated into twenty-five languages, won the Edgar Award of the Mystery Writers of America (1979), and was made into a 1981 United Artists film of the same title starring Kate Nelligan and Donald Sutherland. Other film adaptations include two television miniseries (*The Key to Rebecca* in 1985 and *On Wings of Eagles* in 1986) as well as a 1997 television adaptation of *The Third Twin* (to which CBS purchased the rights for $1.4 million).

By 1989, Follett had more than ninety million readers worldwide. In 2003, as part of the British Broadcasting Corporation series *The Big Read*, the British public voted *The Pillars of the Earth* one of that nation's one hundred best-loved novels. Follett received an honorary doctorate from Exeter University in 2008.

BIOGRAPHY

Kenneth Martin Follett was born in Cardiff, Wales, on June 5, 1949, the son of Lavinia C. Evans and Martin D. Follett. His father worked as an inland revenue clerk and then as a lecturer training tax inspectors. Follett's conservative Christian parents barred television in the home and disapproved of films. There were few books in the Follett home, but the young Follett read avidly the works available in the public library. His family moved to London in 1959. At the age of eighteen, Follett married Mary Emma Ruth Elson, who was pregnant, so their son (Emanuele) would not be born out of wedlock. Elson then worked as a bookkeeper, while Follett studied philosophy at the University of London, becoming involved in left-wing politics, participating in anti-Vietnam War and antiapartheid rallies, and graduating in 1970. He worked as a reporter and rock music columnist for the *South Wales Echo* (Cardiff) until 1973, when his daughter Marie-Claire was born, then switched for one year to covering Scotland Yard and crime in general for the *Evening News* (London) before turning his hand to fiction because of financial necessity.

Follett's first novel, *The Big Needle*, a murder mystery in which the father of a comatose drug user brings down heroin dealers, paid for Follett's car repairs and rent. He went to work for a small London publisher, Everest Books, to find out how to write moneymaking books. After being promoted to deputy managing director in 1976 and writing nine more books (at five thousand dollars per book), some under the pseudonyms Symon Myles, Zachary Stone, and Bernard L. Ross, he finally learned how to turn mediocre novels into popular novels. U.S. literary agent Al Zuckerman, whose correspondence included detailed statements of what Follett was doing wrong and what changes he could make to succeed in the U.S. book market, helped the young writer on the path to becoming a popular novelist. The best work of this period is *The Modigliani Scandal*, a classic caper story about a forged masterpiece and risqué European lifestyles.

Follett finally made his breakthrough with *The Eye of the Needle*, which brought him the fame and fortune needed to retire from journalism and to live comfortably in Surrey. Taxes in the 83 percent bracket, however, drove him to Grasse, France, for a few years. Upon his return, he became involved in Labour Party activities and met Barbara Broer, a Labour official and later a parliamentarian who involved him more deeply in politics. He divorced Elson in September, 1985, and married Broer in November of the same year. He played bass guitar for the bands Damn Right I've Got the Blues and ClogIron and has served as president of the Dyslexia Institute.

ANALYSIS

Though he has varied his writing pattern over the years, Ken Follett often concentrates on a time of international crisis (revolution, war, bank failures, plague, terrorist attacks), then creates a fictive exploration of what could have happened. He mixes invented characters with historical figures and invented action with historical records before returning to some type of epilogue that teases the reader with reference to an actual news story or historical text (like the defeat of the Germans in North Africa during World War II or a newspaper notification of a significant death). His family crises often parallel national or international crises, and middle or working-class outsiders rise to the occasion and dramatically outperform the aristocrats. An impoverished miner or circus performer might gain influence and transform society by behaving with compassion or defending a just cause.

Follett has been proud of his craft and versatility; he has tried new ideas and striven to improve his work. After a series of successful spy thrillers depicting resourceful agents, Follett turned to historical novels, then in the 1990's returned to modern stories centered on high-tech equipment. In the first decade of the twenty-first century, he wrote about World War II, the fourteenth century, biological terrorism, and Cold War espionage. He includes strong heroines who thrive in tough times, and his ongoing goal as a writer has been to produce works in the middle ground between the serious and the popular.

THE EYE OF THE NEEDLE

The Eye of the Needle is a tightly constructed spy story about Germany's long-term top spy in England, Heinrich von Müller-Güden, codenamed Die Nadel (the Needle). Under the alias Henry Faber, this master spy, a dispassionate loner scornful of German authorities and the National Socialist Party, has discovered dummy aircraft and plywood tanks that mean the Allies will invade at Normandy, not Pas-de-Calais, France. He must board a U-boat and take his photographic evidence to Adolf Hitler.

Faber flees aboard a stolen craft that wrecks on Storm Island off the coast of Aberdeen,

Scotland, pursued by medievalist professor Percival Godliman and former Scotland Yard inspector Frederick Bloggs. Bloggs blames Faber's spy reports for his wife's death in a German bombing raid. On the island Faber encounters Lucy and Dave Rose, a dysfunctional couple whose wedding was closely followed by a traffic accident in which David lost both his legs. Lucy and Faber, both emotionally deprived, find kinship and release in each other's arms. Dave, an embittered sheep farmer who has been sexually estranged from his wife since the accident, discovers Faber's photographic negatives and fights him to the death along a cliff top. Lucy remains composed, has sex with Faber, then flees with her son to radio for help. When caught, she axes Faber's hand, knocks out the radio, then shoots Faber when she overtakes him on the beach. In doing so, this lonely, isolated woman determines the fate of millions of people. By humanizing Faber (he falsifies information to save St. Paul's Cathedral from German bombs), Follett establishes a pattern that has become his trademark: balanced portraits of characters on opposite sides of a conflict; understandable villains and flawed heroes.

TRIPLE

Set one year after the Six Day War of June, 1967, *Triple* builds on a striking real-life news story—a 1968 heist of two hundred tons of uranium (enough for thirty nuclear bombs)—to explore a hypothetical explanation of how and why Israel acquired nuclear materials for its weapons program. A newspaper clipping at novel's end suggests readers have the backstory of a world news event. The novel postulates that Israeli intelligence officers, shocked by Egypt's nuclear capability, hijacked the shipload of uranium.

Mossad agent Nat Dickstein, a master of disguise committed to a Jewish homeland, nonetheless loves an attractive Arab woman, Suza Ashford. As Dickstein, aided by a wartime buddy who is now a Mafia don, puts a clever plan in play, a Palestinian triple agent for the Egyptians and Soviets—and a fedayeen, or freedom fighter—Yasif Hassan, and a Russian, David Rostov, seek to thwart the plan. In the process, Dickstein rescues Ashford from Rostov after a hair-raising high-seas chase and sinks the interfering Russian vessel. Follett provides Israeli and Palestinian perspectives, with the Mossad agent suffering strong doubts about his assignment and the Palestinian disturbed at endangering old friends (he went to Oxford with Dickstein and Rostov).

THE KEY TO REBECCA

Set in wartime Cairo and the north African desert lands that German field marshal Erwin Rommel's World War II forces controlled, *The Key to Rebecca* is one of Follett's best works. It is based on the exploits of the real German spy, John Eppler, at the time of Rommel's 1942 move on Alexandria. This well-written, satisfying spy story pits a capable, good-hearted British military intelligence officer against a cruel, psychologically complex spy codenamed Sphinx, who feeds Rommel detailed troop movements. The plot turns on the deciphering of the German spy's secret code, features a young Anwar Sadat, satirizes British *pukka sahibs*, and brings to life the interplay between Cairenes—those from Cairo—and British.

THE MAN FROM ST. PETERSBURG

Set in London just before World War I and amid Russian expatriates, *The Man from St. Petersburg* unravels a Russian anarchist's scheme to keep Russia from signing a treaty supporting England against Germany by assassinating the czarist negotiator. The earl of Walden, who hosts the Russian prince and handles Anglo-Russian treaty negotiations, faces major obstacles, with which a young Winston Churchill assists. The story's focus on eighteen-year-old Lady Charlotte Walden, who rejects her aristocratic roots and plunges into middle-class horrors, brings to the forefront the suffragist movement. In this tale, which is less credible than other Follett stories, the central character is both hero and villain.

LIE DOWN WITH LIONS

Lie Down with Lions depicts the clash of values at work in Afghanistan during the Russian occupation of that country in the 1980's. The idealistic heroine, whose doctor husband spies on Afghan freedom fighters for the Soviets while supposedly engaged in humanitarian relief efforts, has an affair with Central Intelligence Agency operative Ellis Thaler, a 1960's radical poet who hates his new job. Erotic scenes counter images of intolerant Muslim chauvinism, as when the pregnant heroine, upon seeing a young Afghan lose his hand to a mine, wraps the wound with her blouse and then is beaten by Afghanis angry at her exposed upper torso. When she goes into premature labor as a result, an untrained midwife colors the heroine's forehead blue to combat evil spirits before delivering her daughter. The novel even includes a bibliography of Follett's sources.

THE PILLARS OF THE EARTH

The Pillars of the Earth, a massive historical romance, broke new territory for Follett, who considers this his finest work. Very precise details about the forty-year building of a medieval cathedral are the centerpiece of a wide-ranging study of the human sacrifices necessitated by such a monumental effort. Set in the twelfth century, the story depicts the murder of Thomas Beckett, the whipping of Henry II, and the struggle for the Crown as the prior, his master builder, and their community toil on, carving out a living for themselves amid the looting and pillaging of the time.

NIGHT OVER WATER

A wartime thriller, *Night over Water* takes place aboard the last transatlantic voyage of a luxurious Pan American clipper plane bound from Southampton to the United States on the eve of war. Its passenger list provides intriguing subplots even as the plane heads for disaster, a planned crash landing off the coast of Maine facilitated by a blackmailed flight engineer whose wife has been kidnapped. Opposites clashing on board (a Nazi sympathizer and a Jewish scientist, an American gangster and his federal escort, a Russian princess and a jewel thief) make for a tense thirty hours.

A DANGEROUS FORTUNE

A Dangerous Fortune traces several generations of the Pilasters, a late nineteenth century banking family, whose rise to social position and wealth ends with the failure of their bank. Responsible for the failure are the unscrupulous Augusta Pilaster, family matriarch, who contrives to raise her personal fortune and prestige and ruin her enemies; her dissolute son, Edward, whose sexual obsessions result in a deadly sexually transmitted disease, but not before he has entangled the bank in a disastrous South American scheme; and the unscrupulous son of a brutal, power-hungry South American businessman, Micky Miranda, who uses multiple murders and seduction of mother and son to bend the Pilasters to his will.

Hugh Pilaster's instinct for business and strong work ethic make him the only truly reliable member of his extended family, but the failure of his father's bank makes him the poor relation. A number of lives are interlocked by the unexplained death of an English schoolboy, the first in a series of murders disguised as accidents. The novel deals head-on with nineteenth century British anti-Semitism, homosexuality, and the potential horrors of arranged marriages while providing a Pygmalion tale of a Polish-Jewish circus performer-cum-bareback-rider who becomes a woman of prominence and influence among the London aristocracy.

A PLACE CALLED FREEDOM

In *A Place Called Freedom* a young Scotsman flees the permanent servitude in the mines that will result if he continues to work past the age of twenty-one (a regional tradition for youngsters born to mining families, one unsupported by law). He flees to London, encounters more difficulties when he tries to break a monopoly, and is transported as an indentured slave to the American colonies, where he works on a tobacco plantation. He arrives around the time of the American Revolution and gets caught up in the fervor of the struggle for human rights in Virginia.

THE THIRD TWIN

The Third Twin delves into the darker possibilities of biotechnology and genetic research. A university professor, studying twins to test whether or not criminality is genetic, finds the nature-nurture debate played out in the case of law student Steven Logan, accused of sadistic rapes on a peaceful Maryland college campus. His murderous twin is already in jail, but the possibility of a third identical brother raises questions, including: Has Logan been cloned and, if so, by whom?

THE HAMMER OF EDEN

In *The Hammer of Eden*, a radical California cult leader named Priest, upon learning that a power plant, dam, and lake will be constructed above his secret commune and its vineyards, retaliates by stealing a seismic vibrator from an oil company and producing earthquakes that threaten San Francisco. Throughout the story, Follett tries to make understandable Priest's actions.

CODE TO ZERO

Code to Zero takes place in 1958, at the height of the Cold War and on the eve of the first launch of a U.S. satellite, Explorer I. The head scientist wakes up with artificially induced amnesia and must recover his life and memories step-by-step to thwart the Russians, who have him under surveillance to prevent the launch. Not knowing whom to trust or where to turn, he experiences flashbacks that gradually permit him to piece together his past and understand his present.

JACKDAWS

Jackdaws, a wartime thriller in the tradition of the E. M. Nathanson novel *The Dirty Dozen* (1965), pits a female team of six (including a crack shot, an explosives expert, and a cross-dressing telephone operator) against the Gestapo and Nazi intelligence officers. A British agent and a French Resistance leader attack a telephone exchange but fail to cut off German military communications for the region. With D day just days away, the British agent is airdropped into France with her unlikely team (French-speaking Englishwomen with specialized skills), this time to get the job done. They pose as a local cleaning detail and dismantle the telephone exchange.

HORNET FLIGHT

Hornet Flight is an exciting World War II story of Danish amateurs and resistance fighters trying to figure out exactly where the Germans have hidden their new technology: radar stations that identify British bombing formations to facilitate their annihilation. Eighteen-year-old physics student Harald Olufsen, inspired by his brother's wartime efforts as a Danish military pilot, stumbles upon what the British have been seeking, takes photographs, and eventually restores the Hornet's Moth of the title (a wood-and-linen biplane) to carry the evidence and his Jewish girlfriend to England, despite the efforts of local collaborators, such as a Danish police detective who uses cooperation with the Germans to take on longtime family enemies, the Olufsens. Follett demonstrates the insidious ease with which the conquered yielded to German ways, persecuting Jews and enforcing rigid regulations that intimidated the local population.

WHITEOUT

In *Whiteout*, biological terrorism strikes over a wintry Christmas holiday in northern Scotland, as the security head of a boutique pharmaceuticals company discovers two doses of an experimental drug—a potential cure for a deadly virus—stolen from her top-secret laboratory along with a sample of the virus. The associates of the gambling-addicted son of the company's founder have committed the robbery. The son, who is deeply in debt to a mobster, plans to sell the drugs and leave the country. Amid complicated family intrigue, all end up at the Oxenford family estate, trapped by a blizzard, fighting over the stolen materials at midnight on Christmas Eve. This is not a cozy mystery.

WORLD WITHOUT END

World Without End begins two centuries after the completion of the cathedral built in *The Pillars of the Earth*, with the cathedral and priory again at the crossroads of new ideas in conflict with old and the novel set against the backdrop of the Black Plague. According to Follett, the twelfth century monastery, once a positive force for good in medieval society, encouraging education and technological advance, became a wealthy, conservative opponent of change in the fourteenth century. Four children from different social classes witness a murder that affects each differently; between 1327 and 1361, these four become a peasant's wife, a knight, a builder, and a nun, respectively, whose stories the novel traces as it explores continuity and change. Varied topics include the evolution of cloth weaving, the French-English Wars, the corruption of the clergy, and the cruelty and greed of nobles.

Gina Macdonald

OTHER MAJOR WORKS

SCREENPLAYS: *Fringe Banking*, 1978; *A Football Star*, 1979 (with John Sealey); *Lie Down with Lions*, 1988 (adaptation of his novel).

NONFICTION: *The Heist of the Century*, 1978 (with René Louis Maurice; as *The Gentlemen of 16 July*, 1980; revised as *Under the Streets of Nice: The Bank Heist of the Century*, 1986); *On Wings of Eagles*, 1983.

CHILDREN'S/YOUNG ADULT LITERATURE: *The Power Twins and the Worm Puzzle: A Science Fantasy for Young People*, 1976 (as Martin Martinsen); *The Secret of Kellerman's Studio*, 1976; *The Mystery Hideout*, 1991.

BIBLIOGRAPHY

Dean, John W. "Occupational Hazards." *The New York Times Book Review*, January 14, 2001. Dean, a former White House counsel, examines credibility in the works of Follett and fellow novelist Richard North Patterson.

Ramet, Carlos, and Marshall William Fishwick. *Ken Follett: The Transformation of a Writer*. Bowling Green, Ohio: Bowling Green State University Popular Press, 1999. Ramet focuses on the artistic precursors and cultural implications of Follett's literary canon.

Turner, Richard Charles. *Ken Follett: A Critical Companion*. Westport, Conn.: Greenwood Press, 1996. A thorough study of Follett's life, literary influences, and major works, including various critical approaches to his works.

Van Teeffelen, Toine Van. "(Ex)communicating Palestine: From Best-Selling Terrorist Fiction to Real-Life Personal Accounts." *Studies in the Novel* 36, no. 3 (2004): 438-458. Van Teeffelen compares various writers' stories and representations of Palestine and Palestinians, including those of Follett in *Triple*.

FREDERICK FORSYTH

Born: Ashford, Kent, England; August 25, 1938
Also known as: Frederick McCarthy Forsyth

PRINCIPAL LONG FICTION

The Day of the Jackal, 1971
The Odessa File, 1972
The Dogs of War, 1974
The Devil's Alternative, 1979
The Fourth Protocol, 1984
The Negotiator, 1989
The Deceiver, 1991
The Fist of God, 1994
Icon, 1996
The Phantom of Manhattan, 1999
Avenger, 2003
The Afghan, 2006

OTHER LITERARY FORMS

Frederick Forsyth (FOHR-sith) has written and edited short fiction, including *The Shepherd* (1975), one of his most popular short stories. He wrote the screenplay for the 1987 film version of his novel *The Fourth Protocol*. His book sequel to the musical opera *The Phantom of the Opera* (1986), *The Phantom of Manhattan*, is the story of the phantom striking it rich on Wall Street and recruiting his beloved Christine de Chagney to sing at his own opera house. He also has written nonfiction, including *The Biafra Story* (1969), a work based on his experiences in Nigeria. The book was revised as *The Making of an African Legend: The Biafra Story* (1983). He also wrote the biographical *Emeka* (1982; a story of Biafrin president Chukwuemeka Odumegwu Ojukwu) and *I Remember: Reflections on Fishing in Childhood* (1995).

ACHIEVEMENTS

Frederick Forsyth created a new kind of fiction, the docudrama, combining journalistic immediacy, precise technical detail, and the fast-paced, suspenseful style of popular thrillers. More than thirty million copies of his books have been sold. *Avenger, Icon, The Fourth Protocol, The Day of the Jackal, The Odessa File*, and *The Dogs of War* have been made into films. *The Day of the Jackal* received the Edgar Award from the Mystery Writers of America (1971).

BIOGRAPHY

Frederick McCarthy Forsyth, the son of Frederick William Forsyth and Phyllis Green Forsyth, was born in Ashford, Kent, England, on August 25, 1938. His father taught him to love maps and to find the world's trouble spots on those maps, and he told him exciting stories about Borneo headhunters and tiger shoots. Forsyth attended the Tonbridge School in Kent and loves language (he speaks French, German, Spanish, and some Russian and Italian). He quit school at the age of seventeen.

Having qualified for his pilot's license in a Tiger Moth biplane, Forsyth joined the Royal Air Force (RAF) in 1956 and learned to fly a Vampire jet, becoming at the age of nineteen the youngest fighter pilot in the RAF. Two years later, he left the military to work as a journalist for the *Eastern Daily Press* in Norfolk before joining the international news service Reuters and being posted to Paris. There he covered the campaign against French president Charles de Gaulle, the inspiration for his first novel, *The Day of the Jackal*. Forsyth became chief reporter of the Reuters East Berlin bureau, covering East Germany, Czechoslovakia, and Hungary. In 1965, he joined the British Broadcasting Corporation as a radio reporter and then was assistant diplomatic correspondent for BBC television and assigned to cover the Nigerian civil war. The conflict between the official British stance on the war (motivated by Nigeria's rich oil fields) and his personal sympathy with starving Biafrans in general and their leader, Colonel Ojukwu, in particular led to disillusionment. Having offended Sir David Hunt, British high commissioner in Lagos, Forsyth resigned his position, became a freelance journalist, and recorded his war observations, which became his first book *The Biafra Story*. He also helped illegally fly food to save half a million African children.

Forsyth's *The Day of the Jackal*, recounting French political intrigue, was published two years later, followed quickly by *The Odessa File* and *The Dogs of War*. These three novels made his reputation and allowed him to live well, though high English taxes drove him out of the country, first to Spain for one year, then to Ireland, near Dublin, for five years. Returning to England in 1980, he settled in a fashionable section of London with his wife, Carole Forsyth, and their two sons, Frederick and Shane. He later divorced and was remarried. His memoir, *I Remember*, discusses his favorite pastime, fishing, which provides the author with the calm he needs for thinking through his plots.

ANALYSIS

Frederick Forsyth's financially lucrative suspense thrillers set a technically trained professional on, variously, a collision course with a lone-wolf killer, a secret organization, or deadly representatives of a rogue branch of a government bureaucracy; the novels quicken their pace as characters travel widely across national boundaries, experiencing new geographies, customs, and points of view. The shared competence of protagonist and antagonist means readers learn how to do everything from building a bomb or other specialized weapon to correctly employing distinctive Arab gestures to signal regional origins. Forsyth provides the thrill of insider knowledge about current events and a meaningful pattern that unites seemingly disparate news stories. Journalism taught Forsyth how to insinuate into his fiction a persuasive semblance of reality, provide a broad context and significance for seemingly minor incidents, and make credible and seemingly authentic descriptions of events behind the headlines. Plot and structure create suspense and drive the action forward.

Despite attempts to interject feminine perspectives in his later works, Forsyth's stories depend on an underlying sense of shared male interests and attitudes. He told John Mortimer of the *The Times* of London what he aims for in his fiction—depicting the immoral committing immoral acts no different from those committed by an immoral establishment—so compellingly told that at least four copycat crimes have been associated with his books.

THE DAY OF THE JACKAL

The Day of the Jackal tracks the movement of the real, infamous international assassin Carlos the Jackal, a mythic figure thought to have tried to assassinate Charles de Gaulle because de Gaulle supported Algerian independence. (Carlos the Jackal lives on in the works of Robert Ludlum and others.) The novel establishes strategies that became Forsyth's signature: alternating plot lines that promote suspense as the different parties move closer and closer to a deadly encounter, admiration for technically competent professionals, and a contrast between the professional and the amateur.

Forsyth spends a great deal of time on trivial details that prove essential (such as passport forgery), contingency plans that come into play, and logical responses to tight situations. He enables readers to see the action from the perspective of a committed assassin and to appreciate his expertise. Ultimately, however, Commissioner Claude Lebel, a thorough professional, thwarts the Jackal's plan and saves de Gaulle.

THE ODESSA FILE

The Odessa File draws on real-life attempts to track Nazi war criminals. The former SS concentration camp commandant tracked in this story is Captain Eduard Roschmann, a historical figure whose actions Forsyth describes with accuracy. In this story, German crime reporter Peter Miller proves his investigative competence as he skillfully deals with the anti-Nazi underground and the Odessa organization (former members of the SS). Readers learn a great deal about the Holocaust and about the Jewish pursuit of Nazis connected with the concentration camps of World War II.

THE DOGS OF WAR

The Dogs of War is based on Forsyth's Biafran experiences and his indirect involvement in an attempted coup against then-president of Equatorial Guinea, Francisco Macías Nguema. The story depicts attempts to bring down an Idi Amin-like African dictator. The initial motivation is not sympathy for suffering citizens but a desire to take over newly discovered deposits of platinum. Sir James Manson, a British mining company director, hires mercenary Cat Shannon to depose the tyrant and establish a puppet government. Manson plans to take over mining rights, but Shannon and his crew develop a conscience and support the citizens over the greedy, self-interested Manson and the multinational corporations he represents. During this process, readers learn much about the financing and operation of gunrunning, mortar-shell trajectories, and more.

THE DEVIL'S ALTERNATIVE

Unlike its predecessors, *The Devil's Alternative* describes a fictional terrorist takeover of an oil-filled supertanker that leaves no viable alternative: Yielding to terrorist demands could set off a nuclear war; refusing to yield will create the biggest oil spill in history. Typical of Forsyth, real political figures are present, and are thinly disguised: Joan Carpenter as British prime minister Margaret Thatcher, Bill Matthews as U.S. president Jimmy Carter, Stanislaw Poklewski as U.S. national security adviser Zbigniew Brzezinski, and David Lawrence as U.S. secretary of state Cyrus Vance.

The plot features Jewish Ukrainian nationalists with good cause to strike against the Soviet Union. The nationalists are acting at the same time that plant failures lead to fungicide poisoning of the Soviet wheat crop. Failed harvests drive hardliners to contemplate invading Western Europe and the United States to offer food in exchange for military concessions. British security agent Adam Munro finds himself putting a Russian woman he loves at risk to glean insider information to resolve this dilemma.

THE FOURTH PROTOCOL

The Fourth Protocol takes its title from a so-called gentleman's agreement not to take portable nuclear weapons into enemy territory. In this case, the violators of protocol are a rogue Soviet group determined to change the direction of British and Western politics by detonating a small atomic device at a U.S. airbase in England. By blaming the Americans, they hope to put the antinuclear Labour Party in power. The novel includes a memorandum on how British Labour Party politics play into Soviet plans.

To accomplish their goals, the rogue Soviets have put into play a lone-wolf assassin tracked by a nondescript but highly competent police officer. The plot alternates between the two characters in typical Forsyth style, closing the distance for the final encounter. The ease with which a small nuclear bomb can be assembled and employed is shocking, and this plot device became a staple of popular fiction and film, raising legitimate concerns.

THE NEGOTIATOR

Before the novel reached print, the intricate plot of *The Negotiator* was dated by the real-world end of the Soviet Union, a hazard of topical fiction. In this story, Soviet president Mikhail Gorbachev and U.S. president John Cormack negotiate an unprecedented disarmament treaty, cutting arms and military costs by half and ushering in true peace. Conservative Texans and Soviets dependent on a confrontational status quo to retain national pride and power join forces to kidnap and threaten to execute the president's only son. Low-key hostage negotiator Quinn joins federal agent Samantha Somerville to undermine these villains, but negotiations fail, and these two chase and romance their way through Europe, always a little behind the malefactors and plot organizers. Ironically, Quinn and Somerville end up in a wintry Vermont wilderness in alliance with supportive Russian agents after the same villains, and Russians, Americans, and British join forces to defeat the criminals in their respective secret services.

The Deceiver

The Deceiver reflects nostalgically on the Cold War when heroes and villains were more clearly recognizable, their political positions predictably nationalistic. The novel challenges the assertion that perestroika ushered in peaceful coexistence, ending international crises and the need for the derring-do of traditional spies.

The deceiver of the title, aging British agent Sam McCready, began his career as a field agent, rose rapidly through the ranks, and now heads the Deception, Disinformation, and Psychological Operations desk of the Secret Intelligence Service. However, forced retirement is in the offing. McCready challenges accusations that his type of spying is outmoded by East-West cooperation, requesting that his service record be reexamined. The resultant hearings request that he recount and defend the most notorious of his past exploits: four stories divided by Interludes. These stories describe a clandestine crossing of the Berlin Wall, encounters with Russian defectors and Irish Republican Army arms smugglers, and engagements with a far-reaching terrorist network. McCready retires at about the same time that Iraqi dictator Saddam Hussein invades Kuwait, Forsyth's reminder that spies such as McCready will always be needed to provide intelligence and confront enemies behind the scenes.

The Fist of God

The Fist of God focuses on the West's lack of intelligence information about Hussein's closed Iraq and its troop strength and deployment before the Persian Gulf War. To provide insider information about that country, daring British operative Mike Martin of Britain's elite Special Air Service Regiment draws on his childhood experience in the region to go underground as an Arab militant and try to contact a Mossad plant, codenamed Jericho, who is a deep-cover mole in the Baghdad establishment. Once on the move in Iraq, however, Martin discovers more at stake than up-to-date intelligence.

Hussein has an ultimate secret weapon, probably nuclear, codenamed Fist of God—a doomsday bomb to ignite the Middle East. As the novel shifts rapidly from Washington, D.C., and London to Baghdad and Kuwait (Martin's entryway), Martin skates on the edge of discovery and, in the best spy tradition, achieves much with little. Forsyth takes readers behind bland governmental bulletins to demonstrate how real intelligence is gleaned and how behind-the-scenes battles are waged.

ICON

Icon is the story of right-wing Russian fanatic Igor Komarov, who poses as a moderate to seize power but whose neo-Nazi document, the Black Manifesto, exposes his real plans for the nation if elected. A moment of carelessness places the secret document in the hands of a Jewish janitor, who, horrified, passes it on to an American embassy diplomat. Komarov willingly risks all to retrieve this potentially damaging document, while British and U.S. agents and diplomats debate whether or not it is genuine. Former CIA operative Jason Monk returns to Moscow in disguise, where former master British spy runner Nigel Irvine and a Chechen warlord Irvine had once saved help him track down the janitor and tie together the threads of evidence that damn Komarov.

AVENGER

The avenger of this novel's title is Cal Dexter, a Vietnam tunnel rat turned small-town New Jersey attorney and vigilante pursuer who proves unable to save his murdered daughter but is now adept at stalking villains. A billionaire Canadian mining magnate hires Dexter to bring to trial Serbian warlord and mass murderer Zoran Zilic, who brutally butchered the Canadian's idealistic grandson (an aid worker in Bosnia). After searching the United Arab Emirates, Dexter finds Zilic hiding out in a jungle compound in the fictional South American Republic of San Martin, protected by hired security guards and U.S. agents. In the weeks leading up to September 11, 2001, the FBI recruits Zilic to kill Osama Bin Laden, and Dexter pursues Zilic as Zilic pursues Bin Laden. The novel ends on September 10, 2001.

THE AFGHAN

In *The Afghan*, Mike Martin of *The Fist of God* returns from retirement for an even more dangerous mission: to disguise himself as Taliban leader Izmat Khan (imprisoned at Guantanamo Bay) and infiltrate al-Qaeda to learn of a planned strike. Dark-skinned Martin looks like Khan and speaks his language, but he still must convince true believers that he is indeed one of them, anxious to make up for time wasted in prison.

Place, manners, and customs ring true, including a description of the November, 2001, battle to recapture Fort Qala-i-Jangi in northern Afghanistan, highlighting the role of six British Special Boat Service soldiers: Forsyth traveled to Kabul, Islamabad, and Peshawar to collect precise details to bring his story to life. Therein, al-Qaeda plots to bomb world leaders meeting aboard an ocean liner. Their method is to steal and change the shape and name of a small ship, then explode it near the ocean liner outside New York Harbor.

Gina Macdonald and Andrew F. Macdonald

OTHER MAJOR WORKS

SHORT FICTION: *The Shepherd*, 1975; *No Comebacks: Collected Short Stories*, 1982; *Used in Evidence, and Other Stories*, 1998; *The Veteran*, 2001.

SCREENPLAY: *The Fourth Protocol*, 1987 (based on his novel).

NONFICTION: *The Biafra Story*, 1969 (revised as *The Making of an African Legend: The Biafra Story*, 1983); *Emeka*, 1982 (biography of Chukwuemeka Odumegwu Ojukwu); *I Remember: Reflections on Fishing in Childhood*, 1995.

EDITED TEXT: *Great Flying Stories*, 1991.

BIBLIOGRAPHY

Butler, Colin. "The Cold War Revisited." *English Review* 10, no. 1 (September, 1999): 2-8. Butler places Forsyth in the context of other popular Cold War authors, arguing that Forsyth's books are well-constructed documents of their time.

Cabell, Craig. *Frederick Forsyth: A Matter of Protocol*. London: Robson, 2001. An authorized biography of Forsyth and a study of his works. Forsyth was "notoriously reticent" about his own past, yet in this book he is candid about the background to each of his novels and even about his political beliefs.

Jones, Dudley. "Professionalism and Popular Fiction: The Novels of Arthur Hailey and Frederick Forsyth." In *Spy Thrillers: From Buchan to Le Carré*, edited by Clive Bloom. New York: St. Martin's Press, 1990. This chapter in a study of spy thrillers examines Forsyth's contributions to the genre and his focus on experts in conflict.

Leeman, Sue. "Forsyth's Foresight." *Hobart Mercury* (Australia), September 16, 2006. Leeman discusses how Forsyth gathered materials for *The Afghan* and how future events have echoed his fictive predictions.

DASHIELL HAMMETT

Born: St. Mary's County, Maryland; May 27, 1894
Died: New York, New York; January 10, 1961
Also known as: Samuel Dashiell Hammett

PRINCIPAL LONG FICTION

$106,000 Blood Money, 1927 (also known as *Blood Money* and *The Big Knockover*)
Red Harvest, 1927-1928 (serial), 1929 (book)
The Dain Curse, 1928-1929 (serial), 1929 (book)
The Maltese Falcon, 1929-1930 (serial), 1930 (book)
The Glass Key, 1930 (serial), 1931 (book)
Woman in the Dark, 1933 (serial), 1951 (book)
The Thin Man, 1934
Complete Novels, 1999

OTHER LITERARY FORMS

Dashiell Hammett (HAM-eht) first attracted critical attention as the author of short detective fiction published in *Smart Set* and *Black Mask* magazines as early as 1923. The best of his stories were narratives told in the first person by the nameless "Continental Op," a fat, balding operative working out of the San Francisco office of the Continental Detective Agency. The Continental Op is also the narrator and principal character of Hammett's first two novels, both of which were published in magazines before their appearance in book form. A number of his short stories were anthologized in *The Continental Op* (1945) and, after Hammett's death in 1961, *The Big Knockover: Selected Stories and Short Novels* (1966).

ACHIEVEMENTS

Together with his contemporary Raymond Chandler (1888-1959), Dashiell Hammett is credited with defining the form, scope, and tone of the modern detective novel, a distinctly American genre that departs considerably from the earlier tradition inspired by the British. Chandler, although six years Hammett's senior, did not in fact begin publishing detective fiction until 1933 and readily acknowledged the younger writer's prior claim. Together, both authors have exerted considerable influence upon later exponents of the detective genre, notably on Ross Macdonald, their most distinguished successor. Hammett's work in particular has served also as a stylistic model for many novelists working outside the detective genre, among them Ernest Hemingway and John O'Hara.

Unlike his predecessors in the mystery genre, Hammett adopted a starkly realistic, tough-minded tone in his works, sustaining an atmosphere in which questions outnumber

Dashiell Hammett
(Library of Congress)

answers and no one is to be trusted. Hammett's reputation ultimately rests on his creation of two characters who embody the moral ambiguities of the modern world: Sam Spade (*The Maltese Falcon*) and Nick Charles (*The Thin Man*). Widely popularized through film adaptations of the novels in which they appear, Spade and Charles are among the most famous American detectives, known even to those with little more than marginal interest in the mystery genre. Tough-minded if occasionally softhearted, both characters may be seen as particularized refinements of Hammett's Continental Op, professional detectives who remain true to their personal code of honor and skeptical with regard to everything and everyone else.

Partially because of declining health, Hammett wrote no novels after the age of forty. His reputation, however, was by that time secure; even in the following century, his five novels would remain landmarks of the genre, a model for future novelists and a formidable standard of comparison.

BIOGRAPHY

Samuel Dashiell Hammett was born in St. Mary's County, Maryland, on May 27, 1894, into an old but modest Roman Catholic family. Leaving high school at the age of fourteen after less than a year of attendance, Hammett worked indifferently at a variety of odd jobs before signing on with the Pinkerton Detective Agency around the age of twenty. At last, it seemed he had found work that he enjoyed and could do well, with a dedication later reflected in the character and behavior of the Continental Op. With time out for service in World War I, from which he was demobilized as a sergeant, Hammett continued to serve Pinkerton with distinction until failing health caused him to consider other options.

In 1921, Hammett married Josephine Dolan, a nurse whom he had met during one of his recurring bouts with tuberculosis. The couple moved west to San Francisco, where Hammett returned to work for Pinkerton, only to resign in frustration and disgust after an ironic incident in which his detective talents proved too great for his own good: Assigned by Pinkerton to ship out on an Australian freighter in search of stolen gold believed to be hidden aboard, Hammett managed to find the missing gold in a smokestack during a cursory search just prior to departure and was thus denied the anticipated voyage to Australia.

During such spare time as he could find, Hammett had been trying to prepare himself as a writer; upon leaving Pinkerton, he devoted himself increasingly to writing, eventually leaving his family (which by then included two daughters) and moving to a cheap furnished room where he could live and write. Fearing that he had little time left to live, he wrote at a determined pace; encouraged by his first successes, he gradually developed and refined the writing style that was to make him famous. His first story featuring the Continental Op appeared in October, 1923. Increasingly successful, Hammett soon progressed to the writing of longer stories that were in fact independent sections of novels, eventually published as *Red Harvest* and *The Dain Curse*. Both appeared as hardbound editions in 1929. The following year, Hammett achieved both critical recognition and financial independence with *The Maltese Falcon*, an unquestionably mature and groundbreaking work that sold at once to the film industry; director John Huston's landmark 1941 version of *The Maltese Falcon* was the third Hollywood film to be drawn from a Hammett novel.

In 1930, Hammett made the acquaintance of dramatist Lillian Hellman, eleven years his junior, who was to become the most important and influential woman in his life. Although they never married (each was unhappily married to someone else at the time of their first meeting), Hellman and Hammett remained together in an intense, often turbulent, but intellectually rewarding relationship until Hammett's death some thirty years later at the age of sixty-six. *The Thin Man*, Hammett's next and last published novel (*The Glass Key* having already been written by the time he met Hellman), reflects the author's relationship with Hellman in the portrayal of Nick and Nora Charles, represented in the screen version and its sequels by William Powell and Myrna Loy.

Following the success of *The Thin Man* both as book and as film, Hammett moved to Hollywood, where he worked as a writer and script doctor on a variety of screen projects. He became increasingly involved in leftist politics and toward the end of the Depression became a member of the Communist Party. Hammett did not, however, consider his politics an impediment to patriotism; soon after the United States entered World War II, he was back in a sergeant's uniform, despite his advanced age and obviously declining health. Attached to the Signal Corps, he served three years in the Aleutian Islands, where his duties included editing a daily newspaper for his fellow servicemen. By the end of the war, however, his health was more precarious than ever, undermined by years of recurrent tuberculosis and heavy drinking. After an alcoholic crisis in 1948, Hammett forswore drinking for the remainder of his life.

At the same time, Hammett's political past was coming back to haunt him; like his fictional characters, however, he remained loyal to his convictions and his friends, declining to testify against his fellow associates in the Communist Party and other political organizations. In 1951, Hammett spent five months in various prisons for contempt of court as a result of his refusal to testify; around the same time, government authorities determined that he was several years behind in the payment of his income tax. Unable to find work in Hollywood because of his political views, Hammett was further impoverished by the attachment of his remaining income for the payment of back taxes. Increasingly infirm, Hammett spent his last years in the care and company of Hellman. He died at Lenox Hill Hospital in New York City on January 10, 1961.

ANALYSIS

Unlike most of their predecessors in the genre, Dashiell Hammett's detectives live and work, as did Hammett himself, in a world populated with actual criminals who violate the law for tangible personal gain. Significantly, Hammett did all of his creative writing during the years of Prohibition, when lawlessness was rampant and organized crime was rapidly gaining a foothold in the American social structure. Prohibition indeed functions prominently in all of Hammett's published work as background, as atmosphere, and frequently as subject. In *Red Harvest*, Hammett's first novel, a loose confederacy of bootleggers, thieves, and hired killers has set up what appears to be a substitute government, replacing law and order with values of their own; the resulting Hobbesian chaos clearly reflects, however indirectly, Hammett's own developing political consciousness. There is little place in such a world for genteel detectives cast in the mold of Dorothy Sayers's Lord Peter Wimsey; accordingly, Hammett presents in the Continental Op and his successors the kind of detective who can deal routinely and effectively with hardened criminals. As Raymond Chandler observed, "Hammett gave murder back to the kind of people who commit it for reasons."

Within such an evil environment, the sleuth often becomes as devious and mendacious as those whom he is pursuing, remaining faithful nevertheless to a highly personal code of honor and justice. Sam Spade, perhaps the most intriguing of Hammett's literary creations, is so well attuned to the criminal mind that he often appears to be a criminal himself; he is known to have been involved romantically with his partner's wife and is thus a likely suspect after the man is murdered. Still, at the end of *The Maltese Falcon*, he persists in turning over to the authorities the thief and murderer Brigid O'Shaughnessy, despite an acknowledged mutual attraction.

Ned Beaumont, the protagonist of *The Glass Key*, remains similarly incorruptible despite outward appearances to the contrary: A detective by temperament, if not by trade, Ned serves as friend and aide to the rising local politician Paul Madvig, involving himself deeply in political deals and trades; still, he persists in revealing a U.S. senator as the murderer of his own son and insists that the senator stand trial rather than commit suicide. The law of the land, however tarnished, remains a strong value in Hammett's novels, suggesting an abiding need for structure against the threat of anarchy.

With *The Thin Man*, Hammett moved in a new direction. For the first time, humor became a significant element in Hammett's fiction, infusing the novel with a lightness of tone that sets it quite apart from the almost documentary seriousness of *Red Harvest* and *The Glass Key*. Its protagonist, Nick Charles, has retired from the detective trade after his marriage to the rich and pretty Nora, some fifteen years his junior. Released from the need to work, he clearly prefers the carefree life of parties, travel, hotels, and round-the-clock drinking, all the while trading jokes and friendly banter with his attractive wife and other boon companions. Still, some habits die hard, and unpredicted events soon bring Nick's well-honed detective instincts back into operation. Moving back and forth between speakeasies and his lavish hotel suite, getting shot at by enraged gangsters, Nick urbanely unravels the mystery until, to no one's real surprise, one of his many casual friends stands revealed as the culprit. It is no secret that Hammett, in his portrayal of the witty Nora and her relationship with Nick, was more than a little influenced by his own developing relationship with Hellman, who returned the favor in her several volumes of memoirs.

Like Nick, Hammett at the time of *The Thin Man* was approaching middle age without the need to work, free at last to indulge his taste for parties and other carefree pursuits. *The Thin Man*, although certainly not planned as Hammett's final novel, is in a sense a fitting valedictory, an exuberant tour de force in which, ironically, the tensions contained in the earlier novels are finally released and perhaps dissipated. An additional irony exists within the book: Nick and Nora Charles may well be Hammett's best-known literary creations, perpetuated by the film version of the novel as well as by several sequels scripted in Hollywood by Hammett himself.

RED HARVEST

Hammett's first published novel, *Red Harvest*, originally serialized in *Black Mask*, delivers in ample portion the harsh realism promised in its title. Indeed, the high body count of *Red Harvest* may well have set a kind of record to be met or broken by later efforts in the detective genre. Hammett's intention, however, is not merely to shock the reader; seen in retrospect, *Red Harvest* emerges as a parable of civilization and its possible mutations.

Nowhere in *Red Harvest* are Hammett's intentions more evident than in his choice of location, a mythical Western community called Personville, better known as Poisonville. Some fifty years after the lawless days of the Wild West, Personville/Poisonville has yet to be tamed, even as outlaws have been replaced by gangsters with East Coast accents wearing snap-brim hats instead of Stetsons. The Op, sent to Personville at the request of Donald Willsson, makes an appointment with him only to discover that he has been murdered before the planned meeting can take place. Undaunted, the Op proceeds to investigate Willsson's murder, plunging deeper and deeper into the town's menacing and malevolent atmosphere. Among the more likely suspects is Willsson's father, Elihu, the town boss, who may well have tried to put a stop to his son's muckraking activities as publisher of the local newspaper. Other suspects, however, are present in abundance, at least until they begin to kill off one another during internecine combat partially masterminded by the Op.

The Op, it seems, is particularly skillful in setting the various criminal elements loose upon one another, paving the way for eventual martial law and relative peace, "a sweet-smelling and thornless bed of roses." In the process, however, he frequently faces criminal charges himself; at the same time, the authorities who are pressing the charges may well be as corrupt as the more obvious criminals. In such an environment, the closest thing to a moral imperative is the Op's own case-hardened sense of justice.

The major weakness of *Red Harvest* is a bewildering multiplicity of characters and actions; often, a new character will be introduced and established, only to be killed on the following page. The acts of violence, although symptomatic of social ills and not included for their own sake (as in the work of later hard-boiled mystery writers such as Mickey Spillane), are so numerous as to weary even the least squeamish of readers, although a number of scenes are especially effective; in one, the Op, watching a boxing match that he has helped to "unfix," stands helpless as the unexpected winner falls dead in the ring with a knife at the base of his neck.

THE DAIN CURSE

Later in the same year, 1929, Hammett published *The Dain Curse*, another formerly serialized novel featuring the Op as narrator and main character. Less sophisticated in its presentation than *Red Harvest*, *The Dain Curse* is more severely hampered by a multiplicity of characters and plot twists, all turning around the possibility of a family "curse" brought on by incest. Despite some rather skillful and memorable characterizations, *The Dain Curse* is generally agreed to be Hammett's weakest and least effective novel. Significantly, it is the last of Hammett's novels to feature the Op and the last (until *The Thin Man*, a different sort of novel) to be narrated in the first person.

THE MALTESE FALCON

Hammett's third novel, *The Maltese Falcon*, narrated dispassionately in the third person, combines the narrative strengths of his earlier works with a far more developed sense of characterization. Its protagonist, Sam Spade, although enough like the Op to be his slightly younger brother, is a more fully realized character caught and portrayed in all his ambiguity. Clearly the "brains" of the Spade and Archer Agency, he is careful to turn over to Miles Archer the case of a young woman client in whose presence he senses trouble. When Archer, blinded by the woman's flattery, goes forth to his death, Spade is hardly surprised, nor does he take many pains to hide his recent affair with the woman who is now Archer's widow. Spade, meanwhile, has grown tired of Iva Archer and her advances. Himself under suspicion for Archer's murder, Spade delves deeper into the case, learning that the young woman has given a number of aliases and cover stories. Her real name, it appears, is Brigid O'Shaughnessy, and it is not long before Spade connects her to a ring of international thieves, each of whom seems to be competing with the others for possession of an ancient and priceless treasure known as the Maltese Falcon. Supposedly, the football-sized sculpted bird, encrusted with precious stones, has been stolen and repossessed numerous times in the four hundred years of its existence, having surfaced most recently in the hands of a Russian general.

Spade's quest eventually brings him in contact with most of the larcenous principals except for the general himself (who at the end of the novel is found to have substituted a worthless leaden counterfeit for the genuine article). Among the thieves are two particularly memorable characters, interpreted in the John Huston film by Sydney Greenstreet and Peter Lorre, respectively: Casper Gutman, an eloquent, grossly fat manipulator and adventurer, keeps trying to maneuver Spade into his confidence; meanwhile, the other, Joel Cairo, openly gay and a member of the international underworld, repeatedly (and most unsuccessfully) tries to intimidate Spade with a handgun that Spade keeps taking away from him. In 1930, Hammett's frank portrayal of a gay man was considered daring in the extreme; by 1941, it was possible for Huston to apply such a characterization to Gutman as well, whose homosexuality in the novel is little more than latent. The book, for example, mentions that Gutman is traveling with a grown daughter, but the daughter is never mentioned in the Huston film.

In both novel and film, Spade's character develops considerably as he attempts to deal simultaneously with the matters at hand and with his growing affection for the obviously perfidious Brigid O'Shaughnessy. In Brigid, it seems, Spade has at last met his proper match, a woman whose deviousness and native intelligence compare favorably with his own. In her presence, it is all too easy for Spade to forget the cloying advances of Iva Archer or even the tomboyish charms of his secretary, Effie Perine; it is less easy, however, for him to forget the tightening web of circumstantial evidence in which he finds Brigid strongly enmeshed. After the coveted falcon has been revealed as a forgery, Spade confronts Brigid with evidence that she, and not her deceased cohort, Floyd Thursby, fired the bullet that killed Miles Archer. For all Archer's weaknesses and Spade's personal contempt for him, Spade remains true to the code that dictates arrest and prosecution for his partner's murderer. Explaining to an incredulous Brigid that he still thinks he loves her but cannot bring himself to trust her, he declares that he is sending her to jail and may or may not be waiting when she is freed. They are locked in an embrace when the police arrive to take her away.

Considerably more thoughtful and resonant than Hammett's earlier novels, *The Maltese Falcon* is his unquestioned masterpiece. The falcon itself, a contested piece of plunder that, in the novel, has occasioned theft and murder throughout recent history and that in its present form turns out to be a fake, is without doubt one of the strongest and best developed images in contemporary American fiction. Another equally effective device, absent from the Huston film, is the Flitcraft parable that Spade tells to Brigid early in their relationship as a way of explaining his behavior.

Early in his career, Spade recalls, he was hired to find a Seattle resident named Flitcraft who had disappeared mysteriously one day during the lunch hour, leaving behind a wife and two children. Spade later learned that, during the lunch break, Flitcraft had glimpsed his own mortality after a narrow escape from a falling beam. "He felt like somebody had taken the lid off his life and let him look at the works." That same day, he abandoned his family, wandering for two years, after which he fashioned for himself in Spokane a professional and family life very much like the one he had left behind in Seattle. "But that's the part of it I always liked," Spade tells Brigid. "He adjusted himself to beams falling, and then no more of them fell, and he adjusted himself to them not falling." Predictably, Spade's narrative has little effect on Brigid; for the reader, however, it does much to explain Hammett's approach to Spade as character and his own developing sense of the novelist's art. During that stage of his career, Hammett moved from "looking at the works" (*Red Harvest*) to a mature sense of contingency in which one's own deeply held convictions are all that matter.

THE GLASS KEY

Acknowledged to have been Hammett's personal favorite among his five published novels, *The Glass Key* is the only one not to feature a trained detective as protagonist. A rather unlikely hero at first glance, Ned Beaumont is tubercular and an avid gambler without a regular job. His principal occupation is that of friend, conscience, and unofficial assistant to Paul Madvig, an amiable politician forty-five years old who, one suspects, without Beaumont's help would have made even more mistakes than he already has. Himself the father of a grown daughter, Madvig is currently unmarried and in love with Janet Henry, daughter of an aristocratic and powerful U.S. senator. Janet has done little to encourage Madvig's attentions, and Beaumont, for his part, is determined to prevent his friend from making a fool of himself. Complications arise with the brutal murder of Taylor Henry, Janet's brother, who may or may not have been in love with Madvig's daughter,

Opal. As usual in Hammett's novels, there is an underworld connection; Taylor, it seems, was deeply in debt to a professional gambler at the time of his death.

As Madvig's loyal friend and aide, Beaumont sets out to discover the truth behind Taylor Henry's murder, displaying detective instincts worthy of Sam Spade or the Continental Op. Amid serious encounters with angry gangsters and corrupt police, Ned perseveres in his efforts to clear Madvig's name of suspicion in the murder, fully aware that he may well be a suspect himself. Meanwhile, to both Madvig's and Beaumont's consternation, Janet Henry appears to be falling in love with Beaumont, if only because he seems to be proof against her charms. As the action proceeds, it becomes increasingly clear to Beaumont that Taylor Henry could only have been killed by the senator, who has somehow prevailed upon Madvig to accept the burden of suspicion. When Beaumont finally confronts the senator with his suspicions, Henry admits to killing his son in a fit of anger and tampering with evidence at the scene of the crime; he asks only that Beaumont give him five minutes alone with his loaded revolver. Predictably, Beaumont refuses: "You'll take what's coming to you." Beaumont decides to leave town permanently, and, in a surprise twist at the end, he agrees to take Janet with him; the relationship awaiting them can only be surmised.

Like *The Maltese Falcon*, *The Glass Key* is a thoughtful and resonant novel, rich in memorable scenes and images. The glass key itself occurs in a dream that Janet has shortly after the start of her problematical relationship with Ned: She dreams that they arrive at a locked house piled high with food that they can see through the windows, yet when they open the door with a key found under the mat the house turns out to be filled with snakes as well. At the end of the novel, Janet reveals that she has not told Ned all of her dream: "The key was glass and shattered in our hands just as we got the door open, because the lock was stiff and we had to force it." Just as the Maltese Falcon dominates the book bearing its name, the glass key comes to symbolize the dangerous fragility of Janet's life and especially of her relationships with men—Paul Madvig, her father, and finally Ned Beaumont. Born to wealth and privilege, Janet is potentially dangerous to herself and others for reasons that Hammett suggests are outside her control; she does not share in her father's venality and is quite possibly a decent person beneath the veneer of her upbringing.

Not easily deceived, Ned Beaumont has been skeptical about the Henrys from the beginning; early in the book, he warns Paul against deeper involvement with either Janet or her father:

Read about it in the *Post*—one of the few aristocrats left in American politics. And his daughter's an aristocrat. That's why I'm warning you to sew your shirt on when you go to see them, or you'll come away without it, because to them you're a form of lower animal life and none of the rules apply.

To Beaumont, the Henrys are thoughtless and dangerous, much like Tom and Daisy Buchanan as seen by Nick Carraway in F. Scott Fitzgerald's *The Great Gatsby* (1925). Janet, however, develops considerably during the course of the novel, and at the end there is just the barest chance that a change of scenery will allow her to work out a decent life in Ned Beaumont's company.

THE THIN MAN

Fifth and last of Hammett's novels, *The Thin Man* is the only one to have been written during his acquaintance with Hellman, whose witty presence is reflected throughout the novel. Thanks to the successful film version and various sequels, *The Thin Man* is, next to *The Maltese Falcon*, the most famous of Hammett's novels; it is also the least typical.

The narrator and protagonist of *The Thin Man* is Nick Charles (born Charalambides and proud of his Greek extraction), a former detective in his early forties who has married the rich and beautiful Nora, nearly young enough to be his daughter. Contrary to popular belief, the novel's title refers not to Charles himself but to Clyde Miller Wynant, suspected of various crimes throughout the novel until the end, when he is revealed to have been the real killer's first victim: Wynant, an inventor, is described as being tall and painfully thin; at the end of the novel, his bones are found buried with clothes cut to fit a much larger man. In the filmed sequel, however, the title presumably refers to the dapper detective himself.

Peopled with a cast of café-society characters in addition to the usual underworld types, *The Thin Man* is considerably lighter in tone and texture than Hammett's earlier novels. Nick Charles, although clearly descended from Beaumont, Spade, and the Op, is nearly a playboy by comparison, trading lighthearted jokes and double entendres with his wife and boon companions. Close parallels may be drawn between Charles and the author himself, who by the time of *The Thin Man* had achieved sufficient material success to obviate his need to work. Hellman observed, however, that the actual writing of *The Thin Man* took place during a period of abstemious, almost monastic seclusion that differed sharply from Hammett's usual pattern of behavior during those years, as well as from the carefree life ascribed to Nick and Nora in the novel.

Most of the action of *The Thin Man* turns upon the certifiably eccentric personality of the title character, Clyde Wynant, a former client of Nick during his latter years as a detective. Among the featured characters are Wynant's former wife, son, and daughter, as well as his lawyer, Herbert Macaulay. In particular, the Wynants are memorable, deftly drawn characters, nearly as eccentric in their own ways as the missing paterfamilias. Wynant's son, Gilbert, about eighteen years old, is notable for his voracious reading and morbid curiosity concerning such matters as murder, cannibalism, and abnormal psychology. Dorothy Wynant, a year or two older than Gilbert, keeps trying to parlay a former girlhood crush on Nick into something more serious. Their mother, known as Mimi Jorgensen, is a vain, treacherous woman cut from the same cloth as Brigid O'Shaughnessy of *The Maltese Falcon*; she too makes repeated claims upon Nick's reluctant attentions.

Throughout the novel, Mimi and her children coexist uneasily in a state of armed truce that occasionally erupts into open warfare, providing scenes of conflict between parent and child considered rather daring at the time. Among the featured characters, only

Macaulay appears sane or even remotely sympathetic, yet it is he who ultimately stands accused of the financial double-dealing and multiple murders originally attributed to Wynant, not to mention the murder of Wynant himself.

Like Hammett's earlier novels, *The Thin Man* is realistic in its portrayal of urban life during Prohibition, when the criminal element was even more visible and overt in its actions than in later times. Despite the witty urbanity of his characters, Hammett harbors few illusions concerning human nature. When Nora asks Nick at the end of the novel what will become of Mimi and her children, he replies, "Nothing new. They'll go on being Mimi and Dorothy and Gilbert just as you and I will go on being us and the Quinns will go on being the Quinns." The novel ends with Nora telling Nick that his explanation is "pretty unsatisfactory." Perhaps it is, Hammett implies, but that is the nature of life.

Partly because of failing health and the pressures of work in Hollywood, Hammett published no fiction after *The Thin Man*. His reputation thus rests on a small and somewhat uneven body of work, redeemed by frequent flashes of brilliance. Notable for their influence upon the work of Chandler, Macdonald, and a host of lesser-known writers in the mystery genre, Hammett's novels have also exercised an immeasurable influence on novelists and filmmakers outside the genre.

David B. Parsell

OTHER MAJOR WORKS

SHORT FICTION: *Secret Agent X-9*, 1934 (with Alex Raymond); *The Adventures of Sam Spade, and Other Stories*, 1945; *The Continental Op*, 1945; *The Return of the Continental Op*, 1945; *Hammett Homicides*, 1946; *Dead Yellow Women*, 1947; *Nightmare Town*, 1948; *The Creeping Siamese*, 1950; *Woman in the Dark: More Adventures of the Continental Op*, 1951; *A Man Named Thin, and Other Stories*, 1962; *The Big Knockover: Selected Stories and Short Novels*, 1966 (Lillian Hellman, editor); *Nightmare Town: Stories*, 1999 (Kirby McCauley, Martin H. Greenberg, and Ed Gorman, editors); *Crime Stories, and Other Writings*, 2001; *Lost Stories*, 2005.

SCREENPLAYS: *City Streets*, 1931 (with Oliver H. P. Garrett and Max Marcin); *Mister Dynamite*, 1935 (with Doris Malloy and Harry Clork); *After the Thin Man*, 1936 (with Frances Goodrich and Albert Hackett); *Another Thin Man*, 1939 (with Goodrich and Hackett); *Watch on the Rhine*, 1943 (with Hellman).

NONFICTION: *The Battle of the Aleutians*, 1944 (with Robert Colodny); *Selected Letters of Dashiell Hammett, 1921-1960*, 2001 (Richard Layman and Julie M. Rivett, editors).

EDITED TEXT: *Creeps By Night*, 1931 (also known as *Modern Tales of Horror, The Red Brain*, and *Breakdown*).

BIBLIOGRAPHY

Bruccoli, Matthew J., and Richard Layman, eds. *Hardboiled Mystery Writers: Raymond Chandler, Dashiell Hammett, Ross Macdonald*. New York: Carroll & Graf, 2002. A

handy supplemental reference that includes interviews, letters, and previously published studies. Illustrated.

Gale, Robert L. *A Dashiell Hammett Companion*. Westport, Conn.: Greenwood Press,
2000. An encyclopedia devoted to Hammett, featuring a chronology of the major
events in his life and alphabetically arranged entries about his works and characters,
his family, and his acquaintances. Includes bibliographical references and an index.

Gregory, Sinda. *Private Investigations: The Novels of Dashiell Hammett*. Carbondale:
Southern Illinois University Press, 1985. The first chapter discusses Hammett, his
Pinkerton experiences, and the hard-boiled detective genre. Subsequent chapters focus on each of his five major novels. Includes a foreword by Francis M. Nevins, Jr.,
notes, a bibliography, and an index.

Hammett, Jo. *Dashiell Hammett: A Daughter Remembers*. Edited by Richard Layman,
with Julie M. Rivett. New York: Carroll & Graf, 2001. A compelling memoir written
by Hammett's daughter, Jo Hammett. Generously illustrated with photographs drawn
from family archives.

Johnson, Diane. *Dashiell Hammett: A Life*. New York: Random House, 1983. A comprehensive biography of Hammett. Adds considerable information to the public record of
Hammett's life but does not provide much critical analysis of the works. More than
half the volume deals with the years after Hammett stopped publishing fiction and during which he devoted most of his time to leftist political activism.

Layman, Richard. *Shadow Man: The Life of Dashiell Hammett*. New York: Harcourt
Brace Jovanovich/Bruccoli-Clark, 1981. An academic who earlier produced a descriptive bibliography of Hammett, Layman provides lucid interpretations of the
works. While he holds Hammett in high regard as a major figure in twentieth century
American fiction, he does not present a totally admiring portrait.

Mellen, Joan. *Hellman and Hammett: The Legendary Passion of Lillian Hellman and
Dashiell Hammett*. New York: HarperCollins, 1996. Although primarily a biographical study of the relationship of the two writers, this scrupulously researched work provides insight into the backgrounds of Hammett's fiction. Includes detailed notes and a
bibliography.

Metress, Christopher, ed. *The Critical Response to Dashiell Hammett*. Westport, Conn.:
Greenwood Press, 1994. A generous compilation of reviews and general studies, written by leading Hammett scholars, as well as pieces by writers Raymond Chandler,
Ross Macdonald, Dorothy Parker, James M. Cain, and Rex Stout. Includes a comprehensive introduction, a chronology, and a bibliography.

Nolan, William F. *Hammett: A Life at the Edge*. New York: Congdon and Weed, 1983.
Author of the first full-length study of Hammett in 1969, Nolan here builds upon his
earlier work and that of others to present a convincing portrait of a singularly private
man with a code of honor that paralleled those of his detectives. The discussions of the
works are straightforward and sound.

Skenazy, Paul. "The 'Heart's Field': Dashiell Hammett's Anonymous Territory." In *San Francisco in Fiction: Essays in a Regional Literature*, edited by David Fine and Paul Skenazy. Albuquerque: University of New Mexico Press, 1995. A consideration of the importance of history and place in Hammett's fiction. Argues that it is wrong to associate Hammett's concern with expedience, environment, habit, training, and chance with a specifically Wild West tradition.

Wolfe, Peter. *Beams Falling: The Art of Dashiell Hammett.* Bowling Green, Ohio: Bowling Green University Popular Press, 1980. Wolfe surpasses other writers in showing the relationship of each of Hammett's works to the total output. The author of books on other crime-fiction writers (Raymond Chandler, John le Carré, and Ross Macdonald), Wolfe has a knowledge and appreciation of the genre that are apparent in this excellent study.

PATRICIA HIGHSMITH

Born: Fort Worth, Texas; January 19, 1921
Died: Locarno, Switzerland; February 4, 1995
Also known as: Mary Patricia Plangman; Claire Morgan

OTHER LITERARY FORMS

In addition to her novels, Patricia Highsmith wrote several collections of short stories, including *The Snail-Watcher, and Other Stories* (1970), *The Animal-Lover's Book of Beastly Murder* (1975), *Slowly, Slowly in the Wind* (1979), *The Black House* (1981), *Mermaids on the Golf Course, and Other Stories* (1985), and *Tales of Natural and Unnatural Catastrophes* (1987). In 1966, she published a how-to book, *Plotting and Writing Suspense Fiction* (reprinted and expanded three times by the author), which provides a good introduction to her work. She also wrote one children's book, *Miranda the Panda Is on the Veranda* (1958), in collaboration with a friend, Doris Sanders. Although Highsmith wrote prizewinning short stories, she is best known for her novels, especially the Ripley series.

ACHIEVEMENTS

Patricia Highsmith was honored several times. For her first published story, "The Heroine," which was written while she was a student at Barnard College, she was included in the *O. Henry Prize Stories of 1946*. The novel *The Talented Mr. Ripley* was awarded the Grand Prix de Littérature Policière in 1957 and the Edgar Allan Poe Scroll from the Mystery Writers of America. For *The Two Faces of January* she received the Award of the Crime Writers Association of Great Britain.

BIOGRAPHY

Patricia Highsmith's mother, father, and stepfather were all commercial artists. She was born Mary Patricia Plangman a few months after her mother, Mary Coates, and father, Jay Bernard Plangman, were divorced, and she lived the first six years of her life with her grandmother in the house where she was born, in Fort Worth, Texas.

At the age of six, she went to New York City to join her mother and stepfather in a small apartment in Greenwich Village. She later went to high school in New York and on to Barnard College. Life with quarreling parents made her unhappy, but she did inherit from them a love of painting, and she considered it as a vocation. She ultimately decided to be a writer because she could explore moral and intellectual questions in more depth by writing novels than by painting. Highsmith enjoyed early success with a short story she wrote in college that was later published in *Harper's Bazaar* and included in the *O. Henry Prize Stories of 1946*.

Attracted to travel early, Highsmith set out for Mexico in 1943 to write a book. With only part of it written, she ran out of money and returned to New York, where she continued living with her parents and writing comics in the day and fiction at night and on the weekends to save enough money for a trip to Europe. She left for Europe in 1949, after finishing her first novel, *Strangers on a Train*, which was bought and made into a film by Alfred Hitchcock.

The next few years saw Highsmith traveling between Europe and New York and writing novels and short stories that found publishers in New York and throughout Europe. After several visits, she moved permanently to Europe, first to England for four years, then to France (to a small town near Fontainebleau, which became the setting for later Ripley stories), and finally to Switzerland in 1982. When she died in a hospital in Locarno in 1995, she left an estate of more than five million dollars. Highsmith was a solitary figure, shunning reporters and publicity. She lived alone with her favorite cat, Charlotte, working in her garden and painting. She revisited the United States but never returned to live.

ANALYSIS

Patricia Highsmith remains less a household name than other, more traditional crime novelists largely because she wrote about good men who turn bad and bad men who escape punishment. A moral compass is missing in her work, and guilt is hard to assign. She is better known and more interesting to critics in Europe, especially in England and Germany, than in her own country, which she left permanently in 1963. In a final tribute at the time of her death in 1995, critic Michael Tolkin wrote that the Hitchcock adaptation of her first published novel, *Strangers on a Train*, in which only the psychopath is permitted to kill, "is a perfect example of the kind of American cultural repression that I like to imagine as one of the reasons she left."

In Europe, too, her heroes who "kill not without feeling," says critic Susannah Clapp in *London Review of Books*, "but without fear of reprisal" have brought cries of disapproval. In a 1965 review of *The Glass Cell*, one critic declared, "There are not many nastier fiction worlds than Patricia Highsmith's and soon they sicken." Margharita Laski wrote in *The Listener*, "I used to be the only person I knew who loathed Patricia Highsmith's work for its inhumanity to man, but our numbers are growing." On the other hand, a number of respected crime writers, including Julian Symons, consider her among the best crime writers and at least one of her novels a work of true literature. American novelist and critic Gore Vidal wrote, "She is one of our greatest modernist writers."

Highsmith's killers or near killers are middle class and intelligent; they are usually artists or professionals, and they often have sophisticated tastes. In a 1980 interview with Diana Cooper-Clark, Highsmith explained why this is so. Since she believed that most criminals are not particularly intelligent, they do not interest her very much. She chose middle-class characters because she thought writers can write successfully only about their own social milieus. Since "standards of morality come from the society around," pleasant, well-mannered men often commit murder in her fictional world: "The contrast between respectability and murderous thoughts is bound to turn up in most of my books." The five novels about Tom Ripley focus on an otherwise nice young man who gets away with murder. Critics have analyzed this unlikely killer in considerable detail.

The 1980's and 1990's saw a renewed interest in Highsmith as a lesbian writer. In most of her novels women are not the active center; they do not commit murder. When asked about this, she explained that she found men more violent by nature than women. Women seemed passive to her, less likely to create action. Her women characters are among her least admirable. They often seem present only as decor or as a means of furthering the actions of the male characters. There are three novels that represent a degree of exception to this pattern. *The Price of Salt* (later published as *Carol*) is the story of two women who fall in love, and the novel—"a very up-beat, pro-lesbian book," according to its editor, Barbara Grier—has a relatively happy ending. *Edith's Diary*, the only other Highsmith novel with a woman at the center, was viewed more as a commentary of American political and social life in the 1960's than as a suspense novel. Her last book, *Small g: A Summer*

Idyll, about gays, lesbians, and the human immunodeficiency virus (HIV), could not find an American publisher and was published in England to mixed reviews. Feminists find little support in Highsmith's work. Feminist critic Odette L'Henry Evans observed in a 1990 essay that the women are not loving wives and mothers, and it is often the father who loves and cares for the child.

If Highsmith has a philosophy, it could best be described as a negative one, difficult to identify except as a rebellion against the moral status quo. In spite of the disturbing and pessimistic conclusion that readers must draw from her work—that justice is seldom truly important in human affairs, that it is a "manmade conceit," in the words of critic Brooks Peters—she is recognized as a crime writer who has important things to say about human nature and who says them uncommonly well.

Russell Harrison, in the first full-length study of Highsmith, categorized most of the best known of her novels. The early novels may generally be considered stories of American domestic life: *Deep Water, This Sweet Sickness*, and *The Cry of the Owl*. In the 1960's, according to Harrison, Highsmith began to examine U.S. foreign relations and political and social issues in *The Tremor of Forgery, A Dog's Ransom*, and *Edith's Diary*. Finally, he examines the gay and lesbian novels, *The Price of Salt* and *Small g: A Summer Idyll*. Two important novels he does not discuss are *The Glass Cell* and *The Two Faces of January*, which might be grouped with the social-issue novels.

THE TALENTED MR. RIPLEY

The Talented Mr. Ripley was the Highsmith's favorite book, and Tom Ripley is her most popular character. Highsmith once said that writing fiction was a game to her and that she had to be amused to keep writing. The game here is keeping Ripley out of the hands of the police, and much of the fun lies in allowing him to live high on his ill-gotten gains. "I've always had a lurking liking for those who flout the law," Highsmith once admitted. Critic Tolkin described Ripley aptly as "a small-time American crook who moves to Europe and kills his way to happiness." Highsmith was at odds with herself about Ripley's true value. He stands in sharp contrast to stereotypical morality, which is often hypocritical, but he also has almost no conscience and so is, in Highsmith's words, "a little bit sick in the head."

Dickie Greenleaf, a rich young man who has left home and his disapproving parents to become a painter in Italy, is Ripley's first victim. Ripley arrives on the scene, sent by the father to persuade Dickie to return. Ripley decides that he would rather stay and share Dickie's lazy expatriate life. When Dickie becomes angry about Ripley's imitation of him, Ripley decides to eliminate the real Dickie and take his place. Ripley's real talent is this imitation—he once thought of becoming an actor—and he succeeds in deceiving everyone until Freddie, an old friend of Dickie, becomes suspicious. It is necessary for Ripley to murder again in order not to be unmasked. Freddie is killed, but the police suspect Tom/ Dickie of the crime. So Dickie is twice murdered, and Tom Ripley is reborn—along with a fake will in which Dickie leaves him everything. One critic finds this protean man a very contemporary type, one often found in serious literature. Ripley is indeed a classic of his kind, and while Highsmith's touch is almost playful, some readers shudder at Ripley's indifference to his own ghastly crimes. As the Ripley stories multiplied, some readers and critics alike worried that Highsmith had grown too fond of her talented but diabolical hero who is in some ways a monster.

THE GLASS CELL

The dreariness of the style of *The Glass Cell* is the dreariness of its prison atmosphere. There is very little relief from the monotony of wrongfully convicted Philip Carter's life in prison, and there are no scenes of the high life to enjoy. In *Plotting and Writing Suspense Fiction*, Highsmith provides a case history of how three versions of this novel came to be written.

The idea came from a true story, but the story changed as Philip Carter became a Highsmith protagonist. To be interesting, he had to become more active as the novel evolved, and so he kills not once but three times. The alibi he concocts for the murders is coldly calculated; prison has made a ruthless man of him. Highsmith says that she wanted Carter to go free after he commits two postprison murders because he had suffered so much in prison. He had been strung up by his thumbs by a sadistic guard, and he suffers continual physical pain in his hands. The police suspect him of murder but can prove nothing, and Carter and his wife and son are free to go on with their lives together. Highsmith delivers her own kind of justice to a once-innocent man unjustly punished by the courts.

Lucy Golsan

OTHER MAJOR WORKS

SHORT FICTION: *The Snail-Watcher, and Other Stories*, 1970 (also known as *Eleven*); *Kleine Geschichten für Weiberfeinde*, 1974 (*Little Tales of Misogyny*, 1977); *The Animal-Lover's Book of Beastly Murder*, 1975; *Slowly, Slowly in the Wind*, 1979; *The Black House*, 1981; *Mermaids on the Golf Course, and Other Stories*, 1985; *Tales of Natural and Unnatural Catastrophes*, 1987; *The Selected Stories of Patricia Highsmith*, 2001; *Nothing that Meets the Eye: The Uncollected Stories of Patricia Highsmith*, 2002.

NONFICTION: *Plotting and Writing Suspense Fiction*, 1966.

CHILDREN'S LITERATURE: *Miranda the Panda Is on the Veranda*, 1958 (with Doris Sanders).

BIBLIOGRAPHY

Bloom, Harold, ed. *Lesbian and Bisexual Fiction Writers*. Philadelphia: Chelsea House, 1997. Highsmith is one of the writers included in this overview of lesbian, gay, and bisexual fiction writers. Contains a brief biography, excerpts from reviews and criticism, and a bibliography.

Brophy, Brigid. "Highsmith." In *Don't Never Forget: Collected Views and Reviews*. New York: Henry Holt, 1966. Brophy compares Highsmith's artistic achievements to those of Georges Simenon to argue that Highsmith's crime novels, with their moral ambiguity, "transcend the limits of the genre while staying strictly inside its rules."

Cochran, David. "'Some Torture That Perversely Eased': Patricia Highsmith and the Everyday Schizophrenia of American Life." In *America Noir: Underground Writers and Filmmakers of the Postwar Era*. Washington, D.C.: Smithsonian Institution Press, 2000. In his study of underground writers and filmmakers, Cochran describes how Highsmith's amoral Mr. Ripley and other aspects of her fiction challenged the pieties of the 1950's.

Dupont, Joan. "Criminal Pursuits." *The New York Times Magazine*, June 12, 1988. Notes that although Highsmith is a celebrity in the rest of the world, she is relatively unknown in her native United States; suggests that because Highsmith has lived abroad and has never been in the United States to promote her books, she has never developed a strong link with publishers or readers. Others believe it is because her books are not clearly classifiable as thrillers, mysteries, or literature.

Harrison, Russell. *Patricia Highsmith*. New York: Twayne, 1997. This first book-length study of Highsmith in English explores the aesthetic, philosophical, and sociopolitical dimensions of her writing. Harrison focuses on Highsmith's novels, including her gay- and lesbian-focused novels.

Highsmith, Patricia. "Not Thinking with the Dishes." *Writer's Digest* 62 (October, 1983). Highsmith says she follows no set rules for story writing; she begins with a theme, an unusual circumstance or a situation of surprise or coincidence, and creates the narrative around it. Her focus is on what is happening in the minds of her protagonists, and her settings are always ones she knows personally.

Mawer, Noel. *A Critical Study of the Fiction of Patricia Highsmith—From the Psychological to the Political*. Lewiston, N.Y.: Edwin Mellen Press, 2004. An examination of Highsmith's fiction, including the Ripley novels, *The Glass Cell*, and *A Game for the Living*. Although some of Highsmith's novels can be categorized as mystery and detective fiction, Mawer argues that many of her novels explore "the mystery of character," or, how people create their own identities by interacting with others in particular situations.

Summers, Claude J., ed. *Gay and Lesbian Literary Heritage: A Reader's Companion to the Writers and Their Works, from Antiquity to the Present*. Rev. ed. New York: Routledge, 2002. This expanded edition of a book originally published in 1995 includes an excellent essay by Gina Macdonald on Highsmith's life and work to the time of her death in 1995.

Symons, Julian. *Mortal Consequences: A History from the Detective Story to the Crime Novel*. New York: Harper & Row, 1972. Symons calls Highsmith "the most important crime novelist" of her time, a fine writer whose tricky plot devices are merely starting points "for profound and subtle character studies," particularly of likable figures attracted by crime and violence. Highsmith's imaginative power gives her criminal heroes a "terrifying reality" amid carefully chosen settings, and she is at her best describing subtle, deadly games of pursuit.

Tolkin, Michael. "In Memory of Patricia Highsmith." *Los Angeles Times Book Review*, February 12, 1995. A tribute to Highsmith as "our best expatriate writer since Henry James" and an excellent analysis of why her heroes, especially Ripley, are not appreciated in the United States.

Wilson, Andrew. *Beautiful Shadow: A Life of Patricia Highsmith*. New York: Bloomsbury, 2004. The first biography of Highsmith, chronicling the author's troubled life and tracing the roots of her fiction to the works of Edgar Allan Poe, noir, and existentialism. Winner of the 2004 Edgar Award for Best Critical/Biographical Work.

CHESTER HIMES

Born: Jefferson City, Missouri; July 29, 1909
Died: Moraira, Spain; November 12, 1984
Also known as: Chester Bomar Himes

OTHER LITERARY FORMS

Chester Himes was primarily a writer of long fiction, but near the end of his life he published a revealing two-volume autobiography, which, if not wholly accurate about his life, nevertheless is engaging as a testament of survival of a black artist struggling to make his voice heard. Like many writers of his generation, Himes began publishing short fiction in the many periodicals of the time. As his life and career progressed—and the number of publishers declined—Himes worked less in the field. A posthumous collection of his short fiction was published in 1990. Finally, Himes also turned his hand to dramatic writing, both plays and film scripts, the most accessible of which is "Baby Sister," which was published in his book of miscellaneous writings, *Black on Black: "Baby Sister" and Selected Writings* (1973).

Chester Himes
(Library of Congress)

ACHIEVEMENTS

As the title of a biography of Chester Himes suggests, Himes led several lives during the seventy-five years of his troublesome career. He was the youngest son in a rising African American family, who worked his way into the middle class only to fall back again. Himes learned the craft of writing as an inmate in the Ohio correctional system, and after his release from prison he was a writer of angry and violent protest novels, which earned him a reputation as one of the more celebrated black writers in the United States.

Beginning in the mid-1950's, Himes expatriated and became a tangential member of the community of black artists, which included Richard Wright and James Baldwin, who fled American racism to settle in Europe during the period after World War II. In his later years, he wrote a two-volume autobiography and a series of masterful crime novels, the "Harlem domestic" books. The second of the series, *The Real Cool Killers*, won in 1958 the prestigious Grand Prix de la Littérature Policiére for best crime novel published in France. In all of his "lives," Himes struggled to come to grips with the racist American society into which he was born and to realize his place in that society as a black man and as an artist.

From the publication of his first novel, *If He Hollers Let Him Go*, Himes confounded the critics, and they rarely understood his work. Was his fiction too violent or was it merely revealing the realities of American racism? Was Himes sexist or just reflecting the tensions inherent in a community where African American males were desperately searching for a sense of self? Did he compromise his art for the publishing world dominated by white editors when he wrote his Harlem domestic series, or were these hard-hitting yet more mainstream crime novels an extension of his more "artistic" but less popular protest novels? Was his autobiography merely a self-serving complaint against the slights against him or an uncompromising portrait of one black man's struggle for survival?

Perhaps it is because of the contradictions of his life that Himes remains fascinating, and it is through the mixed, often confused, responses to his work that he achieved his measure of importance, not just as a black writer but as an American writer, one who captured something of the truth of America and of its literature.

BIOGRAPHY

Chester Bomar Himes was the youngest of three sons of Joseph Sandy Himes and Estelle Bomar Himes. His father was a teacher of industrial arts and spent the years of Himes's youth as a faculty member at several black institutions predominantly in the South. By the time Himes was in his teens the family had settled in Cleveland, and after his graduation from Glenville High School he entered Ohio State University in the fall of 1926. However, his university career was short-lived, and at the end of the spring quarter, 1927, he was asked to leave because of poor grades and his participation in a speakeasy fight.

Back in Cleveland, Himes slipped into a life on the edges of the city's crime world. After several run-ins with the law he was caught for robbery, convicted, and sentenced to a lengthy term in the Ohio State Penitentiary. For the next seven-and-a-half years Himes served time, and in the enforced discipline of prison life he began to write fiction. His first publication, "His Last Day," appeared in *Abbott's Monthly* in November, 1932. Himes was paroled on April 1, 1936, and the next year he married Jean Johnson. After his prison experience Himes worked at a number of menial jobs while continuing to write.

On April 3, 1953, Himes embarked for Europe, and, except for several brief trips to the United States, he remained an exile for the rest of his life. During these years Himes's writing was devoted mainly to his Harlem detective series featuring Grave Digger Jones and Coffin Ed Johnson. Throughout his years in Europe, Himes traveled extensively, finally settling in Alicante, Spain, with his second wife, Leslie Packard. In 1963, Himes suffered a stroke and in his later years experienced various health problems. He died on November 12, 1984, in Moraira, Spain.

ANALYSIS

In his review of *Lonely Crusade*, James Baldwin hit on the central theme of Chester Himes's work: creating individual black characters who were many faceted and reflected the ambivalence of living in an American society full of contradictions and insecurities. Unfortunately, Baldwin's grasp of the essence of Himes's fiction was not shared by all. Many of the reviewers of Himes's early "protest" fiction either criticized the violence of the books, apologized for it, or merely complained about what they saw as his awkwardness of style. Most reviews simply dismissed the books. Some acknowledged that Himes's portrait of American racism was accurate but deplored his lack of any constructive suggestions for its amelioration. Even when Himes received a certain measure of fame through the republication of his detective novels in the United States, the critical notices, with few exceptions, remained slight. After Himes's death, however, this changed. Himes's literary reputation in France undoubtedly affected his reception in the United States.

Himes once believed that in American letters there was room at the top for only one African American writer at a time, and therefore black writers were always competing against one another for that coveted spot. He felt that he always came in second, initially behind Richard Wright and then behind Baldwin. Certainly this is no longer true (if it ever was). The proliferation of novels, drama, and poetry by such authors as Toni Morrison, Ernest J. Gaines, Gloria Naylor, Derek Walcott, Maya Angelou, Alice Walker, and other black writers suggests that whatever constraints Himes felt as an exiled black writer seem to be loosening. Himes is now being accorded a place beside Wright, Baldwin, and Ralph Ellison, the novelists of his generation who opened the doors for African American writers to be accepted as full-fledged American writers, a part of the native grain.

IF HE HOLLERS LET HIM GO

In *If He Hollers Let Him Go* the central character, Bob Jones, is a black Everyman—as his name would suggest—who comes to represent the experience of all black males who find themselves thwarted while trying to live out their dreams. Jones is an African American who has moved to California to work in the defense plants during World War II. Here he experiences American racism in all its ugly insidiousness and spends the five days covered by the novel's narrative trying to escape the oppressions and humiliations society tries to impose on him.

As an articulate man, with a few years of college, Jones is both better educated and more perceptive than the working-class whites he works with in the aircraft plants. When he is elevated to the position of supervisor at work, he brings out the racism of his coworkers, who are jealous of his success. An altercation on the job, tensions with his white girlfriend, and finally the accusation of rape by a woman at work whose overtures he has rejected, convince Jones that his hopes and dreams will not come true even in Los Angeles, where he thought he would be rid of the racist attitudes of his native South. After his arrest a judge strips him of his military deferment, and as the novel ends he is being sent off to join the U.S. Army.

Himes's first published novel provides the basic themes he would pursue not only in his protest books but also in his crime fiction. In the course of the novel Himes explores the issues of race, class, and sexual positioning and demonstrates how Jones, despite his best efforts, remains trapped within a historically determined social role as a black man trying simply to earn a living, gain some personal respect, and find love. At every turn he finds himself prevented from fulfilling the most basic of American rights and aspirations.

THE PRIMITIVE

The narrative of *The Primitive* focuses on writer Jesse Robinson and his relationship with his white girlfriend, Kriss Cummings. Again in this novel Himes uses a contained time scheme, covering only a few days in the lives of his central characters. After a chance meeting with an old acquaintance, Kriss, Jesse experiences a rapidly accelerating series of seriocomic episodes, which propel him to the novel's conclusion: In an alcoholic fog he stabs Kriss to death in her Gramercy Park apartment. The novel alternates between following Kriss's life and Jesse's thoughts as he tries, in vain, to examine his feelings about his relationship with a white woman and what she stands for in his world, as well as his growing sense of himself as a writer trying to come to grips with his experience as an African American living in a racist culture that will give him recognition as neither an artist nor a man.

The Primitive is often described as one of Himes's "confessional" novels, fiction in which he examines themes that had plagued him since the publication of *If He Hollers Let Him Go*: the rejection he felt as a writer and the obsession with white women often experienced by black men. As critics have pointed out, obsession with white women is a constant theme in Himes's writing and represents attraction, repulsion, and, because of the taboo of miscegenation, long a central anxiety of white Americans, the fear of death and social rejection. Rather than merely striking out against white society, Jesse murders Kriss out of self-hatred for his own desires to join that society, moving the murder beyond the blind killing of Bigger Thomas in Wright's *Native Son* (1940). In the end, Jesse, although still a rejected author, discovers that he has the skills of a fine writer who can put into words his feelings about the conditions of his life.

COTTON COMES TO HARLEM

Cotton Comes to Harlem begins in Harlem at a "back to Africa" rally sponsored by the Reverend Deke O'Malley, who is fraudulently bilking his gullible followers. The rally is interrupted by a gang of thieves who steal the raised money and hide it in a bale of cotton, which they lose on their escape. Into this plot come two African American detectives, Grave Digger Jones and Coffin Ed Johnson, two of the toughest police officers in New York. The rest of the novel involves their attempts to recover the loot, expose the fraud, and make amends to the local residents. The ending of the novel provides an ironic twist, as a poor, old man who found the bale does go to Africa to live out the dream promised by the Reverend O'Malley at the novel's opening.

Cotton Comes to Harlem is one a series of crime novels set in New York's Harlem and featuring two African American detectives, a series Himes called his Harlem domestic books. The series began when his French publisher Marcel Duhamel contracted him to write a novel for Gallimard's La Série Noire, a notable series of crime fiction published in France. In these novels, Himes concentrates as much on the social, political, and economic conditions of the people of Harlem as he does on the solving of crimes. As Himes carefully explores the racism inherent in American culture, he chronicles the world of his characters sympathetically, and without becoming didactic he demonstrates the harmful effects of almost four hundred years of oppression and exploitation of African Americans.

Charles L. P. Silet

OTHER MAJOR WORKS

SHORT FICTION: *The Collected Stories of Chester Himes*, 1990.

NONFICTION: *The Quality of Hurt: The Autobiography of Chester Himes, Volume I*, 1972; *My Life of Absurdity: The Autobiography of Chester Himes, Volume II*, 1976; *Conversations with Chester Himes*, 1995 (Michel Fabre and Robert E. Skinner, editors); *Dear Chester, Dear John: Letters Between Chester Himes and John A. Williams* (John A. Williams and Lori Williams, compilers and editors).

MISCELLANEOUS: *Black on Black: "Baby Sister" and Selected Writings*, 1973.

BIBLIOGRAPHY

Fabre, Michael, and Robert Skinner, eds. *Conversations with Chester Himes*. Jackson: University Press of Mississippi, 1995. A collection of interviews in which Himes speaks candidly about his work, the work of other black writers, racial politics in the United States, the African American community in Harlem, and other topics.

Himes, Chester. *Dear Chester, Dear John: Letters Between Chester Himes and John A. Williams*, compiled and edited by John A. Williams and Lori Williams. Detroit, Mich.: Wayne State University Press, 2008. Himes met Williams, a novice African American writer sixteen years his junior, in 1961, and the two became friends who corresponded for almost thirty years. The letters reveal Himes's personality and his experiences as a black writer. Includes an interview with Himes.

Lundquist, James. *Chester Himes*. New York: Frederick Ungar, 1976. An introductory volume to Himes's life and works, with chapters on the war novels, confessional novels, and detective novels. The first chapter, "November, 1928," describes the armed robbery for which Himes was arrested and the subsequent arrest and trial, in detail. Chronology, notes, bibliography of primary and secondary sources, index.

Margolies, Edward. "Race and Sex: The Novels of Chester Himes." In *Native Sons: A Critical Study of Twentieth-Century Negro American Authors*. Philadelphia: J. B. Lippincott, 1968. A discussion of Himes's major novels. The author sees Himes as considerably different than the group of protest writers following Richard Wright and believes that his European sojourn weakened his writings about the United States. Includes a bibliography and an index.

Margolies, Edward, and Michel Fabre. *The Several Lives of Chester Himes*. Jackson: University Press of Mississippi, 1997. This full-length biography of Himes, written by two people who knew him during the last twenty years of his life, is indispensable for information about his life.

Muller, Gilbert. *Chester Himes*. Boston: Twayne, 1989. An excellent introduction to Himes's life and works. Traces the evolution of his writing, describing how he expressed his grotesque, revolutionary view of life for African Americans in the United States in several literary modes, culminating in his detective fiction. Includes chronology, appendix, index, and annotated bibliographies of primary and secondary works.

Sallis, James. *Chester Himes: A Life*. New York: Walker, 2001. Sallis, a novelist and poet, draws on updated information to provide this detailed recounting of the events of Himes's life and how this life related to his writings.

Silet, Charles L. P., ed. *The Critical Response to Chester Himes*. Westport, Conn.: Greenwood Press, 1999. Reviews and essays analyzing Himes's novels, detective fiction, use of the doppelganger, his anti-Semitism, and his hard-boiled detective tradition. Includes bibliography and index.

Skinner, Robert E. *Two Guns from Harlem: The Detective Fiction of Chester Himes*. Bowling Green, Ohio: Bowling Green State University Popular Press, 1989. Skinner's study presents a comprehensive examination of Himes's mystery and detective novels. He describes how Himes's creation of Coffin Ed Johnson and Grave Digger Jones, two African American police officers, led other writers to create hard-boiled ethnic and female detectives.

Walters, Wendy W. "Harlem on My Mind: Exile and Community in Chester Himes's Detective Fiction." In *At Home in Diaspora: Black International Writing*. Minneapolis: University of Minnesota Press, 2005. Walters describes how Himes's sense of homesickness during his self-imposed exile in Paris led him to write detective novels set in Harlem, even though he never lived there. Himes's Harlem is an imaginary home that reflects both his nostalgia for an African American community and a critique of American racism.

P. D. JAMES

Born: Oxford, England; August 3, 1920
Also known as: Phyllis Dorothy James; Phyllis Dorothy James White

PRINCIPAL LONG FICTION

Cover Her Face, 1962
A Mind to Murder, 1963
Unnatural Causes, 1967
Shroud for a Nightingale, 1971
An Unsuitable Job for a Woman, 1972
The Black Tower, 1975
Death of an Expert Witness, 1977
Innocent Blood, 1980
The Skull Beneath the Skin, 1982
A Taste for Death, 1986
Devices and Desires, 1989
The Children of Men, 1992
Original Sin, 1994
A Certain Justice, 1997
Death in Holy Orders, 2001
The Murder Room, 2003
The Lighthouse, 2005
The Private Patient, 2008

OTHER LITERARY FORMS

Although P. D. James is known principally as a novelist, she is also a short-story writer and a playwright. The great bulk of James's work is in the form of the long narrative, but her short fiction has found a wide audience through its publication in *Ellery Queen's Mystery Magazine* and other popular periodicals. It is generally agreed that James requires the novel form to show her literary strengths to best advantage. Still, short stories such as "The Victim" reveal in microcosm the dominant theme of the long works. James's lone play, *A Private Treason*, was first produced in London on March 12, 1985. In 2000, her eightieth year, *Time to Be in Earnest: A Fragment of Autobiography*, her second work of nonfiction, appeared.

ACHIEVEMENTS

P. D. James's first novel, *Cover Her Face*, did not appear until 1962, at which time the author was in her early forties. Acceptance of James as a major crime novelist, however, grew very quickly. *A Mind to Murder* appeared in 1963, and with the publication of *Un-*

natural Causes in 1967 came that year's prize from the Crime Writers Association. In the novels that have followed, James has shown an increasing mastery of the labyrinthine murder-and-detection plot. This mastery is the feature of her work that most appeals to one large group of her readers, while a second group of readers would single out the subtlety and psychological validity of her characterizations. Critics have often remarked that James, more than almost any other modern mystery writer, has succeeded in overcoming the limitations of the genre. In addition, she has created one of the more memorable descendants of Sherlock Holmes. Like Dorothy L. Sayers's Lord Peter Wimsey and Agatha Christie's Hercule Poirot, James's Adam Dalgliesh is a sleuth whose personality is more interesting than his skill in detection.

BIOGRAPHY

Phyllis Dorothy James was born in Oxford, England, on August 3, 1920. She graduated from Cambridge High School for Girls in 1937. She was married to Ernest C. B. White, a medical practitioner, from August 8, 1941, until his death in 1964. She worked as a hospital administrator from 1949 to 1968 and as a civil servant in the Department of Home Affairs, London, from 1968 to 1972. From 1972 until her retirement in 1979, she was a senior civil servant in the crime department. Since her retirement from the Home Office, James has served as a magistrate in London and as a governor of the British Broadcasting Corporation.

Although she began her career as a novelist rather late in life, by 2008 James had authored eighteen mysteries, most of which had been adapted for broadcast on television. In addition, her heroine Cordelia Gray was featured in a series of television dramas—not adapted from stories actually written by James—produced under the overall title *An Unsuitable Job for a Woman.*

The temperament informing James's fiction seems to be a conservative one, but she has stated that she belongs to no political party. Although not overtly a Christian writer, James, a longtime member of the Church of England, frequently touches on religious themes in her fiction. This tendency is more marked in the later novels and is reflected in several of the works' titles.

James has been the recipient of numerous literary prizes and other honors. In 1991, she was created Baroness James of Holland Park. Since she received her peerage, her political conservatism has become somewhat more apparent in her work. Lady James is the mother of two daughters and has five grandchildren. She divides her time between homes in Oxford, her place of birth, and London, the city so intimately and lovingly described in her fiction.

ANALYSIS

P. D. James's work is solidly in the tradition of the realistic novel. Her novels are intricately plotted, as successful novels of detection must be. Through her use of extremely well-delineated characters and a wealth of minute and accurate details, however, James never allows her plots to distort the other aspects of her novels. As a result of her employment, James had extensive contact with physicians, nurses, civil servants, police officials, and magistrates. She uses this experience to devise settings in the active world where men and women busily pursue their vocations. She eschews the country-weekend murders of her predecessors, with their leisure-class suspects who have little more to do than chat with the amateur detective and look guilty.

A murder requires a motive, and it is James's treatment of motivation that sets her work apart from most mystery fiction. Her suspects are frequently the emotionally maimed who, nevertheless, manage to function with apparent normality. Beneath their veneer, dark secrets fester, producing the phobias and compulsions they take such pains to disguise. James's novels seem to suggest that danger is never far away in the most mundane setting, especially the workplace. She avoids all gothic devices, choosing instead to create a growing sense of menace just below the surface of everyday life. James's murderers rarely kill for gain; they kill to avoid exposure of some sort.

Among James's novels, *The Children of Men* is a generic departure, really more a science-fiction novel than a mystery. It describes a dystopian society of the near future, only some thirty years removed from its 1992 publication date. The society has abandoned all the forms, conventions, and restraints that the author values.

SHROUD FOR A NIGHTINGALE

The setting for *Shroud for a Nightingale* is a nursing hospital near London. The student nurses and most of the staff are in permanent residence there. In this closed society, attachments—sexual and otherwise—are formed, rivalries develop, and resentments grow. When a student nurse is murdered during a teaching demonstration, Inspector Adam Dalgliesh of Scotland Yard arrives to investigate. In the course of his investigation, Dalgliesh discovers that the murdered girl was a petty blackmailer, that a second student nurse (murdered soon after Dalgliesh's arrival) was pregnant but unmarried and had engaged in an affair with a middle-aged surgeon, that one member of the senior staff is committing adultery with a married man from the neighborhood and another is sexually attracted to one of her charges. At the root of the murders, however, is the darkest secret of all, a terrible sin that a rather sympathetic character has been attempting both to hide and to expiate for more than thirty years. The murder weapon is poison, which serves also as a metaphor for the fear and suspicion that rapidly spread through the insular world of the hospital.

Adam Dalgliesh carries a secret burden of his own: His wife and son died during childbirth. He is a sensitive and cerebral man, a poet of some reputation. These deaths have left him bereft of hope and intensely aware of the fragility of human beings' control over their own lives. Only the rules that humankind has painstakingly fashioned over the centuries can ward off degeneration and annihilation. As a policeman, Dalgliesh enforces society's rules, giving himself a purpose for living and some brief respite from his memories. Those who commit murder contribute to the world's disorder and hasten the ultimate collapse of civilization. Dalgliesh will catch them and see that they are punished.

AN UNSUITABLE JOB FOR A WOMAN

In *An Unsuitable Job for a Woman*, published within a year of *Shroud for a Nightingale*, James introduces her second recurring protagonist. Cordelia Gray's "unsuitable job" is that of private detective. Gray unexpectedly falls heir to a detective agency and, as a result, discovers her vocation. Again, James avoids the formularized characterization. Gender is the most obvious but least interesting difference between Dalgliesh and Gray. Dalgliesh is brooding and introspective; although the narratives in which he appears are the very antithesis of the gothic novel, there are aspects of the gothic hero in his behavior. Gray, on the other hand, is optimistic, outgoing, and good-natured, despite her unfortunate background (she was brought up in a series of foster homes). She is a truth seeker and, like William Shakespeare's Cordelia, a truth teller. Dalgliesh and Gray are alike in their cleverness and competence. Their paths occasionally cross, and a friendly rivalry exists between them.

DEATH OF AN EXPERT WITNESS

In *Death of an Expert Witness*, James's seventh novel, Dalgliesh again probes the secrets of a small group of coworkers and their families. The setting this time is a laboratory that conducts forensic examinations. James used her nineteen years of experience as a hospital administrative assistant to render the setting of *Shroud for a Nightingale* totally convincing, and her seven years of work in the crime department of the Home Office serve her to the same effect in *Death of an Expert Witness*. In her meticulous attention to detail, James writes in the tradition of Gustave Flaubert, Leo Tolstoy, and the nineteenth century realists. Because the setting, characterizations, and incidents are so solidly grounded in detail, a James novel tends to be considerably longer than the ordinary murder mystery. This fact accounts for what little adverse criticism her work has received. Some critics have suggested that so profuse is the detail, the general reader may eventually grow impatient—that the pace of the narrative is too leisurely. These objections from some contemporary critics remind the reader once more of James's affinity with the novelists of the nineteenth century.

The laboratory in which the expert witness is killed serves as a focal point for an intriguing cast of characters. Ironically, the physiologist is murdered while he is examining physical evidence connected with another murder. The dead man leaves behind a rather vacant, superannuated father, who lived with him. The principal suspect is a high-strung laboratory assistant, whom the deceased bullied and gave an unsatisfactory performance rating. The new director of the laboratory has an attractive but cruel and wanton sister, with whom he has a relationship that is at least latently incestuous. In addition, Dalgliesh investigates a lesbian couple, one of whom becomes the novel's second murder victim; a melancholy physician, who performs autopsies for the police and whose unpleasant wife has just left him; the physician's two curious children, the elder girl being very curious indeed; a middle-aged babysitter, who is a closet tippler; and a crooked cop, who is taking advantage of a love-starved young woman of the town. In spinning her complex narrative, James draws on her intimate knowledge of police procedure, evidential requirements in the law, and criminal behavior.

INNOCENT BLOOD

The publication in 1980 of *Innocent Blood* marked a departure for James. While the novel tells a tale of murder and vengeance, it is not a detective story. Initially, the protagonist is Philippa Rose Palfrey—later, the novel develops a second center of consciousness. Philippa is eighteen, the adopted daughter of an eminent sociologist and a juvenile court magistrate. She is obsessed with her unremembered past. She is sustained by fantasies about her real parents, especially her mother, and the circumstances that forced them to give her up for adoption. Despite these romantic notions, Philippa is intelligent, resourceful, and tenacious, as well as somewhat abrasive. She takes advantage of the Children Act of 1975 to wrest her birth record from a reluctant bureaucracy.

The record shows that she was born Rose Ducton, to a clerk and a housewife in Essex. This revelation sends Philippa rushing to the dreary eastern suburb where she was born, beginning an odyssey that will eventually lead to her mother. She discovers that her fantasies cannot match the lurid realities of her past. Her father was a child molester who murdered a young girl in an upstairs room of his house. Her mother apparently participated in the murder and was caught trying to take the body away in her car. Her father has died in prison, and her mother is still confined. Though horrified, Philippa is now even more driven to find explanations of some sort and to rehabilitate the image of her mother. She visits Mary Ducton in prison, from which she is soon to be released, and eventually takes a small flat in London, where they will live together.

In chapter 8, James introduces the second protagonist, at which time the novel becomes as much his as it is Philippa's. Norman Scase is fifty-seven and newly retired from his job as a government accounts clerk. Scase is the widowed father of the murdered girl. He retires when he learns of Mary Ducton's impending release, for all of his time will be required to stalk her so that, at the appropriate moment, he may kill her. The murder of young Julia Mavis Scase robbed her father of the same years it stole from Philippa. Philippa is desperately trying to reclaim these lost years by learning to know, forgive, and love her mother. Scase is driven to a far more desperate act.

In form, *Innocent Blood* resembles Tolstoy's *Anna Karenina* (1875-1877; English translation, 1886). Like Anna and Levin, the dual protagonists proceed through the novel along separate paths. Philippa has no knowledge of Scase's existence, and he knows her only as the constant companion of the victim he is tracking all over London. James makes the city itself a character in the novel, and as Philippa shares her London with her mother, it is fully realized in Dickensian detail. Philippa is the more appealing protagonist, but Scase is a fascinating character study: the least likely of premeditating murderers, a little man who is insignificant in everything except his *idée fixe*. James created a similar character in "The Victim," a short story that appeared seven years earlier. There, a dim and diffident assistant librarian stalks and murders the man who took his beautiful young wife away from him. The novel form, however, affords James the opportunity to develop this unpromising material completely into a memorable character. As Scase lodges in cheap hotels, monitors the women's movements with binoculars, and stares up at their window through the night, the reader realizes that the little man has found a purpose that truly animates his life for the first time. He and Philippa will finally meet at the uncharacteristically melodramatic climax (the only blemish on an otherwise flawless novel).

A Taste for Death

Commander Adam Dalgliesh returns in *A Taste for Death* after an absence of nine years. He is heading a newly formed squad charged with investigating politically sensitive crimes. He is assisted by the aristocratic chief inspector John Massingham and a new recruit, Kate Miskin. Kate is bright, resourceful, and fiercely ambitious. Like Cordelia Gray, she has overcome an unpromising background: She is the illegitimate child of a mother who died shortly after her birth and a father she has never known. The title of the novel is evocative. A taste for death is evident not only in the psychopathic killer but also in Dalgliesh and his subordinates, the principal murder victim himself, and, surprisingly, a shabby High Church Anglican priest, reminiscent of one of Graham Greene's failed clerics.

When Sir Paul Berowne, a Tory minister, is found murdered along with a tramp in the vestry of St. Matthew's Church in London, Dalgliesh is put in charge of the investigation. These murders seem linked to the deaths of two young women previously associated with the Berowne household. The long novel (more than 450 pages) contains the usual array of suspects, hampering the investigation with their evasions and outright lies, but in typical James fashion, each is portrayed in three dimensions. The case develops an additional psychological complication when Dalgliesh identifies with a murder victim for the first time in his career and a metaphysical complication when he discovers that Berowne recently underwent a profound religious experience in the church, one reportedly entailing stigmata. Perhaps the best examples of James's method of characterization are the elderly spinster and the ten-year-old boy of the streets who discover the bodies in chapter 1. In the hands of most other crime writers, these characters would have been mere plot devices, but James gives them a reality that reminds the reader how deeply a murder affects everyone associated with it in any way. Having begun the novel with Miss Wharton and Darren, James returns to them in the concluding chapter.

DEVICES AND DESIRES

Devices and Desires possesses the usual James virtues. The story is set at and around a nuclear power plant on the coast of Norfolk in East Anglia. The geographic details are convincing (even though the author states that she has invented topography to suit her purposes), and the nuclear power industry has obviously been well researched. Although the intricate plot places heavy demands of action on the characters, the omniscient narrator analyzes even the most minor of them in such depth that they are believable. Finally, greater and more interesting than the mystery of "who did it" is the mystery of those ideas, attitudes, and experiences that have led a human being to murder. Ultimately, every James novel is a study of the devices and desires of the human heart.

In some ways, however, the novel is a departure. The setting is a brooding, windswept northern coast, the sort of gothic background that James largely eschewed in her earlier novels. *Devices and Desires* is also more of a potboiler than are any of its predecessors. As the story begins, a serial killer known as the Whistler is claiming his fourth victim (he will kill again during the course of the novel). A group of terrorists is plotting an action against the Larksoken Nuclear Power Station. The intrigue is so heavy and so many people are not what they seem that at one point the following tangled situation exists: Neil Pascoe, an antinuclear activist, has been duped by Amy Camm, whom he has taken into his trailer on the headland. Amy believes that she is acting as an agent for an animal rights group, but she has been duped by Caroline Amphlett, personal secretary to the director of Larksoken. Caroline has, in turn, been duped by the terrorists, for whom she has been spying—they plot her death when she becomes useless to them. Eventually, shadowy figures turn up from MI5, Britain's intelligence agency. In this instance, so much exposition and explication is required of James's dialogue that it is not always as convincing as in the previous books.

Adam Dalgliesh shares this novel with Chief Inspector Terry Rickards. Rickards is a mirror image of Dalgliesh. He is less intelligent and imaginative, but he has the loving wife and infant child whom Dalgliesh has lost. While Dalgliesh is on the headland, settling his aunt's estate, he stumbles upon a murder (literally—he discovers the body). Hilary Robarts, the beautiful, willful, and widely disliked and feared acting administrative officer of the station, is strangled, and the Whistler's method is mimicked. As usual in a James novel, the suspects constitute a small and fairly intimate group. The author has totally mastered the detective story convention whereby at some point in the novel each of the suspects will seem the most plausible murderer.

The action of *Devices and Desires* affords James the opportunity to comment on the use and potential misuse of nuclear power, the phenomenon of terrorism, the condition of race relations in London, even the state of Christianity in contemporary Britain. Still, what James always does best is to reveal, layer by layer, the mind that has committed itself to that most irrevocable of human actions, murder.

ORIGINAL SIN

In *Original Sin*, Commander Dalgliesh's investigative team has changed: Although he is still assisted by Kate Miskin, John Massingham has been replaced by Daniel Aaron. Inspector Aaron is a Jew who is exceedingly uncomfortable with his Jewishness—Jewishness that will become a critical factor in the last quarter of the novel. *Original Sin* is replete with religious metaphors, beginning with its title. Again, the reader is reminded that Adam Dalgliesh is the "first," the dominant human being in each of the novels (despite the fact that he makes fewer and briefer appearances in *Original Sin* than in any previous novel). Dalgliesh is the son of a country rector. A minor character, a sister to one of the several members of the Peverell Press to die under mysterious circumstances, is also a sister in a larger sense: She is a nun in an Anglican convent. Frances Peverell, a major character, is a devout Catholic. She is also the near namesake of Francis Peverell, whose sin 150 years earlier has placed a sort of curse upon Innocent House, a four-story Georgian edifice on the Thames that serves as the home of the Peverell Press. Gabriel Dauntsey—a poet whose name suggests the Angel of Revelation—reveals the darkest secret of Innocent House toward the close of the novel.

Innocent House, dating from 1792, is reached by launch and exudes the atmosphere of a Venetian palace. It is the site of five deaths, all initially giving the superficial appearance of suicide. Four are eventually revealed to be murders. Thus, the very name of the building is heavily ironic. Inspectors Miskin and Aaron do most of the detecting, aided by an occasional insight shared or interview perceptively conducted by Commander Dalgliesh. Several of the characters bear the burden of original sin, the sins of their parents and ancestors. The motivation for multiple murders turns out to be events that occurred fifty years earlier in wartime France.

A CERTAIN JUSTICE

In *A Certain Justice*, P. D. James makes use of her whole bag of stylistic tricks, familiar but nevertheless effective. The appropriately ambiguous title refers to either, or both, justice of a particular sort and justice that is sure. The incidents of the novel support both interpretations. The conflicts within and between the members of Dalgliesh's investigative team continue. Kate Miskin is sexually attracted to her boss but dares not acknowledge this fact to herself. Daniel Aaron has left the force, presumably as a result of his unprofessional behavior at the conclusion of *Original Sin*, and has been replaced by Piers Tarrant. As usual, Kate is not sure that she likes her male partner. Also as usual, the murder suspects are members of a small, self-contained professional group—this time, from the Inns of Court, where London's lawyers practice.

As in other of her later novels, James introduces religious overtones. The chief suspect in the second murder, and the victim of the third (there are four in all), is a vicar's widow who has lost her faith. Piers Tarrant has a theology degree from Oxford; he claims that the study of theology is excellent preparation for police work. Detective Sergeant Robbins, who assists Kate and Piers in their inquiries, is a Methodist of impeccable Christian virtue. He combines two apparently paradoxical qualities, a benign view of his fellow human beings and a deeply skeptical view of human nature. The second quality makes him a very good detective. A key conflict in the latter part of the novel involves Father Presteign, a High Church Anglican priest. He initially receives crucial information about the second murder, but under the seal of the confessional.

A Certain Justice is marked by a parallel structure. As the novel begins, an accused killer is acquitted and so is free to kill again. An earlier such instance drives the main plot. Two characters, their intentions unknown to each other, set out to achieve a certain justice outside the law. Both attempts lead to violent death. James experiments with epistolary form in chapter 36, which is written in the form of a long letter left by a murder victim.

DEATH IN HOLY ORDERS

The setting of *Death in Holy Orders* is St. Anselm's Theological College, a High Church Anglican institution in Suffolk. It is the scene of four violent deaths: one on the nearby beach, two on the college grounds, and one in the adjoining church. Commander Adam Dalgliesh investigates, assisted by Kate Miskin and Piers Tarrant.

The influence of religion (Christianity specifically) is a major theme developed throughout the book. Four priests and twenty students reside at St. Anselm's. The visit of an unpleasant archdeacon, one of the murder victims, reflects the occasional bitterness of clerical politics. The reader is reminded that Dalgliesh is the son of a Norfolk rector, that Tarrant read theology at Oxford, and that the fourth member of their team, Sergeant Robbins, is a lay preacher. Important clues are a missing black cloak and a stolen consecrated Communion wafer. The characters run the spiritual gamut from piety to occasional doubt to skepticism to assertive unbelief; these attitudes are reflected in their behavior when they are faced with violent death. The novel postulates that no place, no matter how sanctified, is proof against the power of evil.

James further employs the epistolary form through the text of a long diary entry in the first chapter, launching the mystery, and a long letter in the last, tying up the loose ends. Again, Dalgliesh proves himself to be no armchair detective. He has his flashes of insight, but he and his team usually solve their cases through solid, painstaking police work.

Finally, Dalgliesh meets Dr. Emma Lavenham, a beautiful Cambridge don, who has come to St. Anselm's to present a lecture titled "The Poetic Inheritance of Anglicanism." The two are immediately attracted to each other, and the reader may assume that Dr. Lavenham will reappear in subsequent novels.

THE MURDER ROOM

The Murder Room and *Death in Holy Orders* have several similarities of plot. The latter features St. Anselm's, a small theological college that the Church is about to close. *The Murder Room* features the Dupayne, a small private museum that is on the verge of closing. In *Death in Holy Orders*, Archdeacon Matthew Crampton, who favors closing St. Anselm's, is murdered. In *The Murder Room*, Neville Dupayne, a trustee who favors closing the Dupayne, is murdered. The fates of both St. Anselm's and the Dupayne are complicated by provisions in the founders' wills. Adam Dalgliesh commands the Special Investigations Squad, set up to investigate murders of a "sensitive nature." However, despite the fact that the murders in the two novels do not meet this criterion, Dalgliesh is sent to investigate the crimes—he is sent to St. Anselm's owing to the influence of Sir Alred Treves, a hugely successful businessman, and to the Dupayne because the curator is a sometimes agent of MI5, the British intelligence service.

Here the similarities between the two novels end, however. In *The Murder Room*, Dalgliesh is back on familiar ground, London. The Dupayne is located in the area of London known as Hampstead, and the characters inhabit a London in which James appears to know every street, bus route, tube stop, and train schedule. Detective Inspectors Kate Miskin and Piers Tarrant remain members of the squad. Sergeant Robbins has been promoted and has left. He is replaced by Francis Benton-Smith—handsome, well educated, and resented by Tarrant. The novel is composed of four books. The first introduces the characters; each of the remaining three is devoted to one of the victims.

The museum features exhibits from the period between the world wars, 1918 to 1939. The museum's Murder Room is dedicated to the most notorious cases of the 1920's and 1930's. The crimes in the novel mimic three of those represented in the Murder Room. James employs ambiguity in the novel's title, as she does in many of her works. In the novel, the Murder Room literally becomes a murder room. The suspects are Neville Dupayne's two siblings and six other people connected to the museum.

Dalgliesh continues a problematic romance with Emma Lavenham, Cambridge lecturer in English literature. Each is unsure of the depth of the other's feelings. They live in different worlds, yet with only the distance between Cambridge and London separating them. Kate Miskin is still attracted to Dalgliesh but has accepted the fact that they will never be lovers. The relationship of Dalgliesh and Emma is badly strained when, because of the Dupayne investigation, he must cancel a London weekend with her at the last minute. Dalgliesh solves the murders just before the day of another, and crucial, engagement with Emma. It appears that he will miss this one as well because of his superiors' bureaucratic diddling, but he races through a traffic-snarled London by underground, taxi, and underground again. He intercepts Emma just before she boards her train for a return to Cambridge. Always the writer, he hands her a note expressing his love for her and a proposal of marriage, and stands apart while she reads it. All ends well. Emma joyously accepts, and in the final scene of the novel the lovers embrace on the platform of the Liverpool Street station.

THE LIGHTHOUSE

As is often the case in a James mystery, the setting of *The Lighthouse* is itself one of the major characters. The lighthouse of the title is located on Combe Island off the coast of

Cornwall. Subject to the provisions of a charitable trust, the island is dedicated as a place of rest and seclusion for important men (and women) who seek temporary respite from the rigors of their professional lives. The desired peace is shattered by two murders, however—those of an eminent novelist and an alcoholic priest, the former of whom dies in the lighthouse, the latter in his chapel. James's familiar Christian theme is developed through the character analysis of Adrian Boyde—disgraced and no longer addressed as "Father"—whose body is discovered beneath a cope, an ecclesiastical vestment newly made for him by an admiring seamstress.

The relationships in Dalgliesh's Special Investigations Squad have taken some interesting turns. Piers Tarrant has transferred to the antiterrorist branch, and now that his and Kate Miskin's half-acknowledged professional rivalry no longer exists, they become lovers, at least briefly. Sergeant Francis Benton-Smith, always disliked by Tarrant, has replaced him as the third member of the squad. Kate's admiration for Benton-Smith grows as the murder investigations proceed. The love affair between Adam Dalgliesh and Emma Lavenham continues, passionately but uneasily. Even though Dalgliesh proposed and Emma accepted in the final chapter of *The Murder Room*, there has been no further discussion of marriage. Each is deeply in love but unsure of the seriousness of the other's commitment.

As is customary in a James novel, the descriptive details of the setting subtly create the mood. Each suspect is characterized in depth, so that he or she is no mere plot device. Throughout the investigation, Dalgliesh is tortured by the fear that he may be unworthy of Emma's love. Another, and very serious, complication arises when Dalgliesh contracts SARS (severe acute respiratory syndrome) and for days is desperately ill. Kate and Benton-Smith must conclude the investigation themselves, although their commander furnishes them with crucial deductions from his sickbed.

Emma, shaken by having almost lost Dalgliesh to a fatal illness, announces that they must set the date for Father Martin to marry them. Dalgliesh is exultant as he realizes his years of loneliness and near alienation have come to an end. On the novel's last page, the lovers, like a handsome couple from a Jane Austen novel, face a future the reader knows will be a happy one.

Patrick Adcock

OTHER MAJOR WORKS

PLAY: *A Private Treason*, pr. 1985.

NONFICTION: *The Maul and the Pear Tree: The Ratcliff Highway Murders, 1811*, 1971 (with T. A. Critchley); *Time to Be in Earnest: A Fragment of Autobiography*, 2000.

BIBLIOGRAPHY

Barber, Lynn. "The Cautious Heart of P. D. James." *Vanity Fair*, March, 1993. Presents a profile of James in her seventies—commercially successful, titled, and highly honored as a literary craftsman.

Breen, Jon L. "Murder Most British: P. D. James Strikes Again." *Weekly Standard*, November 29, 2003. Discusses *The Murder Room*, noting that a museum devoted to Great Britain between the world wars is an appropriate setting for one of James's novels, as James is the strongest contemporary link to England's detective fiction of that era.

Gidez, Richard B. *P. D. James*. Boston: Twayne, 1986. Presents an examination of James's place within the tradition of the English mystery novel and discusses in chronological order her first nine novels.

Hoover, Bob. "Mystery Roundup: *Death in Holy Orders*." *Pittsburgh Post Gazette*, April 13, 2001. Faults the novel's plot and some carelessly lost clues but praises James's lyrical descriptions of the English countryside and her effective setting of the mood.

Macintyre, Ben. Review of *A Certain Justice*, by P. D. James. *The New York Times Book Review*, December 7, 1997. Praises James's characterization, observing that each character is himself or herself an embryonic novel. Also notes that, as in other of James's later novels, the protagonist, Dalgliesh, becomes a token presence in the last two-thirds of the book, "oddly distant and preoccupied."

Maslin, Janet. "A Rich Menu of Murder, Garnished with a Small Sprig of Shame." Review of *The Lighthouse*, by P. D. James. *The New York Times Book Review*, December 1, 2005. Perceptive review argues that James is not a garden-variety mystery writer and asserts that *The Lighthouse* is superior to the novel that preceded it, *The Murder Room*.

Maxfield, James F. "The Unfinished Detective: The Work of P. D. James." *Critique* 28, no. 4 (1987): 211-223. Focuses on James's realistic depiction of the challenges facing a female private detective.

Porter, Dennis. "Detection and Ethics: The Case of P. D. James." In *The Sleuth and the Scholar: Origins, Evolution, and Current Trends in Detective Fiction*, edited by Barbara A. Rader and Howard G. Zettler. Westport, Conn.: Greenwood Press, 1988. Discusses James as a writer for whom moral principles are an integral part of the crime and detection story. Focuses on the novels *Death of an Expert Witness*, *An Unsuitable Job for a Woman*, and *Innocent Blood*.

Priestman, Martin. "P. D. James and the Distinguished Thing." In *On Modern British Fiction*, edited by Zachary Leader. New York: Oxford University Press, 2002. Critical essay examines James's work and her place within the broader context of British literature from the late twentieth century onward. Observes that James's undoubted skill as a writer is circumscribed by her choice of genre.

Rowland, Susan. *From Agatha Christie to Ruth Rendell: British Women Writers in Detective and Crime Fiction*. New York: Palgrave Macmillan, 2001. Discusses the works of the most prominent British women writers of mystery novels, including James. Features an interview with James.

Wood, Ralph C. "A Case for P. D. James as a Christian Novelist." *Theology Today* 59, no. 4 (2003): 583-595. Analyzes the moral and social concerns in James's novels as reflective of Christian values.

ELMORE LEONARD

Born: New Orleans, Louisiana; October 11, 1925
Also known as: Elmore John Leonard, Jr.; Dutch Leonard

<small>PRINCIPAL LONG FICTION</small>
The Bounty Hunters, 1953
The Law at Randado, 1954
Escape from Five Shadows, 1956
Last Stand at Saber River, 1959 (also known as *Lawless River* and *Stand on the Saber*)
Hombre, 1961
The Big Bounce, 1969
The Moonshine War, 1969
Valdez Is Coming, 1970
Forty Lashes Less One, 1972
Fifty-two Pickup, 1974
Mr. Majestyk, 1974
Swag, 1976 (also known as *Ryan's Rules*)
The Hunted, 1977
Unknown Man No. 89, 1977
The Switch, 1978
Gunsights, 1979
City Primeval: High Noon in Detroit, 1980
Gold Coast, 1980
Split Images, 1981
Cat Chaser, 1982
LaBrava, 1983
Stick, 1983
Glitz, 1985
Elmore Leonard's Double Dutch Treat: Three Novels, 1986
Bandits, 1987
Touch, 1987
Freaky Deaky, 1988
Killshot, 1989
Get Shorty, 1990
Maximum Bob, 1991
Rum Punch, 1992 (also known as *Jackie Brown*)
Pronto, 1993
Riding the Rap, 1995

Naked Came the Manatee, 1996 (with twelve other Florida writers)
Out of Sight, 1996
Cuba Libre, 1998
Be Cool, 1999
Pagan Babies, 2000
Tishomingo Blues, 2002
Mr. Paradise, 2004
The Hot Kid, 2005
Up in Honey's Room, 2007
Road Dogs, 2009

OTHER LITERARY FORMS

In addition to his novels, Elmore Leonard has published numerous Western short stories as well as several magazine articles on crime writing and police procedure. More significantly, he has developed considerable expertise as a writer of screenplays, both original works and adaptations of other materials, including his own novels.

ACHIEVEMENTS

Elmore Leonard has come to be widely regarded as one of the best crime-fiction writers in the world and is ranked with Dashiell Hammett and Raymond Chandler as a writer who transcends the limitations of category fiction. He is one of those who made hard-boiled crime fiction "respectable," and his storytelling technique has influenced countless others. In 1984, *LaBrava* won the Mystery Writers of America Edgar Allan Poe Award as the best novel of the year. In 1991, the International Association of Crime Writers awarded him the Hammett Prize for *Maximum Bob*, and in 1992 the Mystery Writers of America named him a Grand Master, its highest accolade. For his lifetime achievements, Leonard has received honorary doctorate degrees from Florida Atlantic University (1996), the University of Detroit Mercy (1997), and the University of Michigan (2000).

Leonard also enjoys the distinction of being one of America's most-filmed writers; many of his works have been adapted as screenplays or teleplays by others and by Leonard himself. In addition to such feature films as *3:10 to Yuma* (1957 and 2007), *Hombre* (1967), *The Big Bounce* (1969), *Mr. Majestyk* (1974), *Stick* (1985), *Fifty-two Pick-Up* (1986), *The Moonshine War* (1970), *Cat Chaser* (1989), *Get Shorty* (1995), *Jackie Brown* (1997), *Out of Sight* (1998), and *Be Cool* (2005), and the made-for-television films *Glitz* (1988), *Last Stand at Saber River* (1997), and *Gold Coast* (1997), Leonard's stories have also served as the inspiration for two television series: *Karen Sisco* and *Maximum Bob*. Leonard has provided the original material for four of the top one hundred Western movies as ranked by the Western Writers of America: *3:10 to Yuma* (2007), *The Tall T* (1957), *Hombre* (1967), and *Valdez Is Coming* (1971).

BIOGRAPHY

Elmore John Leonard, Jr., was born in New Orleans, Louisiana in 1925. His father, Elmore John Leonard, Sr., was an executive at General Motors and his mother, Florence Amelia (Rive) Leonard, was a housewife. The Leonard family moved frequently because of Leonard's father's specialty as a manufacturing plant locator, but in the mid-1930's they settled in Detroit, Michigan, a city that would become the backdrop of many of Elmore's crime novels.

Elmore, a Catholic, attended Blessed Sacrament Elementary School and the University of Detroit Jesuit High School, where he picked up the nickname "Dutch," borrowed from Emil "Dutch" Leonard, then a knuckleball pitcher for the Washington Senators baseball team. Elmore graduated from high school in 1943 and was immediately afterward drafted into the U.S. Navy. He served in the Admiralty Islands of New Guinea with the Seabees during World War II.

After the war, Elmore attended the University of Detroit on the G.I. Bill, majoring in English and philosophy. In 1949, the same year that he married for the first time, to Beverly Cline, he began working for the Campbell-Ewald Advertising Agency in Detroit. Following his graduation in 1950, he continued to work as a copywriter, a job he hated, for the advertising agency, eventually becoming assigned primarily to the prestigious Chevrolet account. His growing family (he would eventually father five children by Beverly) made it difficult for him to pursue his ambition to become a freelance writer, but he began writing Western short stories between 5:00 and 7:00 A.M. each day before going to work. He published his first fiction in 1951: the novelette "Trail of the Apache," in *Argosy* magazine. During the ensuing decade, he sold twenty-seven more such stories to pulp magazines and published four Western novels.

After quitting the advertising agency in 1961 to become a freelance writer, for several years Leonard supplemented his fiction income by writing scripts, for one thousand dollars each, for Encyclopædia Britannica educational films. Among the industrial and educational films he authored were *Settlement of the Mississippi Valley, Boy of Spain, Frontier Boy,* and *Julius Caesar.* He also wrote the script for *The Man Who Has Everything,* a recruiting film for the Franciscans. Before he finally became a full-time fiction writer, he ran Elmore Leonard Advertising Company from 1963 to 1966.

Hombre, Leonard's last Western novel, was published in 1961, and four years later Twentieth Century-Fox purchased the film rights for ten thousand dollars; the resulting film, starring Paul Newman, was released in 1967. During his Western writing period, Leonard also sold Columbia Pictures the film rights to his early story "3:10 to Yuma" (the first film adaptation of which was released in 1957; a remake appeared in 2007) and his novelette "The Captives" (which became the 1957 film *The Tall T*). Despite these successes, the market for Western fiction was beginning to dry up, perhaps because the genre had been overly exploited by television.

Leonard, in characteristically pragmatic fashion, switched to writing crime fiction.

This was the turning point in his career, for he had never felt entirely at ease with Westerns, and he made the transition effortlessly. His first non-Western novels, *The Big Bounce* and *The Moonshine War*, were published in 1969; Warner Bros. bought the film rights to the former, and Leonard wrote a screenplay adaptation (his first) of the latter and sold it. A few years later, in 1972, *Joe Kidd*, a film of his first original screenplay, was released. Thus began Leonard's long relationship with the film industry.

In 1974, after twenty years of heavy drinking, Leonard joined Alcoholics Anonymous. In 1977 he and his wife divorced, and he remarried to Joan Shephard in 1979; she died of cancer in January, 1993. He married his third wife later that year, French teacher Christine Kent, who is twenty-four years younger than Leonard. The couple has since made their home in Bloomfield Hills, a northern suburb of Detroit.

From the 1980's onward, Leonard's novels have received widespread critical praise, and he has been described as "the best American writer of crime fiction alive." When *LaBrava* won the Mystery Writers of America Edgar Allan Poe Award in 1984, his reputation as a major crime writer was secured, though he says he writes "novels, not mysteries." He has also been a popular success. In 1985, *Glitz* made *The New York Times* bestseller list, and Warner Books two years later published a first printing of 250,000 copies of *Bandits* in a one-million-dollar deal. A year later, Leonard received three million dollars for *Freaky Deaky*. Film rights purchases continued to be a regular occurrence with Leonard novels, as 1995's *Get Shorty* was a success, and the 1998 film of *Out of Sight* was hailed as one of the year's best.

ANALYSIS

Elmore Leonard's early short stories and novels were conventional in terms of plot and characterization; however, writing Westerns was good training. Knowing nothing about the West, Elmore learned to depend on research that he could embellish with his vivid imagination. This is essentially the method he has employed throughout his writing career, though since the early 1980's, professional researcher Gregg Sutter, rather than the author himself, has collected the raw material, the esoteric facts from which Elmore works. Furthermore, when he switched to crime fiction, he brought some of his hair-trigger, saloon-wrecking cowboy villains into urban settings, with startling effects. Examples of these "redneck monsters" are Raymond Gidre in *Unknown Man No. 89*, Clement Mansell in *City Primeval*, Roland Crowe in *Gold Coast*, and Richard Nobles in *LaBrava*. Another type of displaced Western character is Armand Degas in *Killshot*, a half-blood American Indian turned Mafia hit man.

Placing cowboys and American Indians in modern cities such as Miami and Detroit is only one of the many types of contrast Leonard employs to produce effects. In his crime novels the most violent incidents occur in the most peaceful settings, such as family restaurants, supermarkets, and real estate offices, and the worst villainy is often directed against people whose lives had previously been conventional and uneventful. In *Killshot*, for example, a working-class couple suddenly has their front windows blown out with shotgun blasts; the story ends with a double murder in the cozy breakfast nook of their model kitchen.

In 1959, there were thirty Western series on prime-time television. The public eventually became saturated with saloon brawls and shoot-outs on Main Street, and by the mid-1960's the number of prime-time televised Westerns had dropped to seven. It was not until this six-gun overkill forced Leonard to turn to crime fiction that he began to develop the distinctive approach to storytelling that brought him fame and fortune. That approach was influenced by his own involvement in filmmaking, which has one cardinal rule for writers: "Don't tell us: *Show* us."

Hollywood has long exerted a push-pull effect on fiction writers. The cinematic manner of telling stories through action and dialogue has had an incalculable influence on their conscious and unconscious minds, and the big money to be made from sales of motion-picture rights has provided an irresistible temptation to structure novels so that adaptation from print to film will present no problems. The traits that distinguish Leonard's crime novels are those found in all good films: vivid characterization, believable dialogue, and interesting visual effects. The speeches Elmore places in the mouths of his unique and quirky characters—profane, ungrammatical, ironically humorous, and authentic to place and time—are a particular strength that, combined with plots springing organically from the personalities of the main players and a strong sense of justice, has earned Elmore the sobriquet "the Dickens of Detroit."

The publication of his crime novel *Fifty-two Pickup* in 1974 was the turning point in Elmore's career. He has stated, "I started to realize that the way to describe anywhere, *anywhere*, was to do it from someone's point of view . . . and *leave me out of it*." Perhaps not entirely coincidentally, 1974 was also the year Leonard separated from his first wife and began attending Alcoholics Anonymous meetings. In describing his recovery from alcoholism, he has said, "The key is getting out of yourself." Prior to *Fifty-two Pickup*, Leonard had written his fiction in a conventional manner—that is, mostly in the "voice" of an anonymous narrator who sets the scenes, describes his characters' appearance and behavior, and quotes their verbal interchanges. This objective technique was perfected by Ernest Hemingway, whose Spanish Civil War novel *For Whom the Bell Tolls* (1940) had a permanent effect on Leonard's approach to fiction writing.

Leonard went beyond Hemingway, however, picking up a new mentor in John Steinbeck, particularly that author's novel *Sweet Thursday* (1954), from which he learned to vanish as a narrator and to let his stories be told by the characters themselves. Leonard describes what the viewpoint characters see and hear as well as what they think and feel in language appropriate to each character, so that most of his narration and description reads like dialogue without the quotation marks. It would be inaccurate to call this technique stream of consciousness or interior monologue: It is a modification that Leonard describes as his unique "sound." There are no long passages in italics, no stream-of-consciousness ramblings, nor are there "pebbles in the pond" or other old-fashioned flashback conventions. Since Leonard generally has the reader inside a character's mind, it is easy to move back and forth in time, as he frequently does. The character simply remembers an earlier event, and the reader is instantly transported to the past.

Changing from past to present is simply another of Leonard's ways of deliberately keeping the reader off balance. The one consistent feature of a Leonard novel is that nothing ever stays the same. The writing imitates modern American films, which create the effect of being in continuous motion with changing camera angles, jump cuts, intercuts, tracking shots, aerial shots, flashbacks, and all the other tricks of the trade. Leonard's practice of constantly shifting viewpoints is analogous to modern filmmaking, in which several cameras simultaneously shoot scenes, and strips of film are spliced together to provide visual variety as well as to highlight whatever the director considers most important. Typically, Leonard changes points of view from chapter to chapter; however, he does it within chapters as well, and with effortlessness that makes lesser writers envious.

The average category-fiction writer will describe each character only once, when he or she first appears, and then rely largely on peculiarities of dialogue to differentiate characters from one another for the rest of the book. A standard practice of commercial-fiction writers is to give each character some "shtick"—a cane, a monocle, a pipe, a stammer, a foreign accent—to help the reader remember him or her; still, in many category novels the characters become a hopeless jumble in the reader's mind. The reader's interest in a novel depends on the credibility of the novel's characters. Shootings, bombings, and other forms of violence are not effective unless the reader can believe they are happening to real people. In describing each character's appearance and actions through the eyes of another character, Leonard not only eliminates the need for the "intrusive author" but also characterizes both individuals at once. From beginning to end, he never stops characterizing. He also achieves a strong sense that his characters—often driven, morally ambivalent men from the fringes of society and smart, independent women who are their equals—are actually interrelating, because each is seen in turn through the eyes of someone else. This is one reason Leonard's writing is so much more effective than most category fiction and why he has transcended his genre.

FIFTY-TWO PICKUP

In *Fifty-two Pickup*, Leonard is only partially successful in telling his story through the viewpoints of his characters. The "good guys," a middle-class husband and wife who are being victimized by blackmailers, come alive; however, the "bad guys" are two-dimensional characters exuding the all-too-familiar blend of sadism, cynical humor, and innuendo. Leonard knew that he needed to humanize his villains in order to give his novels balance. In his next novel, *Swag*, he tells the story from the points of view of the "bad guys," two likable young men who take up armed robbery for fun and profit.

SWAG

Swag may be the best novel Leonard has written, although it is far from being his best known. Held in the robbers' viewpoints like a fly in amber, the reader is helplessly but deliciously dragged into one holdup after another and lives out his or her own secret fantasies about walking into a store with a big Colt .45 automatic and walking out with a bag of cash. The reader experiences all the dangers of the profession and ponders all the intangibles: "What if the clerk dives for a gun?" "What if a customer starts screaming?" "What if an alarm goes off?" "What if a cop drives up?" Here, to quote horror writer Stephen King, is "the kind of book that if you get up to see if there are any chocolate chip cookies left, you take it with you so you won't miss anything."

This kind of story has drawbacks. For one thing, the reader is willing to identify with the "bad guys" only as long as they refrain from killing innocent people. Also, stories such as this one, because of the normal reader's ethos for retribution, the need for wrongdoers to be punished for their transgressions, usually end with the protagonists being shot or sent to prison—as in the films *Bonnie and Clyde* (1967) and *Butch Cassidy and the Sundance Kid* (1969). In *Swag*, the antiheroes inevitably become overconfident and walk into disaster. Finally, the viewpoint characters in *Swag* seem less like real criminals than like middle-class young men who are playing at being criminals.

Such a "Robin Hood" plot might serve for a single novel but could not be extended to a career technique. Leonard realized that he needed to learn more about the criminal mentality, and in 1978 he spent two and a half months haunting police headquarters in downtown Detroit, soaking up the atmosphere and listening to the ways detectives, criminals, lawyers, and witnesses really talk. He also established contacts with working detectives, contacts that have continued to prove useful to him. His later novels show a much better balance between protagonists and antagonists.

FREAKY DEAKY

Leonard's highly successful *Freaky Deaky* is an example of his mature technique. A detective who specializes in bomb disposal is pitted against a beautiful but treacherous former antiwar activist ex-convict, in league with an erstwhile bomb builder, who plots to extort a fortune from a pair of multimillionaire brothers whom she suspects of informing on her back in the 1960's, when they were all antiwar activists together. The chapters alternate between the mind of the detective and that of the female extortionist, until all the principals are brought together at the end. The reader sees the world through the terrorists' jaundiced eyes and sympathizes with them; however, the reader also sees the world through the detective's eyes and sympathizes with him a bit more. Leonard has become expert at manipulating the sympathies of his reader, which enables him to create realistic characters. Like people in the real world, the characters in his best novels are not all good or all bad, but mixtures of both.

KILLSHOT

Leonard follows the same blueprint in *Killshot*. The main villain, who is half Native American, is a cold-blooded professional killer; however, the reader achieves a strong identification with and even affection for this lonely, unhappy individual, because the reader spends so much time in the killer's mind. Leonard seems to understand the criminal mentality so well that many people have labored under the erroneous impression that he must have an unsavory past. Whereas he once had trouble making his villains seem credible, his problem later in his career has been making his law-abiding characters seem equally credible. In his next novel, *Get Shorty*, he did away with "good guys" altogether.

GET SHORTY

In *Get Shorty*, for the first time in his career, Leonard sets a novel in Hollywood, California. Here he reaps a rich harvest from his many years of experience as an author of original scripts, adaptations of other authors' novels, and adaptations of his own novels and stories, and as an author of works that have been adapted by others. Among all of his novels, *Get Shorty* most clearly reveals Leonard's intention of making his fiction read like motion pictures. He even incorporates some pages of a screenplay that his sleazy characters are trying to peddle.

Some of the novel's Hollywood characters are so hopelessly immersed in the fantasy world of filmmaking that they see everyone as an actor and every event as a sequence of medium shots, close-ups, and other types of camera shots with varied lighting effects— even when that other character might be coming to shoot them or throw them off a cliff. Leonard is suggesting that Americans are so brainwashed by film and television images that it is becoming impossible for them to distinguish between fantasy and reality.

MAXIMUM BOB

With *Maximum Bob*, his next novel, Leonard returns to familiar turf, southern Florida. The title character is a criminal court judge who, though corrupt to the core professionally and personally, metes out sentences that offenders deserve and easily wins reelection. In contrast to him, Leonard presents capable, dedicated, and honest police officers, assistant district attorneys, and probation officers; however, they fight a losing battle, buffeted not only by corrupt superiors like Judge Bob Isom "BIG" Gibbs, but also by offenders who cannot be rehabilitated. The forces of good frequently confront this dilemma in Leonard novels, sometimes in a contrast between social haves and have-nots.

Like other Leonard books, *Maximum Bob* is peopled by assorted grotesques, notable among them the judge's wife, a onetime underwater dancer who appeared in mermaid costume; she has become a spiritualist with two personalities, one of which is a twelve-year-old 1850's slave girl with a voice like the character Prissy (played by Butterfly McQueen) in the 1939 film *Gone with the Wind*. The major character, however, is completely normal: Kathy Diaz Baker, a young probation officer with carefully honed people skills and analytical crime-solving ability, who narrates most of the novel and is its moral conscience. Baker is not the only narrator, however; other characters also so serve, with the effect that a host of figures are developed more fully than they otherwise would have been. Also, in a curious turn, Leonard relates a portion of an episode from an alligator's point of view.

PRONTO

Leonard again criticizes aspects of law enforcement in *Pronto*, another novel with a Florida setting, though here he focuses primarily on organized crime. The main theme of the book is interdependence. Be it Raylan Givens of the U.S. Marshals Service, Buck Torres of the Miami Beach Police Department, or Federal Bureau of Investigation agent McCormick (whose lack of a first name depersonalizes him), each character's success depends on the cooperation of others, and all grit their teeth when they must enlist the aid of people they consider undesirables. Givens is the focus of a secondary theme, that of fundamental decency. Unimpressed by wealth earned through criminality and corruption, he has a refreshing naïveté tempered only by his determination to redeem a career-damaging error. He is the untainted person of the novel, and that he ultimately prevails—and gets the woman, too—presents an unmistakable thematic message.

Pronto is of special interest in the Leonard canon for two reasons: It introduces Raylan Givens, who returns in the next novel, *Riding the Rap*, and it marks a singular Leonard reversion to a Western trademark. From start to finish, *Pronto* is a chase. The effect of this elementary plot technique is an immediate creation of tension, with momentum and suspense increasing without letup as the narrative moves to climactic shots two pages before the conclusion.

CUBA LIBRE

Leonard also returns to his fictional roots in *Cuba Libre*, a Western complete with a shoot-out and prison escape, albeit set in Cuba in 1898 at the time of the Spanish-American War. The protagonist is an Arizona Territory cowboy and erstwhile bank robber who heads to Cuba in order to sell horses and, not incidentally, to smuggle guns to Cuban rebels. This also is a novel with suspense, fast-paced action, and a collection of grotesque characters that somehow seem credible—no small tribute to Leonard's skills at characterization.

THE HOT KID

A bit of a departure for Leonard, *The Hot Kid*, set during the Great Depression, falls about halfway between his early Westerns and his later contemporary crime novels. Like many of the author's writings, it displays a number of qualities in common with both those extremes of Leonard's creative arts: well-drawn characters, dialogue that rings true, humor (of the deadpan variety), a matter-of-fact tone, and an often violent, breakneck pace.

The novel concerns the exploits of lawman Carlos "Carl" Webster, son of Virgil Webster, who appeared in *Cuba Libre*. Carl is set in opposition to teenage Jack Belmont, son of an oil millionaire, who in emulation of the brazen bandits of the era—Jack aspires to become Public Enemy Number One—falls in with a ruthless gang and attempts to blackmail his father. More straightforward than Leonard's modern-day crime fiction, with fewer outrageous plot twists, *The Hot Kid* nonetheless features the author's usual facility for bringing time and place to vivid life through dialogue and deft scene-setting brushstrokes.

UP IN HONEY'S ROOM

U.S. Marshal Carl Webster, a little older and wiser and married, reappears in *Up in Honey's Room*, which is set in the latter days of World War II. Now the lawman is after a pair of German prisoners of war who have escaped from a detention camp in Oklahoma and made a beeline for Detroit, where they connect with a meat processor who resembles Heinrich Himmler, on their way to joining a German spy ring.

The Honey of the title is the meat processor's ex-wife, Honey Deal. Her unabashed sexuality and wisecracks add considerable spice to a story that, while it has many of the typical Leonard elements—zingy dialogue, wacky secondary characters, bizarre humor, and sufficient action—might otherwise disappoint ardent fans of the author's work. The novel was not a commercial or critical success, owing to its unusually languid pace, uncharacteristically noncompelling plot, unnecessary exaggeration, and uninspired narrative, as well as the flat, uninteresting portrayal of lead character Carl, who did not age well from his previous starring role.

Bill Delaney; Gerald H. Strauss
Updated by Jack Ewing

OTHER MAJOR WORKS

SHORT FICTION: *The Tonto Woman, and Other Western Stories*, 1998; *When the Women Come Out to Dance*, 2002; *The Complete Western Stories of Elmore Leonard*, 2004.

SCREENPLAYS: *The Moonshine War*, 1970 (adaptation of his novel); *Joe Kidd*, 1972; *Mr. Majestyk*, 1974 (adaptation of his novel); *Stick*, 1985 (adaptation of his novel; with Joseph C. Stinson); *Fifty-two Pickup*, 1986 (adaptation of his novel; with John Steppling); *The Rosary Murders*, 1987 (with Fred Walton); *Cat Chaser*, 1989 (adaptation of his novel).

TELEPLAYS: *High Noon Part 2: The Return of Will Kane*, 1980; *Desperado*, 1987.

NONFICTION: *Elmore Leonard's Ten Rules of Writing*, 2007 (illustrated by Joe Ciardiello).

CHILDREN'S LITERATURE: *A Coyote's in the House*, 2004.

BIBLIOGRAPHY

Challen, Paul. *Get Dutch! A Biography of Elmore Leonard*. Toronto, Ont.: ECW Press, 2000. Biography draws on interviews with Leonard and various of his colleagues as well as on the work of scholars who have analyzed Leonard's novels and examined his place within crime fiction and literature in general.

Devlin, James E. *Elmore Leonard.* New York: Twayne, 1999. Literary biography covers a wide range of topics, including Leonard's Westerns, his use of Florida as a locale for his novels, his worldview, his use of genre formulas and pop-culture references, and his film work.

Geherin, David. *Elmore Leonard.* New York: Continuum, 1989. Provides a brief biography and then a critical evaluation of Leonard's works, beginning with his early Western short stories and concluding with more detailed discussion of his novels of the 1980's. Includes chronology, selected bibliography, and index.

Leonard, Elmore. "Dutch in Detroit." Interview by Jeff Zaleski. *Publishers Weekly,* January 21, 2002. In an at-home interview, Leonard discusses his approach to writing and other topics.

_____. "Elmore Leonard." Interview by Stuart Kaminsky. In *Behind the Mystery: Top Mystery Writers.* Cohasset, Mass.: Hot House Press, 2005. Leonard discusses his work, his personal life, and other topics in this interview conducted by Kaminsky, a popular mystery writer.

_____. *Elmore Leonard's Ten Rules of Writing.* New York: William Morrow, 2007. Leonard lists and explains the writing guidelines—including "Never open a book with weather," "Keep your exclamation points under control," and "Try to leave out the parts that readers tend to skip"—that he has developed for himself over the course of more than a half century of writing for publication.

Mendelsohn, Daniel. "Quien es Más Macho? Elmore Leonard or James Lee Burke?" *Esquire,* October, 2004. Compares the recent works of four thriller writers: Leonard, James Lee Burke, Andrew Vachss, and James Patterson.

Rhodes, Chip. "Elmore Leonard: Realism After the End of Ideology." In *Politics, Desire, and the Hollywood Novel.* Iowa City: University of Iowa Press, 2008. Scholarly discussion of Leonard's contribution to the genre of the "Hollywood novel" is part of a larger work of literary criticism that provides close readings of novels that fall into this category, including those of Nathanael West and Raymond Chandler.

Wholey, Dennis, ed. *The Courage to Change: Personal Conversations About Alcohol with Dennis Wholey.* New York: Warner Books, 1986. In a chapter titled "Quitting," Leonard discusses his growing problem with alcohol over two decades and the psychological insights that enabled him to stop drinking. The author's hard-won victory over alcoholism has been an important influence on his writing technique and choice of subjects.

ROSS MACDONALD
Kenneth Millar

Born: Los Gatos, California; December 13, 1915
Died: Santa Barbara, California; July 11, 1983
Also known as: John Macdonald; John Ross Macdonald

OTHER LITERARY FORMS

Ross Macdonald's reputation is based primarily on his twenty-four published novels, particularly on the eighteen that feature private detective Lew Archer. He also published a collection of short stories, *Lew Archer, Private Investigator* (1977), which includes all the stories from an earlier collection, *The Name Is Archer* (1955). *Self-Portrait: Ceaselessly into the Past* (1981) gathers a selection of his essays, interviews, and lectures about his own work and about other writers, including two essays first published in his *On Crime Writing* (1973). *The Archer Files: The Complete Short Stories of Lew Archer, Private Investigator* (2007) collects all the brief Archer fiction, including pieces that remained unfinished. Macdonald also wrote book reviews and articles on conservation and politics.

ACHIEVEMENTS

Ross Macdonald was recognized early in his career as the successor to Dashiell Hammett and Raymond Chandler in the field of realistic crime fiction, and his detective, Lew Archer, was recognized as the successor to Sam Spade and Philip Marlowe. Macdonald's advance over his predecessors was in the greater emphasis he placed on psychology and character, creating a more humane and complex detective and more intricate plotting. He is generally credited with raising the detective novel to the level of serious literature. The Mystery Writers of America awarded him Edgar Allan Poe scrolls in 1962 and 1963. In 1964, *The Chill* was awarded the Silver Dagger by the Crime Writers' Association of Great Britain. The same organization gave his next novel, *The Far Side of the Dollar*, the Golden Dagger as the best crime novel of the year.

Macdonald served as president of the Mystery Writers of America in 1965 and was made a Grand Master of that organization in 1974. In a review of *The Goodbye Look* in *The New York Times Book Review*, William Goldman called the Lew Archer books "the finest series of detective novels ever written by an American." His work has gained popular as well as critical acclaim: *The Goodbye Look*, *The Underground Man*, *Sleeping Beauty*, and *The Blue Hammer* were all national best sellers. Three of his books have been made into successful motion pictures, two starring Paul Newman as Lew Archer: *The Moving Target*, which was made into the film *Harper* (1966), and the film version of *The Drowning Pool*, which was released in 1975. *The Three Roads* was adapted into the film *Double Negative* (1980).

BIOGRAPHY

Ross Macdonald, whose given name is Kenneth Millar, was born in Los Gatos, California, on December 13, 1915. He published his early novels as Millar or John Macdonald or John Ross Macdonald, but settled on the pseudonym Ross Macdonald by the time he wrote *The Barbarous Coast*, in order to avoid being confused with two other famous mystery writers: his wife, Margaret Millar, whom he had married in 1938, and John D. Macdonald.

Ross Macdonald's family moved to Vancouver, British Columbia, soon after he was born, and he was reared and educated in Canada. After he graduated with honors from the University of Western Ontario in 1938, he taught English and history at a high school in Toronto and began graduate work at the University of Michigan in Ann Arbor during the summers. He returned to the United States permanently in 1941, when he began full-time graduate studies at Ann Arbor, receiving his master's degree in English in 1943. During World War II, he served as a communications officer aboard an escort carrier in the Pacific and participated in the battle for Okinawa. In 1951, he was awarded a doctorate in English from the University of Michigan, writing his dissertation on the psychological criticism of Samuel Taylor Coleridge. Macdonald belonged to the American Civil Liberties Union and, as a dedicated conservationist, was a member of the Sierra Club and helped found the

Santa Barbara, California, chapter of the National Audubon Society. He lived in Santa Barbara from 1946 until his death from complications of Alzheimer's disease on July 11, 1983.

Analysis

Ross Macdonald's twenty-four novels fall fairly neatly into three groups: Those in which Lew Archer does not appear form a distinct group, and the Archer series itself may be separated into two periods. His first four books, *The Dark Tunnel, Trouble Follows Me, Blue City,* and *The Three Roads,* together with two later works, *Meet Me at the Morgue* and *The Ferguson Affair,* do not feature Lew Archer. These six novels, especially the first three, are typical treatments of wartime espionage or political corruption and are primarily of interest to the extent that they prefigure the concerns of later works: *The Three Roads,* for example, contains Macdonald's first explicit use of the Oedipus myth as a plot structure and of California as a setting.

The first six Archer books—*The Moving Target, The Drowning Pool, The Way Some People Die, The Ivory Grin, Find a Victim,* and *The Barbarous Coast*—introduce and refine the character of Archer, build the society and geography of California into important thematic elements, and feature increasingly complex plots, with multiple murders and plot lines. Archer still shows traces of the influence of the hard-boiled detectives of Hammett and Chandler (he is named for Miles Archer, Sam Spade's partner in Hammett's *The Maltese Falcon,* 1930, but is closely patterned on Philip Marlowe), but he also shows marks of the sensitivity and patience, the reliance on understanding and analysis, that separate him from his models. Even in these early books, Archer is more often a questioner than a doer.

The Doomsters

The next twelve Archer novels constitute Macdonald's major achievement. Crimes in these books are not usually committed by professional criminals but rather by middle-class people going through emotional crises. They followed a period of personal crisis in Macdonald's own life, during which he underwent psychotherapy. All these novels deal more or less explicitly with psychological issues. *The Doomsters,* although begun before Macdonald's psychoanalysis, presents his first extended treatment of the plot of intrafamilial relations that dominates all the later books.

Carl Hallman, a psychologically disturbed young man, appears at Archer's door after escaping from the state mental hospital. He has been confined there as a murder suspect in the mysterious death of his father. Although he knows himself to be legally innocent, he feels guilty for having quarreled violently with his father on the night of his death. This Oedipal tension between father and son, following the pattern of Sigmund Freud's famous interpretation, often serves as the mainspring of the plot in Macdonald's later novels. After hiring Archer to investigate the death, Carl panics and escapes again as Archer is returning him to the hospital. Carl's brother, Jerry, and sister-in-law, Zinnie, are subsequently murdered under circumstances that appear to incriminate Carl.

As it turns out, the case really began three years earlier, with the apparently accidental drowning of Carl's mother, Alicia. She had forced Carl's wife, Mildred, to undergo an abortion at gunpoint at the hands of Dr. Grantland. Mildred hit Alicia over the head with a bottle when she came out of anesthesia and assumed that she had killed her. Dr. Grantland actually killed Alicia and made it look like a drowning, but he conceals this fact and uses his power over Mildred, who is becoming psychologically unstable, to persuade her to kill Carl's father. He has designs on the family's money, and Mildred is greedy herself. She is also influenced, however, by her hatred of her own father, who deserted her mother, and by her desire to possess Carl entirely, to gain his love for herself by eliminating conflicting familial claims to it. She murders his brother and sister-in-law, his only remaining family, as she increasingly loses touch with sanity.

Women are frequently the murderers in Macdonald's books, and he analyzed the reasons behind this in an interview. He considered that people who have been victims tend to victimize others in turn, and he regarded American society as one that systematically victimizes women. Mildred's difficult childhood and gunpoint abortion provide a clear illustration of this theme.

THE GALTON CASE

While the focus on family psychology constituted a clean break with the Hammett and Chandler school as well as with most of Macdonald's own early work, the next Archer novel, *The Galton Case*, was of even greater importance for Macdonald's career. In *The Doomsters*, the case is rooted in a crime committed three years earlier; in *The Galton Case*, as in most of the novels to follow, the present crime is rooted deeper in the past, in the preceding generation. This gives Macdonald the means to show the long-term effects of the influence of the family on each of its members. The elderly Maria Galton hires Archer to trace her son, Anthony, who had stolen money from his father after a quarrel (reminiscent of that between Carl Hallman and his father) and run off to the San Francisco area with his pregnant wife, Teddy, twenty-three years before. Archer discovers that Anthony, calling himself John Brown, was murdered not long after his disappearance. He also finds a young man calling himself John Brown, Jr., who claims to be searching for his long-lost father. Events lead Archer to Canada, where he learns that the young man is Theo Fredericks, the son of Nelson Fredericks and his wife. Maria Galton's lawyer, Gordon Sable, has planned Theo's masquerade as her grandson to acquire her money when she dies. Yet a further plot twist reveals that Theo really is Anthony Galton's son. Fred Nelson had murdered Anthony twenty-three years before for the money he had stolen from his father and had taken Anthony's wife and son as his own under the name Fredericks.

This summary does not reflect the true complexity of the novel, which ties together a number of other elements, but does bring out the major theme of the son searching for his father, a theme that will recur in later works such as *The Far Side of the Dollar*, *The Instant Enemy*, *The Goodbye Look*, *The Underground Man*, and *The Blue Hammer*. As Macdonald explains in his essay "Writing *The Galton Case*" (1973), this plot is roughly shaped on his own life. His own father left him and his mother when he was three years old. Like Macdonald, John Brown, Jr., was born in California, grew up in Canada, and attended the University of Michigan before returning to California. It is interesting that each man assumed his lost father's name: Macdonald was Kenneth Millar's father's middle name. This transformation of personal family history into fiction seems to have facilitated the breakthrough that led Macdonald to write the rest of his novels about varying permutations of the relations between parents and children.

THE ZEBRA-STRIPED HEARSE

The exploration of the relations between three generations of fathers and sons in *The Galton Case* was followed by examinations of father and daughter relationships in *The Wycherly Woman* and *The Zebra-Striped Hearse*. Macdonald always counted the latter among his favorites for its intensity and range. In *The Zebra-Striped Hearse*, Archer is hired by Mark Blackwell to investigate his daughter Harriet's fiancé, Burke Damis, with a view to preventing their marriage. The implication is made that Mark sees Damis as a rival for his daughter's love. Archer discovers that Damis is really Bruce Campion and is suspected of having murdered his wife, Dolly, and another man, Quincy Ralph Simpson. Suspicion shifts to Mark when it is revealed that he is the father of Dolly's baby and then to Mark's wife, Isobel, who knew Dolly as a child. Harriet disappears and Mark confesses to murdering her, Dolly, and Simpson before committing suicide. Yet Archer believes that Harriet is still alive and tracks her down in Mexico. She had killed Dolly to clear the way for her marriage to Bruce and had also killed Simpson when he discovered her crime. Underlying her motive for Dolly's murder, however, is another Freudian pattern. The child of Mark and Dolly is Harriet's half brother, making Dolly a sort of mother figure and, by extension, making her husband, Bruce, a sort of father figure. Harriet thus symbolically kills her mother and marries her father.

THE CHILL

The Chill features one of Macdonald's most complex plots, but at its center is another basic family relationship, this time between a mother and son. Archer is brought into the case by Alex Kincaid, who hires him to find his wife, Dolly, who has disappeared the day after their wedding after a visit from an unknown man. The visitor turns out to have been her father, Thomas McGee, who has just been released from prison after serving a ten-year sentence for the murder of his wife and Dolly's mother, Constance. Later, it is revealed that he had convinced her of his innocence and told her that Constance was having an affair with Roy Bradshaw.

To learn more about Roy, Dolly has left Alex to go to work for Roy's mother, Mrs.

Bradshaw, as a driver and companion. Shortly thereafter, she is found, hysterical, at the Bradshaws', talking about the murder of her college counselor, Helen Haggerty. Helen is soon discovered murdered and the weapon used is found under Dolly's mattress, though under circumstances that suggest that it may have been planted there. Archer learns from Helen's mother that she had been deeply affected by a death that occurred twenty years before. Luke Deloney had been killed in a shooting that was ruled accidental on the basis of an investigation that was conducted by Helen's father, but Helen was convinced that the facts had been covered up. Luke's widow admits to Archer that there had been a cover-up, that her husband committed suicide. Archer later discovers another connection between the recent death and those of ten and twenty years ago: Roy Bradshaw was the elevator boy at the building in which Luke died.

Investigation of Roy reveals that he has been secretly married to Laura Sutherland, having recently obtained a divorce from a woman named Letitia Macready. Archer confronts Mrs. Bradshaw with the latter fact (though not the former), and after an initial denial she confirms that twenty years ago Roy had briefly been married to a much older woman. Letitia turns out to have been the sister of Luke's wife, and it was rumored that she was having an affair with her sister's husband. Letitia apparently died in Europe during World War II, shortly after Luke's death. Archer eventually draws a fuller story out of Roy: Luke, who was indeed Letitia's lover, found her in bed with Roy. There had been a violent struggle, during which Letitia accidentally shot and killed Luke. Roy married her and took her to Europe, later returning with her to America. He had been leading a secret double life ever since, concealing Letitia, now quite old and sick, from all of his friends as well as from the police and, especially, from his possessive mother. During this confession, Archer answers a telephone call and hears Laura, who believes that she is speaking to Roy, tell him that "she" has discovered their secret marriage. Roy attacks Archer at this news and escapes in his car to attempt to intercept the other woman, who had vowed to kill Laura. Roy is killed when Mrs. Bradshaw's car crashes into his. Archer knows by now that Mrs. Bradshaw is not Roy's mother, but his first wife: She is Letitia Macready.

Roy has acted out the Oedipal drama of the death of a father figure, Letitia's lover Luke, and the marriage to a mother figure, the older woman who posed as his real mother. (Macdonald develops the obverse of this plot in *Black Money*, which pairs a young woman with a much older man.) Letitia murdered Constance McGee because Roy had been having an affair with her and murdered Helen Haggerty in the belief that it was she rather than Laura Sutherland whom Roy was currently seeing.

This unraveling of the plot has come a long way from Alex Kincaid's request that Archer find his wife, but one of the characteristics of Macdonald's later novels is the way in which seemingly unrelated events and characters come together. The deeper Archer goes into a set of circumstances involving people who know one another, the more connectedness he finds. These novels all have large casts of characters and a series of crimes, often occurring decades apart. Once the proper connections are made, however, there is usually only one murderer and one fundamental relationship at the center of the plot. All the disparate elements, past and present, hang together in one piece.

While Freudian themes continued to dominate Macdonald's work, he often combined them with elements adapted from other stories from classical mythology or the Bible. *The Far Side of the Dollar* has been seen as a modern, inverted version of the story of Ulysses and Penelope. Jasper Blevins, the fratricidal murderer of *The Instant Enemy*, explicitly draws the analogy between his story and that of Cain and Abel. He has also murdered one of his stepfathers, adding the Oedipal master plot to the biblical plot, and murdered his own wife in one of the series' most violent books, perhaps reflecting the violence of the Vietnam War period, during which the book was written. The complex events of *The Goodbye Look* are catalyzed by the search for a gold box that is specifically compared to Pandora's box. Again the myth is combined with the primal story of the parricide, this time committed by a child. All three of these books also repeat the quintessential Macdonald plot of a young man's search for his missing father.

THE UNDERGROUND MAN

The search for the absent father also sets in motion the events of *The Underground Man*, probably the most admired of Macdonald's works. This novel, together with his next, *Sleeping Beauty*, also reflects its author's abiding concern with conservation. Each novel examines an ecological crime as well as a series of crimes committed against individuals. In *Sleeping Beauty*, Macdonald uses an offshore oil spill, inspired by the 1967 spill near his home in Santa Barbara, as a symbol of the moral life of the society responsible for it, in particular that of the Lennox family, which runs the oil corporation and is also the locus of the series of murders in the book. In *The Underground Man*, the disaster of a human-made brush fire serves similar ends.

The story begins unexceptionally: Archer is taking a day off at home, feeding the birds in his yard. He strikes up an acquaintance with young Ronny Broadhurst and Ronny's mother, Jean, who are staying at the home of Archer's neighbors. The boy's father, Stanley, disrupts the meeting when he drives up with a young girl, later identified as Sue Crandall, and takes his son to visit Stanley's mother, Elizabeth Broadhurst. They never pay the planned visit, and when Jean hears that a fire has broken out in that area, she enlists Archer to help her look for them. On the way there, Jean explains that her husband has gradually become obsessed by his search for his father, Leo, who apparently ran away with Ellen Kilpatrick, the wife of a neighbor, Brian, some fifteen years ago. It turns out that Stanley, accompanied by Ronny and Sue, obtained a key from Elizabeth's gardener, Fritz Snow, and had gone up to her cabin on a mountain nearby. There, Archer finds Stanley, murdered and half-buried. The fire originated from a cigarillo Stanley dropped when he was killed, creating a causal as well as symbolic link between the personal and ecological disasters.

After an investigation that is complex even by Macdonald's standards, Archer is able to reconstruct the past events that explain those of the present. The seeds of the present crimes are found in the previous generation. Eighteen years ago, Leo Broadhurst got Martha Nickerson, an underage girl, pregnant. She ran away with Fritz Snow and Al Sweetner in a car they stole from Lester Crandall. The incident was planned by Leo and Martha to provide a scapegoat to assume the paternity of her coming child. When they were tracked down, Al went to jail for three years, Fritz was sentenced to work in a forestry camp for six months, and Martha married Lester Crandall.

Three years later, Leo was having an affair with Ellen Kilpatrick. She went to Reno to obtain a divorce from her husband, Brian, and waited there for Leo to join her. While she was gone, however, Leo went up to the cabin with Martha and their child, Sue. Brian, who knew about his wife's affair with Leo and wanted revenge, discovered the renewal of this earlier affair and informed Leo's wife, Elizabeth. She went up to the mountain cabin and shot her husband, believing that she killed him. Stanley, who had followed his mother that night, was an aural witness to the shooting of his father, as was Susan, also Leo's child. Yet Leo had not been killed by the bullet. He was stabbed to death, as he lay unconscious, by Edna Snow, Fritz's mother, in revenge for the trouble that Leo and Martha's affair had caused her son and also as a self-appointed agent of judgment on Leo's adulteries. She forced Fritz and Al to bury Leo near the cabin. Fifteen years later, on almost the same spot, she murders Stanley, who is on the verge of discovering his father's body and Edna's crime. Life moves in a circle as Ronny witnesses Stanley's death in the same place that Stanley witnessed Leo's shooting. The connection is reinforced by Sue's presence at both events.

THE BLUE HAMMER

The last novel Macdonald wrote is *The Blue Hammer,* and whether he consciously intended it to be the last, it provides in certain ways an appropriate conclusion to the series. It is the first time, apart from a brief interlude in *The Goodbye Look,* that Archer has a romantic interest. The effects of a lack of love preoccupy all the Archer novels, and Archer recognizes in this book that the same lack has had its effects on him. He has been single since his divorce from his wife, Sue, which took place before the first book begins. In the last book, he meets and soon falls in love with Betty Jo Siddon, a young newspaper reporter. Yet Macdonald knew that Raymond Chandler was unable to continue the Philip Marlowe novels after marrying off his detective, and perhaps he intended to end his own series similarly. It seems that the genre requires a detective who is himself without personal ties, who is able to and perhaps driven to move freely into and then out of the lives of others. Indeed, the involvement of Betty in the case does create a tension between Archer's personal and professional interests.

Another suggestion that *The Blue Hammer* may have been intended to be the last of the Archer novels lies in its symmetry with the first, *The Moving Target.* In the earlier book, Archer kills a man in a struggle in the ocean, the only such occurrence in the eighteen books and an indication of the extent to which the compassionate Archer differs from his more violent predecessors. In the last book, he finds himself in a similar struggle, but this time manages to save his adversary. Archer specifically parallels the two events and feels that he has balanced out his earlier sin, somehow completing a pattern.

The plot of *The Blue Hammer* is built around the Dostoevskian theme of the double, a theme that Macdonald treated before in *The Wycherly Woman*, in which Phoebe Wycherly assumes the identity of her murdered mother, and in *The Instant Enemy*, in which Jasper Blevins takes on the role of his murdered half brother. The motif is developed here in its most elaborate form and combined with the familiar themes of the crimes of the past shaping those of the present and of the son's search for his true father, forming an appropriate summation of the major themes of MacDonald's entire Archer series.

Thirty-two years ago, Richard Chantry stole the paintings of his supposed half brother, William Mead, then serving in the Army, and married William's girlfriend Francine. William murdered Richard when he returned and assumed his identity as Francine's husband, though he had already married a woman named Sarah and had a son with her named Fred. Seven years later, Gerard Johnson, a friend of William from the Army, appears at William's door with Sarah and Fred, threatening to blackmail him. William kills Gerard and then takes his name, in a doubling of the theme of doubleness. He returns to live with Sarah and Fred and remains a recluse for twenty-five years to hide his crimes.

The case begins for Archer when he is called in to locate a painting that has been stolen from Jack Biemeyer. He learns that it was taken by Fred Johnson, who wanted to study it to determine whether it was a recent work by the famous artist Richard Chantry, who had mysteriously vanished twenty-five years before. If genuine, it would establish that the painter was still alive. Fred had seen similar pictures in the Johnson home and had formed the idea that Chantry might be his real father. William steals the painting, which is one of his own works, in a doubling of his earlier theft of his own paintings from Richard. The painting had been sold by Sarah to an art dealer, and William is forced to kill again to prevent the discovery of his true identity and his earlier murders. By the book's guardedly positive resolution, three generations of men—Fred Johnson; his father, William Mead; and Jack Biemeyer, who turns out to be William's father—have all come to the admission or recognition of their previously concealed identities and have come to a kind of redemption through their suffering.

Macdonald's work, in terms of quantity as well as quality, constitutes an unparalleled achievement in the detective genre. The twenty-four novels, particularly the eighteen that feature Lew Archer, form a remarkably coherent body of work both stylistically and thematically. The last twelve Archer books have received especially high critical as well as popular acclaim and have secured Macdonald's standing as the author of the finest series of detective novels ever written, perhaps the only such series to have bridged the gap between popular and serious literature.

William Nelles

OTHER MAJOR WORKS

SHORT FICTION: *The Name Is Archer*, 1955; *Lew Archer, Private Investigator*, 1977; *Strangers in Town: Three Newly Discovered Mysteries*, 2001 (Tom Nolan, editor); *The Archer Files: The Complete Short Stories of Lew Archer, Private Investigator*, 2007 (Nolan, editor).

NONFICTION: *On Crime Writing*, 1973; *Self-Portrait: Ceaselessly into the Past*, 1981 (Ralph B. Sipper, editor).

BIBLIOGRAPHY

Bruccoli, Matthew J. *Ross Macdonald*. San Diego, Calif.: Harcourt Brace Jovanovich, 1984. Describes the development of Macdonald's popular reputation as a prolific author of detective fiction and his critical reputation as a writer of literary merit. Includes illustrations, an appendix with an abstract of his doctoral thesis, notes, a bibliography, and an index.

Bruccoli, Matthew J., and Richard Layman, eds. *Hardboiled Mystery Writers: Raymond Chandler, Dashiell Hammett, Ross Macdonald*. New York: Carroll & Graf, 2002. A study of the lives and works of Macdonald, Dashiell Hammett, and Raymond Chandler. Includes photographs, reproductions of manuscript pages, interviews, articles, excerpts from earlier studies, letters, and contemporary reviews.

Gale, Robert. *A Ross Macdonald Companion*. Westport, Conn.: Greenwood Press, 2002. A Macdonald reference work with alphabetically arranged entries on his novels, fictional characters, family members, and professional acquaintances. The entries about the novels offer plot summaries, lists of characters, and brief critical commentaries. Includes a select bibliography and a chronology.

Kreyling, Michael. *The Novels of Ross Macdonald*. Columbia: University of South Carolina Press, 2005. An examination of eighteen detective novels by Macdonald. Kreyling compares Macdonald's work to that of Dashiell Hammett and Raymond Chandler, and he argues that Macdonald's books in particular deserve a more serious reading by critics of detective fiction.

Mahan, Jeffrey H. *A Long Way from Solving That One: Psycho/Social and Ethical Implications of Ross Macdonald's Lew Archer Tales*. Lanham, Md.: University Press of America, 1990. Mahan explores the Lew Archer stories and their importance in the detective fiction canon from a variety of perspectives, applying social, ethical, and Freudian theories to Macdonald's fiction. Includes a bibliography.

Nolan, Tom. *Ross Macdonald: A Biography*. New York: Scribner, 1999. The first full-length biography of Macdonald, providing many previously unknown details of his life. Nolan also discusses the origins of Macdonald's novels and critical responses they have received.

Schopen, Bernard A. *Ross Macdonald*. Boston: Twayne, 1990. A sound introductory study that examines Macdonald's development of the Lew Archer character, his mastery of the form of the detective novel, and the maturation of his art culminating in *The Underground Man*. Includes detailed notes and an annotated bibliography.

Sipper, Ralph B., ed. *Ross Macdonald: Inward Journey*. Santa Barbara, Calif.: Cordelia Editions, 1984. This collection of twenty-seven articles includes two by Macdonald—one a transcription of a speech about mystery fiction and the other a letter to a publisher that discusses Raymond Chandler's work in relation to his own.

Skinner, Robert E. *The Hard-Boiled Explicator: A Guide to the Study of Dashiell Hammett, Raymond Chandler, and Ross Macdonald*. Metuchen, N.J.: Scarecrow Press, 1985. An indispensable volume for readers interested in finding unpublished dissertations as well as mainstream criticism on the three writers. Includes brief introductions to each author, followed by annotated bibliographies of books, articles, and reviews.

Speir, Jerry. *Ross Macdonald*. New York: Frederick Ungar, 1978. A good introduction to Macdonald's work, with a brief biography and a discussion of his novels. Includes chapters on his character Lew Archer, on alienation and other themes, on Macdonald's writing style, and on scholarly criticism. Contains a bibliography, notes, and an index.

WALTER MOSLEY

Born: Los Angeles, California; January 12, 1952
Also known as: Walter Ellis Mosley

PRINCIPAL LONG FICTION

Devil in a Blue Dress, 1990
A Red Death, 1991
White Butterfly, 1992
Black Betty, 1994
RL's Dream, 1995
Gone Fishin', 1996
A Little Yellow Dog, 1996
Always Outnumbered, Always Outgunned, 1998
Blue Light, 1998
Walkin' the Dog, 1999
Fearless Jones, 2001
Bad Boy Brawly Brown, 2002
Fear Itself, 2003
Little Scarlet, 2004
The Man in My Basement, 2004
Cinnamon Kiss, 2005
Fear of the Dark, 2006
Fortunate Son, 2006
The Wave, 2006
Blonde Faith, 2007
Killing Johnny Fry, 2007
Diablerie, 2008
*The Right Mistake: The Further Philosophical Investigations of Socrates
    Fortlow,* 2008
The Tempest Tales, 2008

OTHER LITERARY FORMS

In addition to his novels, Walter Mosley (MOHZ-lee) has coedited *Black Genius: African American Solutions to African American Problems* (1999) and has written a critical analysis of capitalism, *Workin' on the Chain Gang: Shaking Off the Dead Hand of History* (2000). In *What Next: A Memoir Toward World Peace* (2003), he contends that the African American experience provides a unique and helpful perspective on the way to achieve world peace. As in his novels, in his nonfiction Mosley transforms social problems into palpable personal ones—in this case by drawing on his own family history. Mosley attacks American provincialism and provides his own idiosyncratic solutions to the problem in *Life Out of Context: Which Includes a Proposal for the Non-violent Takeover of the House of Representatives* (2006). *This Year You Write Your Novel* (2007) provides practical advice for starting and completing a novel within a year. Mosley's short stories have been published in several collections, including *Futureland: Nine Stories of an Imminent World* (2001).

ACHIEVEMENTS

A prolific author of mystery, young adult, and science-fiction novels, Walter Mosley has become one of the most successful African American authors whose work has crossed over into mainstream fiction. His work has been compared favorably to that of classic African American authors such as Chester Himes and John Edgar Wideman. As Frances Smith Foster has observed, however, Mosley surpasses these authors and others in his ability to dramatize the lives of ordinary African Americans with a political consciousness and a sense of social history.

Mosley's first novel, *Devil in a Blue Dress*, was nominated for the prestigious Edgar Award, presented by the Mystery Writers of America, as well as the Shamus Award of the Private Eye Writers of America. In 1996, Mosley won an award from the Black Caucus of the American Library Association as well as an O. Henry Award. *Bad Boy Brawly Brown* was nominated for the International Association of Crime Writers' Hammett Prize. In 2005, Mosley received several honors: the Sundance Institute's Risk-Takers' Award; a Lifetime Achievement Award presented at the Twenty-first Annual Celebration of Black Writing, held by the Art Sanctuary of Philadelphia; and an honorary doctorate presented by the City College of the City University of New York.

BIOGRAPHY

Walter Ellis Mosley was born in January, 1952, and grew up in South Central Los Angeles, which became the setting of many of his novels. Early in his life he became acutely aware of social and political issues, hearing stories from his African American father about life in the American South and from his Jewish mother about anti-Semitism.

Mosley earned a bachelor's degree in political science from Johnson State College in Vermont and then worked as a computer programmer for fifteen years (an experience he puts to good use in his novel *Diablerie*) before enrolling in a creative-writing program at City College of the City University of New York, where he was taught by Edna O'Brien and other important writers. He had long been a keen reader of detective stories, and it is not surprising that he turned to the genre in his first novel—although the initial inspiration for his work was Alice Walker's novel *The Color Purple* (1982). One of Mosley's teachers showed an early draft of Mosley's first novel to her literary agent, who was able to sell it to the publishing company W. W. Norton.

Mosley's most famous character, Easy Rawlins, belongs to Mosley's father's generation, and many of Rawlins's experiences are based on stories that Mosley's father told him about the lives of black people of his generation in both northern and southern areas of the United States. Los Angeles, the main setting of the Rawlins novels, represents the promise and the peril that Mosley's father found in a wide-open and yet highly stratified society full of opportunity but also dangerous for African Americans.

ANALYSIS

Walter Mosley has been praised for his powerful evocation of African Americans and their milieu. His novels show African Americans interacting with each other, creating their own problems and solutions. While the white power structure certainly impinges on these characters, they are not victims. On the contrary, they are accorded their full humanity and the right, so to speak, to commit their own mistakes and achieve their own successes as individuals and as a people.

RL's Dream

RL's Dream has been compared favorably with Ralph Ellison's classic novel *Invisible Man* (1952), an apt comparison, since Mosley, like his illustrious predecessor, writes a prose that is suffused with the rhythms of the blues. Like Ellison, Mosley does not blink at the harshness of the African American experience, and he finds a meaning in suffering, a definition of humanity, that triumphs over degradation.

Robert "RL" Johnson, a legendary blues musician, is the presiding presence in the novel. Atwater "Soupspoon" Wise is an aging African American musician obsessed with memories of RL and determined to recover for posterity the role of the blues in African American life. Kiki Waters, a white girl from Arkansas, befriends the aging Soupspoon, takes care of him, and helps to ensure that he is able to tell his life story.

RL exists only in the memories of those he touched with his music. By dreaming of RL, Soupspoon provides the geography of the blues, explaining to the young Kiki how it was for talented musicians who had to disguise their genius by playing the slack-jawed, clownish Negro—except that RL refused to bow to this form of degradation, paying the physical and mental price for his independence: "Ain't no start to his misery," Soupspoon's book says of RL, "An' death could not never ease his kinda pain."

Life is a tragedy and full of pain, and yet it is a story that is redeemable in the beauty of the blues. This is the story of the blues that Soupspoon conveys to Kiki and a story that he is determined to share with the world. Years earlier, he was asked to provide an account of his career, but his life was too complicated and his suffering too great for him to contemplate telling his own tale. Now confronting certain death, Soupspoon finds that he has the motivation and the perspective to organize his experience into a narrative, which he composes on a tape recorder as he relates his memories to Kiki and others.

Soupspoon regards RL's music as the essence of the blues—perhaps because RL did not permit any event or experience to distract him from the making of music. He is, then, the blues personified, always beset with suffering and yet indomitable and inimitable. The latter point is what Soupspoon emphasizes; that is, he regards himself as a pale imitation of RL because RL is the epitome of a form of music that has allowed a whole people to endure suffering and even to prevail by creating great art.

RL is a "dream" in the sense that he represents the artist's aspirations, the ideal of a great music that transcends life's limitations and the frailties of the artists who perform that music. By recounting his "dream" of RL, Soupspoon is ennobling not only his life but also the strivings of the people blues artists muse about in their music.

WALKIN' THE DOG

Walkin' the Dog is Mosley's second novel in his series featuring Socrates Fortlow, an ex-convict who has settled down to make his quiet way in the world but who is constantly challenged by events in his neighborhood and community that make it difficult for him to remain a peaceful man. Fortlow's difficulty is that he cannot ignore injustice. At the same time, he realizes that for the first time in his life he may actually have the opportunity to live like a normal person with a decent job and home, although he can hardly accept his good fortune—even when he is offered a promotion at the produce market. Fortlow wonders if he wants more responsibility. He values his independence, and a part of him would prefer not to take on more in the form of employment.

Fortlow lives in a high-crime neighborhood but has managed to stay out of jail for nine years. He has a modest and very circumscribed domestic life, which includes a two-legged dog named Killer. It is hard for him to live on an even keel, however, when the police continue to pester him, trying to link him to various crimes in his area. Inured to police suspicion, Fortlow just barely manages to keep his temper—although he stands up for his rights and will not be bullied.

The novel takes the form of various incidents, complete in themselves as short stories but linked by Fortlow's continual troubles with the law, that culminate in his campaign to protest the violent crimes of a cop who has abused and even killed African Americans. Fortlow turns himself into a walking billboard, and though at first he seems destined to be arrested, others who share his concerns soon join him. Ultimately, one man's protest becomes a community's cause, which in turn generates media attention and pressure on the police department to discipline and punish its own. This story is a triumph for Fortlow, since his first impulse was simply to murder the cop. Now he seeks ways to channel his rage into socially responsible behavior. At the same time, he refuses to accept the status quo; he still takes risks that he knows may land him in jail once more.

Mosley has emphasized that in Socrates Fortlow he has created a black thinker, a kind of representative of African American consciousness. This is probably why the Fortlow stories have relatively little plot and action. They are centered, instead, on the development of character and theme. As a result, Mosley's main character does indeed seem like the skeptical philosopher for whom he is named. He doubts the certitudes that others express because he is aware of the precariousness not only of his own position but also that of others, who might, like himself, end up in prison precisely because their worldviews are flawed and do not take in account so many of the forces in society over which they have no control. In this respect, Fortlow has been compared with Tom Joad, the philosopher/ common man of John Steinbeck's *The Grapes of Wrath* (1939). Both men, hemmed in by societal pressures, commit murder, and yet they conceive of a redemptive vision of humanity that transcends their individual fates.

BAD BOY BRAWLY BROWN

In *Bad Boy Brawly Brown*, Easy Rawlins is out to find the title character and keep him out of trouble. The boy's mother and his stepfather (an old friend of Easy) are concerned that Brawly has become involved with a group of black revolutionaries. The setting is the Los Angeles neighborhood of Watts in 1964, the year before the riots that alarmed both the city and the nation. Easy—not a man susceptible to the rhetoric of black power—has to negotiate his way through the duplicity of the black revolutionaries, Brawly's naïve faith in them, and the machinations of law-enforcement agents attempting to infiltrate and destroy political protest groups.

Very much an individualist, Easy is wary of the movement leaders and their zealous lieutenants, but he is hardly any more sanguine about the motives of the white establishment and the police. Easy is no rebel (indeed, he is a World War II combat veteran), but he is also not complacent about the status quo. He provides a critical perspective on all sides of this engrossing political novel, never forsaking his unique experience as a black man but also not overlooking the opportunities his country does offer—provided bitterness, bigotry, and fanaticism do not blind the individual to reality. In this work Mosley skillfully employs the form of the detective novel to get at the psychological roots of radicalism and reaction, since Easy has to keep a clear-eyed, objective attitude if he is to understand the people who have enthralled Brawly and discover how to disengage the young man from his conspiratorial cohort.

DIABLERIE

The title of Mosley's 2008 novel *Diablerie* is also the name of a new magazine that the main character's wife is promoting. Ben Dibbuk is a computer programmer stuck in a rut. He is bored with his routine job, and, even worse, he has withdrawn from his wife, Mona, and is cheating on her even as she herself has taken a lover. Dibbuk reluctantly shows up at the party held to celebrate publication of *Diablerie* and is accosted by a woman who claims knowledge of a murder he committed more than twenty years earlier in Colorado. Dibbuk does not remember the woman or the crime but is disturbed by her allegation because he was drinking heavily at that time in his life and was prone to memory lapses and blackouts.

Acting like a detective, Dibbuk seeks to expose his own life and to come to terms with what has happened to him emotionally. Why has he closed himself off? Why has he settled for such a routine job? His rather heroic self-analysis and his refusal to accept anything less than the truth about himself are the most compelling aspects of the novel. Dibbuk's plight, at least in some respects, is informed by Mosley's own experience of life-changing events that took him out of his dull computer programming job and propelled him toward a writing career.

Carl Rollyson

OTHER MAJOR WORKS

SHORT FICTION: *Futureland: Nine Stories of an Imminent World,* 2001; *Six Easy Pieces: Easy Rawlins Stories,* 2003.

NONFICTION: *Workin' on the Chain Gang: Shaking Off the Dead Hand of History,* 2000; *What Next: A Memoir Toward World Peace,* 2003; *Life Out of Context: Which Includes a Proposal for the Non-violent Takeover of the House of Representatives,* 2006; *This Year You Write Your Novel,* 2007.

YOUNG ADULT LITERATURE: *Forty-seven,* 2005.

EDITED TEXTS: *Black Genius: African American Solutions to African American Problems,* 1999 (with others); *The Best American Short Stories, 2003,* 2003 (with Katrina Kenison).

BIBLIOGRAPHY

Berger, Roger A. "'The Black Dick': Race, Sexuality, and Discourse in the L.A. Novels of Walter Mosley." *African American Review* 31 (Summer, 1997): 281-295. Provides a thoughtful and comprehensive discussion of the Easy Rawlins novels.

Brady, Owen E., and Derek C. Maus, eds. *Finding a Way Home: A Critical Assessment of Walter Mosley's Fiction.* Jackson: University Press of Mississippi, 2008. Collection of essays focuses on the meaning of the concept of home in Mosley's novels and other writings.

Coale, Samuel. "Race, Region, and Rite in Mosley's Mysteries." In *The Mystery of Mysteries: Cultural Differences and Designs.* Bowling Green, Ohio: Bowling Green State University Popular Press, 2000. Examines Mosley's use of black characters within the mystery and detective genre, which has traditionally been dominated by white characters.

Foster, Frances Smith. "Mosley, Walter." In *The Oxford Companion to African American Literature.* New York: Oxford University Press, 1997. Provides a brief biography and discusses the significance of the Easy Rawlins novels, comparing them to works by other notable detective and mystery writers.

Gussow, Adam. "'Fingering the Jagged Grain': Ellison's Wright and the Southern Blues Violences." *Boundary* 30, no. 2 (2003): 137-155. Presents historical background that is essential for an understanding of Mosley's work.

Mosley, Walter. "Anger and Hope Mosley's Formula for Success." Interview by Greg Burchall. *The Age* (Melbourne, Australia), January 31, 1996. Mosley discusses his career, growing up in south Los Angeles, and his belief in the heroism of the black struggle. He also provides information on the literary influences on his work and describes the process he uses in drafting his novels.

Mvuyekure, Pierre-Damien. "Mosley, Walter." In *St. James Encyclopedia of Popular Culture*. Vol. 3. Farmington Hill, Mich.: St. James Press, 2000. Focuses on the importance of the first Easy Rawlins novel, *Devil in a Blue Dress*, with a very brief discussion of Mosley's later work.

Wilson, Charles E., Jr. *Walter Mosley: A Critical Companion*. Westport, Conn.: Greenwood Press, 2003. Good introduction to Mosley's fiction presents discussion of several of his novels, including an analysis of *RL's Dream* that explores the novel's treatment of the blues. A biographical chapter provides background on Mosley's life.

DOROTHY L. SAYERS

Born: Oxford, England; June 13, 1893
Died: Witham, Essex, England; December 17, 1957
Also known as: Dorothy Leigh Sayers

PRINCIPAL LONG FICTION

Whose Body?, 1923
Clouds of Witness, 1926
Unnatural Death, 1927 (also known as *The Dawson Pedigree*)
Lord Peter Views the Body, 1928
The Unpleasantness at the Bellona Club, 1928
The Documents in the Case, 1930 (with Robert Eustace)
Strong Poison, 1930
The Five Red Herrings, 1931 (also known as *Suspicious Characters*)
The Floating Admiral, 1931 (with others)
Have His Carcase, 1932
Ask a Policeman, 1933 (with others)
Murder Must Advertise, 1933
The Nine Tailors, 1934
Gaudy Night, 1935
Six Against the Yard, 1936 (with others; also known as *Six Against Scotland Yard*)
Busman's Honeymoon, 1937
Double Death: A Murder Story, 1939 (with others)
Striding Folly, 1972
"The Scoop" and "Behind the Scenes," 1983 (with others)
"Crime on the Coast" and "No Flowers by Request," 1984 (with others)

OTHER LITERARY FORMS

In addition to the twelve detective novels that brought her fame, Dorothy L. Sayers (SAY-uhrz) wrote short stories, poetry, essays, and plays, and distinguished herself as a translator and scholar of medieval French and Italian literature. Although she began her career as a poet, with the Basil Blackwell publishing house bringing out collections of her verse in 1916 and 1918, Sayers primarily wrote fiction from 1920 until the late 1930's, after which she focused on radio and stage plays and a verse translation of Dante. She also edited a landmark anthology of detective fiction, *Great Short Stories of Detection, Mystery, and Horror* (1928-1934; also known as *The Omnibus of Crime*).

Apart from her fiction, the essence of Sayers's mind and art can be found in *The Mind of the Maker* (1941), a treatise on aesthetics that is one of the most illuminating inquiries

Dorothy L. Sayers
(Library of Congress)

into the creative process ever written; in her essays on Dante; and in two religious dramas, *The Zeal of Thy House* (pr., pb. 1937), a verse play written for the Canterbury Festival that dramatizes Sayers's attitude toward work, and *The Man Born to Be King: A Play-Cycle on the Life of Our Lord and Saviour Jesus Christ*, a monumental series of radio plays first broadcast amid controversy in 1941-1942. The latter work addressed what Sayers regarded as the most exciting of mysteries: the drama of Christ's life and death, the drama in which God is both victim and hero. Of her many essays, the 1946 collection *Unpopular Opinions* and the 1947 *Creed or Chaos?, and Other Essays in Popular Theology* provide a good sampling of the acumen, wit, and originality with which Sayers attacked a variety of subjects, including religion, feminism, and learning.

In 1972, James Sandoe edited *Lord Peter*, a collection of all the Wimsey stories. Two other collections, both published during Sayers's lifetime (*Hangman's Holiday*, 1933, and *In the Teeth of the Evidence, and Other Stories*, 1939), include non-Wimsey stories. At her death, Sayers left unfinished her translation of Dante's *Cantica III: Paradise*, which was completed by her friend and colleague Barbara Reynolds and published posthumously in 1962 as the final volume in the Penguin Classics edition of Dante that Sayers had begun in 1944. An unpublished fragment of an additional novel, to be called "Thrones, Dominations" and apparently abandoned by Sayers in the 1940's, was also left unfinished, as was her projected critical/biographical study of Wilkie Collins. This last fragment was published in 1977. From 1973 to 1977, the British Broadcasting Corporation (BBC) produced excellent adaptations of five of the Wimsey novels for television, thus creating a new audience for Sayers's work.

ACHIEVEMENTS

One of the chief pleasures for readers of Dorothy L. Sayers is the companionship of one of fiction's great creations, Lord Peter Wimsey, that extraordinarily English gentleman, cosmopolite, detective-scholar. Although the Wimsey novels were created primarily to make money, his characterization demonstrates that his creator was a serious, skillful writer. As the novels follow Wimsey elegantly through murder, mayhem, and madness, he grows from an enchanting caricature into a fully realized human being. The solver of mysteries thus becomes increasingly enigmatic himself. Wimsey's growth parallels Sayers's artistic development, which is appropriate, since she announced that her books were to be more like mainstream novels than the cardboard world of ordinary detective fiction.

Lord Peter is something of a descendant of P. G. Wodehouse's Bertie Wooster, and at times he emulates Arthur Conan Doyle's Sherlock Holmes, but in Wimsey, Sayers essentially created an original. Sayers's novels integrate elements of earlier detective fiction—especially the grasp of psychological torment typified by Joseph Sheridan Le Fanu and the fine delineation of manners exemplified in Wilkie Collins—with subjects one would expect from a medieval scholar: virtue, corruption, justice, punishment, suffering, redemption, time, and death. The hallmarks of her art—erudition, wit, precision, and moral passion—provoke admiration in some readers and dislike in others.

Sayers's novels are filled with wordplay that irritates those who cannot decipher it and delights those who can. Her names are wonderful puns (Wimsey, Vane, Freke, de Vine, Snoot, Venables), her dialogue is embedded with literary allusions and double entendres in English, French, and Latin, and her plots are spun from biblical texts and English poetry. Reading a Sayers novel, then, is both a formidable challenge and an endless reward. Hers are among the few detective novels that not only bear rereading, but actually demand it, and Sayers enjoys a readership spanning several generations. To know Sayers's novels is to know her time and place as well as this brilliant, eccentric, and ebullient artist could make them known. Because of her exquisite language, her skill at delineating character, and her fundamentally serious mind, Sayers's detective fiction also largely transcends the limits of its time and genre. Certainly this is true of novels such as *Strong Poison*, *The Nine Tailors*, *Gaudy Night*, and *Busman's Honeymoon*, books that did much toward making the detective novel part of serious English fiction.

BIOGRAPHY

Dorothy Leigh Sayers was born on June 13, 1893, in the Choir House of Christ Church College, Oxford, where her father, the Reverend Henry Sayers, was headmaster. Mr.

Sayers's family came from county Tipperary, Ireland; his wife, the former Helen Mary Leigh, was a member of the old landed English family that also produced Percival Leigh, a noted contributor to the humor magazine *Punch*. Sayers's biographer James Brabazon postulates that her preference for the Leigh side of the family caused her to insist on including her middle initial in her name; whatever the reason, the writer wished to be known as Dorothy L. Sayers.

When Sayers was four, her father left Oxford to accept the living of Bluntisham-cum-Earith in Huntingdonshire, on the southern edge of the Fens, those bleak expanses of drained marshland in eastern England. The contrast between Oxford and the rectory at Bluntisham was great, especially as the new home isolated the family and its only child. Sayers's fine education in Latin, English, French, history, and mathematics was conducted at the rectory until she was almost sixteen, when she was sent to study at the Godolphin School, Salisbury, where she seems to have been quite unhappy. Several of her happiest years followed this experience, however, when she won the Gilchrist Scholarship in Modern Languages and went up to Somerville College, Oxford, in 1912. At Somerville, Sayers enjoyed the congenial company of other extraordinary women and men and made some lasting friends, including Muriel St. Clare Byrne. Although women were not granted Oxford degrees during Sayers's time at Somerville, the university's statutes were changed in 1920, and Sayers was among the first group of women to receive Oxford degrees in that year (she had taken first honors in her examination in 1915).

Following her undergraduate days, Sayers did various kinds of work for several years: first as poetry editor for Blackwell's in Oxford from 1916 to 1918, then as a schoolmistress in France in 1919, and finally in London, where she worked as a freelance editor and as an advertising copywriter for Benson's, England's largest advertising agency. At Benson's, Sayers helped create "The Mustard Club," a phenomenally successful campaign for Colman's mustard. Around 1920, when Sayers's mind was focused not only on finding suitable employment but also on surviving economically, the character of Lord Peter Wimsey was miraculously born, and Sayers's first novel, *Whose Body?*, introduced him to the world in 1923.

Her early years in London were scarred by two bitterly disappointing love affairs, one of which left Sayers with a child, born in 1924. The novelist married Oswald Atherton Fleming, a Scottish journalist, in 1926, and shortly thereafter assumed financial responsibility for him as he became ill and ceased working several years after they wed. Perhaps these pressures encouraged Sayers to keep turning out the increasingly successful Wimsey novels.

By the end of the 1930's, however, Sayers was in a position to "finish Lord Peter off" by marrying him to Harriet Vane, the detective novelist who first appeared in *Strong Poison* and who, like Wimsey, reflected part of Sayers's personality. After the Wimsey novels, Sayers was free to do the kind of writing she had always wanted to do: manifestly serious work such as religious dramas and a translation of Dante that would occupy most of her time from 1944 to 1957. While working on these demanding projects and writing incisive essays on a wide range of issues, Sayers also became something of a public figure, playing the role of social critic and Christian apologist with great brilliance and panache.

On December 17, 1957, Sayers died of an apparent stroke while alone in the house that she had shared with Fleming from 1928 until his death in 1950. Although she left an unpublished autobiographical fragment, "My Edwardian Childhood," much of Sayers's life is reflected in her novels, which depict the Oxford of her college days (*Gaudy Night*), the Fen wastes of her girlhood (*The Nine Tailors*), and the excitement and confusion of the London she knew as a young writer (*Murder Must Advertise*). Excellent though much of her other work is, Sayers will probably be remembered primarily for her novels.

ANALYSIS

If one should wish to know England as it was between the two world wars—how it was in its customs, among its different classes, and in its different regions, how it regarded itself and the world, what weaknesses festered, what strengths endured—there is no better place to learn its soul or to revel in its singular delights and peccadilloes than in the novels of Dorothy L. Sayers. When Harriet Vane marries Peter Wimsey in *Busman's Honeymoon*, she happily realizes that she has "married England," revealing that Sayers herself recognized the symbolic import of her hero. As a survivor of World War I, a war that decimated a generation of young Englishmen and left their society reeling, Wimsey represents England's fragile link with a glorious past and its tenuous hold on the difficult present. His bouts of "nerves" and persistent nightmares dramatize the lasting effects of this "War to End All Wars," while his noble attempts at making a meaningful life represent the difficult task of re-creating life from the rubble.

Sayers's England encompasses tiny villages unchanged for centuries (*Busman's Honeymoon*), the golden-spired colleges of Oxford (*Gaudy Night*), the "gloom and gleam" of London (*Murder Must Advertise*), the deceptive calm of the southern seacoast (*Have His Carcase*), the brooding Fens (*The Nine Tailors*), and the primitive north counties (*Clouds of Witness*). The novelist ranges throughout this varied landscape with some constants: Accompanied by his indefatigable "man," Bunter (who is Jeeves transformed), Lord Peter reasons his way through all but one mystery (he is absent from *The Documents in the Case*). Through Wimsey's well-wrought consciousness, Sayers maintains a certain *Weltanschauung* that seems a peculiar blend of mathematical rigor and lush, witty, insightful language.

Carolyn Heilbrun's praise for Sayers's special blend of "murder and manners" points out to an understanding of both the novelist's appeal and her place in English fiction: Sayers is an inheritor not only of the more literary branch of detective fiction but also of the older tradition of the comedy of manners. She can reveal a character, time, or place in a bit of dialogue or one remark. From a brief sentence, for example, the reader knows the Duchess of Denver: "She was a long-necked, long-backed woman, who disciplined herself and her children." A short speech summarizes all *The Unpleasantness at the Bellona Club*, revealing not only a character but also the values and condition of his world:

> Look at all the disturbance there has been lately. Police and reporters—and then Penberthy blowing his brains out in the library. And the coal's all slate. . . . These things never happened before the War—and great heavens! William! Look at this wine! . . . Corked? Yes, I should think it *was* corked! My God! I don't know what's come to this club!

The character on whom Sayers lavishes most of her considerable talent is Lord Peter. Although it is possible, as some of her critics have said, that Sayers created Wimsey, the perfect mate for an intellectual woman, because actual men had disappointed her, the psychobiographical approach can explain only part of her novels' motivation or meaning. In Wimsey, Sayers dramatizes some significant human problems, including the predicament of the "lost generation," the necessity of every person's having a "proper job," and the imperative synthesis of forces that are often perceived as opposites but are really complementary: intellect and emotion, good and evil, male and female. When viewed in these terms, Sayers's fictional world fits naturally into the entire cosmos of her creation, because it deals with some of the very subjects she addressed in other, more patently serious forms.

It is appropriate to speak of all Sayers's work as one, for, as she concludes in *The Mind of the Maker*, "the sum of all the work is related to the mind [of the artist] itself, which made it, controls it, and relates it to its own creative personality." From beginning to end, Sayers's work investigates the possibility of creative action; for her the creative act consists of establishing equilibrium among competing powers, of drawing together disparate, even warring elements. Of course, given that she writes detective novels, Sayers focuses on the opposite of creative action in the crimes of her villains, crimes that destroy life, property, sanity, peace. Wimsey, who solves the mysteries and thereby makes a life from destruction, is the creative actor.

The Mind of the Maker argues that there is a discoverable moral law, higher than any other, that governs the universe. In a way, Sayers's novels attempt to discover or reveal this universal moral law, which in its most superficial form is reflected in civil codes. This process of moral discovery, however, becomes increasingly complex and ambiguous; if Sayers's subjects are constant, her understanding of them deepens as her art matures. Since Sayers's artistic maturation parallels her hero's development, a comparison of how Wimsey functions in the early and late novels will elucidate both the consistency and the change that mark Sayers's fiction.

WHOSE BODY?

The most striking quality of *Whose Body?* as a first novel is the deftness with which it presents Sayers's hero and his world. In its opening pages, the reader gets to know Lord Peter Wimsey, the dashing man-about-town and collector of rare books (which, amazingly, he seems to read). Keen of mind and quick of tongue, like an exotic bird chirping in a formal English garden that, perhaps, conceals a jolly corpse or two, he is a remarkable personage at birth. Wimsey is also quite marvelously a wealthy man who knows how to spend both his time and his money; his elegant apartment's only acknowledged lack is a harpsichord for his accomplished renditions of Domenico Scarlatti. The product of an older England marked by civility, restraint, and order, Wimsey is accompanied in his first tale by two challengers to his wits and position: his valet, Bunter, and the middle-class Inspector Parker of Scotland Yard, who will make sure that Wimsey never nods during fourteen years of fictional sleuthing. Even his mother, the delightfully balmy Duchess of Denver, is introduced here, and the reader quickly guesses from their relationship that Sayers is interested in how men and women coexist in this world. The Dowager Duchess and her son are as different in appearance as they are similar in character, the narrator remarks, thus signaling that the superficial differences between men and women often conceal more important similarities. Wimsey and his entourage enter the world nearly complete, and their creator has a firm grasp of character, dialogue, and the mystery plot from the beginning of her career.

The theme of *Whose Body?* plants the seeds of one of Sayers's ever-flourishing ideas. Her first and perhaps most horrid villain, Sir Julian Freke, suffers from one of the great problems facing modern people: the disassociation from mind and heart that often renders "civilized" people incapable of moral behavior. The great surgeon Freke, who is aptly named because he is a freakish half-human, denies the importance of intangibles such as the conscience, which he considers akin to the vermiform appendix. With this perfectly criminal attitude, Freke coolly kills and dissects an old competitor, ironically from one of the oldest, least rational of motives, jealousy and revenge. Freke therefore demonstrates Sayers's point: that people, as creatures of both intellect and passion, must struggle to understand and balance both if moral action is to be possible. Freke, the dissector of life, destroys; the destruction he causes awaits the truly healing powers of a creative mind.

The somewhat surprising link between moral action and detective work is suggested by Wimsey, who observes that anyone can get away with murder by keeping people from "associatin' their ideas," adding that people usually do not connect the parts of their experience. The good detective, however, must study the fragments of human life and synthesize the relevant data. This synthesis, the product of imagination and feeling as well as reason, reveals not only "who did it," but how, and why. Thus, according to Sayers's own definitions, her detective pursues moral action in his very sleuthing, not only in its final effects of punishment for the criminal and retribution for society. Wimsey's detective method typifies this creative synthesis by incorporating different aspects of a rich experience: poetry, science, history, psychology, haberdashery, weather reports. When Wimsey finally realizes that Freke is the murderer, he remembers "not one thing, nor another thing, nor a logical succession of things, but everything—the whole thing, perfect and complete . . . as if he stood outside the world and saw it suspended in infinitely dimensional space." In this moment, Wimsey is not merely a successful detective, he is a creator, his mind flashing with godlike insight into human life. The story has moved, therefore, from destruction to creation because disparate aspects of life have been drawn together.

Freke's failure as a human being is exemplified in his failure as a physician, just as Wimsey's successful life is instanced in the skillful performance of his "job," his compulsive "hobby of sleuthing." More than a hobby, detection is actually Wimsey's "proper job." In a crucial discussion with Inspector Parker, Wimsey admits to feeling guilty about doing detective work for fun, but the perceptive Parker warns him that, as a basically responsible person for whom life is really more than a game, he will eventually have to come to terms with the seriousness of his actions. What is clear to the reader at this point is that Wimsey, an English aristocrat displaced by social change and scarred by World War I, is at least carving out a life that is socially useful while it is personally gratifying. He is not simply feeding the Duke of Denver's peacocks.

If Wimsey seems almost too perfect in the early novels, Sayers redeems him from that state by slowly revealing the finite, flawed, and very human man within the sparkling exterior. To make this revelation, she has to create a woman capable of challenging him, which she does in the character of Harriet Vane. By the time he appears in *The Nine Tailors*, Wimsey is less of a god and more of a human being. After all, the great lover has been humiliatingly unsuccessful in wooing Harriet Vane, whom he saved from the hangman four years earlier in *Strong Poison*. The beginning of *The Nine Tailors* finds Wimsey, the supersleuth, wandering about the Fens, that bleak terrain of Sayers's childhood, muttering about the misery of having one's car break down on a wintery evening and dreaming of hot muffins. When offered shelter at the rectory of Fenchurch St. Paul, the great connoisseur of haute cuisine is delighted with tea and oxtail stew. The greatest change in Wimsey's character and in Sayers's fiction, however, is evidenced in the novel's richer, more subtle structure, and in its newly complex view of crime and punishment, of good and evil.

THE NINE TAILORS

Indicative of Sayers's increasing subtlety, *The Nine Tailors* is as much a metaphysical meditation on time and change as it is a murder mystery; there is not even a corpse until Part 2. In place of Lord Peter's jolly but rather macabre singing of "We insist upon a [dead] body in a bath" (in *Whose Body?*), *The Nine Tailors* resonates with the sound of church bells and an explication of campanology (bell or change-ringing). The bells at Fenchurch St. Paul, which are rung for both weddings and funerals, seem ambiguously to stand for both life and death, good and evil. The whole question of good versus evil is quite complicated here, for unlike the wholly innocent victim of the cold-blooded murder in *Whose Body?*, the man killed here is probably the worst person in the book, and he is accidentally killed by the ringing of holy bells. Locked in the church's bell chamber as a precaution by someone who knows of his criminal past, Geoffrey Deacon is killed by the intense sound of the bells, and ultimately by the hands of every man who unwittingly pulls a bell rope that New Year's Eve. This group includes Wimsey, who just happens to be there because of several coincidences.

Although Deacon perhaps deserves to die, not only for his jewel robbery but also because of a generally dishonorable life, his death forces Wimsey to reexamine himself and his motives. In ringing the changes, Wimsey thought he was simply following a set of mathematical permutations to a neat conclusion; in reality, he was taking a man's life. This greatly sobers the old puzzle-solver, who has always had some qualms about attacking life as a game. Indeed, Wimsey's role in Deacon's death is but an exaggerated version of the detective's role in any mystery: He causes the villain or criminal to come to justice, which usually means death. Wimsey cannot ignore the consequences of his actions in *The Nine Tailors*, because they are direct, obvious, and significant in human terms. He voices his concern about the morality of all his "meddling" to the rector, who assures him that everyone must "follow the truth," on the assumption that this path will lead invariably if somewhat indirectly to God, who has "all the facts" in the great case of life. Thus, it is impossible to be too curious, to probe too far, to ask too many questions, even though some answers or consequences may be painful.

In this great novel, Wimsey actually experiences the central Christian paradox, that of good coming from evil or of the two being inextricably linked. The mystery is over when he realizes, in a grisly pun, that Deacon's killers are already hanged, since they are the very bells in the church's tower. As one of the inscriptions on this ancient church says, the nine tailors, or the nine peals, "make a man," suggesting that the bells not only signify a man when they toll his passing but also stand as timeless, disinterested judges of human behavior. The dead man, Deacon, mocked honorable work in his thievery, and thus began the cycle of destruction that ends in his own death, a death that ironically leads to Wimsey's discovery or creative act. From evil thus confronted and comprehended, good may grow. Mr. Venables, the rector, wittily pricks Wimsey with the irony that "there's always something that lies behind a mystery . . . a solution of some kind." For Wimsey, as for Sayers, even the solution to a mystery leads to further mysteries; the answer to the mystery of Deacon's death leads to a more subtle inquiry into one of the essential mysteries of life: how to determine responsibility or meaning for human action. In this paradoxical world, victims may be villains and right action is often based in error, chance, or even transgression.

Wimsey leaves this complex novel with greater insight into himself and the ambiguous nature of life; he is, therefore, finally ready to come to terms with the greatest mystery of his life, Harriet Vane, who is also about ready to accept his inquiry. In *Gaudy Night*, Wimsey reaches his fulfillment, a fulfillment that is expressed in terms of resolving the conflict between man and woman, between intellect and emotion, and between good and evil. In fact, Wimsey's fulfillment represents the culmination of Sayers's search for a resolution of these forces. The novel's subject is also one of Sayers's oldest: the moral imperative for every person to do good work that is well done, and the terrible consequences of not doing so. All of these ideas come into play in this subtle novel, which is on one level the mystery of the "Shrewsbury Poison Pen" and on another, more important one, an unusual and profound love story. Reflecting the subtlety and delicacy with which Sayers spins her tale, there is not even a death in this book; the psychological violence caused by the Poison Pen is alarming, but here evil is banal, and all the more powerful for being so.

GAUDY NIGHT

Gaudy Night takes place at Oxford, which held happy memories for Sayers as the place of her birth and formal education, and the entire novel is a paean to that golden-spired city. Harriet Vane goes to Oxford to attend the Shrewsbury Gaudy, an annual spring homecoming celebration, where she has the opportunity to judge her old classmates and teachers in terms of how well they, as women, have been able to live meaningful lives. Shrewsbury is obviously a fictional version of Somerville, Sayers's college, and just as clearly Vane, a famous detective novelist who is wrestling with the question of "woman's work" and with the problem of rendering reality in fiction, is to some extent Sayers, the self-conscious artist. Having been pursued by Wimsey for five frustrating years, Vane finally accepts him at the end of *Gaudy Night*. She accepts him because the experiences in this book teach her three interrelated things: that Wimsey, as an extraordinary man, will not prevent her from doing her "proper job," a consequence she feared from any relationship with a man; that men and women can live together and not destroy each other, but create a good life; and therefore, that there can be an alliance between the "intellect and the flesh." Vane's discoveries in this novel thus signal the solution of problems that had preoccupied Sayers throughout her career.

Vane learns all of these things through Wimsey's unraveling of the mystery of the Poison Pen, who is a woman frightfully flawed because she has never been able to strike a balance between the intellect and the flesh, and therefore has never done her proper job. Annie Wilson, the Poison Pen who creates so much confusion and instills so much fear in the intellectual women of Shrewsbury, is the victim of sentimentality and a radically disassociated sensibility; she hates all learning because her dead husband was punished long ago for academic dishonesty. Ironically, Harriet Vane suffers from the same problem, but in its other manifestation; she begins the novel capable of trusting only the intellect, and fears any bonds of the flesh or heart. When she finally sees that neither the sentimentality of Annie nor the hyperintellectualism of Shrewsbury can solve the "problem of life," Harriet realizes that it is only through balancing intellect and passion that creative or truly human action is possible.

Wimsey, who solves the mystery because he is able to bring these forces into equilibrium and to acknowledge the potency of both, is rendered acceptable to Vane because of this ability. Her new willingness to admit her feelings reveals to her what Sayers's readers had known for a long time: She loves Wimsey. The man she loves has changed, too. He is no longer an unattainable paragon who sees good and evil as discrete and life as a game, but a middle-aged man who fears rejection and death, who is idiotically vain about his hands, and who, to Harriet's surprise, looks as vulnerable as anyone else when he falls asleep: the man behind the monocle. All of this does not argue that Wimsey is less extraordinary than he was; in fact, perhaps what is most extraordinary about him now is that he seems a real person—flawed, finite, vulnerable—who is yet capable of that rare thing, creative action. Indeed, his very life seems a work of art.

BUSMAN'S HONEYMOON

Wimsey and Vane finally embark upon marriage, that most mundane and mysterious of journeys, in *Busman's Honeymoon*, the final novel that Sayers aptly called a "love story with detective interruptions": The detective novelist had moved that far from the formula. In the closing scene of this last novel, Wimsey admits that his new wife is "his corner," the place where he can hide from a hostile, confusing world and shed tears for the murderer whose execution he caused. This is not the Wimsey who blithely dashed about in the early novels, treating criminals as fair game in an intellectual hunting expedition, but it is the man he could have become after fourteen years of living, suffering, and reflecting. Indeed, it was a masterful stroke for Sayers to create Harriet Vane, a woman who could match Wimsey's wits and passions, because through her and through his loving her, the reader can learn the most intimate facts of this once-distant hero. If a man is to cry in front of anyone, that witness should most likely be his wife, especially if she is an extraordinary person who understands his tears. The early Wimsey may have been the kind of man that an intellectual woman would imagine for a mate, but the mature Wimsey is one with whom she could actually live. The unpublished fragment of a later novel to be called "Thrones, Dominations" indicates that the Wimsey-Vane marriage was just this workable.

Finally, the marriage of Wimsey and Vane symbolizes the paradoxical and joyful truth of good coming out of evil, for if Harriet had not been falsely accused of murder, they would never have met. She quiets Wimsey in one of his familiar periods of painful self-scrutiny about his "meddling" by reminding him that if he had never meddled, she would probably be dead. The point seems clear: Human actions have consequences, many of which are unforeseen and some painful, but all of which are necessary for life. It is not difficult to imagine a novelist with this vision moving on shortly to the drama of Christ's crucifixion and resurrection, or even the next step, her study and translation of that great narrative of good and evil, desire and fulfillment, mortality and eternity, Dante's *La divina commedia* (c. 1320; *The Divine Comedy*, 1802). Indeed, all of Sayers's work is of a piece, creating that massive unity in diversity by which she defined true art.

Catherine Kenney

OTHER MAJOR WORKS

SHORT FICTION: *Hangman's Holiday*, 1933; *In the Teeth of the Evidence, and Other Stories*, 1939; *Lord Peter*, 1972 (James Sandoe, editor).

PLAYS: *Busman's Honeymoon*, pr. 1937 (with Muriel St. Clare Byrne); *The Zeal of Thy*

House, pr., pb. 1937; *The Devil to Pay, Being the Famous Play of John Faustus*, pr., pb. 1939; *Love All*, pr. 1940; *The Just Vengeance*, pr., pb. 1946; *The Emperor Constantine*, pr. 1951 (revised as *Christ's Emperor*, 1952).

POETRY: *Op 1*, 1916; *Catholic Tales and Christian Songs*, 1918; *Lord, I Thank Thee—*, 1943; *The Story of Adam and Christ*, 1955.

RADIO PLAY: *The Man Born to Be King: A Play-Cycle on the Life of Our Lord and Saviour Jesus Christ*, 1941-1942.

NONFICTION: *The Greatest Drama Ever Staged*, 1938; *Strong Meat*, 1939; *Begin Here: A War-Time Essay*, 1940; *Creed or Chaos?*, 1940; *The Mind of the Maker*, 1941; *The Mysterious English*, 1941; *Why Work?*, 1942; *The Other Six Deadly Sins*, 1943; *Making Sense of the Universe*, 1946; *Unpopular Opinions*, 1946; *Creed or Chaos?, and Other Essays in Popular Theology*, 1947; *The Lost Tools of Learning*, 1948; *The Days of Christ's Coming*, 1953 (revised 1960); *The Story of Easter*, 1955; *The Story of Noah's Ark*, 1955; *Further Papers on Dante*, 1957; *Introductory Papers on Dante*, 1957; *The Poetry of Search and the Poetry of Statement, and Other Posthumous Essays on Literature, Religion, and Language*, 1963; *Christian Letters to a Post-Christian World*, 1969; *Are Women Human?*, 1971; *A Matter of Eternity*, 1973; *Wilkie Collins: A Critical and Biographical Study*, 1977 (E. R. Gregory, editor); *The Letters of Dorothy L. Sayers, 1937-1943*, 1998.

TRANSLATIONS: *Tristan in Brittany*, 1929 (of Thomas the Troubadour's romance); *The Heart of Stone, Being the Four Canzoni of the "Pietra" Group*, 1946 (of Dante's poems); *The Comedy of Dante Alighieri the Florentine*, 1949-1962 (*Cantica III* with Barbara Reynolds); *The Song of Roland*, 1957.

CHILDREN'S LITERATURE: *Even the Parrot: Exemplary Conversations for Enlightened Children*, 1944.

EDITED TEXTS: *Oxford Poetry 1917*, 1918 (with Wilfred R. Childe and Thomas W. Earp); *Oxford Poetry 1918*, 1918 (with Earp and E. F. A. Geach); *Oxford Poetry 1919*, 1919 (with Earp and Siegfried Sassoon); *Great Short Stories of Detection, Mystery, and Horror*, 1928-1934 (also known as *The Omnibus of Crime*); *Tales of Detection*, 1936.

BIBLIOGRAPHY

Brabazon, James. *Dorothy L. Sayers: A Biography*. New York: Charles Scribner's Sons, 1981. Authorized biography draws on Sayers's private papers and contains an introduction by her only son, Anthony Fleming. Demonstrates that Sayers's real desire was to be remembered as an author of poetry and religious dramas and as a translator of Dante.

Brown, Janice. *The Seven Deadly Sins in the Work of Dorothy L. Sayers*. Kent, Ohio: Kent State University Press, 1998. Links Sayers's literary and religious works by analyzing the author's representations of the seven deadly sins in her mystery fiction and religious plays. Includes bibliography and index.

Coomes, David. *Dorothy L. Sayers: A Careless Rage for Life*. New York: Lion, 1992. Concentrates on reconciling the author of religious tracts with the detective novelist in order to provide a portrayal of a more "complex Sayers." Draws heavily on Sayers's papers at Wheaton College.

Dale, Alzina Stone. *Maker and Craftsman: The Story of Dorothy L. Sayers*. Rev. ed. Wheaton, Ill.: H. Shaw, 1992. Revised edition of a work originally published in 1978 recounts the events of Sayers's life and describes her many and varied writings.

_____, ed. *Dorothy L. Sayers: The Centenary Celebration*. New York: Walker, 1993. Collection of memoirs and essays situates Sayers within the history of detective fiction. Includes an essay by mystery writer Anne Perry about Sayers and Dante, a brief biography, and an annotated bibliography.

Downing, Crystal. *Writing Performances: The Stages of Dorothy L. Sayers*. New York: Palgrave Macmillan, 2004. Presents an analysis of Sayers's writing from the perspective of performance theory. Argues that Sayers was a modernist whose work anticipated postmodernist irony.

Gaillard, Dawson. *Dorothy L. Sayers*. New York: Frederick Ungar, 1981. Brief volume seeks to establish a link between Sayers's detective fiction and her other literary works. Devotes four chapters to her mystery novels, one to her short stories, and a sixth to a summary of Sayers's literary virtues.

Hall, Trevor H. *Dorothy L. Sayers: Nine Literary Studies*. Hamden, Conn.: Archon Books, 1980. Nine critical essays discuss topics such as the connection between Sayers's creation, Lord Peter Wimsey, and Arthur Conan Doyle's creation, Sherlock Holmes. Also speculates in some detail on the influence of Sayers's husband, Atherton Fleming, on her writing.

McGregor, Robert Kuhn, and Ethan Lewis. *Conundrums for the Long Week-End: England, Dorothy L. Sayers, and Lord Peter Wimsey*. Kent, Ohio: Kent State University Press, 2000. Focuses on how Sayers used the character of Wimsey to comment on British society in the period between the two world wars.

Reynolds, Barbara. *Dorothy L. Sayers: Her Life and Soul*. New York: St. Martin's Press, 1993. Recounts Sayers's life story through the author's letters and conversations and through passages from her writings, depicting a woman of great intellect and generosity.

GEORGES SIMENON

Born: Liège, Belgium; February 13, 1903
Died: Lausanne, Switzerland; September 4, 1989
Also known as: Georges Joseph Christian Simenon; Georges Sim; Christian Brulls

PRINCIPAL LONG FICTION

Au pont des Arches, 1921 (as Georges Sim)
Au rendez-vous des terreneuves, 1931 (*The Sailors' Rendezvous*, 1940)
Le Charretier de la "Providence," 1931 (*The Crime at Lock 14*, 1934; also known as *Maigret Meets a Milord*, 1963)
Le Chien jaune, 1931 (*A Face for a Clue*, 1939; also known as *Maigret and the Yellow Dog*, 1987; also known as *The Yellow Dog*, 1940)
Un Crime en Hollande, 1931 (*A Crime in Holland*, 1940)
La Danseuse du Gai-Moulin, 1931 (*At the "Gai-Moulin,"* 1940)
La Guinguette à deux sous, 1931 (*The Guinguette by the Seine*, 1940)
M. Gallet, décédé, 1931 (*The Death of Monsieur Gallet*, 1932; also known as *Maigret Stonewalled*, 1963)
La Nuit du carrefour, 1931 (*The Crossroad Murders*, 1933; also known as *Maigret at the Crossroads*, 1964)
Le Pendu de Saint-Pholien, 1931 (*The Crime of Inspector Maigret*, 1933; also known as *Maigret and the Hundred Gibbets*, 1963)
Pietr-le-Letton, 1931 (*The Strange Case of Peter the Lett*, 1933; also known as *Maigret and the Enigmatic Lett*, 1963)
Le Relais d'Alsace, 1931 (*The Man from Everywhere*, 1941)
La Tête d'un homme, 1931 (*A Battle of Nerves*, 1939)
L'Affaire Saint-Fiacre, 1932 (*The Saint-Fiacre Affair*, 1940; also known as *Maigret Goes Home*, 1967)
Chez les Flamands, 1932 (*The Flemish Shop*, 1940)
L'Écluse numéro un, 1932 (*The Lock at Charenton*, 1941)
Le Fou de Bergerac, 1932 (*The Madman of Bergerac*, 1940)
Liberty Bar, 1932 (English translation, 1940)
L'Ombre chinoise, 1932 (*The Shadow in the Courtyard*, 1934; also known as *Maigret Mystified*, 1964)
Le Passager du "Polarlys," 1932 (*The Mystery of the "Polarlys,"* 1942; also known as *Danger at Sea*, 1954)
Le Port des brumes, 1932 (*Death of a Harbour Master*, 1941)
Le Coup de lune, 1933 (*Tropic Moon*, 1942)
Les Fiançailles de M. Hire, 1933 (*Mr. Hire's Engagement*, 1956)
Les Gens d'en face, 1933 (*The Window over the Way*, 1951)

Le Haut Mal, 1933 (*The Woman in the Gray House*, 1942)
La Maison du canal, 1933 (*The House by the Canal*, 1948)
L'Homme de Londres, 1934 (*Newhaven-Dieppe*, 1942)
Le Locataire, 1934 (*The Lodger*, 1943)
Maigret, 1934 (*Maigret Returns*, 1941)
Les Suicidés, 1934 (*One Way Out*, 1943)
Quartier Nègre, 1935
Les Demoiselles de Concarneau, 1936 (*The Breton Sisters*, 1943)
L'Assassin, 1937 (*The Murderer*, 1949)
Le Blanc à lunettes, 1937 (*Talatala*, 1943)
Faubourg, 1937 (*Home Town*, 1944)
Chemin sans issue, 1938 (*Blind Alley*, 1946)
L'Homme qui regardait passer les trains, 1938 (*The Man Who Watched the Trains Go By*, 1945)
Monsieur la Souris, 1938 (*The Mouse*, 1950)
Les Inconnus dans la maison, 1940 (*Strangers in the House*, 1951)
Il pleut, bergère . . . , 1941 (*Black Rain*, 1949)
Le Voyageur de la Toussaint, 1941 (*Strange Inheritance*, 1950)
Les Caves du Majestic, 1942 (*Maigret and the Hotel Majestic*, 1977)
Cécile est morte, 1942 (*Maigret and the Spinster*, 1977)
La Maison du juge, 1942 (*Maigret in Exile*, 1978)
Oncle Charles s'est enfermé, 1942 (*Uncle Charles Has Locked Himself In*, 1987)
La Veuve Couderc, 1942 (*Ticket of Leave*, 1954; also known as *The Widow*, 1955)
Félicie est là, 1944 (*Maigret and the Toy Village*, 1978)
L'Inspecteur cadavre, 1944 (*Maigret's Rival*, 1979)
Signé Picpus, 1944 (*To Any Lengths*, 1958)
L'Âiné des Ferchaux, 1945 (*Magnet of Doom*, 1948)
La Fuite de Monsieur Monde, 1945 (*Monsieur Monde Vanishes*, 1967)
Trois Chambres à Manhattan, 1946 (*Three Beds in Manhattan*, 1964; also known as *Three Bedrooms in Manhattan*, 2003)
Le Clan des Ostendais, 1947 (*The Ostenders*, 1952)
Lettre à mon juge, 1947 (*Act of Passion*, 1952)
Maigret à New York, 1947 (*Maigret in New York's Underworld*, 1955)
Maigret se fâche, 1947 (*Maigret in Retirement*, 1976)
Maigret et son mort, 1948 (*Maigret's Special Murder*, 1964)
La Neige était sale, 1948 (*The Snow Was Black*, 1950; also known as *The Stain in the Snow*, 1953; also known as *Dirty Snow*, 2003)
Pedigree, 1948 (English translation, 1962)
Les Vacances de Maigret, 1948 (*Maigret on Holiday*, 1950; also known as *No Vacation for Maigret*, 1953)

Les Fantômes du chapelier, 1949 (*The Hatter's Ghosts,* 1956)
Le Fond de la bouteille, 1949 (*The Bottom of the Bottle,* 1954)
Maigret chez le coroner, 1949 (*Maigret at the Coroner's,* 1980)
Mon Ami Maigret, 1949 (*My Friend Maigret,* 1956)
La Première Enquête de Maigret, 1949 (*Maigret's First Case,* 1958)
Les Quatre Jours du pauvre homme, 1949 (*Four Days in a Lifetime,* 1953)
L'Amie de Mme Maigret, 1950 (*Madame Maigret's Own Case,* 1959; also
    known as *Madame Maigret's Friend,* 1960)
L'Enterrement de Monsieur Bouvet, 1950 (*The Burial of Monsieur Bouvet,* 1955)
Maigret et la vieille dame, 1950 (*Maigret and the Old Lady,* 1958)
Les Volets verts, 1950 (*The Heart of a Man,* 1951)
Maigret au "Picratt's," 1951 (*Maigret in Montmartre,* 1954)
Maigret en meublé, 1951 (*Maigret Takes a Room,* 1960)
Maigret et la grande perche, 1951 (*Maigret and the Burglar's Wife,* 1969)
Les Mémoires de Maigret, 1951 (*Maigret's Memoirs,* 1963)
Une Vie comme neuve, 1951 (*A New Lease on Life,* 1963)
Maigret, Lognon, et les gangsters, 1952 (*Inspector Maigret and the Killers,*
    1954; also known as *Maigret and the Gangsters,* 1974)
Le Révolver de Maigret, 1952 (*Maigret's Revolver,* 1956)
Antoine et Julie, 1953 (*The Magician,* 1955)
Feux rouges, 1953 (*The Hitchhiker,* 1955; also known as *Red Lights,* 1975)
Maigret a peur, 1953 (*Maigret Afraid,* 1961)
Maigret et l'homme du banc, 1953 (*Maigret and the Man on the Bench,* 1975)
Maigret se trompe, 1953 (*Maigret's Mistake,* 1954)
Crime impuni, 1954 (*The Fugitive,* 1955)
Le Grand Bob, 1954 (*Big Bob,* 1954)
L'Horloger d'Everton, 1954 (*The Watchmaker of Everton,* 1955)
Maigret à l'école, 1954 (*Maigret Goes to School,* 1957)
Maigret chez le ministre, 1954 (*Maigret and the Calame Report,* 1969)
Maigret et la jeune morte, 1954 (*Maigret and the Dead Girl,* 1955)
Les Témoins, 1954 (*The Witnesses,* 1956)
Les Complices, 1955 (*The Accomplices,* 1964)
Maigret et le corps sans tête, 1955 (*Maigret and the Headless Corpse,* 1967)
Maigret tend un piège, 1955 (*Maigret Sets a Trap,* 1965)
Un Échec de Maigret, 1956 (*Maigret's Failure,* 1962)
En cas de malheur, 1956 (*In Case of Emergency,* 1958)
Le Petit Homme d'Arkangelsk, 1956 (*The Little Man from Archangel,* 1966)
Maigret s'amuse, 1957 (*Maigret's Little Joke,* 1957)
Dimanche, 1958 (*Sunday,* 1960)
Maigret voyage, 1958 (*Maigret and the Millionaires,* 1974)

Les Scrupules de Maigret, 1958 (*Maigret Has Scruples*, 1959)
Une Confidence de Maigret, 1959 (*Maigret Has Doubts*, 1968)
Maigret et les témoins récalcitrants, 1959 (*Maigret and the Reluctant Witnesses*, 1959)
Maigret aux assises, 1960 (*Maigret in Court*, 1961)
Maigret et les vieillards, 1960 (*Maigret in Society*, 1962)
L'Ours en peluche, 1960 (*Teddy Bear*, 1971)
Betty, 1961 (English translation, 1975)
Maigret et le voleur paresseux, 1961 (*Maigret and the Lazy Burglar*, 1963)
Le Train, 1961 (*The Train*, 1964)
Maigret et le client du samedi, 1962 (*Maigret and the Saturday Caller*, 1964)
Maigret et les braves gens, 1962 (*Maigret and the Black Sheep*, 1976)
La Porte, 1962 (*The Door*, 1964)
Les Anneaux de Bicêtre, 1963 (*The Patient*, 1963; also known as *The Bells of Bicêtre*, 1964)
La Colère de Maigret, 1963 (*Maigret Loses His Temper*, 1964)
Maigret et le clochard, 1963 (*Maigret and the Bum*, 1973)
La Chambre bleue, 1964 (*The Blue Room*, 1964)
Maigret et le fantôme, 1964 (*Maigret and the Apparition*, 1975)
Maigret se défend, 1964 (*Maigret on the Defensive*, 1966)
La Patience de Maigret, 1965 (*The Patience of Maigret*, 1966)
Le Petit Saint, 1965 (*The Little Saint*, 1965)
Le Confessional, 1966 (*The Confessional*, 1968)
Maigret et l'affaire Nahour, 1966 (*Maigret and the Nahour Case*, 1967)
La Mort d'Auguste, 1966 (*The Old Man Dies*, 1967)
Le Chat, 1967 (*The Cat*, 1967)
Le Voleur de Maigret, 1967 (*Maigret's Pickpocket*, 1968)
L'Ami de l'enfance de Maigret, 1968 (*Maigret's Boyhood Friend*, 1970)
Maigret à Vichy, 1968 (*Maigret in Vichy*, 1969)
Maigret hésite, 1968 (*Maigret Hesitates*, 1970)
La Main, 1968 (*The Man on the Bench in the Barn*, 1970)
La Prison, 1968 (*The Prison*, 1969)
Maigret et le tueur, 1969 (*Maigret and the Killer*, 1971)
Novembre, 1969 (*November*, 1970)
La Folle de Maigret, 1970 (*Maigret and the Madwoman*, 1972)
Maigret et le marchand de vin, 1970 (*Maigret and the Wine Merchant*, 1971)
La Cage de verre, 1971 (*The Glass Cage*, 1973)
La Disparition d'Odile, 1971 (*The Disappearance of Odile*, 1972)
Maigret et l'homme tout seul, 1971 (*Maigret and the Loner*, 1975)
Maigret et l'indicateur, 1971 (*Maigret and the Informer*, 1972)

Les Innocents, 1972 (*The Innocents*, 1973)
Maigret et Monsieur Charles, 1972 (*Maigret and Monsieur Charles*, 1973)

OTHER LITERARY FORMS

Georges Simenon (see-muh-NOHN) is known primarily for his fiction. Throughout his career as a novelist, however, he frequently displayed mastery of shorter forms as well, both with and without the presence of his famous character Inspector Maigret. Originally published for the most part in periodicals, his short stories and novellas have been collected in such volumes as *Les Dossiers de l'Agence O* (1943), *Nouvelles exotiques* (1944), and in English translation as well. In his late thirties, erroneously informed by his doctors that he had but a short time to live, Simenon began writing his autobiography as a memoir for his infant son. At the urging of the eminent novelist André Gide (1869-1951), he soon abandoned the project, incorporating its best portions into the novel *Pedigree*, published in 1948. After publicly renouncing the practice of fiction shortly before his seventieth birthday, Simenon published his recollections in *Mémoires intimes* (1981; *Intimate Memoirs*, 1984).

ACHIEVEMENTS

Georges Simenon is among the most prolific fiction writers of his generation. During fifty years of sustained creative activity, he published upward of three hundred novels under his own name, exclusive of lesser efforts for which he employed a variety of pseudonyms. Although best known for his novels featuring Inspector Maigret of the Paris police, Simenon in fact published more titles outside the detective genre and was justly acclaimed both in France and abroad for his keen analysis of human character in mainstream fiction.

Simenon was a gifted student of human nature and a born raconteur whose keen powers of observation, linked to a highly retentive memory, have furnished the world with a vast array of memorable characters both within and outside the mystery genre. Incredibly, the sheer quantity of Simenon's work had little, if any, negative effect on its quality; throughout most of his career, Simenon was taken seriously, as a "serious" novelist, by general readers and critics alike.

Heir apparent to the tradition of French naturalism that flourished a quarter of a century before his birth through the works of Émile Zola, Guy de Maupassant, and Edmond and Jules de Goncourt, Simenon brought the best features of naturalism into the twentieth century. Unlike some other novelists and playwrights of his own generation, who pretended to "psychological realism" by parroting forth, as if undigested, the latest insights of Sigmund Freud and Carl Jung, Simenon evolved throughout his career a mode of psychological observation and recording that is all the more credible, and convincing, for its lack of cant or visible erudition. In most of his novels, Simenon appears to be suggesting that it is unnecessary to read Freud or Jung to gain an understanding of the criminal or psychotic mind, that all one need do is observe others closely, with understanding and compassion.

Maigret, among the most convincing and memorable of modern fictional detectives, is an "instinctive" psychologist who solves many initially baffling murders by focusing his attention on the victims, attempting to figure out what they might have done to invite violent death. In the non-Maigret novels, it is Simenon himself, as unseen and frequently omniscient narrator, who portrays apparently "normal" characters driven to sudden crime and violence by inevitable forces that they themselves can barely comprehend. Seldom, in either type of novel, does the action appear forced or the characters' behaviors unconvincing—a fault that hampers, if only infrequently, even the finest narratives of Zola and Maupassant.

It can be argued that Simenon's Maigret has contributed as much to the development of the mystery novel as did Sherlock Holmes himself, implicitly awarding to psychology the role in detection that Arthur Conan Doyle, writing a half century earlier, had attributed to the then-innovative scientific method. To Simenon and Maigret, as to their contemporary readers, it is usually more important (as well as entertaining) to understand *why* a crime was committed than precisely *how* it was done.

Of perhaps equal importance is Simenon's role in helping to create, through his Maigret novels, the subgenre of detective fiction known as the police procedural, now widely read and written the world over. Departing from the frequently romantic private detective whose dazzling insights make law officers look like buffoons, Simenon and his many followers in the subgenre focus instead on the grueling routines of police work itself, featuring career detectives whose profiles often fall far short of the heroic. Maigret is a case in point—a portly, balding, dedicated civil servant in late middle age with a durable, affectionate, but unfortunately childless marriage. Assisted in his many investigations by a recurring cast of subordinates and his voluble physician friend, Pardon, Maigret puts in long and frequently fruitless hours in his efforts to look at and through the crime to the mind of the criminal. Among the least judgmental of fictional detectives, Maigret on occasion comes to "understand" the crime so well that he either lets the perpetrator go free or agrees to testify in the person's defense.

At the risk of belaboring the obvious, it is perhaps appropriate to observe that the main difference between Simenon's Maigret novels and his "mainstream" works (by far the larger part of his production) is that in the latter, Maigret does not appear. Without Maigret's avuncular presence to tie up the loose ends of the characters' lives, the loose ends remain untied—frequently with disastrous results. As Lucille Frackman Becker has observed, the

> reassuring presence of Maigret . . . convinces us that there is an order, a structure, and a meaning to life. In the other novels, there is no Maigret to whom the protagonist can confess, there is no one to understand or with whom to communicate, leaving him immured in his solitude, stifled and suffocated by repressed confessions.

Indeed, the usual and highly credible atmosphere is one of utter solitude, alienation, and estrangement in which the characters, fully comprehensible to the author and hence to the reader, are just as fully incomprehensible to one another.

Among twentieth century French novelists, perhaps only the Nobelist François Mauriac—a possible source for some of Simenon's novelistic predicaments—has rendered as convincingly as Simenon the heart-wrenching predicaments of cross-purposes and unheard cries for help that often reverberate through life and love. In Mauriac's fictional universe, however, there is always the promise, secured only by the author's personal religious faith, of a better life to come in the next world. In those of Simenon's novels without Maigret, by contrast, hell on earth is most often simply hell. In his own defense, Simenon argued with some justice that in the twentieth century the novel came to fulfill much the same function that tragedy did for the ancient Greeks. People's destinies are played out in repeated dialogue between author and audience, the one compelled to exorcise inner demons and the other to see its best hopes and worst fears replicated in the characters' behavior. After readers are thus reassured—presumably by a catharsis similar to that emerging, in Aristotle's view, from the viewing of a classical tragedy—they are able to address themselves to life with renewed vigor, aware of their limitations but better suited to savor the sights, sounds, and smells of everyday life.

Literary critics have most often reproached Simenon, like Zola before him, for his lack of literary style. Advised early in his career by the novelist Colette, then serving as one of his editors, to pare his work down to the barest essentials, Simenon soon perceived that his most effective style was one that favored the literal over the figurative, the concrete over the abstract. Over the years, that decision served him well, especially in the creation of plausible atmospheres in which to place his often hapless characters.

BIOGRAPHY

Born in 1903 in Liège, Belgium, the elder of two brothers, Georges Joseph Christian Simenon enjoyed an urban childhood that was sufficiently middle class that he recalled being disgruntled when his mother felt herself obliged to take in boarders in order to make ends meet. The failing health of his father, an insurance clerk, obliged the young Simenon to cut short his formal education and join the workforce at about age sixteen. After false starts as apprentice to a pastry cook and subsequently as a salesclerk, Simenon found steady work as a journalist at a still-precocious age and thereafter earned his living through writing, either as a journalist or as a secretary-speechwriter. Married in 1923 to Régine Renchon, Simenon later in that year began selling short stories to newspapers and soon expanded to the novel as well, publishing more than two hundred potboilers under various pseudonyms between 1925 and 1934, by which time his own name, thanks in part to Maigret, was beginning to ensure brisk sales.

According to Becker, Simenon originally attempted the detective novel "as a bridge between the popular potboilers he had been writing and the more serious literary efforts to which he aspired but for which he did not consider himself ready." His proposal accepted by the publisher Fayard, Simenon contracted in 1929 to write eighteen Maigret novels, which in time would expand to eighty-three in addition to shorter Maigret adventures. Curiously, Simenon's talent and fame as a mainstream novelist developed almost simultaneously with his reputation as a mystery writer, with several examples of each type of novel published annually throughout the 1930's to generally good sales and reviews.

In the mid-1930's, Simenon traveled extensively throughout the world; the "exotic" novels resulting from these voyages are justly famous among readers and scholars, although they constitute a small fraction of his literary output and depend more heavily on character than on atmosphere for their overall effect. Shortly after the outbreak of World War II, already involved in refugee relief work, Simenon began writing his memoirs in the erroneous belief that he was soon to die of a respiratory ailment; after revision, those memoirs would form the basis of the major novel *Pedigree*, completed during 1943 but not published until five years later. Toward the end of the hostilities, Simenon traveled extensively in North America and met the Canadian Denise Ouimet, who, after his divorce in 1950, would become his second wife. Residing first in Arizona, Simenon settled in northern Connecticut following his marriage to Ouimet; there he would write a number of his best-remembered novels, many with American settings and characters.

After returning to Europe in 1955, Simenon spent most of his time in the Lausanne area of Switzerland, where he was to die in 1989. Around 1972, Simenon renounced the writing of fiction, preferring instead to record on tape the most salient excerpts of his photographic memory. In 1981, he published his massive autobiography, *Intimate Memoirs*, notable for its sensational disclosures with regard to his unconventional sex life and his obsession with the suicide of his daughter, Marie-Jo. Despite its self-advertised candor, it is a strangely unrevealing work; Simenon the man remains elusive.

ANALYSIS

Named by the highly regarded André Gide as the greatest modern French novelist, Georges Simenon indeed compiled an enviable record of achievement, producing a body of work equally remarkable for its quality as for its quantity. The apprenticeship he served in writing his so-called potboilers appears to have served him well, allowing him to write fluently while maintaining rigorous standards of content and characterization. Simenon's demonstrated proficiency in the mystery genre alone would no doubt suffice to secure his position in the history of modern letters; nevertheless, he further confirmed his reputation with a solid list of mainstream titles valued for their psychological insights.

Simenon's prodigious accomplishment may be explained, at least to a point, by acknowledging that his fictional universe remains essentially the same regardless of whether Maigret is involved in the action; in both types of novel, the true protagonists are hounded, uncommunicative creatures with little more than the most marginal knowledge of what makes them behave as they do. The main difference, as Becker has observed, lies in the thoughtful, reconciling presence of Maigret, who functions almost as a psychoanalyst in "solving" the mystery of behavior to the satisfaction of characters and readers alike; in the mainstream novels, the characters remain in their own private hells, understood (if at all) only by the narrator and his reader. Rarely, and then with remarkable effect, does Simenon surprise the reader with his conclusions; even then, as elsewhere in Simenon's novels, the denouement soon appears inevitable, amply prepared for by what he has revealed of the characters' makeup and motivations.

MAIGRET NOVELS

By his own admission, Simenon "discovered" Maigret at a time when, still unsure of his skills as a novelist, he was seeking a viewpoint character who could move about in space and time as the conventional narrator (or novelist) could not; eventually, he settled on a policeman as ideally suited to his needs and proposed the Maigret series, initially planned for eighteen volumes. The result, by now almost legendary, was one of the most durable characters in the history of detective fiction, further established by his omnipresent pipe, his childless wife, and cold meals ordered "to go" during the late-night hours from the obliging Brasserie Dauphine. Modeled on Simenon's own pensive, easygoing father, Maigret is on occasion so appealing that he makes the prospect of crime seem nearly attractive to the reader. The eminent playwright Jean Anouilh paid indirect homage to Maigret with *L'Arrestation* (pr., pb. 1975; *The Arrest*, 1978), in which an aging gangster, mortally wounded in a motor accident, is fortunate enough, in his final moments, to have his entire life explained to him by an even older inspector who has devoted his own career to studying the gangster's lifestyle and habits. Habitual criminals are, however, rather rare quarry for Maigret; more commonly, the crimes with which he deals are perpetrated by inhabitual offenders, seemingly normal people suddenly propelled toward violence by an accumulation of privation or resentment.

Maigret's murderers frequently kill for love or for its cherished memory. In *Maigret and the Loner*, one of Simenon's later Maigret adventures, more than twenty years elapse before a lovesick painter avenges his girlfriend's murder with the apparently gratuitous killing of his erstwhile rival, who has since become a homeless derelict. To Maigret, as to his creator, the painter could not possibly have behaved otherwise, his crime having long since been predetermined. Indeed, Maigret solves easily half of his initially baffling mysteries by reconstructing the lives of the victims in search of signs of irregularity or stress that could have engendered violence. Simenon himself claimed that, upon study of the evidence, "there are at least eight crimes in ten in which the victim shares to a great extent the responsibility of the murderer." Similar cases abound throughout Maigret's career, from nagging spouses and sadistic lovers to the "public enemy" Fumal in *Maigret's Failure*, who himself victimized so many people that Maigret is hard put to choose among them as he reluctantly searches for Fumal's killer.

Occasionally, as in *Maigret Sets a Trap*, the identity of the murderer is known early in the novel, lacking only Maigret's deductive analysis to render the case against him (or her) conclusive. Identified by a police "plant" and hemmed in by circumstantial evidence, the admittedly unlikely mass murderer, a mild-mannered interior decorator named Moncin, eludes conviction only because an additional, identical murder was committed after he was taken into custody. As Maigret, following a hunch, delves deeper into Moncin's life and career, he finds a spoiled and highly intelligent man dominated by his wife and mother, who compete ceaselessly for top billing in his life. Either woman, Maigret reasons, would have had both motive and capacity to commit the "decoy" murder; in fact, it was the wife who did it, thus scoring a final, irrefutable "point" against her husband's mother.

STRANGERS IN THE HOUSE

Generally similar in theme and subject matter to the novels featuring Maigret, Simenon's mainstream titles likewise abound in ill-adjusted characters who live in quiet desperation, occasionally bursting out in violence. The expository method employed is frequently similar to that of the detective novel, with one or more characters attempting to solve the mystery in their lives. A case in point is that of Loursat in *Strangers in the House*, an intriguing novel perhaps even more timely in the twenty-first century than when it first appeared. A once-promising attorney, Loursat has responded to his wife's desertion by hiding out for years, bottle in hand, in the sanctuary of his personal library. A gunshot and the discovery of a body in his attic one night forces his attention to the fact that his adolescent daughter, Nicole, who lives in the same house but whom he has seen only at mealtimes, is in fact the leader of a housebreaking ring and that their accumulated loot is stored in Loursat's own attic. The dead man proves to have been a criminal who was blackmailing Nicole's band. Nicole's lover, Émile Manu, a poor young man who proves a convenient but innocent suspect, is arrested. As Loursat—his professional instincts and sense of justice awakened from long dormancy by what he knows is an unjust arrest—attempts to track down the real killer, he proceeds as well toward a long-overdue assessment of his own strengths and weaknesses; in time, Loursat discovers the true murderer and obtains Manu's freedom, proceeding thereafter to resume the life and career that he had abandoned years earlier.

UNCLE CHARLES HAS LOCKED HIMSELF IN

Such happy endings are rare in Simenon's work; more frequently, the self-knowledge reached through deduction is then used for self-serving means, with little prospect of true liberation. Such is the case in *Uncle Charles Has Locked Himself In*, in which deduction leads a petty embezzler toward the even greater satisfaction of "invisible" blackmail.

Mild-mannered and unprepossessing, like many of the criminals ferreted out by Maigret, "Uncle" Charles Dupeux has for years nursed a grudge against his overbearing employer and brother-in-law, Henri, occasionally feeding that grudge with small thefts that, carefully managed, have grown into a considerable fortune; presumably, he will one day make his "break," supported by the embezzled nest egg. Before that can happen, however, Charles discovers that Henri is being blackmailed, and with good cause: Henri, although not legally responsible for his late partner's early death, in fact conspired to bring it about. Armed with this knowledge, Charles retreats to the attic, where he keeps his hoard of stock certificates, trying to decide how best to use what he has learned. To Henri's consternation, he refuses a generous offer for his silence, knowing that Henri does not even suspect him of embezzlement. Instead, Charles prefers "the revenge of the underdog"—to hold over Henri's detested head the potential threat of exposure and thus avenge himself, albeit in secret, for what he regards as years of exploitation.

The Witnesses

Yet another of Simenon's memorable character studies is *The Witnesses*, which recalls the Maigret series as it carefully considers the often fragile foundations of justice. *The Witnesses* presents the tale of two men, the judge and the accused, and of circumstances that might, on occasion, be assessed as "circumstantial evidence." Little but the judicial bench, indeed, separates Judge Lhomond from Lambert in the dock; both men have notoriously bad marriages and have lately been prone to irregular behavior. As Lhomond successfully enjoins his jury to allow for "reasonable doubt" in Lambert's case, he is sure that the man would be convicted were not he, Lhomond, sitting on the bench that day.

Tropic Moon

Simenon's exotic novels of the 1930's, although few in number, contain some of his best-remembered insights and descriptions; as elsewhere in his work, however, the setting is of interest to Simenon almost solely for its effects on human behavior. Joseph Timar, the ill-starred protagonist of *Tropic Moon*, arrives in the Congo only to find that the company that hired him is about to go bankrupt, that his job lies ten days upriver, and that his predecessor is still in place, having threatened to kill anyone who might be sent in to replace him. Soon thereafter, somewhat corrupted by an older woman of his acquaintance, Timar goes more than a little mad; aboard the ship that has been sent to fetch him home, he confidently declares that "there is no such place as Africa."

Quartier Nègre

Hardly more fortunate is the engineer Dupuche of *Quartier Nègre*, who, like Timar, discovers upon arriving at the site of a new job that his position has been abolished as a result of the firm's bankruptcy. Set in Panama, *Quartier Nègre* is perhaps even richer in atmosphere than *Tropic Moon*. In any case, both novels resulted in lawsuits against Simenon by residents of the Congo and Panama, respectively, who considered themselves ill represented in his works. Unlike Timar, Dupuche never leaves the tropics. Necessarily separated from his wife, who finds employment while he does not, Dupuche gradually but definitively goes native, residing in a tumbledown shack with his black mistress and their several children until he eventually dies, still young, of a tropical disease. Somewhat more fortunate is Ferdinand Graux, the title character of *Talatala*, who survives both the heat and his infatuation with a wanton Englishwoman long enough to rebuild his life and career with the help of his wife, Emmeline.

PEDIGREE

Unique among Simenon's many works outside the detective genre is the novel *Pedigree*, successfully mined by many of his critics in search of clues to his life and technique. Covering scarcely sixteen years in the life of Simenon's alter ego Roger Mamelin, *Pedigree* memorably chronicles the sights, sounds, and smells of Liège during the author's youth, adding unforgettable portraits of "Roger's" parents, aunts, and uncles. Implicit throughout the novel is the author's satiric attack on his German-descended mother and her representation of the lower-middle class, which would sooner starve than eat the cheap, abundant food favored by "peasants." Included as well are detailed portraits of his mother's boarders, many of whom had already appeared, or would soon appear, with slight fictional disguise, in Simenon's novels. Of Roger's parents, the ailing father is by far the more wise and sympathetic, if less forceful and therefore less significant; later, in *Lettre à ma mère* (1974; *Letter to My Mother*, 1976), the septuagenarian Simenon would give even fuller vent to his resentment of his mother. In any case, it is clear from *Pedigree* that were it not for the influence of his mother, Simenon would never have had the determination and perseverance to become a writer and that without his father, he would never have acquired the patience, skill, and compassion that made his work as successful as it is.

SUNDAY

Among Simenon's later novels, *Sunday* is one of the most memorable and impressive, rivaled perhaps only by *The Old Man Dies*. As befits its title, the events of the novel take place on a particular Sunday, the day that Émile, an accomplished chef, has selected in advance for the murder of his wife, Berthe, who is also his employer. Impotent in marriage, released from his affliction only in the arms of a wild and uncultured young waitress, Émile remains unaware of his abiding dependence on the domineering Berthe. So great, in fact, is Berthe's hold on Émile that when he learns that she has outsmarted him, feeding to his young mistress the poisoned lunch intended for herself, he meekly heeds her suggestion that he is already late for the regional soccer match. By the time he returns, all traces of the girl and his act will be gone, and everything will be restored to order.

THE OLD MAN DIES

In *The Old Man Dies*, similarly concerned with the running of a restaurant, the heir apparent, Antoine, is portrayed initially as an unsympathetic character, but he divides with his brothers, upon their father's death, a supposed "legacy" that is in fact wholly composed of his own funds. The true legacy, Simenon implies, is the restaurant itself, a business long since spurned by Antoine's brothers.

Simenon still stands virtually unchallenged in the territory that he claimed as his own between the two world wars. Faulted by some observers for his essentially negative, deterministic view of human nature and by others for his implied derogation of women and marriage, Simenon nevertheless remains among the most accomplished observers and chroniclers of his generation, his own legacy a challenge to any aspiring successors.

David B. Parsell

OTHER MAJOR WORKS

SHORT FICTION: *Les 13 coupables*, 1932 (*The Thirteen Culprits*, 2002); *Les Dossiers de L'Agence O*, 1943; *Les Nouvelles Enquêtes de Maigret*, 1944 (*The Short Cases of Inspector Maigret*, 1959); *Nouvelles exotiques*, 1944; *Maigret et l'inspecteur malchanceux*, 1947 (also known as *Maigret et l'inspecteur malgracieux*); "La Pipe de Maigret," 1947 ("Maigret's Pipe," 1977); *Un Noël de Maigret*, 1951 (*Maigret's Christmas*, 1951).

NONFICTION: *Le Roman de l'homme*, 1958 (*The Novel of Man*, 1964); *Quand j'étais vieux*, 1970 (*When I Was Old*, 1971); *Lettre à ma mère*, 1974 (*Letter to My Mother*, 1976); *Mémoires intimes*, 1981 (*Intimate Memoirs*, 1984); *Mes apprentissages: Reportages, 1931-1946*, 2001.

BIBLIOGRAPHY

Assouline, Pierre. *Simenon: A Biography.* Translated by Jon Rothschild. New York: Alfred A. Knopf, 1997. Presents a wealth of biographical information, providing an honest and often unflattering portrait of the writer.

Becker, Lucille Frackman. *Georges Simenon, Revisited.* New York: Twayne, 1999. Begins with a biographical chapter and then analyzes Simenon's novels, which are divided into novels of crime and detective, novels of crime and deviance, and exotic novels. Also discusses Simenon's "gift of narration" and reviews the film versions of his novels. Includes notes and bibliography.

Bresler, Fenton. *The Mystery of Georges Simenon.* Toronto, Ont.: General, 1983. Well-written, informative biography gives a strong sense of Simenon's roots and the development of his literary career. Includes conversations between Bresler and Simenon.

Carter, David. *The Pocket Essential Georges Simenon.* Harpenden, England: Pocket Essentials, 2003. Concise guide to Simenon's prolific body of fiction includes discussion of his Maigret mystery novels, the adaptation of his fiction to film, and critical opinions of the author.

Eskin, Stanley. *Simenon: A Critical Biography.* Jefferson, N.C.: McFarland, 1987. Provides a comprehensive narrative of Simenon's life and a meticulous analysis of his work, accompanied by detailed and helpful notes and a bibliography.

Franck, Frederick. *Simenon's Paris.* New York: Dial, 1970. Basically a book of illustrations of Paris, but informative in that it reveals a good deal about the way Simenon chose locations for his fiction.

Freeling, Nicolas. "Georges Simenon." In *Criminal Convictions: Errant Essays on Perpetrators of Literary License.* Boston: D. R. Godine, 1994. Examines how Simenon's works question the meaning of redemption and suffering. Part of a collection of essays in which Freeling, a crime novelist, analyzes the crime writing of other authors.

Marnham, Patrick. *The Man Who Wasn't Maigret: A Portrait of Georges Simenon.* London: Bloomsbury, 1992. Accessible and thorough study of Simenon's turbulent life and times is based in part on Marnham's analysis of Simenon's voluminous memoirs. Includes bibliographical references and index.

Raymond, John. *Simenon in Court.* New York: Harcourt Brace and World, 1968. Classic work provides an excellent overview of Simenon's fiction.

Simenon, Georges. "The Art of Fiction: Georges Simenon." Interview by Carvel Collins. *The Paris Review* 9 (Summer, 1993): 71-90. The author discusses both his career and his fictional methods in this wide-ranging interview.

SCOTT TUROW

Born: Chicago, Illinois; April 12, 1949
Also known as: Scott Fredrick Turow; L. Scott Turow

PRINCIPAL LONG FICTION
Presumed Innocent, 1987
The Burden of Proof, 1990
Pleading Guilty, 1993
The Laws of Our Fathers, 1996
Personal Injuries, 1999
Reversible Errors, 2002
Ordinary Heroes, 2005
Limitations, 2006

OTHER LITERARY FORMS

Early in his career, while an undergraduate at Amherst College, Scott Turow (tuh-ROH) published short stories. In 1977, he published *One L: An Inside Account of Life in the First Year at Harvard Law School*, a compelling nonfiction account of his first year as a law student. *One L* became required reading for prospective law students and eventually sold more than three million copies. Turow has continued to write and publish various works of nonfiction, including book reviews, articles for legal journals, and newspaper articles on topics ranging from politics to sports.

ACHIEVEMENTS

Scott Turow received the Crime Writers' Association Silver Dagger Award in 1988 for *Presumed Innocent*. Paperback rights to *Presumed Innocent* sold for a record three million dollars, and Turow was paid one million dollars for the motion-picture rights, an unprecedented amount for a first novel. Turow's remarkable success with *Presumed Innocent*, coupled with his determination to remain a practicing lawyer, started an interest in legal fiction written by lawyers, especially Turow and novelist John Grisham. Turow's success helped to create a new market for courtroom drama, and scores of lawyers and law students began tinkering with writing fiction. Turow is often hailed as having transcended his genre, producing consistently literary works with mass audience appeal.

BIOGRAPHY

The eldest of two children, Scott Fredrick Turow was born into an upper-middle-class Jewish family in Chicago, the son of a physician and a former public school teacher. When he was in his teens, his family moved from a largely Jewish neighborhood in the city to the suburbs. Turow's father, a former U.S. Army doctor, treated depression and devoted most of his time to his work, so Turow's relationship with him was somewhat strained. Largely inspired by his mother, who had written unpublished short stories and novels and published a self-help book, Turow decided to pursue a career as a writer. He enrolled in Amherst College in Massachusetts in 1966, where he majored in English and studied with Tillie Olsen, a noted writer of Jewish and feminist short stories. Turow graduated summa cum laude and in 1970 entered the master's program in creative writing at Stanford University, where he continued to study with Olsen as well as with the well-known novelist Wallace Stegner.

In 1971, Turow married Annette Weisberg, a painter and teacher who also had grown up in the suburbs of Chicago; the couple would eventually have three children. Turow was awarded the appointment of E. H. Jones Lecturer in Creative Writing at Stanford, but after three years as a teacher he began to feel that life in academia kept him too far removed from the real world. Turow had become interested in the law, intrigued by research into legal matters he had done for his first novel, "The Way Things Are" (which was eventually rejected by twenty-five publishers). He was accepted into Harvard Law School in 1975. Turow felt that the legal system was to some degree taking on the role once played by organized religion in American culture; he saw practitioners of the law as vital modern-day arbiters of truth and defenders of right against wrong. Receiving his law degree in 1978, he accepted a job as an assistant U.S. attorney in the U.S. Court of Appeals in Chicago. There, he became involved with "Operation Greylord," an investigation into corruption in the court system, and helped prosecute police officers, lawyers, and judges.

Often noted for his remarkable discipline, Turow successfully juggled his legal career, growing family, and literary pursuits, writing *Presumed Innocent* during the hours he traveled on a commuter train between his office and his suburban home. Realizing that he could not both maintain his grueling work schedule and complete the book, on his wife's advice Turow resigned his job with the U.S. Attorney's Office and accepted a position with Sonnenschein Nath and Rosenthal, a private Chicago law firm. Before starting work there, he took three months off to finish *Presumed Innocent*.

Presumed Innocent's record-breaking success made Turow a wealthy man. Although he continued to work as a lawyer and was determined to maintain his two careers, soon after the publication of *Presumed Innocent* he asked Sonnenschein Nath and Rosenthal to allow him to work part time. He still does legal work with the firm as well as pro bono legal work while writing his best-selling novels.

ANALYSIS

Typically, Scott Turow draws on his own firsthand experiences of the courtroom, of police procedures, and of political maneuvering and corruption to create realistic and gripping characters and scenes. He tends to return to several compelling themes: the technical and moral intricacies of legal practice, the elusive quality of truth and how well truth can be revealed by the legal process, and the notions that anyone can be corrupted and that everyone has at least one dark secret. Heroes can be quite flawed, and even villains act because of understandable human motives. These ideas are central to all of Turow's fiction, although each work takes a different approach to exploring these themes. Turow's later novels introduce a greater range of characters, examine these characters' failures in greater depth, and address more convoluted aspects of courtroom tactics, crime, and criminal behavior. Each book features a corpse, but the mystery of "whodunit" has increasingly become secondary to Turow's delight in legal maneuvering and his concerns with larger questions of character.

PRESUMED INNOCENT

Upon its publication, *Presumed Innocent* was an astonishing critical and popular success. Drawing on Turow's experiences as a prosecutor in the U.S. Attorney's Office in Chicago, the novel presents a detailed, realistic portrait of Rusty Sabich, a chief deputy prosecutor in the fictional midwestern Kindle County. The particularity of this world, especially the rendition of the murder trial central to the book, figures heavily in its appeal.

As the novel opens, Sabich's beautiful, ambitious colleague, Carolyn Polhemus, has just been raped and murdered, apparently by someone she trusted. Her murder embarrasses Sabich's boss, chief prosecuting attorney Raymond Horgan, who is up for reelection, so Horgan asks Sabich to head the investigation. When Sabich fails to uncover the murderer and Horgan loses the election, Horgan conspires to frame his deputy for the murder. Sabich, who had had a brief affair with Polhemus and pursued her obsessively for months afterward, is charged with her murder and brought to trial, with attorney Alejandro "Sandy" Stern defending him. The courtroom scenes and Sabich's consultations with his lawyer offer fascinating insights into real-world legal tactics and explore a theme that Turow revisits in later works: the ambiguity and simple human recalcitrance that plague the search for the truth.

A long-past bribery scam and Polhemus's affairs with Horgan and the judge, Andrew Lyttle, complicate everyone's motives, and Horgan testifies against Sabich to hide his own connection to Polhemus. When Stern discredits prosecution witnesses, suggests that Sabich might have been framed for Polhemus's murder, and lets the judge know indirectly that he is willing to bring in the judge's connection to Polhemus, the case is dismissed. Thus, *Presumed Innocent* creates a many-layered world where motives and perceptions shift depending on point of view and current knowledge, with nearly every noble act countered by the reprehensible.

Even after the murderer's identity is revealed, what really happened remains unknowable as Sabich and his friend Lipranzer disagree about the murderer's intentions. The final revelation of the killer is deeply satisfying and thematically apropos, as the title signals: There is no real innocence, only "the presumption of innocence," a legal term acknowledging the ineffability of human motive and thus the impossibility of establishing clearcut culpability. Trials may or may not end in justice, but they rarely reveal the full truth.

Truth in *Presumed Innocent* emerges not from Sabich's trial but from his first-person meditations, revealing his brooding, philosophical temperament, and readers must repeatedly reexamine thoughts and actions based on new pieces of the whole. This disturbing moral ambiguity indicates that readers are not in hackneyed thriller country but rather in literature territory.

THE BURDEN OF PROOF

The Burden of Proof opens with the suicide of defense lawyer Alejandro "Sandy" Stern's wife of thirty-one years, Clara. In the rest of the novel, Stern, Rusty Sabich's defense attorney in *Presumed Innocent*, unravels the reasons for Clara's death and comes to terms with his own life. Stern soon learns that Clara had been unfaithful, acquired a venereal disease, and wrote a check to an unknown payee that almost depleted her estate. He fails to connect his wife's suicide with the troubles of his brother-in-law, Dixon Hartnell, the owner of a brokerage house and Stern's most significant client (Stern is defending Hartnell on charges of illegal trading).

In this novel Turow explores the psyche and the complex family ties of the hero as this reserved, formal, middle-aged Argentine immigrant and Jew returns to society, engages in a reinvigorated sex life, and finds love with the married, pregnant federal prosecutor investigating Hartnell's case. Stern's strained relationships with his three children eventually lead him to understand the death of his wife and the burden of proof—in both the technical legal sense and as the weight he must carry by unraveling his wife's inexplicable behavior.

PLEADING GUILTY

A detective story about human greed written in a modern epistolary style—in the contents of six Dictaphone tapes—*Pleading Guilty* is the first-person narrative of McCormack "Mack" Malloy, a policeman turned lawyer, tasked with finding a missing law partner, star litigator Bert Kamin. Kamin might have absconded with more than five million dollars, the settlement for a class-action suit and the funds intended to be shared as profits. The tapes are Malloy's report to the Management Oversight Committee, but they are also an indictment of the law firm that pays him. The narrative provides a kaleidoscope view of actions whose nature changes as the point of view shifts and professional integrity yields to self-interest and betrayal of public trust.

THE LAWS OF OUR FATHERS

Turow's fourth novel, *The Laws of Our Fathers*, continues his move away from the page-turning intensity of *Presumed Innocent*. Ghetto gang leader and drug dealer Ordell Trent, known as Hardcore, meets a white woman who comes to his neighborhood to see him for unclear reasons; before she can explain, she is gunned down, and a teenage girl wounded. The murdered woman is June Eddgar, ex-wife of State Senator Loyall Eddgar. Hardcore turns state's evidence to reduce the sentence for his own seeming involvement in the murder, claiming that June Eddgar's son Nile set up the meeting and conspired to have his mother killed.

The murder and Nile's trial reintroduce a secondary character from an earlier work, just as *The Burden of Proof* does with *Presumed Innocent*'s defense attorney Sandy Stern. Here, Sonia "Sonny" Klonsky, a prosecuting attorney and love interest for Stern in *Burden of Proof*, has moved on: Several years later, she is divorced from her poet husband, struggling with single motherhood, and sitting as a state court judge in Kindle County, feeling out of place even among her clerical staff.

The trial also reunites Sonny with several people from the late 1960's, when Sonny and the Eddgars, then leftist revolutionaries, lived in the same apartment building. Seth Weissman was Sonny's uneasy boyfriend, trying to wring some kind of commitment out of a determinedly distant Sonny. Seth's best friend Hobie Tuttle, an African American who has become a successful defense attorney representing Nile Eddgar, once flirted with black separatism, while Seth now writes a syndicated column about the faded 1960's idealism.

Hobie's showboating defense (despite indignant screaming by prosecuting attorney Tommy Molto, who first appeared in *Presumed Innocent*) drags the proceedings into theatrics, and Sonny declares a mistrial. Three-quarters through the novel, the trial is suddenly over, but it has been simply a vehicle for reuniting the Eddgars, Seth, Sonny, and Hobie and examining the people they have become, told from either Seth's or Sonny's point of view, shifting backward and forward from the 1960's to 1995. No one knows the full truth about the Eddgars and Hardcore, neither judge nor journalist; the legal process has not uncovered the events that led to June Eddgar's death. The book's last few chapters cut quickly to interior points of view of Hardcore, Nile, Loyall Eddgar, and June Eddgar, allowing the reader to learn why June met Hardcore and why she was killed. Much of this novel is devoted to the characters' struggles—not always successful—to leave behind the legacies of their parents and find happiness by improving on or rejecting the past.

PERSONAL INJURIES

In *Personal Injuries* Turow draws on his experiences as a federal prosecutor in Operation Greylord, creating the fictionalized Project Petros, a federal investigation of Kindle County judges suspected of bribery. U.S. Attorney Stan Sennett, who heads the investigation, has evidence against personal injury attorney Robert "Robbie" Feaver, who failed to report a slush fund. To escape a long prison term for tax fraud, Feaver reluctantly agrees to assist in a sting operation against the judges, with agent Evon Miller of the Federal Bureau of Investigation as his watchdog. When Feaver hires defense attorney George Mason, who understands the contrasting roles of prosecution and defense and, like Feaver, sees the law in shades of gray rather than in the black-and-white divisions of Sennett's conception, he has an ally.

The operation has Feaver bringing fake personal injury cases before key judges and then offering them bribes to rule in his supposed clients' favor. The novel makes clear the difficulty of gathering evidence of corruption sufficient to survive defense challenges, as video surveillance fails, recordings are muddled, and judges prove cautious. Feaver's beautiful wife, Rainey, is dying of Lou Gehrig's disease, and a jail sentence will leave her without care and protection. Miller, a lesbian from a Fundamentalist Christian religious background, is attracted to the charming Feaver despite his cynicism, relativism, lies, and borderline criminality (he does not really have a law degree). Turow's point is that people do not fit into the narrow legal categories on which Sennett insists; rather, they are complex beings, mixtures of good and bad, more gray than any black or white extreme. Sennett cannot make his case because of the rigidity of his outlook and is to some degree responsible for Feaver's death. In contrast, Miller learns to see the gray areas of life and acts humanely to assist Rainey.

REVERSIBLE ERRORS

In *Reversible Errors*, Turow fictionalizes the discussion of capital punishment that he raises in his nonfiction work *Ultimate Punishment: A Lawyer's Reflections on Dealing with the Death Penalty* (2003) to make his case against capital punishment and to show precisely how easily justice can miscarry. Corporate attorney Arthur Raven has been assigned the final appeal of Rommy Gandolph, convicted of murdering a popular restaurateur based on circumstantial evidence and a confession produced under pressure. Despite Gandolph's marginal developmental disability and disagreeable nature, Raven comes to believe him innocent. To prove his case, he must face detective Larry Starczek, who was responsible for Gandolph's confession, and Muriel Wynn, the prosecutor, both of whom seem unbending. These two were once lovers, and a continuing attraction affects their professional judgment. They do not question their own behavior and are skeptical about defense ploys; they believe they have acted justly and take pride in the conviction.

Ironically, the former judge who sentenced Gandolph, Gillian Sullivan, was herself imprisoned for taking bribes and now helps Raven's defense. Her vulnerability brings out the best in Raven, who begins an affair with her. Turow thus shows personal and emotional states affecting both prosecution and defense: Wynn permits Starczek great leeway in his conduct of the investigation, and Raven more zealously defends Gandolph to show his new lover his masculine power. Ultimately, it is revealed that the true culprit and motive were never a part of the original investigation. In this novel, Turow captures the complexity of human behavior and motive so well, describing the best efforts of highly competent and basically honorable people, that the reader remains unsure. While many errors can be reversed, death by execution cannot. In this case, only random happenstance—the illness of the true culprit—brings justice.

ORDINARY HEROES

Ordinary Heroes departs physically and thematically from Kindle County, although the action begins and ends there and briefly returns. The premise is that reporter Stewart

Dubinsky, a very minor character in *Presumed Innocent*, is wrestling with his feelings about his recently deceased father, David Dubin, a judge advocate general (JAG) lawyer in World War II Europe who has been closed-mouthed about his war service. (The son has resurrected the original Russian family name that his father had Americanized.) Stewart, now retired early and searching for a freelance writing project, discovers love letters his father wrote home to a fiancé, Grace Morton, a WASP-ish fellow student he met at Easton College in Kindle County who is very different from Gilda Dubin, Stewart's mother, rescued by his father from a German concentration camp while he was on JAG assignment in the war. Shocked by this unknown and out-of-character fiancé, Stewart realizes how little he really knows about his father. His mother claims ignorance of David's life before she met him, and Stewart is further shaken to learn from documents that his father was court-martialed toward the end of the war. His father's defense attorney, "Bear" Leach, is aged but still lucid and in possession of a long manuscript of David's describing the events leading up to the court-martial. The novel shifts to David's story of his 1944 European experiences, returning occasionally to Stewart in the early 2000's. Stewart plans to publish his father's memoir and is rewriting parts, so we hear the father's tale as edited by the son. As in *The Laws of Our Fathers*, the action shifts back and forth in time and place, but the difference is more than fifty years and on two continents.

The theme of stories is central to *Ordinary Heroes*, which deals with stories told and stories withheld, the latter especially by parents being less than totally candid with their children. In fact, the layers of tales is even greater than one generation, since some of the best yarns were told to a youthful Scott Turow by his father David D. Turow, a field surgeon commanding a military medical company, notably of parachuting at low altitude at night into a Bastogne under German siege and losing excretory control out of sheer terror. (Turow insists that though the stories and travels around the front are his father's, David Turow is in no way David Dubin.) The last line of the book, "And when we tell our parents' tales to the world, or even to ourselves, the story is always our own," addresses both Turow's retelling of his father's history and Stewart's reworking of his fictional father's narrative.

David Dubin feels guilty to be avoiding combat as a JAG lawyer but also relieved. He is conducting courts-martial in France just behind General George S. Patton's advance, punishing American soldiers who have abused French civilians. His investigation of an American expatriate, Robert Martin, a former union organizer on the French railways who now works for the Office of Strategic Services (OSS), the secret operations agency that became the Central Intelligence Agency (CIA), and who is suspected of being a communist with Soviet sympathies, aims at ascertaining Martin's true loyalties. In fact, he finds his own understanding of himself so altered that he begins to question his role as a JAG lawyer. A love triangle intensifies his self-doubts as the pursuit continues. Dubin finds out later that even Martin's London OSS handler is not quite sure whether Martin is a patriot or a double agent. This is classic Turow—characters filled with passionate obsession but clouded by an indeterminate truth. Dubin witnesses the Battle of the Bulge, the brotherhood that combat creates, and the liberation of a Nazi concentration camp. The large-screen scope of *Ordinary Heroes* makes the exactitude of Turow's courtroom novels impossible to sustain, producing a fine read, but short of the author's past successes.

LIMITATIONS

Limitations, which was serialized in sixteen issues of *The New York Times Magazine* beginning April 23, 2006, has a tightness of plot, a highly focused central theme, and an economy of telling that set it apart from Turow's more expansive novels. It ends abruptly, leaving readers wishing for more about its attractive central character. George Mason, first seen as a defense attorney in *Personal Injuries*, representing Robbie Feaver and crossing swords with federal prosecutor Stan Sennett, is the perfect counter to Sennett's prosecutorial zeal, a transplanted Virginian distantly related to the original George Mason of colonial times, a Founding Father and Bill of Rights originator. Mason's philosophy perceives reality in shades of gray, finding human motive complex and even unfathomable, in utter contrast to prosecutor Sennett's insistence on the polar opposites: guilty or not.

At fifty-nine, Judge Mason has done very well, landing an appeals court position in which he has thrived, raising a happy family, and earning the respect of his superiors, his peers, and his court staff. He faces three problems, however, which intermingle: His wife, Patrice, is undergoing treatment for a cancer on her thyroid; he has received e-mailed death threats escalating in intensity; and a sexual assault case before his court, *Warnovits et al.*, in which a high school ice hockey team raped an unconscious girl, recalls a personal sexual encounter, Mason's first, in which the young woman was helplessly drunk. Mason's term of service as judge is up shortly, and he must commit to standing for an assured reelection even as he doubts his right to sit in judgment of a crime he may well have committed himself, no matter that standards of the time were different. Mason is no longer sure who he is, and he even asks Rusty Sabich, the defendant in *Presumed Innocent* but now chief judge, "Who are we to judge?"—an unpromising question for a distinguished senior jurist up for reelection.

The plot unfolds neatly, with several candidates introduced as possible origins of the death threats, sharp and convincing portraits of Mason's staff and coworkers, an assault that rings of authenticity for any urban resident, and nuanced meditations on culpability and how it can be sorted out by the all-or-nothing force of the law: Should the rapists be freed because the statute of limitations period has passed? How can real justice be served without resort to simply ignoring the rule of law and exercising personal judgment, as some of Mason's appeals court colleagues seem to do? The title *Limitations* resonates with meanings: that of the statutory period but also the more general sense of human constraints and insufficiencies. Mason's age allows Turow to present a retrospective of changing sexual mores in the last half of the twentieth century and the ways in which the law has attempted to adapt to new attitudes.

Andrew F. Macdonald

OTHER MAJOR WORKS

NONFICTION: *One L: An Inside Account of Life in the First Year at Harvard Law School*, 1977; *Ultimate Punishment: A Lawyer's Reflections on Dealing with the Death Penalty*, 2003.

EDITED TEXTS: *Guilty as Charged: A Mystery Writers of America Anthology*, 1996 (also known as *Guilty as Charged: The Penguin Book of New American Crime Writing*); *The Best American Mystery Stories, 2006*, 2006.

BIBLIOGRAPHY

Diggs, Terry K. "Through a Glass Darkly: John Grisham and Scott Turow Lay Down the Law for Millions of Americans." *American Bar Association Journal* 82 (October, 1996): 72-75. Compares the realities of the legal life with its representation in the novels of Turow and John Grisham.

Gray, Paul. "Burden of Success: As a High-Powered Lawyer and Novelist, Scott Turow Has Become the Bard of the Litigious Age." *Time*, June 11, 1990. Discusses aspects of Turow's legal fiction and Turow's influence on public perceptions of the legal system.

Lundy, Derek. *Scott Turow: Meeting the Enemy*. Toronto, Ont.: ECW Press, 1995. Presents an admiring examination of Turow's background, his work, and his personal views on life, authorship, fame, and the law. Also provides analysis of his early short stories and his first three novels.

Macdonald, Andrew, and Gina Macdonald. *Scott Turow: A Critical Companion*. Westport, Conn.: Greenwood Press, 2005. Provides an examination of Turow's life and literary influences as well as discussion of his major works, including the topics of characterization, themes, and plot structure. Includes bibliography and glossary.

_____. "Scott Turow's *Presumed Innocent*: Novel and Film—Multifaceted Character Study Versus Tailored Courtroom Drama." In *It's a Print! Detective Fiction from Page to Screen*, edited by William Reynolds and Elizabeth Trembley. Bowling Green, Ohio: Bowling Green State University Popular Press, 1994. Discusses the differences between the novel and its film adaptation, focusing in particular on the film's failure to capture the psychological complexity of the novel.

Turow, Scott. "Building a Legal Thriller: Scott Turow Finds Compelling Stories in the Gray Areas Between What's Legal and What's Moral." Interview by Elfrieda Abbe. *Writer* 188 (May, 2005): 18-22. Turow discusses his approach to the creation of a legal thriller.

_____. "Scott Turow: Nothing Is More Moving to Me than What Happens in the Average Life." Interview by Nancy Bunge. In *Master Class: Lessons from Leading Writers*. Iowa City: University of Iowa Press, 2005. Turow addresses his writing methods and techniques.

Watson, Jay. "Making Do in the Courtroom: Notes on Some Convergences Between Forensic Practice and Bricolage." *Studies in Law, Politics, and Society* 14 (1994): 119-137. Discusses how the American judicial process is portrayed in works of fiction.

JOSEPH WAMBAUGH

Born: East Pittsburgh, Pennsylvania; January 22, 1937
Also known as: Joseph Aloysius Wambaugh, Jr.

OTHER LITERARY FORMS

In addition to several nonfiction works, including *The Onion Field* (1973), *Echoes in the Darkness* (1987), and *Fire Lover: A True Story* (2002), Joseph Wambaugh (WAHM-baw) has written screenplays for the film adaptations of his works *The Onion Field* (1979) and *The Black Marble* (1980) and teleplays for *Echoes in the Darkness* (1987) and *Fugitive Nights* (1993). He has also served as creative consultant for the television production of his novel *The Blue Knight* and for the television series *Police Story.*

ACHIEVEMENTS

Joseph Wambaugh is widely regarded as an outstanding storyteller and the most respected and prolific American novelist in the field of police procedure novels. All of his fiction and nonfiction works have been best sellers, and, given his cinematic feel for character and scene, many of his works have been developed into television and film projects. With works defined by gritty realism and realistic and vivid characters, Wambaugh has received a range of prestigious genre awards, most notably the Mystery Writers of America's Special Edgar Allan Poe Award for Nonfiction in 1974 (for *The Onion Field*) and the 2004 Grand Master Award, a lifetime achievement recognition presented by the same organization.

Critics have long praised Wambaugh's ability to combine objectivity and empathy in realistic depictions of contemporary life on an urban police force. Few genre novelists

Joseph Wambaugh
(Library of Congress)

have so effectively conveyed the feelings of horror, isolation, despair, frustration, and helplessness experienced daily by police officers, as well as their reactions to these intense psychological pressures. Wambaugh vividly brings to life the heroism and cowardice, anger and compassion, dedication and laziness, insight and ignorance of the average police officer on the beat. His believable portraits of police officers, both men and women, are matched by cogent explorations of the sociopathic personalities of the criminals they battle, all of which draw the reader into a complete and compelling world of drugs, crime, alcoholism, and social and moral decay.

BIOGRAPHY

Joseph Aloysius Wambaugh, Jr., was born in 1937 in East Pittsburgh, Pennsylvania, the son of a small-town police chief. Following in his father's footsteps was not young Wambaugh's original intention. He entered the U.S. Marine Corps in 1954 and soon thereafter married his high school sweetheart, Dee Allsup. Discharged from the military in 1957, Wambaugh settled in Ontario, California, where he became a steelworker and went to college part time at night. He planned to be a teacher and eventually completed both a B.A. and an M.A. in English. In 1960, however, while in his senior year at California State College in Los Angeles, Wambaugh decided instead to become a policeman.

Over the next fourteen years, he worked his way up to detective in the Los Angeles Police Department (LAPD) and was eventually promoted to sergeant, despite several well-publicized run-ins with his superiors. Many of these conflicts were occasioned by the publication of Wambaugh's first novel (and best seller), *The New Centurions*, in which the hierarchy of the LAPD is irreverently satirized.

Wambaugh continued to be both detective and novelist until 1974. By that time, he had become so famous that his celebrity status had begun to limit his job effectiveness. He regretfully gave up police work for full-time writing. In 1983 Wambaugh moved from Los Angeles, dividing his time between the suburban areas of Orange County and Palm Springs. In 1993 he moved farther south to the Point Loma district of San Diego. Then, for more than a decade, Wambaugh turned to true-crime writing, most notably his account of a California serial arsonist who was also an arson investigator, *Fire Lover*, which brought Wambaugh his second Edgar Allan Poe Award for best fact crime in 2003. His return to fiction—and to stories of the LAPD—in 2006 was hailed by critics and by fans.

Wambaugh continues to pursue numerous projects, such as the adaptation of his 2006 novel *Hollywood Station* as a television series. In addition, recognizing the impacts that film and television have had on the development of police fiction and the public perception of the process of criminal investigation, he regularly guest lectures on screenwriting and screen adaptation at the University of California at San Diego.

ANALYSIS

All of Joseph Wambaugh's novels deal with police officers, primarily in Southern California. Their environment is completely outside the experience of most middle-class Americans, for it is populated with drug dealers, drifters, pimps, prostitutes, addicts, panhandlers, murderers, and thieves. Supplementing the bad guys are the outcasts, outsiders, and victims: welfare mothers and their families, abused children, old and disabled pensioners, illegal immigrants, the mentally incompetent, and the chronically disaffected. Middle-class values have disappeared, and what are usually considered normal attitudes and behaviors seem nonexistent. In the cultures of the barrio and the ghetto, and even among the wacky rich, police officers are charged with representing and upholding a legal system overwhelmed by the morass of modern society. Because Wambaugh himself is a veteran of the streets, the reader experiences his world through the mind of a policeman: It is full of darkness, desolation, and, above all, a sense of helplessness, for the fate of an individual, as well as the solution to a case, often turns upon trivial, capricious accidents.

This depressing background of urban decay sets the stage on which Wambaugh presents several themes. The most persistent is that real police work is very different from typical public perceptions influenced by television, motion pictures, and traditional police stories, which depict cops as superheroes who always get the bad guys and put them away. Again and again, Wambaugh's police officers express their frustration with juries who demand to know why it takes three officers with nightsticks to subdue a single, unarmed suspect, or why a police officer did not "wing" a fleeing felon rather than shoot him to death. Everyday people who have never been involved in real fistfights or attempted to aim a weapon at a moving target simply do not understand the realities of these situations. Police officers are not superhuman; they are normal people thrown into extremely abnormal situations.

Often, it seems as if the police are at war with a judicial system that elevates form over substance and technicalities over the determination of guilt or innocence. To the average patrol officer, vice-squad officer, or homicide detective, the courts are arenas where shifty, politically motivated defense lawyers and prosecutors conspire to overturn common sense, where judges and juries view police procedures and conduct with twenty-twenty hindsight, and where the rights of defendants have triumphed over the suffering of victims. It is the average officer who most often encounters the anguish and suffering of those victims. These experiences alienate and isolate police officers from the rest of normal society.

Within the police force itself, the officers on the street are responsible to a hierarchy of brass who, for the most part, have never themselves worked a beat. In Wambaugh's view, the brass are primarily concerned with ensuring their own advancement and have little concern for the welfare of their officers. He paints high-level officers, often with brutal humor, as buffoons who spend much of their time trying to seduce female officers, avoiding real responsibility, and protecting their reputations. That acerbic critique of authority continues in Wambaugh's later fiction when he specifically looks at the consequences of bureaucratic directives to compel political correctness and sensitivity in the wake of a bruising series of scandals involving the LAPD in the late 1990's.

Given that he is a street veteran himself, Wambaugh's sympathies clearly lie with his former comrades, yet what makes his novels extraordinary is his realistic appraisal of these officers, warts and all. Many of them are crude racists, many abuse alcohol, and most resent the forced acceptance of women within their ranks, which began in the 1960's. Attempting to shield themselves from the sheer terror and pain intrinsic to their jobs, they exude cynicism and disgust with nearly everything and everybody, even themselves. They respond to the daily brutality they encounter, and that they must occasionally employ, with gallows humor, sexual promiscuity, alcoholism, and, far too often, "eating their pieces"—suicide. Only in his later novels, after his hiatus from fiction in the late 1990's, does Wambaugh's evident compassion for streetwise cops permit a celebration of the profession. Indeed, his later fiction evidences his own reinvestigation of the police procedural itself—he shifts his attention from the intricacy of investigation and the dogged pursuit of solution and the focus on a single complex criminal act to a more character-driven narrative with embedded anecdotes that reflect less Wambaugh as a seasoned cop and more Wambaugh as a gifted storyteller.

THE NEW CENTURIONS

Wambaugh's first novel, *The New Centurions*, follows the progress of three rookies from their training at the Los Angeles Police Academy in the summer of 1960 to their accidental reunion during the Watts riots of August, 1965. Serge Duran is a former athlete and former marine who has attempted to escape his Chicano heritage, Gus Plebesly is an undersized overachiever who is exceedingly afraid of failure, and Roy Fehler thinks of himself as a liberal intellectual making merely a temporary detour from an academic career in criminology. In their development as police officers, all three face situations that force them to examine their beliefs about themselves. Initially assigned as a patrolman in a barrio precinct, Duran meets a Hispanic woman who teaches him not to be ashamed of his ethnic identity. Under the tutelage of a veteran patrolman, Kilvinsky, Plebesly gains the professional and personal assurance to become a competent officer. Fehler, however, fails to reconcile his intellectual views with the emotional realities of race relations on the street: He blinds himself to his own prejudices, tying himself into a psychological knot. His failure is dramatically symbolized at the end of the novel, when he is shot and dies.

The plot of *The New Centurions* develops chronologically and in episodes focusing on each of the rookies in turn. As Duran, Plebesly, and Fehler receive new assignments, Wambaugh takes the opportunity to display the operational peculiarities of the various divisions within the police force—street patrols, vice, homicide, juvenile, and narcotics—as well as to introduce a host of minor characters, both police and civilians, who reveal all the quirks and propensities of their world. Whenever a new character appears, Wambaugh adds believability and depth by interrupting the narrative to discuss some incident that has shaped this person's life and attitudes. These brief digressions are often darkly humorous and also allow Wambaugh to illustrate further the vicissitudes of life in the LAPD.

It is apparent that Wambaugh regards the Watts riots as a kind of watershed for civilized society and the rule of law. Until the summer of 1965, the Los Angeles police force generally dealt with specific crimes committed by and against individuals. The Watts riots, however, represented a fundamental rejection of the structures of lawful authority by almost the entire black community, and the department was astonished and overwhelmed by the senseless violence of mobs of ordinarily law-abiding citizens. At the end of the book it is clear that, though a few officers seem to have guessed that some sort of qualitative change in social attitudes has occurred, most assume that the situation will soon return to normal.

THE BLUE KNIGHT

One of the main themes of *The Blue Knight*, Wambaugh's second novel, is that the situation did not, in fact, return to normal. Hostile media coverage of the riots focused on the LAPD's lack of community-relations efforts, incompetence, and alleged brutality, while government investigations reported widespread racism and corruption throughout the department. Stung by criticism, department executives became increasingly image-conscious and ordered significant changes in training and operational procedures. One result was that the time-honored tradition of the individual policeman walking his beat was replaced by the two-person patrol-car unit. In the past, officers generally had been granted a large amount of latitude in dealing with situations on their beats and were usually trusted to keep order as they saw fit. The wise policeman developed a commonsense attitude, allowing certain kinds of violations to slide while dealing with others immediately and often severely. The new breed of patrol officer, however, was supposed to stay close to his unit, maintain constant radio communication with his precinct, and limit his activities to those precisely within the law. The new policy was intended to ensure both the safety and the good behavior of officers, whose individual initiative was drastically curtailed.

The Blue Knight takes place in the midst of the transition from the old to the new; its main character is a traditional beat officer, William H. "Bumper" Morgan, a twenty-year veteran on the brink of retirement. Wambaugh examines Bumper's last three days on the police force, using the first-person viewpoint to help the reader perceive events directly through Bumper's eyes and ears. Though Bumper has been forced to trade walking his beat for driving a police unit, he insists on working alone and spends most of his shift out of his car and out of radio contact with his precinct.

Bumper's long experience has made him something of a sociologist and philosopher, and his observations represent Wambaugh's slightly irreverent tribute to the old police view of the world. As he makes his rounds, Bumper recalls for the reader many of the events of his twenty years on the force, as well as what he learned from them. Through these recollections, he reveals the essence of his approach to successful police work: Never give or accept love, and always remain impersonal and uninvolved on the job. Unfortunately, Bumper's philosophy is a self-delusion. The excitement and danger of police work isolate him from everything and everyone outside his beat, the only environment in which he is truly in control. In fact he is so completely involved that his life is nothing but his job. Thus, at the end of the story, despite postretirement plans for marriage and a cushy position as a corporate head of security, Bumper decides that he cannot give up his badge.

Though Bumper is clearly meant to be a sympathetic character, Wambaugh also endows him with flaws. He is overweight and indulges himself in vast feasts provided free by the restaurateurs on his beat. He is crude and flatulent, angry and vengeful, egotistical and very expansive in interpreting his powers as a representative of the law. He imbibes copious amounts of liquor and is certainly no paragon of sexual morality. Sometimes, despite his experience, he even makes stupid mistakes, such as allowing himself to be drawn alone into a dangerous confrontation with student demonstrators. Bumper is softhearted but also tough, violent, and often frustrated. Ultimately, he appears as a tragic figure, unable to break with a career that casts him as a permanent outsider.

THE CHOIRBOYS

After leaving the LAPD in 1974, Wambaugh apparently felt the need to give free rein to some of the anguish and bitterness he felt about his career as a police officer. These emotions are expressed in his third novel, *The Choirboys*, which differs significantly from his previous works in both style and substance. In its structure, grim humor, and overall feeling of hopelessness, *The Choirboys* resembles Joseph Heller's *Catch-22* (1961), with the LAPD substituted for Heller's Army Air Corps. Like the military officers in *Catch-22*, the ten officers who make up the choirboys are losers and misfits: several alcoholics, a sadist, a masochist, a violent racist, and the like. Each chapter introduces a new character and relates a series of especially harrowing incidents that lead to the calling of a "choir practice," in which the group meets in a park to get drunk and vie for the sexual favors of two overweight waitresses. Choir practice allows the officers to let off steam and serves as a coping device against the horrifying realities they have faced. The sessions frequently get out of hand, however, and eventually lead to the unintended death of a civilian and the suspension of several of the group.

With its uninhibited street language, unrestrained cynicism, emotional violence, and unrelieved sense of futility, *The Choirboys* is saved only by the brutal hilarity of its bumbling protagonists and the ironies they suffer. The situations into which Wambaugh's policemen stumble are so outrageous that the reader cannot take them very seriously. Thus, even though Wambaugh's characters are incisive and believable, the world in which they operate is so impossibly awful that the reader maintains the objectivity necessary for laughter

THE BLACK MARBLE

After *The Choirboys*, Wambaugh's novels became both more conventional in structure and more sentimental in tone. His main characters are still losers, and the sense of blind fate and the prominence of coincidence continue to dominate his plots, but, in the end, his protagonists seem to be at least somewhat redeemed; the climaxes always result in some kind of catharsis. Each of his succeeding books revolves around a single case, a kind of puzzle that is resolved not through brilliant police work but through dogged determination and serendipitous accidents. An excellent example is his next novel, *The Black Marble*, whose hero is Sergeant Andrei Mikhailovich Valnikov, an absentminded, broken-down alcoholic who is also a consummate and very touching gentleman. Valnikov was once a top homicide detective, but after he investigated a string of cases of sexually abused and brutally murdered children, he developed constant nightmares and started drinking to forget. Eventually, he suffered a breakdown and was reassigned to the robbery division.

Valnikov is paired with Natalie Zimmerman, an ambitious female detective who is bitter generally about the discriminatory attitude of the LAPD toward women and specifically about being stuck with Valnikov. She believes that her Russian-born partner is not only a drunk but crazy as well, especially when he begins to devote all of his still-considerable abilities to the solution of a case she regards as ridiculous: the theft of a prize schnauzer. Wambaugh follows their misadventures in discovering that the dog has been stolen by a trainer seeking to extort money from the owner, a formerly wealthy divorcée now unable to pay the ransom. As always in a Wambaugh novel, along the path to the solution of the case the reader becomes acquainted with a cast of wacky police officers and civilians, until Valnikov finally catches the criminal and wins the love and respect of his partner.

All of Wambaugh's subsequent novels have followed the pattern established by *The Black Marble*: the often-coincidental solution of a crime by not-very-heroic police officers or former officers. Though he himself regards *The Choirboys* as his best work, it is not representative of his style. In later novels Wambaugh solidified his reputation as a master of the crime novel with stories featuring the flawed characters, dark humor, intricate plots, and dangerous constructions exhibited in his earlier works.

THE GLITTER DOME

Few Wambaugh novels reflect the dark urgency of his outraged moral sensibility (rooted in his Catholic upbringing) better than *The Glitter Dome*—this is a novel, as Wambaugh suggests in his own foreword, full of venom. As such, it holds a particular place in Wambaugh's development: It is something of a nadir; from this point, his novels will follow a steady trajectory toward affirmation more appropriate to the procedural genre in which, traditionally, complex mysteries yield to resolution and a moral order is confirmed in the end.

The Glitter Dome, like other Wambaugh works, is a character-driven procedural, an ensemble narrative that traces four sets of partners who work the seedy districts of Hollywood. There, amid the world of the sordid and the kinky, officers struggle to assert a code of morality. It is Wambaugh's conviction, however, that the police are at best a fragile stay against the moral confusions and brutality of the criminal element. Here police careers follow a grim trajectory from cockiness to compromise and ultimately to despair; successes are rare and often the result not of brilliant police work but rather of guesswork and luck. Indeed, the novel starts with a cold case, a killing that has eluded solution—a film studio executive has been shot in a bowling alley parking lot.

The narrative focus rests on partners Aloysius Mackey and Martin Welborn. Wambaugh again examines the psychological effects of police work: the two partners represent the extremes, the hard-souled survivor (Mackey) and the idealistic innocent (Welborn). The borderline alcoholic Mackey, at forty-three years old paying alimony to multiple ex-wives and living with a cat, toys with the idea of suicide but survives by virtue of his cynicism and his grim sense of humor (the Glitter Dome is a raucous bar where cops go to vent). Welborn, however, struggles in a moral miasma—a lapsed seminarian who finds the order and ritual of the Catholic Church comforting, he seeks that same order in the night-world of Hollywood. He is haunted by memories: of an informant whose name he accidentally revealed who is subsequently murdered; of a child abuse victim, a bed wetter, whose penis was cut off by his father. Like the elaborate contraption he uses to try to repair his back injury, Welborn sees police work as a way to correct failures that Wambaugh sees, with unsettling honesty, are uncorrectable parts of the twisted human psyche.

As Welborn and Mackey investigate, they stumble into a plan to make a so-called snuff film (a film of a real killing) in Mexico, and they become entangled in the seamiest reaches of Hollywood, coming into contact with child pornographers, drug dealers, and sadomasochists. Here, Mackey points out, there is no evil—evil has a dignity and grandeur. Rather, this is simple opportunism and garden-variety greed. By the same token, there are no noble forces of good—detective work here is the product of coincidence and chance executed by imperfect officers who struggle with demons of their own. Appropriately, the final break in the case is entirely capricious—as it turns out, the studio executive was the victim of a spontaneous burglary that had simply gone wrong, and that information only comes from the dying confession of one of the robbers after he is shot. The reader is then denied the satisfying feeling of a case solved—it is merely closed—and that is further complicated by Welborn's suicide as he is overwhelmed by his own surrender to the amorality of the streets (the reader is given disturbing evidence that he may have participated in the robber's shooting as a way to assert some viable moral force). Although the case is technically cleared, like the smog that hangs about the Hollywood streets, a pall of uneasiness hangs about the narrative.

THE GOLDEN ORANGE and FUGITIVE NIGHTS

With *The Golden Orange* and *Fugitive Nights*, Wambaugh enters into the "ex-cop" phase of his work in the persons of Winnie Farlowe and Lynn Cutter, both former officers and heavy drinkers who become drawn into complicated crimes requiring considerable application of their skills. All the while they must strive to surmount the accumulation of personal demons engendered and nurtured by years of police work. In both novels the upscale settings—Newport Harbor in *The Golden Orange* and Palm Springs in *Fugitive Nights*—serve as effective foils for the trademark cop chatter and streetwise daring of the heroes.

In the ex-cop's world, saloons serve as substitute offices where former officers and off-duty policemen congregate to conduct business and male bonding on the side. Wambaugh's ex-cops are tough yet vulnerable, especially when they place their trust in others who, on the surface, seem worthy of it. In *The Golden Orange*, the moment arrives for one of the author's gritty veterans to address what he terms the Cop's Syllogism, a condition that could be applied to nearly all of Wambaugh's fictional constructions. It simply states, "People are garbage. I am a person. Therefore——." Once the syllogism is avowed, only something bad can happen. It "has led thousands of burned-out, overwhelmingly cynical members of the law enforcement business into alcoholism or drug addiction, police corruption, or suicide." It affirms why, in an interview, the author took issue with the notion that his works are police procedurals. "I was the first person, I think, to write a book about cops that was not a police procedural," he said. "A police procedural is a novel that attempts to show how a cop acts on the job. I wasn't interested so much in that. So, I turned it around. I thought I'd like to show how the job acts on the cop."

FINNEGAN'S WEEK

In *Finnegan's Week* another of Wambaugh's hero-detectives, Finbar Finnegan, teams up with Nell Salter, a district attorney's office investigator, and Bobbie Ann Doggett, a navy law enforcement official, to solve a crime involving a stolen truck loaded with lethal pesticide. As usual, the drinks, jokes, sexual repartee, salty dialogue, and verbal and physical clashes flow freely. At times they almost career out of control, whipsawing the reader to a conclusion that is judicious and sensible.

FLOATERS

Floaters features an aquatic theme, as Wambaugh pairs a couple of harbor cops and vice officers in an investigation of a scheme by a business tycoon to sabotage a competitor's entry in the America's Cup yachting race. As in previous works, the author demonstrates a knack for juxtaposing characters who are very different. In addition to the unlikely cops, the characters include a yachting enthusiast, an expensive call girl and masseuse, a vicious pimp, and a band of rowdy Australian crewmen. Though the plot is slow paced at the beginning, the events leading up to the climax are vintage Wambaugh. In all his fiction, Wambaugh has explored essentially the same themes: the basic humanity of police officers and the pressures they face, the decline of traditional values in modern society, and the haphazard and accidental nature of fate.

HOLLYWOOD STATION

After more than a decade working exclusively on documentary treatments of true crimes, a series of successful (and controversial) best sellers in the manner of Truman Capote's *In Cold Blood* (1966), Wambaugh returned to fiction in 2006. It was less a return to form than a reinvention of it. Intrigued by requests from longtime fans and respected colleagues to revisit the LAPD in the wake of nearly a decade of scandals (very public investigations of botched procedures, coerced confessions, evidence tampering, excessive violence, racial profiling, and illegal searches), Wambaugh hesitated only because he was not sure he was still in touch with the psyche of the contemporary street cop. To reignite his fictional sensibility, Wambaugh hosted a series of dinners with a range of LAPD officers and listened to their conversations about life on the streets—he found the process cathartic as he gathered a wealth of vivid anecdotal material, and in the resulting novel, *Hollywood Station*, Wambaugh acknowledges the nearly fifty cops who participated.

Although on the surface *Hollywood Station* is a familiar Wambaugh novel—an ensemble novel set in the gritty underworld of Hollywood—it is a striking departure. It lacks a riveting central investigation: Here, a small-time criminal, a methamphetamine freak who is marginally competent as a thief, ends up tangling with a Russian crime lord (who is himself something of a clownish presence) and a succession of more daring and more dangerous thefts. It is a slender plot—Wambaugh is far more interested in creating the psychological lives of the investigating officers, a collection of vivid characters led by the

Oracle, a fifty-ish captain who centers the novel with a steadying moral vision in a universe of chaos and absurdities. The anecdotes that the characters tell, full of streetwise humor, underscore Wambaugh's Irish love of storytelling. Given the range of characters (each with defining interests and signature dialogue—one a new mother, another an aspiring actor, two others veteran surfers), the compelling humor, and the episodic vignettes of these officers struggling to assert some measure of dignity and order, the novel recalls less the traditional police procedural and more Joseph Heller's *Catch-22*, by Wambaugh's admission a seminal text in his evolution as a writer.

Wambaugh (like Heller) is motivated not only by an instinct for compelling stories but also by a caustic critique of what he sees as bureaucratic absurdities—specifically, a complex of federal regulations that tried to create a politically correct environment but that undercut the effectiveness of the street cops and made the old-school camaraderie of the force strained and artificial. Unlike his earlier fictions, however, in which cops are imperfect and at times overwhelmed by the insidious pull of the criminal world they patrol, *Hollywood Station* presents a clear endorsement not only of the LAPD but also of police work generally. Public scandals trained attention, Wambaugh argues, on a slender element of the LAPD—and, as the Oracle says, there is no work more fun than police work. It is that spirited endorsement of the profession that distinguishes Wambaugh's return to fiction. Writing in his seventies, Wambaugh enthusiastically praises the work, determination, compassion, and moral authority of the cops he has chronicled for more than forty years.

Thomas C. Schunk; William Hoffman
Updated by Joseph Dewey

OTHER MAJOR WORKS

SCREENPLAYS: *The Onion Field*, 1979 (adaptation of his book); *The Black Marble*, 1980 (adaptation of his novel).

TELEPLAYS: *Echoes in the Darkness*, 1987 (adaptation of his book); *Fugitive Nights*, 1993 (adaptation of his novel).

NONFICTION: *The Onion Field*, 1973; *Lines and Shadows*, 1984; *Echoes in the Darkness*, 1987; *The Blooding*, 1989; *Fire Lover: A True Story*, 2002.

EDITED TEXT: *The Best American Crime Writing, 2004*, 2004.

BIBLIOGRAPHY

Dunn, Adam. "Burning Down the House." *Book* 22 (May/June, 2002): 19. Provides background information on Wambaugh's first book after a six-year hiatus.

Jeffrey, David K. "Joseph Wambaugh: Overview." In *St. James Guide to Crime and Mystery Writers*, edited by Jay P. Pederson. 4th ed. Detroit, Mich.: St. James Press, 1996. Focuses on critical analysis of Wambaugh's work, but also provides some biographical information.

Marling, William. "Joseph Wambaugh." In *Hard-Boiled Fiction*. June, 2007. Case Western Reserve University. http://www.detnovel.com/Wambaugh.html. Accessed January 29, 2009. Presents helpful analysis of the principal themes in Wambaugh's work that place his novels within the tradition of police procedurals.

Van Dover, J. Kenneth. *Centurions, Knights, and Other Cops: The Police Novels of Joseph Wambaugh.* San Bernardino, Calif.: Brownstone Books, 1995. Presents a critical study of Wambaugh's first fourteen books. Includes an excellent chronology of his life.

Wambaugh, Joseph. Interviews, May 17, 2002, and March 28, 2008. Bookreporter.com. Http://www .bookreporter.com/authors/au-wambaugh-joseph .asp. Accessed January 29, 2009. Wambaugh provides extensive discussion of his methods for creating believable police officers in his fiction and for maintaining readers' sympathy for these characters in an era of scandals involving police misconduct. Also examines the relationship between his fiction and his extensive catalog of nonfiction works.

_____. "Ship to Shore with Joseph Wambaugh: Still a Bit Paranoid Among the Palms." Interview by Andy Meisler. *The New York Times,* June 13, 1996. Wambaugh offers his observations on what he considers the erosion of the American judicial system in the late twentieth century and also provides an overview of his own career as a Los Angeles detective and novelist.

BIBLIOGRAPHY

Every effort has been made to include studies published in 2000 and later. Most items in this bibliography contain a listing of secondary sources, making it easier to identify other critical commentary on novelists, movements, and themes.

THEORETICAL, THEMATIC, AND HISTORICAL STUDIES

Altman, Janet Gurkin. *Epistolarity: Approaches to a Form*. Columbus: Ohio State University Press, 1982. Examines the epistolary novel, explaining how novelists use the letter form to develop characterization, further their plots, and develop meaning.

Beaumont, Matthew, ed. *Adventures in Realism*. Malden, Mass.: Blackwell, 2007. Fifteen essays explore facets of realism, which was critical to the development of the novel. Provides a theoretical framework for understanding how novelists attempt to represent the real and the common in fiction.

Brink, André. *The Novel: Language and Narrative from Cervantes to Calvino*. New York: New York University Press, 1998. Uses contemporary theories of semiotics and narratology to establish a continuum between early novelists and those of the postmodern era in their conscious use of language to achieve certain effects. Ranges across national boundaries to illustrate the theory of the development of the novel since the seventeenth century.

Brownstein, Rachel. *Becoming a Heroine: Reading About Women in Novels*. New York: Viking Press, 1982. Feminist survey of novels from the eighteenth century through the latter half of the twentieth century. Examines how "becoming a heroine" defines for women a sense of value in their lives. Considers novels by both men and women, and discusses the importance of the traditional marriage plot.

Bruzelius, Margaret. *Romancing the Novel: Adventure from Scott to Sebald*. Lewisburg, Pa.: Bucknell University Press, 2007. Examines the development of the adventure novel, linking it with the medieval romance tradition and exploring readers' continuing fascination with the genre.

Cavallaro, Dani. *The Gothic Vision: Three Centuries of Horror, Terror, and Fear*. New York: Continuum, 2005. Study of the gothic novel from its earliest manifestations in the eighteenth century to the early twenty-first century. Through the lenses of contemporary cultural theories, examines readers' fascination with novels that invoke horror, terror, and fright.

Doody, Margaret Anne. *The True Story of the Novel*. New Brunswick, N.J.: Rutgers University Press, 1996. Traces the roots of the novel, traditionally thought to have been developed in the seventeenth century, to classical Greek and Latin texts that exhibit characteristics of modern fiction.

Hale, Dorothy J., ed. *The Novel: An Anthology of Criticism and Theory, 1900-2000*. Malden, Mass.: Blackwell, 2006. Collection of essays by theorists and novelists. Includes commentary on the novel form from the perspective of formalism, structuralism, poststructuralism, Marxism, and reader response theory. Essays also address the novel through the lenses of sociology, gender studies, and feminist theory.

_____. *Social Formalism: The Novel in Theory from Henry James to the Present*. Stanford, Calif.: Stanford University Press, 1998. Emphasizes the novel's special ability to define a social world for readers. Relies heavily on the works of contemporary literary and cultural theorists. Provides a summary of twentieth century efforts to identify a theory of fiction that encompasses novels of many kinds.

Hart, Stephen M., and Wen-chin Ouyang, eds. *A Companion to Magical Realism*. London: Tamesis, 2005. Essays outlining the development of Magical Realism, tracing its roots from Europe through Latin America to other regions of the world. Explores the political dimensions of the genre.

Hoffman, Michael J., and Patrick D. Murphy, eds. *Essentials of the Theory of Fiction*. 2d ed. Durham, N.C.: Duke University Press, 1996. Collection of essays by influential critics from the late nineteenth century through the twentieth century. Focuses on the essential elements of fiction and the novel's relationship to the world it depicts.

Lodge, David. *The Art of Fiction: Illustrated from Classic and Modern Texts*. New York: Viking Press, 1993. Short commentaries on the technical aspects of fiction. Examples from important and minor novelists illustrate literary principles and techniques such as point of view, suspense, character introduction, irony, motivation, and ending.

Lynch, Deirdre, and William B. Walker, eds. *Cultural Institutions of the Novel*. Durham, N.C.: Duke University Press, 1996. Fifteen essays examine aspects of long fiction produced around the world. Encourages a redefinition of the genre and argues for inclusion of texts not historically considered novels.

Moretti, Franco, ed. *The Novel*. 2 vols. Princeton, N.J.: Princeton University Press, 2006. Explores the novel from multiple perspectives, including as an anthropological, historical, and sociological document; a function of the national tradition from which it emerges; and a work of art subject to examination using various critical approaches.

Shiach, Morag, ed. *The Cambridge Companion to the Modernist Novel*. New York: Cambridge University Press, 2007. Essays explaining the concept of modernism and its influence on the novel. Detailed examination of works by writers from various countries, all influenced by the modernist movement. Includes a detailed chronology.

Vice, Sue. *Holocaust Fiction*. New York: Routledge, 2000. Examines controversies generated by novels about the Holocaust. Focuses on eight important works, but also offers observations on the polemics surrounding publication of books on this topic.

Zunshine, Lisa. *Why We Read Fiction: Theory of Mind and the Novel*. Columbus: Ohio State University Press, 2006. Applies theories of cognitive psychology to novel reading, explaining how experience and human nature lead readers to constrain their interpretations of a given text. Provides numerous examples from well-known novels to illustrate how and why readers find pleasure in fiction.

DETECTIVE AND MYSTERY FICTION

Bertens, Hans, and Theo d'Haen. *Contemporary American Crime Fiction.* New York: Palgrave, 2001. Surveys the work of crime and detective writers of the 1990's. Discusses ethnic crime literature, police procedurals, private detectives, and American fiction exploring other countries and historical periods. Special focus on the writing of women and people of color.

Priestman, Martin, ed. *The Cambridge Companion to Crime Fiction.* New York: Cambridge University Press, 2003. Essays examine the nature and development of the genre, explore works by writers (including women and ethnic minorities) from several countries, and establish links between crime fiction and other literary genres. Includes a chronology.

Scaggs, John. *Crime Fiction.* New York: Routledge, 2005. Provides a history of crime fiction, explores key subgenres, and identifies recurring themes that suggest the wider social and historical context in which these works are written. Suggests critical approaches that open crime fiction to serious study.

Laurence W. Mazzeno

GLOSSARY OF LITERARY TERMS

absurdism: A philosophical attitude, pervading much of modern drama and fiction, that underlines the isolation and alienation that humans experience, having been thrown into what absurdists see as a godless universe devoid of religious, spiritual, or metaphysical meaning. Conspicuous in its lack of logic, consistency, coherence, intelligibility, and realism, the literature of the absurd depicts the anguish, forlornness, and despair inherent in the human condition. Counter to the rationalist assumptions of traditional humanism, absurdism denies the existence of universal truth or value.

allegory: A literary mode in which a second level of meaning, wherein characters, events, and settings represent abstractions, is encoded within the surface narrative. The allegorical mode may dominate an entire work, in which case the encoded message is the work's primary reason for being, or it may be an element in a work otherwise interesting and meaningful for its surface story alone. Elements of allegory may be found in Jonathan Swift's *Gulliver's Travels* (1726) and Thomas Mann's *Der Zauberberg* (1924; *The Magic Mountain*, 1927).

anatomy: Literally the term means the "cutting up" or "dissection" of a subject into its constituent parts for closer examination. Northrop Frye, in his *Anatomy of Criticism* (1957), uses the term to refer to a narrative that deals with mental attitudes rather than people. As opposed to the novel, the anatomy features stylized figures who are mouthpieces for the ideas they represent.

antagonist: The character in fiction who stands as a rival or opponent to the *protagonist*.

antihero: Defined by Seán O'Faoláin as a fictional figure who, deprived of social sanctions and definitions, is always trying to define himself and to establish his own codes. Ahab may be seen as the antihero of Herman Melville's *Moby Dick* (1851).

archetype: The term "archetype" entered literary criticism from the psychology of Carl Jung, who defined archetypes as "primordial images" from the "collective unconscious" of humankind. Jung believed that works of art derive much of their power from the unconscious appeal of these images to ancestral memories. In his extremely influential *Anatomy of Criticism* (1957), Northrop Frye gave another sense of the term wide currency, defining the archetype as "a symbol, usually an image, which recurs often enough in literature to be recognizable as an element of one's literary experience as a whole."

atmosphere: The general mood or tone of a work; atmosphere is often associated with setting but can also be established by action or dialogue. A classic example of atmosphere is the primitive, fatalistic tone created in the opening description of Egdon Heath in Thomas Hardy's *The Return of the Native* (1878).

bildungsroman: Sometimes called the "novel of education," the bildungsroman focuses on the growth of a young *protagonist* who is learning about the world and finding his or her place in life; typical examples are James Joyce's *A Portrait of the Artist as a*

Young Man (1914-1915, serial; 1916, book) and Thomas Wolfe's *Look Homeward, Angel* (1929).

biographical criticism: Criticism that attempts to determine how the events and experiences of an author's life influence his or her work.

bourgeois novel: A novel in which the values, preoccupations, and accoutrements of middle-class or bourgeois life are given particular prominence. The heyday of the bourgeois novel was the nineteenth century, when novelists as varied as Jane Austen, Honoré de Balzac, and Anthony Trollope both criticized and unreflectingly transmitted the assumptions of the rising middle class.

canon: An authorized or accepted list of books. In modern parlance, the literary canon comprehends the privileged texts, classics, or great books that are thought to belong permanently on university reading lists. Recent theory—especially feminist, Marxist, and poststructuralist—critically examines the process of canon formation and questions the hegemony of white male writers. Such theory sees canon formation as the ideological act of a dominant institution and seeks to undermine the notion of canonicity itself, thereby preventing the exclusion of works by women, minorities, and oppressed peoples.

character: Characters in fiction can be presented as if they were real people or as stylized functions of the plot. Usually characters are a combination of both factors.

classicism: A literary stance or value system consciously based on the example of classical Greek and Roman literature. While the term is applied to an enormous diversity of artists in many different periods and in many different national literatures, "classicism" generally denotes a cluster of values including formal discipline, restrained expression, reverence for tradition, and an objective rather than a subjective orientation. As a literary tendency, classicism is often opposed to *Romanticism*, although many writers combine classical and romantic elements.

climax/crisis: The term "climax" refers to the moment of the reader's highest emotional response, whereas "crisis" refers to a structural element of plot, a turning point at which a resolution must take place.

complication: The point in a novel when the *conflict* is developed or when the already existing conflict is further intensified.

conflict: The struggle that develops as a result of the opposition between the *protagonist* and another person, the natural world, society, or some force within the self.

contextualist criticism: A further extension of *formalist criticism*, which assumes that the language of art is constitutive. Rather than referring to preexistent values, the artwork creates values only inchoately realized before. The most important advocates of this position are Eliseo Vivas (*The Artistic Transaction*, 1963) and Murray Krieger (*The Play and Place of Criticism*, 1967).

conventions: All those devices of stylization, compression, and selection that constitute the necessary differences between art and life. According to the Russian Formalists, these conventions constitute the "literariness" of literature and are the only proper concern of the literary critic.

deconstruction: An extremely influential contemporary school of criticism based on the works of the French philosopher Jacques Derrida. Deconstruction treats literary works as unconscious reflections of the reigning myths of Western culture. The primary myth is that there is a meaningful world that language signifies or represents. The deconstructionist critic is most often concerned with showing how a literary text tacitly subverts the very assumptions or myths on which it ostensibly rests.

defamiliarization: Coined by Viktor Shklovsky in 1917, this term denotes a basic principle of Russian Formalism. Poetic language (by which the Formalists meant artful language, in prose as well as in poetry) defamiliarizes or "makes strange" familiar experiences. The technique of art, says Shklovsky, is to "make objects unfamiliar, to make forms difficult, to increase the difficulty and length of perception. . . . Art is a way of experiencing the artfulness of an object; the object is not important."

detective story: The so-called classic detective story (or mystery) is a highly formalized and logically structured mode of fiction in which the focus is on a crime solved by a detective through interpretation of evidence and ratiocination; the most famous detective in this mode is Arthur Conan Doyle's Sherlock Holmes. Many modern practitioners of the genre, however, such as Dashiell Hammett, Raymond Chandler, and Ross Macdonald, have de-emphasized the puzzlelike qualities of the detective story, stressing instead characterization, theme, and other elements of mainstream fiction.

determinism: The belief that an individual's actions are essentially determined by biological and environmental factors, with free will playing a negligible role. (See *naturalism.*)

dialogue: The similitude of conversation in fiction, dialogue serves to characterize, to further the *plot*, to establish *conflict*, and to express thematic ideas.

displacement: Popularized in criticism by Northrop Frye, this term refers to the author's attempt to make his or her story psychologically motivated and realistic, even as the latent structure of the mythical motivation moves relentlessly forward.

dominant: A term coined by Roman Jakobson to refer to that which "rules, determines, and transforms the remaining components in the work of a single artist, in a poetic canon, or in the work of an epoch." The shifting of the dominant in a *genre* accounts for the creation of new generic forms and new poetic epochs. For example, the rise of *realism* in the mid-nineteenth century indicates realistic conventions becoming dominant and *romance* or fantasy conventions becoming secondary.

doppelgänger: A double or counterpart of a person, sometimes endowed with ghostly qualities. A fictional character's doppelgänger often reflects a suppressed side of his or her personality. One of the classic examples of the doppelgänger motif is found in

Fyodor Dostoevski's novella *Dvoynik* (1846; *The Double*, 1917); Isaac Bashevis Singer and Jorge Luis Borges, among others, offer striking modern treatments of the doppelgänger.

epic: Although this term usually refers to a long narrative poem that presents the exploits of a central figure of high position, the term is also used to designate a long novel that has the style or structure usually associated with an epic. In this sense, for example, Herman Melville's *Moby Dick* (1851) and James Joyce's *Ulysses* (1922) may be called epics.

episodic narrative: A work that is held together primarily by a loose connection of self-sufficient episodes. *Picaresque novels* often have episodic structure.

epistolary novel: A novel made up of letters by one or more fictional characters. Samuel Richardson's *Pamela: Or, Virtue Rewarded* (1740-1741) is a well-known eighteenth century example. In the nineteenth century, Bram Stoker's *Dracula* (1897) is largely epistolary. The technique allows for several different points of view to be presented.

euphuism: A style of writing characterized by ornate language that is highly contrived, alliterative, and repetitious. Euphuism was developed by John Lyly in his *Euphues, the Anatomy of Wit* (1578) and was emulated frequently by writers of the Elizabethan Age.

existentialism: A philosophical, religious, and literary term, emerging from World War II, for a group of attitudes surrounding the pivotal notion that existence precedes essence. According to Jean-Paul Sartre, "Man is nothing else but what he makes himself." Forlornness arises from the death of God and the concomitant death of universal values, of any source of ultimate or a priori standards. Despair arises from the fact that an individual can reckon only with what depends on his or her will, and the sphere of that will is severely limited; the number of things on which he or she can have an impact is pathetically small. Existentialist literature is antideterministic in the extreme and rejects the idea that heredity and environment shape and determine human motivation and behavior.

exposition: The part or parts of a fiction that provide necessary background information. Exposition not only provides the time and place of the action but also introduces readers to the fictive world of the story, acquainting them with the ground rules of the work.

fantastic: In his study *The Fantastic* (1970), Tzvetan Todorov defines the fantastic as a *genre* that lies between the "uncanny" and the "marvelous." All three genres embody the familiar world but present an event that cannot be explained by the laws of the familiar world. Todorov says that the fantastic occupies a twilight zone between the uncanny (when the reader knows that the peculiar event is merely the result of an illusion) and the marvelous (when the reader understands that the event is supposed to take place in a realm controlled by laws unknown to humankind). The fantastic is thus essentially unsettling, provocative, even subversive.

feminist criticism: A criticism advocating equal rights for women in political, economic, social, psychological, personal, and aesthetic senses. On the thematic level, the feminist reader should identify with female characters and their concerns. The object is to provide a critique of phallocentric assumptions and an analysis of patriarchal ideologies inscribed in a literature that is male-centered and male-dominated. On the ideological level, feminist critics see gender, as well as the stereotypes that go along with it, as a cultural construct. They strive to define a particularly feminine content and to extend the *canon* so that it might include works by lesbians, feminists, and women writers in general.

flashback: A scene in a fiction that depicts an earlier event; it may be presented as a reminiscence by a character in the story or may simply be inserted into the narrative.

foreshadowing: A device to create suspense or dramatic irony in fiction by indicating through suggestion what will take place in the future.

formalist criticism: Two particularly influential formalist schools of criticism arose in the twentieth century: the Russian Formalists and the American New Critics. The Russian Formalists were concerned with the conventional devices used in literature to defamiliarize that which habit has made familiar. The New Critics believed that literary criticism is a description and evaluation of its object and that the primary concern of the critic is with the work's unity. Both schools of criticism, at their most extreme, treated literary works as artifacts or constructs divorced from their biographical and social contexts.

genre: In its most general sense, this term refers to a group of literary works defined by a common form, style, or purpose. In practice, the term is used in a wide variety of overlapping and, to a degree, contradictory senses. Tragedy and comedy are thus described as distinct genres; the novel (a form that includes both tragic and comic works) is a genre; and various subspecies of the novel, such as the *gothic* and the *picaresque*, are themselves frequently treated as distinct genres. Finally, the term "genre fiction" refers to forms of popular fiction in which the writer is bound by more or less rigid conventions. Indeed, all these diverse usages have in common an emphasis on the manner in which individual literary works are shaped by particular expectations and conventions; this is the subject of genre criticism.

genre fiction: Categories of popular fiction in which the writers are bound by more or less rigid conventions, such as in the *detective story*, the *romance*, and the *Western*. Although the term can be used in a neutral sense, it is often used dismissively.

gothic novel: A form of fiction developed in the eighteenth century that focuses on horror and the supernatural. In his preface to *The Castle of Otranto* (1765), the first gothic novel in English, Horace Walpole claimed that he was trying to combine two kinds of fiction, with events and story typical of the medieval romance and character delineation typical of the realistic novel. Other examples of the form are Matthew Gregory

Lewis's *The Monk: A Romance* (1796; also known as *Ambrosio: Or, The Monk*) and Mary Wollstonecraft Shelley's *Frankenstein: Or, The Modern Prometheus* (1818).

grotesque: According to Wolfgang Kayser (*The Grotesque in Art and Literature*, 1963), the grotesque is an embodiment in literature of the estranged world. Characterized by a breakup of the everyday world by mysterious forces, the form differs from fantasy in that the reader is not sure whether to react with humor or with horror and in that the exaggeration manifested exists in the familiar world rather than in a purely imaginative world.

Hebraic/Homeric styles: Terms coined by Erich Auerbach in *Mimesis: The Representation of Reality in Western Literature* (1953) to designate two basic fictional styles. The Hebraic style focuses only on the decisive points of narrative and leaves all else obscure, mysterious, and "fraught with background"; the Homeric style places the narrative in a definite time and place and externalizes everything in a perpetual foreground.

historical criticism: In contrast to *formalist criticism*, which treats literary works to a great extent as self-contained artifacts, historical criticism emphasizes the historical context of literature; the two approaches, however, need not be mutually exclusive. Ernst Robert Curtius's *European Literature and the Latin Middle Ages* (1940) is a prominent example of historical criticism.

historical novel: A novel that depicts past historical events, usually public in nature, and features real as well as fictional people. Sir Walter Scott's Waverley novels established the basic type, but the relationship between fiction and history in the form varies greatly depending on the practitioner.

implied author: According to Wayne Booth (*The Rhetoric of Fiction*, 1961), the novel often creates a kind of second self who tells the story—a self who is wiser, more sensitive, and more perceptive than any real person could be.

interior monologue: Defined by Édouard Dujardin as the speech of a character designed to introduce the reader directly to the character's internal life, the form differs from other kinds of monologue in that it attempts to reproduce thought before any logical organization is imposed on it. See, for example, Molly Bloom's long interior monologue at the conclusion of James Joyce's *Ulysses* (1922).

irrealism: A term often used to refer to modern or postmodern fiction that is presented self-consciously as a fiction or a fabulation rather than a mimesis of external reality. The best-known practitioners of irrealism are John Barth, Robert Coover, and Donald Barthelme.

local colorists: A loose movement of late nineteenth century American writers whose fiction emphasizes the distinctive folkways, landscapes, and dialects of various regions. Important local colorists include Bret Harte, Mark Twain, George Washington Cable, Kate Chopin, and Sarah Orne Jewett. (See *regional novel*.)

Marxist criticism: Based on the nineteenth century writings of Karl Marx and Friedrich Engels, Marxist criticism views literature as a product of ideological forces determined by the dominant class. However, many Marxists believe that literature operates according to its own autonomous standards of production and reception: It is both a product of ideology and able to determine ideology. As such, literature may overcome the dominant paradigms of its age and play a revolutionary role in society.

metafiction: This term refers to fiction that manifests a reflexive tendency, such as Vladimir Nabokov's *Pale Fire* (1962) and John Fowles's *The French Lieutenant's Woman* (1969). The emphasis is on the loosening of the work's illusion of reality to expose the reality of its illusion. Other terms used to refer to this type of fiction include "irrealism," "postmodernist fiction," "antifiction," and "surfiction."

modernism: An international movement in the arts that began in the early years of the twentieth century. Although the term is used to describe artists of widely varying persuasions, modernism in general was characterized by its international idiom, by its interest in cultures distant in space or time, by its emphasis on formal experimentation, and by its sense of dislocation and radical change.

motif: A conventional incident or situation in a fiction that may serve as the basis for the structure of the narrative itself. The Russian Formalist critic Boris Tomashevsky uses the term to refer to the smallest particle of thematic material in a work.

motivation: Although this term is usually used in reference to the convention of justifying the action of a character from his or her psychological makeup, the Russian Formalists use the term to refer to the network of devices that justify the introduction of individual *motifs* or groups of motifs in a work. For example, "compositional motivation" refers to the principle that every single property in a work contributes to its overall effect; "realistic motivation" refers to the realistic devices used to make a work plausible and lifelike.

multiculturalism: The tendency to recognize the perspectives of those traditionally excluded from the canon of Western art and literature. In order to promote multiculturalism, publishers and educators have revised textbooks and school curricula to incorporate material by and about women, members of minority groups, persons from non-Western cultures, and homosexuals.

myth: Anonymous traditional stories dealing with basic human concepts and antinomies. According to Claude Lévi-Strauss, myth is that part of language where the "formula *tradutore, tradittore* reaches its lowest truth value. . . . Its substance does not lie in its style, its original music, or its syntax, but in the story which it tells."

myth criticism: Northrop Frye says that in myth "we see the structural principles of literature isolated." Myth criticism is concerned with these basic principles of literature; it is not to be confused with mythological criticism, which is primarily concerned with finding mythological parallels in the surface action of the *narrative*.

narrative: Robert Scholes and Robert Kellogg, in *The Nature of Narrative* (1966), say that by "narrative" they mean literary works that include both a story and a storyteller. The term "narrative" usually implies a contrast to "enacted" fiction such as drama.

narratology: The study of the form and functioning of *narratives*; it attempts to examine what all narratives have in common and what makes individual narratives different from one another.

narrator: The *character* who recounts the *narrative*, or story. Wayne Booth describes various dramatized narrators in *The Rhetoric of Fiction* (1961): unacknowledged centers of consciousness, observers, narrator-agents, and self-conscious narrators. Booth suggests that the important elements to consider in narration are the relationships among the narrator, the author, the characters, and the reader.

naturalism: As developed by Émile Zola in the late nineteenth century, naturalism is the application of the principles of scientific *determinism* to fiction. Although it usually refers more to the choice of subject matter than to technical conventions, those conventions associated with the movement center on the author's attempt to be precise and scientifically objective in description and detail, regardless of whether the events described are sordid or shocking.

New Criticism: See *formalist criticism.*

novel: Perhaps the most difficult of all fictional forms to define because of its multiplicity of modes. Edouard, in André Gide's *Les Faux-monnayeurs* (1925; *The Counterfeiters*, 1927), says the novel is the freest and most lawless of all *genres*; he wonders if fear of that liberty is the reason the novel has so timidly clung to reality. Most critics seem to agree that the novel's primary area of concern is the social world. Ian Watt (*The Rise of the Novel*, 2001) says that the novel can be distinguished from other fictional forms by the attention it pays to individual characterization and detailed presentation of the environment. Moreover, says Watt, the novel, more than any other fictional form, is interested in the "development of its characters in the course of time."

novel of manners: The classic examples of this form might be the novels of Jane Austen, wherein the customs and conventions of a social group of a particular time and place are realistically, and often satirically, portrayed.

novella, novelle, nouvelle, novelette, novela: Although these terms often refer to the short European tale, especially the Renaissance form employed by Giovanni Boccaccio, the terms often refer to that form of fiction that is said to be longer than a short story and shorter than a novel. "Novelette" is the term usually preferred by the British, whereas "novella" is the term usually used to refer to American works in this *genre*. Henry James claimed that the main merit of the form is the "effort to do the complicated thing with a strong brevity and lucidity."

phenomenological criticism: Although best known as a European school of criticism practiced by Georges Poulet and others, this so-called criticism of consciousness is also propounded in the United States by such critics as J. Hillis Miller. The focus is less on individual works and *genres* than it is on literature as an act; the work is not seen as an object but rather as part of a strand of latent impulses in the work of a single author or an epoch.

picaresque novel: A form of fiction that centers on a central rogue figure, or picaro, who usually tells his or her own story. The plot structure is normally *episodic*, and the episodes usually focus on how the picaro lives by his or her wits. Classic examples of the mode are Henry Fielding's *The History of Tom Jones, a Foundling* (1749; commonly known as *Tom Jones*) and Mark Twain's *Adventures of Huckleberry Finn* (1884).

plot/story: "Story" refers to the full *narrative* of *character* and action, whereas "plot" generally refers to action with little reference to character. A more precise and helpful distinction is made by the Russian Formalists, who suggest that "plot" refers to the events of a narrative as they have been artfully arranged in the literary work, subject to chronological displacement, ellipses, and other devices, while "story" refers to the sum of the same events arranged in simple, causal-chronological order. Thus story is the raw material for plot. By comparing the two in a given work, the reader is encouraged to see the narrative as an artifact.

point of view: The means by which the story is presented to the reader, or, as Percy Lubbock says in *The Craft of Fiction* (1921), "the relation in which the narrator stands to the story"—a relation that Lubbock claims governs the craft of fiction. Some of the questions the critical reader should ask concerning point of view are the following: Who talks to the reader? From what position does the narrator tell the story? At what distance does he or she place the reader from the story? What kind of person is he or she? How fully is he or she characterized? How reliable is he or she? For further discussion, see Wayne Booth, *The Rhetoric of Fiction* (1961).

postcolonialism: Postcolonial literature emerged in the mid-twentieth century when colonies in Asia, Africa, and the Caribbean began gaining their independence from the European nations that had long controlled them. Postcolonial authors, such as Salman Rushdie and V. S. Naipaul, tend to focus on both the freedom and the conflict inherent in living in a postcolonial state.

postmodernism: A ubiquitous but elusive term in contemporary criticism, "postmodernism" is loosely applied to the various artistic movements that followed the era of so-called high modernism, represented by such giants as James Joyce and Pablo Picasso. In critical discussions of contemporary fiction, the term "postmodernism" is frequently applied to the works of writers such as Thomas Pynchon, John Barth, and Donald Barthelme, who exhibit a self-conscious awareness of their modernist predecessors as well as a reflexive treatment of fictional form.

protagonist: The central *character* in a fiction, the character whose fortunes most concern the reader.

psychological criticism: While much modern literary criticism reflects to some degree the impacts of Sigmund Freud, Carl Jung, Jacques Lacan, and other psychological theorists, the term "psychological criticism" suggests a strong emphasis on a causal relation between the writer's psychological state, variously interpreted, and his or her works. A notable example of psychological criticism is Norman Fruman's *Coleridge, the Damaged Archangel* (1971).

psychological novel: A form of fiction in which *character,* especially the inner lives of characters, is the primary focus. This form, which has been of primary importance at least since Henry James, characterizes much of the work of James Joyce, Virginia Woolf, and William Faulkner. For a detailed discussion, see *The Modern Psychological Novel* (1955) by Leon Edel.

realism: A literary technique in which the primary convention is to render an illusion of fidelity to external reality. Realism is often identified as the primary method of the novel form: It focuses on surface details, maintains a fidelity to the everyday experiences of middle-class society, and strives for a one-to-one relationship between the fiction and the action imitated. The realist movement in the late nineteenth century coincides with the full development of the novel form.

reception aesthetics: The best-known American practitioner of reception aesthetics is Stanley Fish. For the reception critic, meaning is an event or process; rather than being embedded in the work, it is created through particular acts of reading. The best-known European practitioner of this criticism, Wolfgang Iser, argues that indeterminacy is the basic characteristic of literary texts; the reader must "normalize" the text either by projecting his or her standards into it or by revising his or her standards to "fit" the text.

regional novel: Any novel in which the character of a given geographical region plays a decisive role. Although regional differences persist across the United States, a considerable leveling in speech and customs has taken place, so that the sharp regional distinctions evident in nineteenth century American fiction have all but disappeared. Only in the South has a strong regional tradition persisted to the present. (See *local colorists.*)

rhetorical criticism: The rhetorical critic is concerned with the literary work as a means of communicating ideas and the means by which the work affects or controls the reader. Such criticism seems best suited to didactic works such as satire.

roman à clef: A fiction wherein actual people, often celebrities of some sort, are thinly disguised.

romance: The romance usually differs from the novel form in that the focus is on symbolic events and representational characters rather than on "as-if-real" characters and events. Richard Chase says that in the romance, character is depicted as highly stylized, a function of the plot rather than as someone complexly related to society. The romancer is more likely to be concerned with dreamworlds than with the familiar world, believing that reality cannot be grasped by the traditional novel.

Romanticism: A widespread cultural movement in the late eighteenth and early nineteenth centuries, the influence of which is still felt. As a general literary tendency, Romanticism is frequently contrasted with *classicism*. Although many varieties of Romanticism are indigenous to various national literatures, the term generally suggests an assertion of the preeminence of the imagination. Other values associated with various schools of Romanticism include primitivism, an interest in folklore, a reverence for nature, and a fascination with the demoniac and the macabre.

scene: The central element of *narration*; specific actions are narrated or depicted that make the reader feel he or she is participating directly in the action.

science fiction: Fiction in which certain givens (physical laws, psychological principles, social conditions—any one or all of these) form the basis of an imaginative projection into the future or, less commonly, an extrapolation in the present or even into the past.

semiotics: The science of signs and sign systems in communication. According to Roman Jakobson, semiotics deals with the principles that underlie the structure of signs, their use in language of all kinds, and the specific nature of various sign systems.

sentimental novel: A form of fiction popular in the eighteenth century in which emotionalism and optimism are the primary characteristics. The best-known examples are Samuel Richardson's *Pamela: Or, Virtue Rewarded* (1740-1741) and Oliver Goldsmith's *The Vicar of Wakefield* (1766).

setting: The circumstances and environment, both temporal and spatial, of a *narrative*.

spatial form: An author's attempt to make the reader apprehend a work spatially in a moment of time rather than sequentially. To achieve this effect, the author breaks up the *narrative* into interspersed fragments. Beginning with James Joyce, Marcel Proust, and Djuna Barnes, the movement toward spatial form is concomitant with the *modernist* effort to supplant historical time in fiction with mythic time. For the seminal discussion of this technique, see Joseph Frank, *The Widening Gyre* (1963).

stream of consciousness: The depiction of the thought processes of a *character*, insofar as this is possible, without any mediating structures. The metaphor of consciousness as a "stream" suggests a rush of thoughts and images governed by free association rather than by strictly rational development. The term "stream of consciousness" is often used loosely as a synonym for *interior monologue*. The most celebrated example of stream of consciousness in fiction is the monologue of Molly Bloom in James Joyce's *Ulysses* (1922); other notable practitioners of the stream-of-consciousness technique include Dorothy Richardson, Virginia Woolf, and William Faulkner.

structuralism: As a movement of thought, structuralism is based on the idea of intrinsic, self-sufficient structures that do not require reference to external elements. A structure is a system of transformations that involves the interplay of laws inherent in the system itself. The study of language is the primary model for contemporary structuralism. The structuralist literary critic attempts to define structural principles that operate intertextually throughout the whole of literature as well as principles that operate in *genres* and in individual works. One of the most accessible surveys of structuralism and literature available is Jonathan Culler's *Structuralist Poetics* (1975).

summary: Those parts of a fiction that do not need to be detailed. In *Tom Jones* (1749), Henry Fielding says, "If whole years should pass without producing anything worthy of . . . notice . . . we shall hasten on to matters of consequence."

thematics: According to Northrop Frye, when a work of fiction is written or interpreted thematically, it becomes an illustrative fable. Murray Krieger defines thematics as "the study of the experiential tensions which, dramatically entangled in the literary work, become an existential reflection of that work's aesthetic complexity."

tone: The dominant mood of a work of fiction. (See *atmosphere*.)

unreliable narrator: A narrator whose account of the events of the story cannot be trusted, obliging readers to reconstruct—if possible—the true state of affairs themselves. Once an innovative technique, the use of the unreliable narrator has become commonplace among contemporary writers who wish to suggest the impossibility of a truly "reliable" account of any event. Notable examples of the unreliable narrator can be found in Ford Madox Ford's *The Good Soldier* (1915) and Vladimir Nabokov's *Lolita* (1955).

Victorian novel: Although the Victorian period extended from 1837 to 1901, the term "Victorian novel" does not include the later decades of Queen Victoria's reign. The term loosely refers to the sprawling works of novelists such as Charles Dickens and William Makepeace Thackeray—works that frequently appeared first in serial form and are characterized by a broad social canvas.

vraisemblance/verisimilitude: Tzvetan Todorov defines vraisemblance as "the mask which conceals the text's own laws, but which we are supposed to take for a relation to reality." Verisimilitude refers to a work's attempts to make the reader believe that it conforms to reality rather than to its own laws.

Western novel: Like all varieties of *genre fiction*, the Western novel—generally known simply as the Western—is defined by a relatively predictable combination of *conventions*, *motifs*, and recurring themes. These predictable elements, familiar from many Western films and television series, differentiate the Western from *historical novels* and idiosyncratic works such as Thomas Berger's *Little Big Man* (1964) that are also set in the Old West. Conversely, some novels set in the contemporary West are regarded as Westerns because they deal with modern cowboys and with the land itself in the manner characteristic of the *genre*.

Charles E. May

GUIDE TO ONLINE RESOURCES

WEB SITES

The following sites were visited by the editors of Salem Press in 2009. Because URLs frequently change, the accuracy of these addresses cannot be guaranteed; however, long-standing sites, such as those of colleges and universities, national organizations, and government agencies, generally maintain links when sites are moved or updated.

American Literature on the Web
http://www.nagasaki-gaigo.ac.jp/ishikawa/amlit

Among this site's features are several pages providing links to Web sites about specific genres and literary movements, southern and southwestern American literature, minority literature, literary theory, and women writers, as well as an extensive index of links to electronic text collections and archives. Users also can access information for five specific time periods: 1620-1820, 1820-1865, 1865-1914, 1914-1945, and since 1945. A range of information is available for each period, including alphabetical lists of authors that link to more specific information about each writer, time lines of historical and literary events, and links to related additional Web sites.

Books and Writers
http://www.kirjasto.sci.fi/indeksi.htm

This broad, comprehensive, and easy-to-use resource provides access to information about hundreds of authors throughout the world, extending from 70 B.C.E to the twenty-first century. Links take users from an alphabetical list of authors to pages featuring biographical material, lists of works, and recommendations for further reading about individual authors; each writer's page also includes links to related pages on the site. Although brief, the biographical essays provide solid overviews of the authors' careers, their contributions to literature, and their literary influences.

The Canadian Literature Archive
http://www.umanitoba.ca/canlit

Created and maintained by the English Department at the University of Manitoba, this site is a comprehensive collection of materials for and about Canadian writers. It includes an alphabetical listing of authors with links to additional Web-based information. Users also can retrieve electronic texts, announcements of literary events, and videocasts of author interviews and readings.

A Celebration of Women Writers

http://digital.library.upenn.edu/women

This site presents an extensive compendium of information about the contributions of women writers throughout history. The "Local Editions by Authors" and "Local Editions by Category" pages include access to electronic texts of the works of numerous writers, including Louisa May Alcott, Djuna Barnes, Grazia Deledda, Edith Wharton, and Virginia Woolf. Users can also access biographical and bibliographical information by browsing lists arranged by writers' names, countries of origin, ethnicities, and the centuries in which they lived.

Contemporary Writers

http://www.contemporarywriters.com/authors

Created by the British Council, this site offers "up-to-date profiles of some of the U.K. and Commonwealth's most important living writers (plus writers from the Republic of Ireland that we've worked with)." The available information includes biographies, bibliographies, critical reviews, news about literary prizes, and photographs. Users can search the site by author, genre, nationality, gender, publisher, book title, date of publication, and prize name and date.

Internet Public Library: Native American Authors

http://www.ipl.org/div/natam

Internet Public Library, a Web-based collection of materials, includes this index to resources about writers of Native American heritage. An alphabetical list of authors enables users to link to biographies, lists of works, electronic texts, tribal Web sites, and other online resources. The majority of the writers covered are contemporary Indian authors, but some historical authors also are featured. Users also can retrieve information by browsing lists of titles and tribes. In addition, the site contains a bibliography of print and online materials about Native American literature.

LiteraryHistory.com

http://www.literaryhistory.com

This site is an excellent source of academic, scholarly, and critical literature about eighteenth, nineteenth, and twentieth century American and English writers. It provides numerous pages about specific eras and genres, including individual pages for eighteenth, nineteenth, and twentieth century literature and for African American and postcolonial literature. These pages contain alphabetical lists of authors that link to articles, reviews, overviews, excerpts of works, teaching guides, podcast interviews, and other materials. The eighteenth century literature page also provides access to information about the eighteenth century novel.

Literary Resources on the Net

http://andromeda.rutgers.edu/~jlynch/Lit

　　Jack Lynch of Rutgers University maintains this extensive collection of links to Internet sites that are useful to academics, including numerous Web sites about American and English literature. This collection is a good place to begin online research about the novel, as it links to hundreds of other sites with broad ranges of literary topics. The site is organized chronically, with separate pages for information about the Middle Ages, the Renaissance, the eighteenth century, the Romantic and Victorian eras, and twentieth century British and Irish literature. It also has separate pages providing links to Web sites about American literature and to women's literature and feminism.

LitWeb

http://litweb.net

　　LitWeb provides biographies of more than five hundred world authors throughout history that can be accessed through an alphabetical listing. The pages about each writer contain a list of his or her works, suggestions for further reading, and illustrations. The site also offers information about past and present winners of major literary prizes.

The Modern Word: Authors of the Libyrinth

http://www.themodernword.com/authors.html

　　The Modern Word site, although somewhat haphazard in its organization, provides a great deal of critical information about writers. The "Authors of the Libyrinth" page is very useful, linking author names to essays about them and other resources. The section of the page headed "The Scriptorium" presents "an index of pages featuring writers who have pushed the edges of their medium, combining literary talent with a sense of experimentation to produce some remarkable works of modern literature." The site also includes sections devoted to Samuel Beckett, Umberto Eco, Gabriel García Márquez, James Joyce, Franz Kafka, and Thomas Pynchon.

Novels

http://www.nvcc.edu/home/ataormina/novels/default.htm

　　This overview of American and English novels was prepared by Agatha Taormina, a professor at Northern Virginia Community College. It contains three sections: "History" provides a definition of the novel genre, a discussion of its origins in eighteenth century England, and separate pages with information about genres and authors of nineteenth century, twentieth century, and postmodern novels. "Approaches" suggests how to read a novel critically for greater appreciation, and "Resources" provides a list of books about the novel.

Outline of American Literature

http://www.america.gov/publications/books/outline-of-american-literature.html

This page of the America.gov site provides access to an electronic version of the ten-chapter volume *Outline of American Literature*, a historical overview of prose and poetry from colonial times to the present published by the U.S. Department of State. The work's author is Kathryn VanSpanckeren, professor of English at the University of Tampa. The site offers links to abbreviated versions of each chapter as well as access to the entire publication in PDF format.

Voice of the Shuttle

http://vos.ucsb.edu

One of the most complete and authoritative places for online information about literature, Voice of the Shuttle is maintained by professors and students in the English Department at the University of California, Santa Barbara. The site provides thousands of links to electronic books, academic journals, association Web sites, sites created by university professors, and many, many other resources about the humanities. Its "Literature in English" page provides links to separate pages about the literature of the Anglo-Saxon era, the Middle Ages, the Renaissance and seventeenth century, the Restoration and eighteenth century, the Romantic age, the Victorian age, and modern and contemporary periods in Britain and the United States, as well as a page focused on minority literature. Another page on the site, "Literatures Other than English," offers a gateway to information about the literature of numerous countries and world regions.

ELECTRONIC DATABASES

Electronic databases usually do not have their own URLs. Instead, public, college, and university libraries subscribe to these databases, provide links to them on their Web sites, and make them available to library card holders or other specified patrons. Readers can visit library Web sites or ask reference librarians to check on availability.

Canadian Literary Centre

Produced by EBSCO, the Canadian Literary Centre database contains full-text content from ECW Press, a Toronto-based publisher, including the titles in the publisher's Canadian fiction studies, Canadian biography, and Canadian writers and their works series, *ECW's Biographical Guide to Canadian Novelists*, and *George Woodcock's Introduction to Canadian Fiction*. Author biographies, essays and literary criticism, and book reviews are among the database's offerings.

Literary Reference Center

EBSCO's Literary Reference Center (LRC) is a comprehensive full-text database designed primarily to help high school and undergraduate students in English and the humanities with homework and research assignments about literature. The database contains massive amounts of information from reference works, books, literary journals, and other materials, including more than 31,000 plot summaries, synopses, and overviews of literary works; almost 100,000 essays and articles of literary criticism; about 140,000 author biographies; more than 605,000 book reviews; and more than 5,200 author interviews. It also contains the entire contents of Salem Press's MagillOnLiterature Plus. Users can retrieve information by browsing a list of authors' names or titles of literary works; they can also use an advanced search engine to access information by numerous categories, including author name, gender, cultural identity, national identity, and the years in which he or she lived, or by literary title, character, locale, genre, and publication date. The Literary Reference Center also features a literary-historical time line, an encyclopedia of literature, and a glossary of literary terms.

MagillOnLiterature Plus

MagillOnLiterature Plus is a comprehensive, integrated literature database produced by Salem Press and available on the EBSCO*host* platform. The database contains the full text of essays in Salem's many literature-related reference works, including *Masterplots*, *Cyclopedia of World Authors*, *Cyclopedia of Literary Characters*, *Cyclopedia of Literary Places*, *Critical Survey of Long Fiction*, *Critical Survey of Short Fiction*, *World Philosophers and Their Works*, *Magill's Literary Annual*, and *Magill's Book Reviews*. Among its contents are articles on more than 35,000 literary works and more than 8,500 writers, poets, dramatists, essays, and philosophers, more than 1,000 images, and a glossary of more than 1,300 literary terms. The biographical essays include lists of authors' works and secondary bibliographies, and almost four hundred overview essays offer information about literary genres, time periods, and national literatures.

NoveList

NoveList is a readers' advisory service produced by EBSCO. The database provides access to 155,000 titles of both adult and juvenile fiction as well information about literary awards, book discussion guides, feature articles about a range of literary genres, and "recommended reads." Users can search by author name, book title, or series title or can describe the plot to retrieve the name of a book, information about the author, and book reviews; another search engine enables users to find titles similar to books they have enjoyed reading.

Rebecca Kuzins

GEOGRAPHICAL INDEX

CATEGORY INDEX

SUBJECT INDEX